THE VICTORIOUS LIFE

MESSAGES FROM THE SUMMER CONFERENCES

AT

Whittier, California, June
Princeton, New Jersey, July
Cedar Lake, Indiana, August

INCLUDING ALSO SOME MESSAGES FROM
THE 1917 CONFERENCE AT PRINCETON
AND OTHER MATERIAL

WIPF & STOCK · Eugene, Oregon

Wipf and Stock Publishers
199 W 8th Ave, Suite 3
Eugene, OR 97401

The Victorious Life
Messages from the Summer Conferences
at Whittier, California, June.
Princeton, New Jersey, July.
Cedar Lake, Indiana, August.
Including Also Some Messages From
The 1917 Conference at Princeton and Other Material.
By McQuilken, Robert C.
ISBN 13: 978-1-5326-8468-5
Publication date 3/13/2019
Previously published by The Board of Managers,
Victorious Life Conference, 1918

CONTENTS

The Conference and Its Message....................	1
A Foreword by the Editorial Committee	
The Conference at Whittier in June...................	7
Robert C. McQuilkin, Presiding at sessions of the three Conferences	
The Conference at Princeton in July..................	13
Philip E. Howard, President and Publisher of The Sunday School Times	
The Conference at Cedar Lake in August..............	18
Charles Gallaudet Trumbull, Editor of The Sunday School Times	
"The Master is Here": Mr. McQuilkin................	24
The Gospel of Victory...............................	35
Professor W. H. Griffith Thomas, D.D., of Wycliffe College, Toronto	
The Holy Spirit in Daily Life: Dr. Griffith Thomas....	49
What is "Justification"? Dr. Griffith Thomas.........	61
What is "Sanctification"? Dr. Griffith Thomas.........	69
Prayer and the Christian Life: Dr. Griffith Thomas....	78
The Bible and the Christian Life: Dr. Griffith Thomas.	91
Our Lord's Second Coming: Dr. Griffith Thomas......	103
Victory's First Step: Salvation (The first of six addresses on the Victorious Life by Charles Gallaudet Trumbull)	112
Some Victory Tests: Mr. Trumbull...................	124
God's Threefold Work of Grace: Mr. Trumbull.......	134
Unconditional Surrender: Mr. Trumbull..............	144
Victory by Faith: Mr. Trumbull.....................	157
Going on in Victory: Mr. Trumbull..................	168
The Spirit's Fire in Korea............................	183
Jonathan Goforth, D.D., Missionary in Honan, China	

God's Overflow in Korea: Dr. Goforth................ 195

Philippine Trophies 201
    The Rev. E. J. Pace, formerly Missionary to the Philippines. Acting Director of Missionary Course Moody Bible Institute. Author of Lesson Cartoons in The Sunday School Times

Africa from the Watch Tower.......................... 213
    Dr. H. Virginia Blakeslee, Missionary in British East Africa

Missions' War Challenge............................... 226
    Mrs. Alice E. McClure, Missionary in the Punjab, India. Temporarily Student Volunteer Secretary in America

Apostolic Faith in China............................... 235
    Miss Louisa Vaughan, for seventeen years Missionary in China

Testing God's Method: Miss Vaughan................. 243

Ding Li Mei—China's Moody: Miss Vaughan........... 246

The Jews and Their King.............................. 250
    The Rev. A. E. Thompson, Missionary in Palestine

Prayer that Prevails................................... 262
    Howard Agnew Johnston, D.D.

The Next Belgian Invasion............................. 274
    Edith Fox Norton (Mrs. Ralph C.), Missionary to Belgium

Reaching Belgium's Soldiers........................... 286
    Ralph C. Norton, Director of British and Allied Soldiers' Evangelistic Campaign, conducting the Belgian Gospel Mission

Outdoor Evangelism in New York...................... 293
    Arthur J. Smith, D.D., General Secretary New York Evangelistic Committee

"This Man Receiveth Sinners"......................... 302
    W. B. Anderson, Corresponding Secretary, United Presbyterian Board of Foreign Missions. For ten years Missionary in India

The Price of a Revival................................. 312
    W. L. McClenahan, Missionary in Egypt

The Leaders' Testimonies............................ 320
    Dr. Griffith Thomas; Miss Vaughan; Mr. McClenahan; Benjamin F. Culp, Director of Conference Music; Dr. Virginia Blakeslee; Mr. Pace; Mrs. McClure; Mr. Trumbull; Mr. McQuilkin; Mrs. Norton; Mr. Norton; Addison Raws, Manager of Keswick Colony of Mercy, Conference Cornetist; Miss Bessie E. Stockwell, Stenographic Reporter of Conference Messages; Oliver R. Heinze, Director of Christian Life Literature Fund, in charge of Conference literature

A Business Man's Victory............................ 337
    J. Harvey Borton, President and General Manager of the Haines, Jones & Cadbury Plumbing Company, Chairman of Conference Board of Managers

Fighting College Doubts............................. 340
    J. A. Morris Kimber, Professor of Bible, Whittier College, Whittier, California

In the Army Camps.................................. 343
    Philip E. Howard, Jr., Pocket Testament League and Y. M. C. A. worker. In charge of Recreation in the Conference at Princeton

Looking Unto Jesus: Mr. McQuilkin.................. 346

At the "Say-So" Meetings........................... 351

"Am I Ready for His Coming?": Mr. McQuilkin...... 364

Resurrection Days: Mr. Philip E. Howard............ 371

A Call to Prayer for Future Conferences............. 375

Selected Lists of Literature.......................... 379

CONFERENCE MOTTO

"To Me to Live is Christ"

THE VICTORIOUS LIFE

THE CONFERENCE AND ITS MESSAGE

A Foreword by the Editorial Committee

THE beginnings of the Victorious Life Conference, which in the summer of 1918 grew into three gatherings in different parts of the country, may be placed in the years 1911 and 1912, when several young Christian workers in Philadelphia were led out into an experience in Christ which transformed their lives. A group of three young women and three young laymen began in 1912 to meet together for prayer and asked God to open the way for a summer conference where others might be led into the experience that was meaning so much to them. After months of prayer, in a notable way that showed the Spirit's direct hand, a conference was arranged through the young people's societies of the city in which the members of the little group were working.

Several places were suggested as possibilities for the gathering, among them Princeton, New Jersey, but it was finally settled that the little country town of Oxford, Pennsylvania, should be the meeting place.

About a week or two before the conference there were so few delegates actually registered,—less than twenty-five, including the workers themselves,—that a young business man who was asked to help at the Conference asked the business manager if he was sure that the Lord wanted this Conference. The business manager, on whom rested the chief burden of arrangements, Robert P. Regester (now Dr. Regester, in the service in France), told his friend something of the prayer preparation and the way the Lord had been guiding in the program, and the answer came: "This thing is of the Lord. That's all I want to know. I'm right with you." About seventy-five delegates were in attendance from out-of-town,—

The Conference and Its Message

most of them young people,—beside the Oxford friends. The Bible hour in the morning was conducted the first four days by Henry W. Frost, of the China Inland Mission, and the last four days by Dr. W. H. Griffith Thomas, who had recently come to Toronto from Oxford, England. Among other speakers were Dr. C. A. R. Janvier, now of India, Dr. Charles R. Watson, Samuel W. Foster, Dr. Thomas C. Pollock; the sessions were presided over by Dr. J. Alvin Orr, whose warm spiritual touch and remarkable understanding of young people had much to do with the utterly unexpected outpouring of definite blessing at this first Conference,—that is, utterly unexpected to all except the little group who had been praying through the months.

It was clearly seen that the Conference had outgrown Oxford the first year, and without knowing that it had been in the mind of the Committee, Mr. Frost and Dr. Griffith Thomas each suggested Princeton as an ideal meeting place for a summer Conference. The authorities of Princeton Seminary graciously gave over their entire plant for the Conference in 1914, and each year since then the Victorious Life Conference has met the third full week in July at Princeton.

After Oxford, 1913, it seemed clear to all that God wanted the Conference continued from year to year along the same general lines. The aim of the Conference was later stated as follows: "To bring men and women into a life of fellowship with God, victory over sin, and fruit-bearing, through the presentation of the Bible message concerning the Life that is Christ." The Victorious Life Conferences are preaching no new or strange Gospel, nor is any new teaching regarding the Lord Jesus and his work for us being presented. The purpose has been, as will be seen from the messages in this book, simply to press home upon Christians that the whole of the old Gospel so marvelously pictured in the New Testament is really for us and is intended by God to be lived to-day.

In the presenting of this message the leaders of the Conference have been keenly conscious of failure at a thousand points and they stand in wonder at the over-ruling Grace of God which has brought blessing in spite of the weakness and mistakes of management and of teaching. The managers have been grateful to God for criticism, and are seeking to learn from the criticism both of those in full sympathy with

A Foreword by the Editorial Committee

the Conference and its message and of those who are sincerely antagonistic to it.

The Victorious Life teaching has been subjected to the keenest analysis by master minds in theology, but after every allowance has been made for human fraility and limitation in the stating of God's truth, the thing which abides is the seal of God's Spirit in his transforming power upon thousands who in simple faith have surrendered and believed. The Conference began not first of all with a system of teaching which resulted in a life-experience, but with a life-experience which was followed by more or less accurate attempts to formulate a full explanation of it. The experience itself, indeed, rested upon a "teaching,"—not on a logical "system" but on simple statements of the Word of God which pointed the way to Christ who is himself the Victory. This does not mean that accurate theological statement should be discounted, and it is the endeavor of the Victorious Life Conference to use every aid that the long centuries of consecrated thinking can give to Bible problems. But it is earnestly urged that after the last word that theology can speak has been spoken, there will remain the impossibility of the human intellect compassing in our logical systems the great truths of salvation. There is God's side and man's side, and much that is God's side must remain his secret; the things that are revealed belong to us. The question as to *how* God gives victory can lead to endless and fruitless discussion; the great fact that he *does* give victory, and tells in simple ways how each Christian may take the Life and enjoy it, is the glad tidings with which this book is concerned.

The personal experience of individual Christians should never be used as a basis for doctrine, nor should a Christian seek to copy the details of the personal experience of another. When it is said that the Conference at Oxford began with a definite experience in the lives of certain Christians it is not intended that this experience should be the norm to judge every Christian by. But a reason for the blessing of God upon the Victorious Life message is because it is addressed to many Christians who are in just the place of defeat, and of ignorance of the walk of Faith and the meaning of Grace, that those young people were in who heard the glad tidings of victory.

It has been a matter of deep concern and grief to the Conference leaders that some of the delegates, particularly

The Conference and Its Message

younger Christians, have been led by Satan into a critical spirit toward others. They have testified to the experience of Victory in Christ in such a way as to lead earnest and mature fellow-Christians to feel that there was a note of judgment of others who did not have such an experience. Every effort is made by the speakers to guard the young Christian against these dangers. It is strongly urged that the testimony should be given far more by the life than by the lips, and that when the Lord does give opportunity to testify to what He has done we should never testify, "I have the Victorious Life," but rather speak of what the Lord Jesus has done for us and that we are trusting him to continue to live his life in us. Warning is needed also against a spirit of separation from other Christians, or leaving the commonplace tasks that the Lord has committed to us in our own churches. It is in these everyday matters that there is finest opportunity to display the grace of the Lord in kindness toward others, which is a distinctive mark of the Life that is Christ. The least intrusion of spiritual pride is a complete contradiction of the Victorious Life. Yet it is one of the subtle dangers.

Christ the Saviour sufficient for the individual's every need cannot be divorced from Christ the sufficient Saviour for the lost world's need. In every Victorious Life Conference the missionary passion of our Lord has had central place, as will be seen from the messages in this volume. Scores of young people have volunteered for the mission field at these Conferences. Several of them are now at work in the fields of their choice, and a number of others are in training to go forth. At all of the Conferences in 1918 thank-offerings for missions were given and the money is being used to spread the Gospel in places that are as yet entirely untouched by the missionary. The Corresponding Secretary, Robert C. McQuilkin, and his wife have sailed for British East Africa as Conference missionaries, being supported the first year by the thank offering given for this purpose at the 1917 Conference at Princeton. All six of the original group of young people who prayed and planned the Conference into being were missionary volunteers, and all were led into their experience of Victory in Christ directly or indirectly through a missionary Conference.

This reaching of young Christians with life largely before

A Foreword by the Editorial Committee

them has been one of the distinctive features of the Conferences. They are not confined in any sense to young people but the program is planned with their needs in mind, with wholesome recreation and fun a real part of the Conference week.

In 1917 the managers of the conference grounds at Cedar Lake, Indiana, invited the managers of the Victorious Life Conference at Princeton to hold a similar conference at Cedar Lake in the summer of 1918, using as far as possible the same speakers and leaders. After months of prayer the way opened to accept this invitation and the result was a Victorious Life Conference for the Middle West at Cedar Lake, an account of which is given on page 18 of this book. A number of Christian workers who had been in touch with the Conferences in the East were praying for a similar gathering in Southern California, and in December of 1917 a committee was formed which arranged for the Conference at Whittier, a sketch of which is given on page 7. The purpose of this volume is to give the messages and the spirit of these three Conferences so far as that may be done by the printed page. Most of the addresses included are those given at Princeton and Cedar Lake in 1918, which were stenographically reported, but a number of the addresses, or the substance of them, were given also at Whittier. Some of the striking messages given at the 1917 Conference at Princeton are also included. It was possible to include only such addresses given at Whittier as were repeated at Princeton or Cedar Lake, and among others Dr. Blanchard's messages are omitted. Some of the rich material he gave is in his book, "Getting Things from God." The plan has been followed of noting the books or leaflets by the speakers which supplement their messages, and at the close of the volume will be found the book lists and prices.

Grateful acknowledgment is made by the Board of Managers to The Sunday School Times and its Directors for a co-operation with the conference movement without which much of its wide extension would not have been possible. The Sunday School Times is not officially related in any way to the Conferences (though members of its editorial force are upon the Board of Managers), but it was through the message of its Editor that the original group of young people

The Conference and Its Message

were brought into victory, and this has led to a continuance of the close fellowship.

Of the speakers whose messages are included here no less than six quite independently of one another have centered attention upon the Christian life as lived in the apostolic church and described in the Acts of the Apostles. May we not take this as the central message of the book and of the Conferences,—to get back in individual experience and in the corporate life of the Body of Christ to that apostolic standard. Will you not add your petitions to many others that the Holy Spirit may use this volume to help toward that end, that many individuals in every land may find the Victorious Christ of Paul to be his present, powerful Lord; that such a Spirit-produced yearning for the world-wide revival in the body of Christ may go up to the throne of Grace that God can give what he so desires to give; that the glad Day of Christ's return may be hastened. Along with this oft repeated challenge of the conditions in the apostolic Church, which God intended to continue so long as the author of those conditions—the Holy Spirit—continued with and in his people, there was presented in the Conferences the challenge of present-day miracles of revival grace wrought in India, Korea, China and other parts of the world, told by the lips of those who were in the midst of and shared these revivals. Let us be satisfied with nothing less for the church of Christ in America.

This volume goes forth with the earnest prayer that whatever may be the errors or weaknesses that are discovered in its messages, these mistakes may not be permitted to shut out any Christian from the fulness of the blessing of the Gospel of Christ.

THE CONFERENCE AT WHITTIER

Robert C. McQuilkin

A FEW days after the opening of the Victorious Life Conference the first week of June in Whittier, California, I received a letter from a friend who had been one of the workers in the little Conference held at Oxford, Pennsylvania, in 1913. This gathering at Oxford was the beginning of the Victorious Life Conference held since 1914 in Princeton, New Jersey. My friend was recalling those early days at Oxford, and suggested that this first conference at Whittier would also be a rather small gathering, but prayed that it might be filled with the same power. There were about seventy-five delegates from out of town attending the conference at Oxford. What was the surprise of the friends in the East to learn that before the close of the conference at Whittier over a thousand had enrolled, and hundreds more had attended some of the meetings without registering their names. On the matter of mere numbers that were directly touched by the meeting, not to speak of the thousands upon thousands indirectly reached, the first Victorious Life Conference on the Pacific coast went beyond the expectations and rebuked the faith of most of the intercessors.

Day after day the beautiful campus of the Friends' College at Whittier, which hospitably opened its doors to house the conference, was dotted with the automobiles that had traveled thirty, sixty, and a hundred miles from all the surrounding country. Whittier is about fourteen miles from Los Angeles, and the electric cars and buses from the city brought their quota. Most of the visitors arrived for the nine o'clock meeting in the morning, when informal heart to heart messages on the Victorious Life were given, and remained for the day, attending the mission study groups at ten o'clock, Dr. Griffith Thomas' Bible hour at eleven, a platform meeting soon after dinner addressed each day by different speakers, and the two evening meetings, out-door vespers at seven and the closing platform at eight. The little college chapel seated about four hundred and fifty, and for most of the meetings through the week it was comfortably filled, the attendance averaging be-

---

This article, giving a sketch of the Conference at Whittier, together with that by Mr. Howard, on the Conference at Princeton, and that by Mr. Trumbull on the Conference at Cedar Lake, are reprinted from The Sunday School Times.

A Sketch of the Conference

tween three hundred and four hundred. On Friday evening when Dr. Griffith Thomas gave a message on the Second Coming it was necessary to move into the large auditorium of the Whittier Friends' Church, where the meetings on the closing Sunday were also held. Perhaps about a hundred of the delegates lived in the dormitories and had their meals in the college dining-room. Many brought their lunches or patronized the excellent restaurants in the town.

The remarkable unity of the conference seemed entirely unaffected by the shifting crowd from day to day. Over the entrance of the main college building was stretched a sign with these words in large letters: "Ye are all one in Christ Jesus." The number attending the conference was not less a surprise to some of the leaders than was the beautiful realization of this oneness in Christ and this unity of the Spirit throughout the meetings. For in Southern California many sad seeds of dissension have been sown among the Lord's own people, not to speak of the bewildering array of Satan's religious cults for which the Pacific coast is famed.

There were many shades of doctrine and opinion among the Christians who shared the conference, but there was one note in all the messages, and in the prayers and testimonies throughout the conference, which gathered to itself the varying notes among the true believers. It was not a doctrine held up at the conference that brought about this blessed unity, but a Person. The Victorious Life was presented as the Life that is Christ. The conference motto hung over the platform in the chapel gave the keynote: "To me to live is Christ." A young pastor gave his grateful testimony that for a number of years he had been preaching a particular theory on the life of holiness, but was puzzled many times to adjust his experience to his theory, and keep that personal experience just where it ought to be. During the conference Christ had been revealed to him as the secret of victory in a way that cleared up the problems of his experience and revealed some of the dangers of his theory. This young pastor went back with the conviction that he had a new message not only for his own congregation but for the brother pastors in his own denomination who may be in danger of that same bondage to a "theory" of holiness.

Another surprise to those who were not expecting God to answer prayer so abundantly was the number of ministers included among the delegates. The list of delegates is not

at Whittier in June

at hand, but there must have been well over a hundred pastors at one or more of the meetings. One delegate counted on one day twenty-three brother-ministers of his own denomination with whom he was personally acquainted. Reports came from here and there in the surrounding country that these pastors were giving their people the conference messages and telling them of the blessing to their own lives.

But the ministers were not the only missionaries that went out from the Conference with a new message. There was a young married woman who in her girlhood days had looked forward to missionary work, and she indeed found it in her home in Salt Lake City, Utah. Surrounded by the awful pressure of the heathenism of that Mormon city, as well as by the deadly inertia of the Christians, this worker had come to the conference with a hungry heart and with an eager desire to get the refreshment that she might pass on to her fellow-Christians. She got more than her note-book filled, for the message went home with new power and clearness to her heart on the first day of the conference.

At the close of one of the meetings a young woman asked an interview with one of the leaders. A few moments' conversation revealed that though a consecrated Christian worker, she did not know the secret of complete victory in her own life. For one thing she could not understand how any Christian could be kept free from worry and anxiety under all circumstances. "Now, just suppose," she said, "that if you or I received word now that one of our babies was taken seriously ill. You just could not help being anxious."

"But it is possible to have the experience that the Psalmist spoke of, 'He shall not be afraid of evil tidings: his heart is fixed, trusting in the Lord.'"

They talked together of the simple secret of complete surrender and receiving by faith the fact of His all-sufficiency, and the Christian mother took God at his word and thanked Him for the victory. The next morning at the close of one of the meetings she came with the word that she was unexpectedly called away from the conference. Her youngest child, a little girl of just eighteen months, had been taken suddenly ill and two physicians had been in consultation over the case. Her husband was trying to reach her the night before at the very hour she was speaking of this test of victory.

The impressive experience of the young mother was brought before the conference, at the next morning's meeting, and

A Sketch of the Conference

there was united prayer for the little girl's recovery. (The plan was followed each day of remembering special requests unitedly in prayer. Each day the boys in the training camps and in Europe were thus remembered, particularly the sons of the scores of parents present at the conference.) The following day this word came from the mother: "We never can make a mistake to leave everything in His hands. He gave me perfect peace, when I heard my baby was so sick—and He brought me home to a perfectly well child. She seemed to have every symptom of scarlet fever only the night before, when you and I were talking together, and praying. How wonderfully He works. He tested me through the very thing suggested by myself, proving Himself the 'Wonderful Saviour.' I had accepted in cold faith the Victory. He brought it to a heart test. Praise His name! I know you prayed as you said you would. God answered."

One of the ministers who came for a personal interview had been blessedly used in home missionary work, but was grieved at heart because the experience of joy and peace and power that he once possessed had gone from him and for over ten years he had been hungry for the lost blessing. He spoke of just what it was that he longed for in his life.

"Do you believe that God wants to give you that experience?" he was asked.

"Yes, I do."

"Let us ask Him to do it."

The two men knelt and asked the God of all grace to give his servant the fulness of the Spirit, with all that this meant.

The pastor prayed very definitely for the blessing.

"Do you believe God heard that prayer?"

"Yes, He surely did."

"Is it according to His will that you should receive the blessing you have asked for?"

The pastor agreed that there was no doubt of this.

"Well, God's Word says, 'If we ask anything according to his will, he heareth us: and if we know that he heareth us whatsoever we ask, we know that we have the petitions which we have asked of him.'"

The minister did this very thing, and accepted by faith the answer to his prayer because God's Word clearly told him it was answered. The two men had not been together more than ten minutes, and as the minister looked up after his prayer and thanksgiving, he just laughed, laughed at the

at Whittier in June

simplicity of it all, a very earnest laugh at his own folly of going hungry ten years just because he kept on praying and asking God and never taking that which God had granted.

These are but a few of the hundreds whom the Spirit of God touched. At the Say-So meeting on the closing Sunday afternoon one hundred and sixty-five others gave their happy testimony to what the Lord Jesus had done for them through the conference. There were between three and four hundred at this meeting, only a fraction of those who had been blessed in the conference. The hundred and sixty-five who testified included twenty or more who came to a decision to surrender and accept victory during that very meeting. There were no long testimonies, and sometimes into one sentence was packed a whole life story. Several had never testified before, and stood and spoke only by His enabling grace.

The out-door vespers each day also offered an opportunity for the redeemed of the Lord to "say so." A memorable vesper meeting was that in which a number of those who had been richly blessed at the Victorious Life Conference at Princeton gave their testimony. There were a dozen at the Whittier Conference who had been blessed at one or more of the conferences at Princeton, half of them missionary volunteers through the influence of the Victorious Life messages.

Notable among the testimonies at the vesper services was that of Professor Morris Kimber, the young Corresponding Secretary of the Conference at Whittier. Mr. Kimber told of his struggle with doubts and questions through a period of half a dozen years, and how grateful he was that one of the leaders at the conference in Princeton held him steadily to this question, "Is it true that God is supplying all your needs,— or is God a liar?" In vain he attempted to bring in other problems to settle, the question of the inspiration of the Scriptures and such things, but he was forced to make the plain choice as to whether he believed God was supplying all his needs. And on this simple statement he entered into the life of victory which not only solved his own problem but led in a remarkable way to the actual beginning of the Victorious Life Conference for the Pacific coast.

At another vesper meeting a young business man, Mr. Warren Pike, told how his life was revolutionized two years ago, when he went East unexpectedly and while there attended the conference at Princeton. He returned home with a great desire to extend this message on the Pacific coast.

A Sketch of the Conference

There were others upon whom God had put this same burden, and in His own wonderful way these men came together in prayer about six months ago and planned for the conference at Whittier. Mr. Pike became the business manager, and upon him and Professor Kimber, two young men under thirty, the burden of the conference rested. And so this first conference on the Pacific coast, just as the conference in the East, was begun in such a way that man could not glory, for in both cases God has worked, not through well-known leaders but through the young people whose chief preparation was their deliverance out of a life of defeat into a new life of victory in Christ.

The blessed unity of the conference extended to the messages of the speakers. President Charles A. Blanchard, of Wheaton College; Professor W. H. Griffith Thomas, and the writer of this article, were the three speakers from the East. George W. Davis, of the Christian and Missionary Alliance, and Dr. F. W. Farr, were other speakers. Among the missionaries who were blessedly used in the conference were Mr. and Mrs. A. R. Saunders, of the China Inland Mission; Miss Anna McKee, of Korea; Miss Roe Williams, of Egypt; Miss Edna Alger, and Miss Moran, of China. A beautiful inspiration were Mr. and Mrs. Saunders, he almost blind and she almost deaf, lovingly assisting each other in the work of speaking and hearing and seeing. They indeed bore about in their bodies the marks of their fellowship with Christ's suffering. Two of their little children were massacred in the Boxer outrages, and they themselves almost killed. Full of joy was their testimony to God's grace.

There were no enrolment fees charged at the conference, but voluntary offerings were taken up to meet the expenses. Here once more God met the need according to His "exceeding abundant" measure. The offering beyond the amount needed for the expenses was to be given to the three largest unreached fields in the world, central Africa, central Asia, and central South America.

Prayers and plans are already under way for the Victorious Life Conference next year at Whittier, if the Lord will. And the committee feel that one piece of equipment that will probably be needed is a conference tent large enough to seat several thousands. But beyond every other equipment in spreading the message of His sufficient Grace are prayer warriors. Will you be one?

THE CONFERENCE AT PRINCETON

Philip E. Howard

IN THE quiet of the early morning the Seminary campus was waking to the song of birds. The shadows reached out across the shaded lawn in the old quadrangle, but the sunlight seemed to have touched the faces of the company of men and women, younger and older, that had gathered in the chapel for morning prayer. There was no sound of traffic, no restless haste, but a brooding peace that only the Spirit can bring to those who have gone apart for a little time to give themselves to prayer.

Then came a moment in the meeting when every voice was silent. For stealing through the songs of birds and the rustle of leaves in the breezes came the notes of a morning hymn, pouring out over the campus, and into open windows and into waiting hearts,—a hymn more prayed than played by the cornetist, as he himself says, yet played with such silvery sweetness that one knew in that moment how pure music can be. Who can ever forget the restfulness, the worship, the praise, the sheer joy in the morning call sounding over the Seminary campus?

It is a happy company that streams over to the Princeton Inn for breakfast. If you want to know what "the morning face" can be at its best, stand where you can watch the three or four hundred conference members as they pass out of the Seminary gate. Did you ever see a happier crowd, a crowd of young people from school and college and home and office, more alert, more eager, and normal, and just glad to be alive? A crowd of mature men and women more earnestly thoughtful, and keenly interested in the doings of the Conference day? Folks from California, Alaska and Saskatchewan, Ontario, New Orleans, and China, Japan, India, Egypt, Africa, the Philippines, and some very likely from your own home town in Jersey, or Massachusetts, or Pennsylvania, or Virginia,— oh, real folks from almost everywhere! And you will be sure to glimpse the young aviator, one of our best American fliers, on week-end leave, and the powerfully built sailor near him,

---

An article reprinted from The Sunday School Times. See note on page 7.

A Sketch of the Conference

and the big Y. M. C. A. secretary just alongside. What could bring such a crowd to old Princeton these hot July days, and keep them there, most of them, for eight days?

Well, some of them have had (to them) a new experience of the grace and mercy of the Lord Jesus Christ in dealing with the power of sin in this life, and have been telling others what it has meant to them in such a definite way that a widening circle of earnest Christians, and some who had not accepted Christ, have wanted to hear the story. Others have been unclear as to much Scripture teaching, and out of a longing to get at the heart of God's Word in more than one of its aspects have undertaken the journey in order to talk over with men and women who are themselves still learning, some of the fundamentals of the Christian faith and life. And the Victorious Life Conference at Princeton is a true conference in the most satisfying sense. It is a time of close and humble fellowship in the Spirit between the leaders and the led, with the positions often reversed as it is given to one Bible student or another to let the light in upon a truth under consideration.

The way of it is this: Dr. Griffith Thomas conducts a Bible study hour in the morning, unfolding meanings, warning against misconceptions, digging down around the Hebrew and the Greek roots so that anybody can understand the original significance of the words, and bringing pure scholarship to bear, in the most spiritual and vivid and sensibly balanced fashion, upon such a series of studies as he gave on Prayer, and on the Holy Spirit. Then in the afternoon on certain days, Dr. Thomas sits under a big tree out on the campus, and forty or fifty of the folks with hard questions crowding for answer, get around him and bombard him. It is a beneficent attack, for his return fire brings such a relieved and satisfied look to so many faces!

There is a great scattering after Dr. Thomas' morning hour to various mission study classes, when for another hour such topics as these are really studied: Ancient Peoples at New Tasks, led by A. E. Thompson, of Jerusalem; South American Problems, led by E. J. Pace, formerly missionary to the Philippines; The Moslem World, led by W. J. McClenahan, of Egypt; The Lure of Africa, led by Dr. H. Virginia Blakeslee, of British East Africa; The Call of a World Task, led by Mrs. Alice E. McClure, of India. Now wouldn't you be likely

at Princeton in July

to get into one of those classes, under such leadership, if you could?

The Conference comes together again for Mr. Trumbull's hour, for studies in the Victorious Life. But "for studies" is a very inadequate way to put it. It isn't a theory, or an academic body of speculative truth with which Mr. Trumbull is concerned. You can't listen to him for five minutes without realizing that you are face to face with a decision for your own will, your own faith, your own life. But he won't let you look at yourself even when you want to. It is Christ your Victory about whom he is talking, and to whom he is looking straight past many of the questions you at first want to ask. So his keen analysis of God's Word and your need, and Christ's glorious sufficiency to take care of your problem of sin, not only past but present, leads you up face to face with the question: Do I believe that Christ is meeting all my need now? You are going to answer that question, too, one way or the other, not publicly perhaps, but in your own heart, before you get through with the Conference. No one knows how many personal interviews with Mr. Trumbull follow during the Conference days, but they are many and very searching, and joyously revolutionizing, when one learns by them to "let go, and let God."

In the afternoons there is no program of meeting. Recreation is planned for; there is ample time for rest, and conversation, and study. And on the edge of the evening, after supper, comes the vesper service, out-of-doors, with song, and testimony, and prayer, conducted chiefly by the young people, but shared by all alike.

The general meetings in the evenings open out wide horizons of spiritual longing, and opportunities for service. The Nortons tell of their work among the Belgians; Dr. Arthur Smith speaks on the street meeting evangelism in city work. Mr. Thompson deals with prophecy and its fulfilment with reference to the Jews; Mrs. McClure gives a message of missionary service that must be faced and fulfilled by this generation, and Mr. Pace gives us a wonderful picture of missionary work in the Philippines; Dr. Blakeslee presents the missionary call in one great meeting, when at the close the eight or ten missionaries and all the volunteers are gathered on and around the platform, an impressive company of nearly seventy persons, who join with us (so far as we can manage our voices at all) in singing "O Zion, haste, thy mission high

A Sketch of the Conference

fulfilling," and many of these young people for the first time declare their missionary decision at this Conference.

After the evening sessions, the prayer groups. There is the secret of the quiet spirit, the steady poise, the joyousness, the convincing results, the life-changing effects of this Victorious Life Conference. The Board of Managers, under Mr. J. Harvey Borton's leadership, at prayer, prolonged prayer, day by day, prayer on the part of some of the leaders lasting far into the early morning hours; prayer, individual and in groups, night after night. And a quiet prayer-room apart, where, undisturbed, any one may go at any time to pray. Do you wonder that when the Conference comes to its closing meetings there are grateful testimonies that simply must be put into words?

That explains the "Say So" meeting out on the lawn on the afternoon of the last Sunday. Everybody is there. Robert McQuilkin is leading, as he has in the general meetings throughout the Conference. His glad smile is a testimony in itself, and he carries that meeting so cheerily, so joyously that no one seems to mind the necessary brevity of time for individual testimony. All the gathered gratitude of a week of new vision, blessed experiences, victory realized, freedom taken from Christ's own loving hand,—all this breaks forth in the "Say So" meeting. There isn't any shouting, somehow. Some voices are so low you cannot hear them clearly. You can see the hesitancy in some who start to rise, and then having risen, and given praise in a single sentence, the countenance breaks up into lines of ease and rest and joy. Perhaps a hundred and fifty that afternoon "Said So." And that night at the supper table, a clean-visaged Christian business man from a big concern in Pittsburgh, leaned over to some friends and said with intense earnestness, "It's the real thing. You simply can't get around those testimonies."

As the twilight sent its shadows over the campus, we gathered under the trees for a communion service. Mr. McQuilkin conducted that service, and pointed us in his Spirit-filled words to our returning Lord. It was dark when the communion elements were taken by that glad and humiliated and grateful company of the Lord's followers, and the stillness and restfulness and fellowship of that hour are not soon to pass from the memory of any of us who gathered about the Lord's table. After the meeting we were loth to go. Little groups stood about in quiet conversation under the

at Princeton in July

trees. Some went away to pray. And by and by Addison Raws took up that silvery instrument of his and played, while we listened, "Where he leads me I will follow." Then we turned toward our night of rest, and a new day of new disclosures of our Christ.

THE CONFERENCE AT CEDAR LAKE

Charles Gallaudet Trumbull

MANY a Christian needs to be rescued from himself. Either he is trusting in himself, or he is mistakenly thinking that he must learn to trust himself better than he has yet done. Of course, while he labors under this delusion, he is a defeated Christian. He is unconsciously commiting the commonest and most disastrous sin of the Christian,—the sin of unbelief. He needs to be rescued, real Christian though he is, from himself and his unbelief.

Many a discouraged, defeated, and wearied Christian has been rescued from himself and his unbelief during this past summer. How did it come to pass? Through a transcontinental chain of three links, three Victorious Life Conferences or "Rescue Missions for Christians," reaching from the Pacific to the Atlantic. The first of these was held in Whittier, Cal., in June. The second was at Princeton, N. J., in July. The middle link of the chain came last, at Cedar Lake, Ind., during the last week of August, on the large conference grounds known as "Restawhile" [from our Lord's word, "Come ye yourselves apart . . . and rest a while" (Mark 6: 31)] of the Moody Church of Chicago. Would you glimpse what the Lord did for those who went apart with him to rest with and in him? He can do the same for you to-day, in a conference of just Himself and yourself.

It was seven o'clock one morning, and many of the delegates were gathering in the tent of meeting, as was their custom, for the early prayer-meeting with which every day commenced. The silver-toned cornet "prayed" (not merely played) by Addison Raws had sounded its clear, sweet call over the entire grounds; and hearts were hushed in prayer, waiting on God. Miss Louisa Vaughan of China was there,—she has sometimes been called "the Evan Roberts of Shantung Province" by those who know of God's use of her intercessory work there; and the leader of the prayer-meeting had asked Miss Vaughan to give the message this morning. She waited, as one after another was led out into praise and thanksgiving and worship and intercession. The minutes

---

An article reprinted from The Sunday School Times. See note on page 7.

at Cedar Lake in August

passed; still a volume of praise and prayer went up. Hymns were quietly sung, without announcement; and the prayer-meeting went on. After the hour was over the leader expressed his regret to Miss Vaughan that she had not been given an opportunity for her message. "I am the most honored person in this conference," was her quiet reply; "the Holy Spirit has taken my time on the program."

It *was* the Holy Spirit's Conference, as was overwhelmingly shown to all. God seemed to be building upon the blessings he had so lavishly given at the earlier Victorious Life conferences of the summer. Praying "in the Spirit" became a frequent privilege and experience. How God rejoices to answer prayers offered by any of his children, in the Spirit, and in the name of Jesus!

Stop trying, and trust: that was the key-note of the conference. The key-note, that is, when we add the single word "Jesus." *Stop trying, and trust Jesus.* Stop trying to help Jesus win your victories; praise him and trust him that he has won and is winning them all.

Rest, instead of restlessness, was what many a Christian found. Glad-hearted testimonies breathed restfulness in Christ. A young woman stenographer told, at a Vesper Service under the trees by the lakeside, how the earlier years of her business life had been lived under the constant pressure of speed, speed, speed. Whether in business school or commercial office, she was always urging forward to work harder and faster. Then she told how, step by step, God had brought her to see the very practical method of resting in Christ Jesus. Did she lose her speed as a stenographer? No; she consecrated it to the Lord for him to use as he would; and to-day she has the deserved reputation of being able to "take" the addresses of speakers whose messages are like chain lightning in their tumultuous speed! But she definitely commits every such reporting task in special prayer to the Lord Jesus; and she prays again before she transcribes her notes; and her stenographic service is being honored by God to readers the world around as souls are saved and Christians rescued through her reporting ministry.*

---

*This volume, containing the addresses of the Conferences, consists chiefly of this worker's stenographic reports, and will carry added blessing because of her prayer ministry in this work. Her own testimony will be found on page 333.

A Sketch of the Conference

God brought prepared people to the conference. A minister who had read about it wanted to attend, and commenced praying that he might. He had no money for the trip. One day, when he had finished preaching in a certain church, he was handed twenty-five dollars for his services; the payment was entirely unexpected, and he said they owed him no such amount, but he was told that it was his. A little later he received in the mail fifty dollars, with no intimation of its sender. His wife told him that God certainly wanted him to attend the Cedar Lake Conference; and he started by way of another place where he was to spend a week or so of vacation first. As the time for the conference approached, he was tempted to stay right where he was for the remainder of his vacation. Then he saw what a sin of unbelief this would be; he went on to the conference; and the joy of his radiant testimony to his finding of Christ as his sufficiency and rest and victory those who heard it will never forget.

A young married woman had gone to Cedar Lake the week before the conference, solely for a vacation. She did not know that a Victorious Life Conference was to be held there. Attending some meetings during the days before the conference began, she was not particularly interested, and had decided to leave on the Saturday when the conference itself opened. But she attended a conference meeting, and now she stayed on. Day by day she drank in all that she could of the messages and truths there given. The day came when she must leave. There were unanswered questions that were troubling her; she asked one of the leaders for a personal interview.

As they talked together, it came out that she had been "healed" by Christian Science. And she had been supposing, during that week of the conference, that the truth of victory in Christ and the teachings of Christian Science were fundamentally the same! She was surprised, then startled, then shocked to learn of the abhorrent and blasphemous repudiations of the Word of God that are the foundations of "Science." But she saw the truth. The Holy Spirit was clearly speaking to her; she went away rejoicing in a new vision of her Lord, and saved from the deadly poison that she had been unconsciously taking in.

Very clearly and definitely it was shown at this conference that Christian Science denies the reality of sin (a thing that God knows is so real that it cost him the life of his Son),

at Cedar Lake in August

denies the need of the atonement, denies the reality of the atonement through the shed blood of Jesus, denies the death of Christ, denies the resurrection of the body of Christ, denies the personality of the Holy Spirit,—and with these denials leads souls away from the truth of God and the Gospel of Jesus Christ into death and hell.

Christians were shown how to turn away from their unbelief and rest everything on Christ. A minister's wife, hungering for victory, said despairingly to a friend that she *knew* that faith was the secret of victory, but she did not have the necessary faith, and could not get it. The friend asked her what she thought about Christ. She was sure that *He* was all right. Then her friend reminded her that she already had all the faith she needed, if she was sure of *Christ*. She had been making the mistake of looking at her faith, instead of looking at Jesus. She and many another Christian there were led to turn away from everything and every one else, and see Jesus only.

Dr. Griffith Thomas told of the long-time search of the great missionary John G. Paton for a word to use for faith, or belief, when he was making a translation of the Scriptures into the language of those to whom he was seeking to bring Christ. Apparently there was no native word for "believe." For a long time Dr. Paton was well-nigh baffled. One day, while working on the translation, a native came into his study, and, tired out, flung himself down on a chair, rested his feet on another chair, and lay back full length, saying as he did so something about how good it was to lean his whole weight on those chairs. Instantly Dr. Paton noted the word the man had used for "lean his whole weight on." The missionary had his word for "believe"! He used it once, and thereafter, in translating the Scriptures. Try it for yourself and see, in any verse that uses the word "believe." "For God so loved the world, that he gave his only begotten Son, that whosoever leans his whole weight on him should not perish, but have eternal life" (John 3: 16). "What must I do to be saved? . . . Lean thy whole weight on the Lord Jesus, and thou shalt be saved" (Acts 16: 30, 31).

As belief is the secret of victory as well as of salvation, so leaning our whole weight on Jesus brings victory. Many a Christian at Cedar Lake wondered and rejoiced at the simplicity of it, as we all may do.

The victorious life can no more be selfish than Christ can

A Sketch of the Conference

be selfish. Therefore the victorious life is the missionary life. The day verse chosen for Friday, at the end of the week, was this: "Pray ye therefore the Lord of the harvest, that he send forth laborers into his harvest" (Matt. 9: 38), but it had not been announced, and those at the seven o'clock prayer-meeting that morning did not know what it was. A minister, who had been spending an hour in prayer in the tent before the seven o'clock meeting, now was led to intercede for the lost world. Miss Vaughan of China followed this prayer with intercession for each country, and pleaded with the Lord to send forth laborers; she quoted Matthew 9: 38. One after another of those who were present prayed in a burden of intercession for missions; and all this in spite of the fact that few knew that missions was to be emphasized that day. But the Holy Spirit knew, and led on; the evening brought a great missionary meeting; and victory encircled the world that night through intercessions that God gave and that God will answer.

On the closing Sunday afternoon came the "Say-so Meeting" of testimonies. In the first sixty minutes there were sixty testimonies, with songs and prayers interspersed. One man said that it only took a moment to glance from the seventh chapter of Romans to the eighth; but he had been twenty years getting out of the life of struggle described in the seventh and into the restfulness and victory of the eighth.

A minister confessed that God had shown him his own unbelief; and that while there had been some results in his ministry, "a few sick people healed," Christ had been able to do no mighty works there because of his own unbelief.

Another minister told of the sins of which the Holy Spirit had been convicting him, one of which was laziness, another meanness; and now, he said, God had been awakening him early every morning and he had been spending an hour in the tent in prayer before the seven o'clock prayer-meeting started.

A radiant testimony came from a woman who said that she was now trusting the Lord for victory and for the supply of her every need; and she had only come to this place of victory since the testimonies in that Say-so meeting had started. The Lord had shown her that the grace the others were testifying to belonged to her as well as to any one else; that it was foolish for her to wait longer before quietly taking God at his word. Another told how, coming to the conference

at Cedar Lake in August

on the opening Monday, he was under conviction by the time the first hymn was sung.

Even at the close of this powerful testimony meeting quite a number took the step of complete surrender and "leaned their whole weight on Christ."

Victory is "just Himself." After yielding our lives utterly to his mastery, we are simply to believe on Jesus for all the rest. Shall we, if we have not yet done so, let God deliver us this moment from all unbelief in our Lord and Saviour? Shall we—if we must be cautious and move slowly in the matter—do this by taking the five steps that Dr. Griffith Thomas urged upon all? Here they are:

I must believe.
I may believe.
I can believe.
I will believe.
I do believe.

For it is safe, and it is easy, and it is Victory, to believe Jesus.

"THE MASTER IS HERE"

Robert C. McQuilkin

"THE Master is here and calleth thee." The Master is here: let our expectations for our meeting to-night, and for our Conference, be according to that great fact.

There may be those here at Princeton who have come to listen to the messages of some particular servant of God whom he has blessed and wonderfully used. Some of us remember how two years ago we looked forward to Dr. Scofield's coming to Princeton to give us Bible messages. Dr. Scofield came on the opening Sunday, then took sick, and could not give his other messages. A few came to the conference because this noted Bible teacher was announced, and they feared, on his departure, that the meetings would not bring to them what they expected. This year some of us have been looking forward to the coming of Miss Louisa Vaughan of China, who has blessed us through her messages on the prayer of faith. Miss Vaughan is ill and does not expect to come. If we are here because of this or that human leader, let us remember to-night that the Master is here, and desires to speak. This is not a conference of great men but of a great Lord.

The Master is here and calleth *thee.* It is a personal call. We lose a great deal sometimes because of the change from "thee" to "you," and very often we listen to messages given in our churches as addressed to "you," the congregation in general. This message from the Master is for *"thee."*

"Oh, if she were only here!" perhaps you are saying of some friend. "If I could have persuaded him to come; this is just the message he needed, the message I have been longing for him to get!" Will you just commit that loved one to Him to-night, and remember that God has brought *thee* here, and that the Master is here to give a message to thee?

One thing that has impressed me at all the conferences I have gone to in the past years, is the temptation of the leaders

---

This was the opening address at Princeton, Saturday evening, July 20, and the same message with some changes was given also at the opening meeting at Cedar Lake, Saturday, August 24.

Mr. McQuilkin

and the speakers, and those who have attained to a deep experience in the Christian life to pray that the Lord would bring others into the blessing that they have received, that the Lord would somehow bring up the conference to the level of their blessing. So we take part in the meetings with our eyes upon those others who need the message, rather than expecting a fresh message for ourselves. Are we not tempted sometimes in our churches to think, "Oh, if God could only get hold of these indifferent Christians and make them earnest and on fire for God!" May I say this to you to-night, that I believe the heart of the Lord Jesus Christ is more concerned about getting the earnest, consecrated Christians where he wants them to be. For if God can do this, he can pour out unmeasured blessing on those cold and indifferent Christians, and those Christians who are not hungry, who would not think of coming to a Victorious Life conference. In a real sense God's problem has always been with the leaders. A great historian wrote that all that was left of the Christian Church in the eighteenth century were the funeral rites. So dead and cold had professing Christians become that they said it was hardly possible to find any true faith in England,—the great mass of the people going after the pleasures of the world, and those who did come to the houses of worship coming in a formal way, not being touched by the Spirit of God. "Oh, if God would only touch the hearts of the indifferent ones!" must have been the heart cry of earnest Christians. But I think that at that time God was not first of all concerned about those indifferent ones, but was looking down on a few of the most earnest men in England, the men whose hearts were hungry for God, the men who, at any cost, wanted to go the whole way with God. And as he looked down on John Wesley, Charles Wesley, Whitefield, and others I believe that on God's heart was this thought, "If I can only get them to go the whole way with me! If I can only get those men to the place where I want them to be!" God did get them in a great measure where he wanted them to be, and you know how he poured out the revival fires all over England, and the fire caught all over the world. Now to-night, as the eyes of God go to and fro throughout the whole earth to show himself strong in behalf of those whose hearts are perfect toward him, he is longing that the consecrated, earnest, hungry Christians, such a group as we have here at Princeton, may

"The Master is Here"

come to the place where he wants us to be; and if we get there, then how abundantly he can pour out his blessing on those others who do not want to come to Victorious Life conferences!

Will you remember then that the Master is here and calleth thee? I am sure that if you listen to *my* message some of you will go out and say, "Well, I haven't heard anything new. I have heard all of that before. I have read all of that in The Sunday School Times,—nothing new." My dear friends, if you listen to my message you will go out and say that; but if you remember that the Master is here and calleth thee, he will give thee a new message to-night. And to those of you who know the most about the life of victory in Christ, and the life of intercession, to those who have gone thousands of miles beyond the speaker in the knowledge of the Lord Jesus Christ, there will come to-night that fresh message direct from the Master himself.

And so I bring these words of Martha to her sister Mary in that Bethany home where the Lord Jesus loved to come, as very appropriate words for the opening message of a Victorious Life Conference: "The Master is here and calleth thee."

He is here to give thee resurrection life. To speak of "the call" of Christ suggests that he is calling to us to do something for him; but his call to-night is a call for us to receive something from him. God is a great deal more concerned that we should receive from Jesus Christ what he has for us, than he is that we should do things for the Lord Jesus Christ. For if he can just get us to receive what he has for us, he will take care of what we do for him, or rather what he does through us.

One of the young women who expects to come to the Conference this week has for a number of years been a leader in other conferences that have brought great blessing. The first year she came here to Princeton some of her friends asked just what was the difference between those other gatherings where she had been a leader, and a Victorious Life conference. She said, "Well, it seems to me that at those conferences I learned better what I could do for God; when I came to Princeton I learned what God wanted to do for me." These conferences on the Victorious Life are first of all concerned that we should get from the Lord Jesus

Mr. McQuilkin

what he longs to give to us. I believe that the call of Christ the Christian Church needs to-day is not first of all the call to service, but the call to the resurrection life, the life of victory in the Lord Jesus Christ.

What is this resurrection life? It is remarkable that out of the twenty-five times the Apostle Paul mentions the resurrection, twenty-four times he connects the resurrection directly or indirectly with the present life of believers. If we want to find what the resurrection life means, I know of no better way than to look at the lives of those early disciples, and compare what they had after they received the resurrection life with what they were before the ascension of the Lord Jesus and the outpouring of the Holy Spirit.

As we read the book of Acts, one of the words that keeps coming to our minds, whether the word is there in the book or not, is "joy." Their life was a life of joy. The resurrection life is *a life of joy*, abiding, unbroken joy, the kind of joy that has a heart full of praise. At midnight, in the prison, with feet bound in the stocks, and with the blood running down the back from the stripes that have been laid on, the two disciples of the Lord sing,—under the very circumstances where we would suppose they could have no joy in the heart.

In the midst of persecution the disciples praised God and counted it all joy that they were counted worthy to suffer for the Lord Jesus. Do you have to-night this joy of the Lord, joy that may continue unbroken, even in the midst of sorrow? Remember that it was the man of sorrows and acquainted with grief, on the road to the cross, who said to his disciples, "These things have I spoken unto you, that my joy may be in you, and that your joy may be made full."

The resurrection life is *a life of the peace of God that passeth all understanding*. We may be sure that when Paul said "the peace of God . . . shall guard your hearts and your thoughts in Christ Jesus," he was speaking not only out of the knowledge of the grace of Christ; he was speaking out of a personal experience of that peace that passeth all understanding.

Another word that goes all through the Acts of the Apostles is the word "boldness." The disciples had boldness before men, and they had boldness before God. They came to the throne of grace with boldness in the name of the Lord Jesus Christ, and they gave their testimony with all boldness.

"The Master is Here"

Those timid, shrinking, cowardly disciples were changed into the most courageous men that have ever lived, men who defied the two greatest human powers on earth at that time,— the religious power represented in the Jewish rulership, and the great military power represented in Rome. And those timid disciples, who before the crucifixion one and all forsook Jesus and fled, had the boldness to withstand those two great powers, *because they had resurrection life.*

A fourth mark of resurrection power in the lives of these disciples was this: they worked miracles in the name of the Lord.

At a conference not long ago, a Christian woman came to me and said that she was in a little prayer-meeting where the leader, a missionary, read this verse in the fourteenth chapter of John: "He that believeth on me, the works that I do shall he do also; and greater works than these shall he do; because I go to the Father." After reading the verse the missionary looked around on that group of earnest Christian women, and asked, "Where are your 'greater works?' Greater works than the Lord Jesus worked in the days of his flesh,—where are they?" As those words sank down into the ears and the hearts of those Christian women, this woman said she was convicted for the first time in her life of the awful sin of unbelief; because Christ had said, *"He that believeth on me,"* these works shall he do, and greater works.

As the Master is here to-night, speaking to thee and to me, he is asking us, "Where is the proof that you believe in the Lord Jesus Christ? Not only believe in him for redemption from your sins, but believe in him for these miracle works."

Those early disciples did accomplish miracles in the name of the Lord Jesus, and they did not accomplish those miracles because they were apostles, they did not accomplish those miracles because they were great scholars; they accomplished those miracles, our Lord Jesus Christ said, "Because I,"— mark it, not because of what *they* were, not because of what *they* did,— but *"because I go to the Father."* You remember that if Jesus had not gone to the Father he could not have poured out the Holy Spirit; but he went to the Father, he poured out the Holy Spirit, and those disciples had resurrection life. That is why, not the disciples, but the Lord Jesus

Mr. McQuilkin

dwelling in them, was able to do these greater works than he was able to do in the days of his flesh.

Let us note just one other mark of the resurrection life. (Will you let the Holy Spirit search your heart and ask you whether you have these signs of the resurrection life of victory in Christ?) These disciples had *supernatural victory over sin*. The apostles taught as the birthright of Christians, complete, supernatural victory over sin; and if we learn their secret of complete victory over sin we shall also know the secret of joy, and peace, and boldness, and power, for at the heart of the whole problem is the sin question.

At the close of a week's meetings on the Victorious Life in a small college a student came to me for an interview. He told me frankly that some of his friends thought he would enjoy having a talk, and that was why he came. Then he said something like this: "At these Y. M. C. A. conferences, and other college conventions, they always invite the students to come and talk with the leaders about their problems. But I haven't any problems." That did not seem a very promising start for the interview. This student was an earnest, true Christian, trusting the Lord Jesus Christ for salvation.

"Do you have complete victory over sin?" I asked him.

"Well, that depends on what you mean by 'sin.'"

"Do you ever get angry at people? Do you ever have angry thoughts in your heart?"

"What do you mean, get 'peeved' at people?"

"Yes."

"Why, sure I do," he said.

"And do you ever worry about things?"

"Worry about things? I should say I do; everybody does," he answered.

"Do you ever have impure thoughts in your heart?"

He was honest and said, "Yes, I do."

I asked him two or three other questions that went to the root of those subtle sins of jealousy, pride, irritation, impatience. And my friend went down at every count. Then I said, "Those things are sins, aren't they?"

"Yes, I suppose they are," he admitted.

"Those are the things that put the Lord Jesus Christ on the cross, and you tell me that you have all of those things in your life, and yet you say you have no problem?"

We knelt together in prayer, and as we came before the

"The Master is Here"

Lord he learned that he did have a problem, and he learned what God wants us to learn at this conference, that the problem of all problems is the sin problem. And if we as Christians have in our lives these "common sins," as we call them, of impatience, irritation, worry, jealousy, impurity, pride, covetousness, if we have those things in our hearts, and our hearts are not broken because those things that put the Lord Jesus Christ on the cross are there, we are not likely to find the secret of victory this week. Let us pray that God himself will bring a great conviction of the real meaning of sin, and then we shall be in the place to receive the resurrection life of victory over sin.

Notice with me in the second place that not only is the Master here to give thee resurrection life, but he is here to give thee resurrection life *now*. Some, perhaps, are thinking, "Yes, when I hear these messages on the Victorious Life, and have all my questions answered, perhaps toward the close of this conference, I shall learn the secret of victory in Christ." But the Master is here to give thee resurrection life *now*, to-night.

You remember when Jesus came to Martha that Martha said, "Lord, if thou hadst been here, my brother had not died" (and we can understand the heart cry of Martha as she said it). "And even now I know that whatsoever thou shalt ask of God, God will give thee." She expected that Jesus would bring comfort to their sorrowing hearts, and she was not prepared for what he answered: "Thy brother shall rise again." Martha said, "I know that he shall rise again in the resurrection at the last day." And what said the Lord to her? *"I am* the resurrection, and the life."

I suppose all of our hearts are looking forward to that wonderful day when the Lord Jesus Christ shall come, and when we shall get the bodies of our resurrection glory; but sometimes in looking forward to that glorious day, do we not forget that to-day, as he has given us the earnest of the Spirit, the earnest of that great day to come, do we not forget that the Lord of resurrection life is here to-night, and that he wants to give us that life *now?* It was too good to be true, Martha thought, and Mary too, that the one great desire of their hearts should be granted. But that is what the Lord said, and what he is saying to us to-day. Satan's great word in talking to us about the Victorious Life, and about all the blessings that our hearts are craving to-night, is "not now,

Mr. McQuilkin

but later"; he tells us that we must never expect complete victory over sin until we get our resurrection bodies. Perhaps many of us, when we get those glorious bodies, and when we look back on the pathway of life over which we have come, in imagination will see ourselves walking along a desert road; and just alongside of this desert road are wonderful green pastures, and still waters,—and paths of sorrow, too, but the Lord Jesus Christ is there in the path. As we see that desert road along which we have come, we see that with just one step we might have stepped over into the abundant life of green pastures and still waters, that we might have had this life of peace, and joy, and power, and victory. And we shall exclaim, "Oh, I never knew that I could have those wonderful riches *down there.*"

It is even so. The Master is here to give thee resurrection life, and to give it to thee *now.* He does not want you to wait until the end of the conference, or until you have all your questions answered.

Now, who is entitled to this resurrection life? What are the conditions for receiving it? What were the conditions in that Bethany home? There was just one qualification. There was death in that home, and the Lord of Resurrection Life came to give life. The only qualification for the resurrection life is the letting go of the self life. We call it "surrender," and we shall hear a great deal about it during these conference days. But you do not need to have your questions about surrender answered. Just tell the Lord Jesus Christ to-night that all you are, and all you have, are his, and you surrender yourself for crucifixion death. Because without crucifixion death there cannot be resurrection life.

Every one of us who is trusting the Lord Jesus Christ for salvation has been crucified with Christ. Nineteen hundred years ago when he died, we died; when he was buried we were buried; when he arose we arose; and when he ascended to heavenly places, we ascended with him. This is the position and the privilege of every Christian. But alas, not every Christian is enjoying the fruits of this in experience. That is what the Master wants to give to-night, the actual experience of this resurrection life; and before it can be our actual experience, the crucifixion death must be an actual experience. We can make it so by surrender. We shall learn through the week and I hope we shall learn to-night, that the Holy Spirit is very definite; when he asks us to surrender

"The Master is Here"

there is nothing vague about it. If you are holding anything back from the Lord Jesus Christ to-night, and this is keeping you from blessing, you can know what it is you are holding back from him.

At one of our conferences, a girl who was rejoicing in victory was praying about a friend who was in deep distress; she did not have joy or peace, she did not have victory, and she was having a very miserable time of her Christian life, although she was in a Bible Institute studying to prepare herself for service. She had not come to the meetings on the Victorious Life, but her friend brought her for an interview.

As we talked together she said she was holding something back from the Lord Jesus. She was not willing to do a certain thing.

"Well, if you knew the Lord wanted you to do it wouldn't you do it?"

"No," she said, "I do not want to do it."

"Why?"

"Well, I suppose there is pride in my heart," she replied.

"And you are not willing to give that up?"

"No, I cannot."

We talked together, and I said to her, "Whom do you belong to?"

She was a true Christian, and she said, "I belong to Christ."

"And what price did he pay for you?"

"Why, he died for me. He gave his own life."

"Well," I said, "Jesus bought you and you belong to him, but you are saying you are going to hold something back from your Lord. What are you doing?"

Tears came into her eyes, and she said, "I suppose I am crucifying him afresh."

I had not thought of it just that way, but I said, "Yes, you are robbing Jesus."

Will a man rob God? Will a Christian rob Christ? Is not Christ saying to-day, as he looks down on the blood-torn world, "You have robbed me, even this whole Christian Church," for we are holding back something more serious than tithes and offerings, we are holding back the living sacrifice that the Lord Jesus Christ asks of us. That young Christian girl was still not willing to yield. I asked her if she would kneel down and say, "Lord, thou hast purchased me with thine own blood, I belong to thee; but Lord, I am

Mr. McQuilkin

robbing thee, and I am going to keep on robbing thee." She shrank back from such a thought as that. I said, "Well, that is just what you are saying to Jesus, whether you kneel down and put it into words or not."

Will you remember this, as the Master is here speaking to us, that if you, as you sit in that seat, are consciously holding back anything from the Lord Jesus Christ, you are saying to him, "Lord, I am robbing thee, and I am going to keep on robbing thee?"

We knelt to pray, and after some moments of prayer we waited, and waited, while that young Christian girl struggled. Then in a very quiet way, without any great emotion, she told the Lord Jesus that she wanted to stop robbing him, and she would do anything that he told her to do. She surrendered, she offered herself a living sacrifice, she offered herself for crucifixion death, and that girl rose with her face shining with radiant joy. The Lord Jesus Christ had brought the evidence of resurrection life, when she was ready to offer herself for crucifixion death.

And now what was the final word of the Master to his dear friends in the Bethany home before he worked the resurrection miracle? Dr. Howard Agnew Johnston in that striking message on the meaning of faith which he brought at the 1916 Conference, told us how Christ tried to build up the faith of the needy ones so that he might create an "atmosphere of spiritual power" in which he could work miracles. So in this case, Dr. Johnston suggested, Jesus was trying to teach Mary and Martha to expect that miracle of resurrection. You remember when he came to the grave and told them to roll away the stone, Martha said, "Lord, by this time the body decayeth," and the Lord Jesus turned, and probably in a tone of gentle rebuke, said, "Said I not unto thee, that, if thou believedst, thou shouldest see the glory of God?" Dr. Johnston told us that he believed the Lord Jesus was trying to build up the faith of Martha. I have wondered if Mary, that Mary who sat at the feet of Jesus, was not expecting that miracle; did not Mary, who did not tell the Lord not to roll away the stone, have in her heart at least a great hope and expectation? And the Lord Jesus took hold of that faint faith that was just beginning to stretch out to him, and, linking it with his own mighty faith, he spoke the word of power.

"The Master is Here"

This, then, is the final word in the matter of accepting the resurrection life of the Lord Jesus: Believe.

The Master is here and calleth for thee, to give thee resurrection life, to give it to thee *now*, to give it to thee if all of self is yielded. And after we have yielded everything to him, what shall we do? Shall we wait to see whether we shall have resurrection life? That is what Satan wants us to do, because, as Mr. McConkey has said, the world's motto is, "Seeing is believing." But, as Mr. McConkey puts it, "Faith says, 'Believing is seeing.'"

"Said I not unto thee, that, if thou believedst, thou shouldest see?" Shall we accept to-night his gift of resurrection life? The Master is not here to-night to scold you. The Master is not here to-night to ask you to do a hard and difficult thing. The Master is here to-night to give thee resurrection life.

The Master is here to-night, just as he was in the Bethany home that day, to supply the deepest desire of your heart The very thing that you are longing for as a Christian, the Master is here to give to thee to-night. It may seem too good to be true, as it seemed to Martha and Mary too good to be true that that supreme desire, the life of their brother, should be granted to them; it may seem too good to be true that that thing your heart has been longing for for years, is what Jesus waits to give you. But that is just like the Master—to do things that are "too good to be true." Just believe his Word, and as you believe, he is working now his miracle of resurrection life in you.

Two addresses on the Victorious Life given by Mr. McQuilkin at Cedar Lake, and the series of addresses given at Whittier are not included in this volume. The substance of several of them will be found in the book, "Victorious Life Studies," and in leaflet form. See page 379.

THE GOSPEL OF VICTORY

Professor W. H. Griffith Thomas, D. D.

SOME years ago in the North of England a Salvation Army lassie met a clergyman in the street of a little Durham city, and not knowing who he was, she asked him whether he was saved. With his very beautiful smile that was characteristic of him, he looked at her rather quizzically, and said do you mean *Esothen*, or *Sozomenos,* or *Sothesomai?* It was Bishop Westcott, the great scholar, and he asked her in Greek, "Do you mean I was saved, or do you mean I am being saved, or do you mean I shall be saved?" I have no doubt that before they left one another that lassie had learned a great deal more about salvation than she knew when she asked the question.

Salvation is one of the greatest words of the Bible, and it does, as Bishop Westcott implied, cover the whole of our life, past, present and future. In regard to the past, a Christian can say, "I was saved," or "I have been saved;" that is, from the penalty of sin. In regard to the present, a Christian can say, "I am being saved;" that is, from the power of sin. In regard to the future the Christian can say, "I shall be saved;" that is, from the presence of sin.

Now this Victorious Life Conference has to do particularly with the second of these aspects of salvation. It assumes and takes for granted the first, "I was saved;" "I have been saved from the condemnation, the guilt, the penalty of sin." It looks forward, as we shall see to-morrow, to the coming of the Lord and all that that means in the future, as we say, "I shall be saved from the very presence of sin;" but the Victorious Life means, "just in between I am being saved from the power of sin," and that is the Gospel for to-day.

You know that the word "Gospel" means Good News, and if we had not Good News for the past, the present and the future it would not be worth while. If you told a man that he was saved from the past, that would be good news. If

---

In this message, given on the second Saturday evening at Cedar Lake, and given also at Whittier, Dr. Griffith Thomas gathers up the Scripture message on the Victorious Life, and many of the expositions given in the addresses on the Holy Spirit, and in other messages that are omitted from this volume, are here touched upon.

The Gospel of Victory

you told a man that he would be saved from the very presence of sin hereafter, that would be good news; but if you could not tell him that there was a salvation in between, you see how you would rob him of a great deal of the good news.

In order that we may realize this, let us look at it from the Scriptural point of view, and perhaps it may be well first of all to refer briefly to the passage in Romans 5: 10, where the apostle says that we have been reconciled, that is, there has been salvation for the past, but goes on to say, "If when we were enemies we were reconciled to God by the death of his Son, much more, being reconciled, we shall be (as Bishop Moule of Durham suggests) *kept safe* in his life." So his death blots out the penalty, his coming will deal with the presence of sin, and in between, his resurrection life has to do with our being saved from the dominion, the power, the bondage, the thralldom of sin.

If this is the case, let us look at it point by point, and let us follow the matter step by step; and I want first of all that we should all face this,—THE POSSIBILITY OF VICTORY.

It is not very long ago that some of the leading military men told us that it was impossible to see victory on the Western front for either side, that the power of Germany was such that the Allies could never break through, that the power of the Allies was such that Germany could never break through, that the condition was rapidly passing to what is called one of stale-mate in which neither side could get the victory. I am not concerned with that except that it is an illustration of what so many think to-day in the spiritual warfare. They think that victory is impossible in the Christian life, they think that Romans 7 tells us of a struggle between good and evil, and that spiritually we are in a position of stale-mate, "The good that I would do I do not, and the evil that I would not that I do. I see a law on the one side tending toward God, and on the other side turning toward evil. How shall I overcome the evil? How shall I do the good? I cannot do either." Then people say, "We must do the best we can and hope for the best; but complete and constant victory is obviously impossible."

Now I want to say that *the Bible is absolutely opposed to that*. Victory is possible. Listen to these passages from Scripture. I do not want to put forth my own ideas tonight, but only God's ideas, and anything I may say, if it is not supported by the Word of God, will be worse than

Dr. Griffith Thomas

useless: Let not sin reign in your mortal bodies; Be not overcome of evil; This is the victory that overcometh the world; Ye have overcome the wicked one; They shall reign in life; That grace may reign through righteousness; Thanks be unto God who always causeth us to triumph; To him that overcometh; They overcame him by the blood of the Lamb and the word of their testimony; Thanks be to God who is giving us the victory; In all these things we are more than conquerors through him that loved us.

If these passages mean anything at all, they clearly teach the possibility of victory, and before I take another step tonight I want everyone here to face these simple Scripture passages. I want to say again, that if this victory were not possible, the only other alternative is just this, that sin is inevitable; and if sin were inevitable your conscience and mine would never condemn us. I know of course there are people who excuse themselves; I know there are Christians who say, "Well, this or that is inevitable." I was talking to a man the other day, and he spoke of an infirmity, but really he was referring to a sin, although he called it an "infirmity."

Now I believe in following the Bible and calling a spade a spade, and not an instrument of husbandry. I do not believe in calling your wife the partner of your joys and sorrows, but your wife. And you may gloss over sin by sesquipedalian words as much as you like, sin is sin. If there is anyone here to-night who is hiding behind any excuse, who is calling a sin "an infirmity," or who is allowing himself or herself to be deceived in this way, depend upon it there will be no victory for you; but if you face the problem as the Bible faces it, that sin is sin, and that notwithstanding all its power there is the possibility of victory over it, then you have taken the first step toward victory.

I read only this evening, these words of Rear Admiral McGowan, Pay-Master General of the United States Navy, who has had a little card printed and circulated in his department, bearing the words in gray type: "It can't be done;" and then in bold black type underneath is printed "But here it is." The card is designed to prevent some of the clerks in his department who are easily discouraged, from giving way to their natural besetment, and no doubt it helps in that direction. The same thing is true with things spiritual. There are any number of Christians who say, "It can't be done," but in the Bible, "Here it is," and not only in the

The Gospel of Victory

Bible, but in the experience of thousands of Christians, "Here it is." The apostle Paul says, "I can do all things in him who is strengthening me, empowering me." So let us face this possibility of victory.

Secondly, if we have taken this step, the next is fairly easy,—THE PROMISE OF VICTORY. I only call your attention to one promise, and that is enough, Romans 6: 14: "Sin shall not have dominion over you."

Not long ago an article was written on the subject of the Victorious Life, denying the teaching, and if I have not mistaken the matter, this passage was never quoted once from beginning to end. Now here it is, "Sin shall not have dominion over you." Look at every word of it. "Sin,"—however powerful, however deadly, however long it may have been in your life. "Sin shall not!" there is no doubt about it,—whether you call it "shall not," or "will not," the truth is the same, certain, without any question, "shall not." "Have dominion,"—that means literally "Lord it,"—sin shall not be your Lord and master. "Over you," and that means every Christian.

That is the promise, "Sin will not—sin shall not have dominion over you." It is a promise from God. You and I make promises, but we do not keep them. God always keeps his promises, because he is able and willing so to do.

If that is right, then this is the third step, THE PROVISION FOR VICTORY, and there is this general provision in that very same verse, "for ye are not under law, but under grace." Now, without going too much into detail, I want to ask you to notice that wherever the word "law" occurs, it always means the effort of self, and whenever you see the word "grace" it always means the act of God. When it says you are not under law, it means you are not under self, but you are under God, and self cannot overcome sin. Self is powerless, and this effort of self to overcome sin is just the expression of an utter impossibility. I can quite understand people feeling this impossibility, and if they would only feel this it would be a great and glorious mercy. I remember hearing some years ago of a man who was under deep conviction of sin. He went to a clergyman in England and said, "I feel I am a great sinner." "Praise God," the minister said. "What! are you praising the Lord for my being a sinner?" asked the man. "No, I praise the Lord that you know it," was the reply. If you and I in our Christian life know that we are powerless, it is a mercy, it is a matter for thanksgiving, because it means that we have come to the end of ourselves. If our self-effort is powerless, grace, which is God's act and action, is powerful, and that is the meaning of 2 Corinthians 9: 8, "God is able to make all grace abound toward you; that ye always having all sufficiency in all things, may abound to every good work." God seems almost, as it were, to pile on the word "all" in regard to this assurance that his grace is sufficient for us.

Now, going a little more into detail, especially for those who are here to-night for the first time, I want to ask you to notice the marvelous way in which God has provided for this victory, and given to us in his Word the absolute assurance of its reality. You will remember the familiar passage in Romans 8: 1-4, and if you take those verses just as they stand I think we shall be able to see together how wonderfully God provides for victory.

First of all he starts in this way, "There is no condemnation." You must settle the question of salvation first of all, and Romans 8: 1 says, "There is therefore now no condemnation." Very often people come to conferences like this who have never settled the question of salvation. They want to be better, they want to be holy, they have preached perhaps, or have had before them in their college or university wonderful ideals that they want to attain to, and they cannot attain to them. Such people who want to be better, but have never yet settled the question of salvation, are very much like people who are trying to take the second step before they have taken the first. It is impossible for anyone to be holy and to have victory over sin unless he has settled this question of salvation,—freedom from condemnation.

"There is therefore now no condemnation." Secondly, when that is settled,—*no bondage*, verse 2, "For the law of the Spirit of life in Christ Jesus hath made me free from the law of sin and death." There are two laws, the one dragging us down, and the other lifting us up. A friend of mine has written of an interesting glass case he saw in the north of England; in this glass case you can see a key which seem to be hanging on nothing. But when you look more closely you will find that there is, in the top of the case, a large magnet, which has drawn the steel key towards itself. But why does the key hang suspended in the middle of the case? There is a thread, which, fastened on the key, and fastened to the bottom of the case, keeps it from flying up to the magnet. Now there is the law of gravitation which would draw that key to the bottom of the case, but because of the more powerful law of attraction it is held there, and if somebody were to snap the thread it would fly up without any hesitation to the magnet. Ah, dear friends, there are two laws in our life,—there is the law of sin and death dragging us down, and there is the law of the Spirit of life in Christ Jesus, that is lifting us up. You may speak of one as the lower law, and the other the higher law.

Another illustration, very simple, pictures the difference between the law of gravitation and the law of what is called volition, or the will. If I drop this book, by the law of gravitation it falls, but as it falls I put forth my hand and catch it and stop it from falling. That is to say, the lower law of gravitation is counteracted by the higher law of my will, and the book does not fall to the ground.

So it is with the believer, there is no bondage,—he has been set free from the lower law by the higher law of the Spirit of life in Christ Jesus. We have been talking this week in various addresses and Bible readings of this great and wonderful law of the Spirit of life in Christ Jesus, which sets us free from the law of sin and death.

Then in the third place, you will notice "no weakness." That is verse three, "For what the law could not do (what self could not do—put the word "self" in, and you get it); for what self could not do, God did in the person of his Son." No weakness, because the Lord Jesus Christ has done what self could not do in regard to sin.

Then in verse four, no failure, "that the righteousness of the law might be fulfilled in us,"—that the very righteousness required by the law of God, the law of Moses, is fulfilled when we walk not after the flesh but after the Spirit.

Look at these four things. You will see God's provision for victory,—no condemnation, no bondage, no weakness and no failure. No condemnation, because of the death of Christ; no bondage, because of the life of Christ; no weakness, because of the grace of Christ; and no failure, because of the Spirit of Christ; and if you will look again you will see that these four verses are the very heart of Christian holiness. Verse one looks back over chapter five—no condemnation;

Dr. Griffith Thomas

verse two looks back over chapter six—no bondage; verse three looks back over chapter seven—no weakness; and verse four looks forward over chapter eight—no failure. Romans eight, as someone has said, commences with no condemnation, ends with no separation, and in the middle there is no defeat. Glory to God for the provision of victory. Nothing less is required.

When the Lord Jesus Christ died and rose again, and sent the Spirit, he provided everything that pertains to life and godliness (2 Peter 1: 3), and you and I have only just to appropriate that and use it for ourselves. A man once was asked what he had learned by going to the Keswick convention, a similar gathering to the one we have been having this week. He said, "I learned how to cash my checks." That is what many Christians do not know how to do,—there is the infinite wealth of grace in the Lord Jesus Christ, and they do not know how to present their checks and get them cashed, "the check-book of faith," to use Spurgeon's phrase, that by means of which we can appropriate to ourselves everything we need for time and eternity, for life and godliness.

Now that is the *provision* for victory.

My fourth point is THE PROOF OF VICTORY. We want to know how this works. There is first of all what we may call the negative proof, Ephesians 6: 13. "Take up the whole armor of God, that ye may be able to withstand in the evil day, and having done all, to stand." It is a glorious thing to be able to withstand evil, and to keep on standing, notwithstanding all the trouble that may surround you. That is the negative proof.

Now then the positive proof; I wonder whether you have ever seen it: "That he would grant unto us, that we being delivered out of the hand of our enemies might serve him without fear, in holiness and righteousness before him, all the days of our life" (Luke 2: 74, 75). We are delivered, therefore, in order that we may serve, and we are to serve without fear.. Ah, that is the trouble, there is so much fear in our life. We are afraid of this, that and the other. "My life," a man once said, "has been always surrounded by trouble, most of which has never come." I told you the other day about the old lady who went on deck, in a storm, and asked a sailor, "Is there any fear?" "Yes madam," he

The Gospel of Victory

answered, "plenty of fear, but no danger." That is often the case in the Christian life, there is plenty of fear, but there is really no danger.

"Without fear, in holiness"—that is towards God, "and righteousness"—towards men. Is that true of us to-night, dear friends? Are we right with God,—holiness? Are we right with our fellows,—righteousness? Can you look into your own heart and say, "There is not a single being on this earth that I am wronging to-night? You husbands, are you all right with your wives? You wives, are you all right with your husbands? You folk here, are you all right with your trades-people? Do you pay your debts? Are you right with your fellowmen?

A friend of mine once asked in England, "Is So-and-so a Christian?" "Yes," was the answer, "he is all right towards God, but he is a little twistical towards men." That is not right. If a man is right towards God he will not be "twistical" towards men. Some people say, "Is Christianity individualistic or socialistic?" It is both,—individual in relation to God, and social in relation to our fellows; and the trouble is that very often we fail to keep these together, and that which God hath joined together not one of us must put asunder.

What does this proof of victory mean for ourselves? First of all our thoughts will be right. Some people think this is impossible. Thoughts are so very elusive, so variable, that it is impossible for us to have our thoughts right and true to God. Is that the case? Have you ever looked at Second Corinthians 10: 5. "Bringing every thought into captivity to the obedience of Christ." Have you ever looked at Philippians 4: 6, 7 and seen the connection? "In nothing be anxious; . . . and the peace of God . . . shall guard your . . . thoughts." Let no one say therefore, that the thoughts, however elusive, however changeable, cannot be brought into captivity—in harmony—with the obedience of Christ.

The same thing is true of words. "Is it possible," someone asks, "that our words may be always all right?" Well, according to Colossians 4: 6, "Let your speech be always with grace." As I said the other morning, there is all the difference in the world between lightness and brightness. We are called upon to be bright, but not to be light. Levity, especially levity in sacred things, is to be avoided. The cheapening of sacred things in the present age, to my mind is something awful. "Holy and reverend is his name." "If you call on him as Father"—what? "Pass the time of your sojourning in fear." That is the way to deal with the fatherhood of God, and the New Testament, with all its glory of grace and freedom and fellowship, never forgets that. "It is a fearful thing to fall into the hands of the living God."

Yes, our words can be right. "Let your speech be always with grace," and if the words are all right, of course the actions will be all right. "Whatsoever ye do, do all to the glory of God" (1 Cor. 10: 31). Now this is reality, this is proof of Christianity, and we want this evening to face the question, with all its intensity, and with all its seriousness. These things are possible. If they were not possible we may close this Book and never open it again. If in our thoughts, and our words, and our deeds we cannot have victory, then Christianity is not only a farce, it is not only futile, it is fatal; and yet there are people who are excusing themselves for this or that wrong-doing. There are those who sometimes speak of crosses, when they ought to speak of sins. A lady once said to my friend Prebendary Webb-Peploe, "Mr. Peploe, I assure you there is no fault in my case, because I never lose my temper unless I am provoked." I think he answered that the Devil does about the same thing. I heard the other day of a man who, when he was speaking about something that he thought was not quite according to the New Testament, said, "You are too much under the law and not under the Gospel." The fact is, dear friends, there is a real danger of mistaking liberty for license. We rejoice with all our hearts in the liberty of the Spirit, but that is not license to do wrong, it is not license to think or to say what is wrong, and if there is anything in your life or mine that does not stand square with the Word of God, as we find it in the New Testament, you and I can make all the excuses we like, but when we get into the presence of God those excuses will have to go.

Now if that is the case, my next point follows naturally, THE POWER OF VICTORY. What is the power? Faith is the secret of this Victorious Life. Someone says, "Why is it that all this week you and other speakers have emphasized faith?" I will tell you why: faith is the only, as it is the adequate response of the soul to God. Faith enters into every part

The Gospel of Victory

of our life from the earliest days to the latest. The child goes to school, and the very first day trust is shown. The teacher says, "That is A," and the child believes it. The child does not say, "I want you to demonstrate beyond all question that that is A." The child believes it, and believes the whole alphabet from A to Z; and then it begins to verify, and put C and A and T together, and finds it spells cat, and D and O and G together, and finds it spells dog. That is the verification of faith; but it is faith first of all.

Faith is the only answer that we can give to God's revelation of himself. That is why Hebrews 11: 6 is true, "Without faith it is impossible to please him." If I say to my son, "My boy, I know something, which, if you will do it, will make a man of you," and that boy says, "I won't believe you," there is a barrier. But if he says, "Yes, father, I believe it, and will do what you tell me," I can work on and through that boy and make a man of him, if he does what I tell him. God comes to you and me, and says, "Will you believe?" and if you say "No," there is a barrier between you and God, and nothing can take that down unless you and I do it ourselves. But if we say, "Yes Lord, I am prepared to believe," that is the word of faith: "I believe God, that it shall be."

Faith covers everything in the Christian life. By faith we are justified, Romans 5: 1: "Being justified by faith." By faith we are saved, Ephesians 2: 8: "By grace are ye saved through faith." By faith we live, Galatians 2: 20: "I live by faith in the Son of God," is the true meaning of it; "I live by faith in him who is the Son of God, who loved me and gave himself for me." By faith we walk, 2 Corinthians 5: 7: "We walk by faith, and not by sight." Our hearts are purified by faith, Acts 15: 9; we receive the Holy Ghost by faith, Galatians 3: 14; we are sanctified by faith, Acts 26: 18. The Victorious Life Conference is intended to show that just as we bring the Gospel to bear upon the sinner, and make it as simple as we can, so this Gospel for the saint is intended to be equally simple, and they are both by faith. It is not justification by faith and sanctification by fighting; it is not justification by faith and sanctification by struggling, it is justification and sanctification by faith in the same Lord Jesus Christ. I Corinthians 1: 30, "Christ Jesus is made of God unto us wisdom"—that is the whole thing, but that wisdom is broken up into three parts,—righteousness for the

Dr. Griffith Thomas

guilty past, sanctification for the sin-stained present, and redemption for the future when sin shall be no more,—Christ Jesus, by faith for past, present and future (1 Cor. 1: 30). That is the meaning of the words "The just shall live by faith." When that passage is quoted in Romans 1, it is *"the righeous* by faith shall live;" when quoted in Galatians 3 it is "the righteous *by faith* shall live;" and when quoted in Hebrews 10 it is "the righteous by faith *shall live."* From beginning to end, the emphasis is on the life of the believer through faith.

Someone asks, "What is faith?" Well, faith takes various forms. In Matthew 7: 7, and elsewhere, in prayer: "Ask, and it shall be given you," "believe . . . and ye shall have." Faith believes God's Word, John 16: 31. You take God at his word, and that is another element of faith. I got a letter about a year ago, and it had on the top these words, "God said it, Jesus did it, I believe it, that settles it; Amen." That is faith. That is for the sinner, and it is also, thank God, for the saint.

Faith receives the grace of God, 2 Corinthians 6: 1: "We . . . beseech you also that ye receive not the grace of God in vain." "To as many as received him, to them gave he authority to become the sons of God;" we receive grace in receiving Christ by faith.

Then faith *reckons,* Romans 6: 11,—reckons on God's faithfulness. The Christian life, a well known commentator has said, is just like a metaphor taken from accounts. There are the two columns of accounts, debtor and creditor. On the one side everything that I owe, as long a list as you like, and on the other side put the Lord Jesus Christ; everything he is, and everything he has done, and is doing, is reckoned to my account, and there is a great and glorious reckoning. God reckons, and I reckon. God reckons that Jesus Christ has covered everything, and I reckon the same; I keep on reckoning, and he keeps on reckoning; I reckon myself dead unto sin, and alive unto God; and that faith is the secret of victory. Faith recognizes the promises of God, faith appropriates the facts of God such as we have been hearing about this week, faith is everything, and it is underneath act and attitude, and is what we have said again and again,—letting go and laying hold,—faith is allowing the Victor to come in. "If any man hear my voice, and open the door, I will come in to him, and will sup with him, and he with me" (Rev. 3: 20).

The Gospel of Victory

Therefore faith simply means the lordship of Jesus Christ. Faith means, as someone has said, "First of all you are to submit; then you are to admit; then you are to permit; then you are to commit; and then you are to transmit." Now that is faith. Faith submits to Christ, faith permits Christ to be everything, faith commits everything to Christ, faith admits Christ to every part of the life; and then faith transmits Christ to other people. And the question for every one of us to-night is, "Is that true of me?"

Oh, my brother, or sister, I would like the opportunity of asking that question of everyone here personally. Is the Lord Jesus Christ the Lord of your life? "To this end Christ both died, and lived again, that he might be Lord." So here is the question to-night: either sin is lording it over you, or Jesus Christ is lording it over you; under which lord are you to-night? who is your Lord, my brother, as you look into your own heart? As you review your past life, as you think of the last few days and weeks and months, have you been under the lordship of Jesus Christ, or have you been under the lordship of self and sin?

If Jesus Christ is your Lord, depend upon it, victory is yours. If he is not, you will never have victory. If you are prepared to-night to crown Jesus Christ as the Lord of your life, you have instant and constant victory, and if Jesus Christ is not Lord of all, Jesus Christ is not Lord at all; if Jesus Christ is not the Master of everything in your life, your hopes, those tendencies of yours, that will of yours, those insistent desires and yearnings, and determinations, everything,—if Jesus Christ is not Lord of those, Jesus Christ is not Lord of your life at all.

Over thirty years ago there were some riots in London, in that place known as Trafalgar Square, which from time immemorial has been like Madison Square in New York, the place for everybody to air his grievances, to speak freely in open air gatherings, without let or hindrance. But when there came rioting, it was another matter, and the government was perplexed. They wanted to avoid the rioting, but wanted to avoid any constraint or restraint on the liberty well known in connection with that place. For some time the government was perplexed to know what was to be done. Someone urged the government to take strong and drastic action, but the government wanted to find out, if possible, an

Dr. Griffith Thomas

easier way of overcoming the difficulty, when someone found out that Trafalgar Square belonged to the Crown, to the then reigning monarch, who was Queen Victoria. When that was brought to the government's notice, they saw at once that that settled the question, and they asserted the rights of the Crown over that area. Freedom of speech went on, and they are having their open air meetings there now, and always will have, apart from exceptional times like the present war; but in normal days Trafalgar Square is the scene of the most perfect freedom of speech, but no rioting, because everyone knows that belongs to the Crown.

Dear friends, your nature and mine is full of rioting, full of the incursions of evil, full of the assertions of our evil nature, full of determination to go the wrong way, and there is only one way of settling this, and that is the assertion of the Crown rights of the Lord Jesus Christ. "Of the increase of his government and peace,"—notice the order, first government, and then peace. When there is good government there is always peace, and when the Lord's government is ours, then there is always peace, and the government is to be upon his shoulder. The question is whether the government of our life is on him. To-night, the Lord asks for the control of our life.

> "O who this day, will rejoicing say,
>   With a grateful heart and free,
> 'Thou King Divine, my life shall be thine,
>   I consecrate all to thee.'
>
> "We daily live, and we daily give
>   For some object near the heart;
> Some purpose bold, some name we hold
>   Where the gushing life springs start;
>
> "But O, it is wise, when the heart can rise
>   And carry its wealth away,
> Where the angels fall: He deserveth all
>   That we at his feet can lay.
>
> "A life that serves where a love deserves
>   The life and the love that give,
> Is a life sublime on the fields of time,
>   A life it is grand to live.

The Gospel of Victory

> "Then let each this day, rejoicing say,
> With a grateful heart and free,
> 'Thou King Divine, my life shall be thine,
> I consecrate all to thee.'"

I am going to mention several steps into the Victorious Life. I want you to face these steps and find out whether what I now say is true. This is the first step: "Jesus, I *must* trust thee." Then, if we have taken that step, take the next, "Jesus, I *may* trust thee." There is no doubt about his willingness and readiness to help, and to bless, to receive and welcome,

> "Just as I am, thou wilt receive,
> Wilt welcome, pardon, cleanse, relieve,
> Because thy promise I believe."

That is true of the Christian as well as of the sinner, "I may trust thee." Then there is the next, "Jesus, I *can* trust thee." There is no reason why we should not. His power is sufficient, his grace will meet every need, his Word is true, an absolute guarantee for every need, under every conceivable circumstance, "Jesus, I can trust thee." The next is the crucial one, Jesus, I *will* trust thee." "I think, I feel, I ought, I will,—my mind thinks, my heart feels, my conscience says I ought, and when mind, and heart, and conscience combine, then the will should act,—"I will." When Rebecca was asked whether she would go with that man for the long distance to Isaac, she answered "I will." Are we ready to-night to say, "Jesus I will trust thee?" If so, then the fifth and last step will be true of us, "Jesus I do trust Thee,"—a present, blessed, glorious reality, "I do trust thee."

THE HOLY SPIRIT IN DAILY LIFE

Professor W. H. Griffith Thomas, D. D.

THERE are many differences between the methods of God's revelation of himself in the Old Testament and in the New Testament, and a fair number of them are perfectly obvious. But the most important and far reaching contrast (I think we may say "contrast") between the old and the new dispensations, is connected with the revelation of the Holy Spirit. You will remember this, or you can see it easily, if you take your concordance. There are singularly few references to the Spirit in the Old Testament. The term "Holy Spirit" only occurs, if I remember rightly, three times; but the general teaching about the Spirit of God in the Old Testament is almost impressive by its rareness. There is more, of course, in the Gospels, but it is especially in the latter part of the New Testament that we find the teaching so striking.

In the New Testament the Holy Spirit may be regarded as a characteristic of Christianity. John 7: 39 is one of the foundation texts, "This spake he of the Spirit, which they that believe on him should receive: for the Holy Ghost was not yet; because Jesus was not yet glorified." And as you know, the concluding discourses of our Lord in John 14 to 16 were almost wholly concerned with "that day," the day of the Holy Ghost. And yet, dear friends, with all this, it is strange that there are Christians to-day whose experience is still on the level of the Old Testament, or on the level of the Gospel.

There is a very striking illustration of this. I do not use it for more than as an illustration. You remember that Paul went to Ephesus, and met twelve men, and he said, "Did ye receive the Holy Ghost when ye believed?" And they answered, "We did not know that the Holy Ghost was given." It is a great mistake to think that they said, "We did not think there was a Holy Ghost." That is not the point,—"We

---

At Princeton Dr. Griffith Thomas gave four Bible studies on the Holy Spirit, of which this is the opening study. The other studies took up the Holy Spirit in Galatians, in Ephesians, and in Romans. While these are not published here, many of the important truths touched upon are covered in the addresses that are included in this volume. See page 379 for notice of Dr. Thomas' book on the Holy Spirit.

The Holy Spirit in Daily Life

did not know that the Holy Ghost was given." That is to say, they had never heard of Pentecost. They were disciples of the Baptist who had promised and prophesied the Spirit, but that the fact had ever been realized was of course outside their ken.

Now I think we may say (using that strictly as an illustration), there are people today who, though they may know these things intellectually, are really living on a plane of spiritual experience the other side of Pentecost. So I want to describe the dispensations this morning very briefly, in order that we may lead up to our subject.

First, will you notice there is *the dispensation of the Father*, from Abel to John the Baptist. We may call that generally, the dispensation of the Father. Now what were the marks of the believer's life during that dispensation? First of all there was a great fear of God. Six hundred times in the Old Testament is the word "fear" found. There is no doubt that those disciples of the Old Testament dispensation were moved with fear rather than love,—not to the exclusion of love, but certainly fear was the predominant thought.

Secondly, there was a sense of sin. You will see that all through the Old Testament sin was real, and with sin came sorrow; and yet, for the most part there was a good deal of powerlessness and hopelessness in the face of sin.

Third, there was a belief in the Messiah. The Jews looked forward to the coming of the Christ. They were thoroughly orthodox in their belief, all looking forward to their Messiah.

Fourth, there was a consciousness of immortality. They did believe in a future life. Perhaps they did not know much about it, but they looked forward to it, and I suppose they were certain that there was such a place, and that they by and by would go there.

Fifth, there was a spirit of separateness. The Jews were exclusive, and there was very little diffusion of religion. The Jewish religion was not in any true sense of the word what we should call "missionary."

These are the five elements of the Old Testament dispensation, and, dear friends, I want to suggest that they represent the life of a great many Christians today. There are many people today who are dominated with the thought of the fear of God. They are oppressed with the thought of sin, and

Dr. Griffith Thomas

they are powerless and hopeless in regard to sin. They are thoroughly orthodox in their belief about Jesus Christ, they are looking forward to the future and expect to go to heaven when they die. And there is a good deal of exclusiveness or separateness. This is the position generally that many Christians this side Pentecost really occupy.

Second, there is *the dispensation of the Son*. This is the period of our Lord's ministry on earth, and this represents a distinct advance on the old dispensation, and we want to look at the life of the godly, especially the disciples of Jesus Christ during those years of ministry.

The first element of it is this: it was a time of great power in the Word. The Lord Jesus Christ as a teacher was very impressive, and the Word, as taught by him, was very real and true. Sin was repressed rather than overcome, and all through the ministry there was that thought of, "His Word was with power."

Secondly, there was a good deal of variableness of experience. You will see the contrast between Peter on the Mount of Transfiguration and Peter at the time of the cock-crowing, and that is only one instance of many showing the variableness,—sometimes on the mountain top, sometimes in the valley.

Then there was a good deal of what we call the dominion of tradition. Things had been, and things were. "We saw," said the apostles, "a certain man; but he followeth not us." There was the idea of the traditional,—what may be called "an orthodox way of looking at things." They could not break the bonds of tradition even to the very end.

Fourth, there was a good deal of contentiousness. This is one of the sad things in the Gospels,—the disciples were contending to the very end; and at the time of the Last Supper they were still contending as to their particular places. Strife was based upon ignorance.

Then you will remember that this was also the time that the Holy Ghost was promised. The Lord promised them the Holy Ghost. He spoke of the Holy Ghost as the Comforter, as the Spirit of Truth, as the one who would bear witness. But all this was looking forward.

Now I want to say that this too represents the spiritual experience of a great many today. The Word is a power, the Bible is a reality,—they do not for a moment question it,

The Holy Spirit in Daily Life

and they see a good deal that is powerful in it; but their experience is variable, sometimes here, sometimes there, sometimes on the mountain, sometimes in the valley. There is a good deal of the dominion of tradition, "as it was in the beginning, is now, and ever shall be." There is also, we may say, a good deal of the spirit of contention. God's people are often ready to have strife, to throw bricks at one another, very largely through ignorance—until they throw the brick, and then they begin to see; but it is a little late then. Then there is always the expectation of something,—the promise of the Spirit, looking forward.

So there are people today (it is a most astonishing thing), living this side of Pentecost, whose experiences are practically those of the disciples, or of the people of the Old Testament.

My third point is this, *the dispensation of the Spirit*. Pentecost marked a difference, and I want to try to point out to you for your own meditation and study, some of the outstanding facts of the Acts of the Apostles in relation to the Spirit, that will enable us to see where we are, and, I trust, to get where we ought to be, so that we shall no longer be living in the dispensation of the Father, or in the dispensation of the Son, but in the dispensation of the Spirit.

And yet I want you to notice this, lest I should give a wrong impression. All these elements of the first dispensations will be found to be united and caught up and included in this. Everything that was right and true in the Old Testament and the Gospels, will be found here, but with wonderful additions and amplifications.

I take the Acts of the Apostles today, because, as you know, that book gives us the record of the first thirty years of the Christian Church. If I started with the Epistles people might say, "Well, that is just the ideal to which we are to strive," and so I start with the Acts, because this has to do with reality.

Someone has said that the name of the fifth book of the New Testament is called The *Acts* of the Apostles. Their resolutions have not come down to us; it is not what they resolved, but what they *did*. That is the idea I want to emphasize. This is the Christian life as *lived*. Now what is it?

(1) First of all it was a life of *rich personal experience*. This is the first element in the Christian life in the Acts. I

Dr. Griffith Thomas

do not suppose I can do much more than suggest passages, but I want you to look at these. We are told first of the fulness of faith. "These men were full of faith"—Stephen (6: 5), Barnabas (11: 24), both mentioned in connection with the Holy Ghost and faith.

Wisdom is another part of the experience (6: 3), "They could not resist the wisdom." Then you will remember Acts 15: 28, in the Council, "It seemed good to the Holy Ghost, and to us," and I do not think we have ever fathomed the depth of that phrase. It seems almost beyond possibility for any company of believers to say, "It seemed good to the Holy Ghost and to us."

Then you will find there is not only the fulness of faith, and the fulness of wisdom, but the *fulness of joy.* "The disciples were filled with joy and the Holy Ghost" (13: 52). Here you will allow me, perhaps, to make, I won't say a correction, but a little explanation. I was distinguishing the other morning between joy and happiness, and I said that we could not be happy always, because happiness depends upon what happens, circumstances, joy is independent of circumstances, and is the state of the soul in relation to God. A friend said, "What about the phrase in the Psalms, 'Happy are the people that have the Lord for their God?'" I was glad to have that correction, because the word "happy" as used in that connection always means blessed. It is the same word that is found in the first Psalm, "Blessed is the man." So I still think I am right in saying you cannot be happy always, but you can be blessed always, because blessedness is that element of Christian joy that comes from relation to God, and I think that if you will study the Beatitudes you will see that almost every Beatitude in the Gospels or in the Psalms has to do with our relation to God. Blessedness today is very largely associated with what we have, but in the Psalms this blessedness relates to what we are. There are in the Bible (I just mention this to those who might like to write a book on the subject), three sections of Beatitudes. I have often longed to see them put in a book,—the Beatitudes of the Psalms (twenty or more), the Beatitudes of the Sermon on the Mount, and the Beatitudes of Revelation.

Joy, then, was one of the outstanding features of the life of the early disciples. If you want to run through this book of Acts you would probably be surprised to find how many references there are to joy and blessedness, from Acts two on

The Holy Spirit in Daily Life

the day of Pentecost, onward. Joy has always been the mark of the true Christian life. All through Christian history you will find that wherever the Gospel has been purely preached and fully received, joy has been the result; while on the other hand, in the dark ages, joy has receded and has been absent from Christian experience. There is nothing more striking than to trace back the history of Christianity all through the centuries and see how joy burst out in the Reformation, how it receded in those dry and dread days of the sixteenth and seventeen centuries, came back in the evangelical and Methodist revival, and has been seen on the mission field and at home all through the recent centuries. That is the joy of the Holy Ghost.

Then there is *hope*. Stephen looked up and saw the Lord Jesus (Acts 7: 55), because he was full of the Holy Ghost.

Now it is this rich personal experience of faith, and wisdom, of joy and of hope that needs to be emphasized as one of the essential features of the Christian life; and when we examine ourselves in the light of it, O dear friends, don't you feel how rebuked and humiliated we are as we see how different our lives are from the lives of those early believers?

(2) It was a life of *great personal courage*. Mark: first the experience, and then the courage. There was great courage of speech (Acts 2). Just imagine Peter, the man who had been frightened by a servant maid seven weeks before, now stands out and tells those people frankly, "You put Him to death; God raised Him from the dead." The boldness of speech! Look at 4: 31. When the apostles came back from their trial, or so-called trial, they had a prayer-meeting, and the prayer-meeting was for strength and protection, "Now, Lord, behold their threatenings: and grant" that we may keep silence and be very well behaved and not say too much? "Now, Lord, behold their threatenings, and grant unto thy servants that with all boldness they may speak thy word" (4: 29).

There was also boldness of action. Again look at 4: 31. Not only were they to speak, but to act. Look at 13: 9, Paul, filled with the Holy Ghost, *said* to Elymas the sorcerer, and *did* something to Elymas beyond all question. Look at 8: 29 about Philip, and you will see again boldness of speech, and boldness of action.

Here again, courage is one of the essential features of the

Dr. Griffith Thomas

Christian life,—first experience, and then courage. It is because we are not courageous enough that we need to look at these things. Of course we need hardly tell you that with courage there should be tact. We must be very careful about that. What is the meaning of tact? "Getting in touch with people." Some people have plenty of courage, but have no tact. Just like the clergyman over in England who wanted the church graveyard enlarged. He thought it would be nice to take in a plot of ground, and did not know how to get it. At last he said to one of the officers of the church, "Don't you see our cemetery is filling up nicely?" He thought he would get his wish that way. You know, dear friends, many of us spoil our courage by want of tact. Of course there is always the danger lest, in our so-called tactfulness, we should be nervous and not faithful. I do not know which of the two is the worse. It is a little difficult to say which is the worse, courage without tact, or tact without courage, but they both hinder the cause of Christ. At any rate, here are these people who were able to say, "We cannot but speak the things we have seen and heard."

(3) It was a life of *splendid personal service*,—the experience and the courage expressing themselves in service, the service of preaching, "They were all filled with the Holy Ghost, and began to speak" (2: 4). That is a good way of beginning to speak, isn't it? If we did not speak unless we were filled with the Holy Ghost it would be all the better for the people and for ourselves, and for our message. "They were all filled with the Holy Ghost, and began to speak." Not only was there service of speech, but service of living. In 9: 31 you will find it, and in 4: 31, 32, that favorite text, they were one in heart; and you will find this thought of the Holy Ghost in all their service.

Just think for a moment: Peter was filled with the Holy Ghost (4: 8); Stephen was filled with the Holy Ghost (7: 55); Paul was filled with the Holy Ghost (9: 17, 18; 13: 4). You will find the Holy Ghost connected with comfort (9: 31); with power (10: 38) as well as with those elements I have mentioned; but they have their expression as well as their experience, faith, joy and wisdom.

Now let us look particularly at the phrase or the word connected with being filled. I know that some of my expressions will not necessarily find endorsement by everybody,

The Holy Spirit in Daily Life

but I can only pass on what I think. I do not know that these things are more than phraseology, but I want to suggest that you need to be particularly careful when you talk about the "baptism" of the Holy Ghost. The baptism of the Holy Ghost is a phrase not found in Scripture. You read of Christians receiving the baptism of the Holy Ghost, but whilst our experience may be right, I think sometimes our expression may be wrong. My point is this. I take baptism in the Holy Ghost to be exactly the same as baptism in water,—never repeated. People are never baptized in water twice,—at least they ought not to be; and so I think the baptism of the Spirit is an elementary and initial act that is never repeated. But I do believe with all my heart, in what has been said, "One baptism, many fillings," and it is a very striking thing, that the word "baptism" connected with the Holy Ghost, is never associated in the New Testament with anything except the beginning of an experience. "Ye shall be baptized with the Holy Ghost," referred to the day of Pentecost. When the Holy Ghost fell on Cornelius Peter remembered the word, "Ye shall be baptized." So the falling of the Spirit reminded Peter of the word "baptism"; so that baptism means "falling," and you will remember in First Corinthians 12: 13 (that passage I think is worthy of very careful consideration), "for by one Spirit are we all baptized into one body." That is to say, "when we first accepted Jesus Christ as our Saviour, the Holy Ghost baptized us." That is not *water*, that is the Holy Ghost; "We were baptized by the Holy Ghost" and put into the Body of Christ, that is, the Church.

Now when you have settled that, here comes the question. In the Acts of the Apostles you find a variety of wonderful experiences about the filling. "They were all filled with the Holy Ghost on the day of Pentecost" (2: 4); Peter was filled with the Holy Ghost again when he had some special work to do, in chapter four. We are told this of the disciples in Iconium (Acts 13), "They kept on being filled," they were being continually filled (*eplerounto*). Then there is the adjective "full" of the Holy Ghost, the normal position and condition; but I think the most beautiful of all is this, "Stephen, being permanently full of the Holy Ghost" (7: 55). All you who know the Greek will remember it is *huparchou pleres,* and I think it is a wonderful thing, not only were they *pleres,* "full," but *huparchou pleres,* Stephen was "permanently full" of the Holy Ghost. And that ought to be

Dr. Griffith Thomas

true of me, and of every other Christian, "permanently full" of the Holy Ghost.

That is the Holy Ghost in the Book of the Acts along those three lines,—a rich personal experience, a great personal courage, and a splendid personal fulness; and if you will look through all the chapters from Acts one to twenty-eight, you will find that that is true. So I have just these three points to emphasize as we draw to a close.

(1) First, this is God's *purpose for all;* this is not a luxury for a few. That is where we sometimes make our mistake. You know I have said again and again, there are no luxuries in the New Testament. A luxury is a thing you can do without, and Mr. Hoover is reminding us of things we can do without. But there are no things in the New Testament spiritual life that you can do without. There is no distinction between luxuries and necessities,—everything is a necessity, but thank God it is a luxury too, in the sense that we enjoy it. Everything is luxurious in that sense, but it is absolutely necessary. Now let us get rid of this idea that the fulness of the Holy Ghost is for a favored few.

You will find five typical bestowments of the Holy Ghost in Acts, showing that this is universal. There was the gift of the Holy Ghost to the Jews (Acts 2); there was the gift of the Holy Ghost to the Samaritans (8); there was the gift of the Holy Ghost to the persecutor (9); there was the gift of the Holy Ghost to the Gentiles (10); and there was the gift of the Holy Ghost on half educated and half ignorant believers (19). So you will see these are representative bestowments, indicating that the Holy Ghost is for all. That is God's purpose. And not only for all, but for all times.

For all times, for all circumstances, we read of the promise of the Spirit. We read of being baptized with the Spirit, we read of the gift of the Spirit, we read of the fulness of the Spirit, we read of the witness of the Spirit, we read of the anointing of the Spirit; so that this is not for special occasions, but for all occasions. In the Old Testament the Holy Ghost seemed to come upon special men, for special work, at special times; but now we may say, for *all* his saints.

You will find the Holy Ghost connected with boldness, and we need that at all times; we find him connected with obedience, and we need that under all circumstances; we find the

The Holy Spirit in Daily Life

Holy Ghost connected with wisdom, and who knows the moment we may not want wisdom? We notice the Holy Ghost in connection with faith, and comfort and joy; but I think the most delightful thing of all is this: "Look ye out among you seven men of honest report, full of the Holy Ghost and wisdom, whom we may appoint over this business" (6: 3). What is that? What we call secular work. The Holy Ghost was absolutely required for those people to do secular work. To my mind that is one of the most inspiring things in our life.

Of course the preacher needs the Holy Ghost to preach, but we need the Holy Ghost to add up that column of figures in the office, to do that bit of work, however secular. Don't let us be too hard and fast in our distinction between the sacred and the secular. I like the words of the Archbishop of Canterbury, "Nothing is secular but what is sinful." There is no real distinction between the sacred and the secular. In this sense of the word we need the Holy Ghost for everything.

> "Teach me, my God,
> In all things Thee to see;
> And what I do in anything,
> To do it as to Thee."

Secondly, *God's plan*. How may this thing be? Oh, may God enable me to speak to you as I want to speak to myself, and just find out how can this thing be ours.

First, faith obtains. That means, "Resist not the Spirit." Barnabas is described in a wonderful way, "A good man, full of the Holy Ghost and faith." Have you noticed that? It sounds to me like an epitaph. It seems as though Barnabas must have been dead when those words were written; but there is no need to wait for the epitaph. I like the man who said, "A penny worth of taffy is better than a shilling's worth of epitaphy." "A good man, full of the Holy Ghost and faith." "A good man," there is his character. "The Holy Ghost," there is the secret, "and faith" was the means by which he received the Holy Ghost. Barnabas had faith and the Holy Ghost,—faith obtains.

I should like to say that faith means faith, not feeling. There are many people who seem to think that the Holy Ghost is invariably associated with great tides of emotion.

Dr. Griffith Thomas

Not necessarily. Emotions are very largely temperamental. Some people are matter of fact stolid old English people that do not know much about emotion. There are wonderfully enthusiastic Welsh people who are simply always in emotion. You cannot expect that the Holy Ghost will work the same way among entirely different people, the warm hearted enthusiastic Celts, and the phlegmatic Saxons. The Holy Ghost must deal with them differently. But you see where it comes in—faith is as necessary for the Celt as for the Saxon, "that we might receive the promise of the Spirit through faith." Faith obtains.

Secondly, *faithfulness maintains.* Faith obtains, and faithfulness maintains. That means, "Grieve not the Holy Spirit." When we have, with the act of faith, obtained, then we so yield ourselves to God that we maintain by faithfulness. The act becomes an attitude, and the Holy Ghost, without any necessary tides of emotion, is simply and solely lived day by day.

Fellowship retains. That means, "Quench not the Spirit." In First Thessalonians 5: 19, 20 it says, "Quench not the Spirit. Despise not prophesyings." That is to say, "Keep close to the Bible and listen to what God says, and in fellowship with that you will obtain, and maintain, and retain the Holy Ghost."

So, dear friends, I will say again in a very simple way, this secret of the Holy Ghost is only possible as we are close to our Bibles. God speaks through the Word; God's Spirit uses the Word, and just as in regard to faith, we are to resist not, as regards faithfulness we are to grieve not, as regards fellowship we are to quench not the Spirit. This is God's plan, very simple, and yet very satisfying.

My last point is this, *God's power.* This is God's power in the Christian life. Have you noticed that there are twenty-eight chapters in the book of the Acts? In the first eleven chapters of Acts you have the Spirit of God; in the next nine you have the Word of God; and in the next eight you have the man of God. If you work it out you will see that in the first eleven chapters the Holy Ghost is mentioned thirty-eight times and the Word of God only fifteen; in the next nine chapters the Spirit of God is mentioned seventeen times, but the Word of God twenty-three times; and in the last eight chapters the Spirit of God is mentioned I think three times,

The Holy Spirit in Daily Life

but it is the man of God that is prominent. Paul's conversion is found, and the story of his life.

What is the meaning of that? The Spirit of God is our power; the Word of God is our message; the man of God is the channel through which the message can be sent home with power. But you will notice the order,—the Spirit first, the Word second, the man last. Not as you and I would have it,—the man first, the Word second and the Spirit last; but the Spirit comes first, and there are eleven chapters for the Spirit, nine chapters for the Word, eight chapters for the man. Although that is a little artificial, I think it does really represent the substance, the relation, the proportion in that book.

That is the thing I want to emphasize this morning, that the Spirit of God is God's power by means of which He, through the Word, uses the man of God; and when you and I have a message in our hearts from the Word of God, and it is illuminated by the Spirit of God, then we realize what this Book means.

Our Lord and Saviour Jesus Christ, in the same night in which he was betrayed, took bread, and when he had done this, he brake it, and said unto his disciples, "Take." And they took, didn't they? Our Saviour Jesus Christ, the same night that he rose from the dead, breathed on his disciples and said "Take," exactly the same word. "Take, eat, this is my body." "Take ye the Holy Ghost." And surely we may believe that as they took the bread on that night, they also took the Holy Ghost. They took, and if you and I are willing to take him this morning, as we are, and as definitely as we take the bread into our hands, that is the "taking" of faith, and the Holy Ghost comes into our lives, and fills us with wisdom, power, blessing, joy, faith, courage, and everything for life, character and service.

WHAT IS "JUSTIFICATION"?

Professor W. H. Griffith Thomas, D. D.

WHEN once the Bible is seen to be a revelation from God, the question that immediately follows is as to the relationship of man to God in response to his revelation, and the fundamental inquiry is practically that which is found in Job: "How can man be just with God?" (9: 2.) This implies that man is not "just" or "right" with God, and every religion, ancient and modern, bears its testimony to this solemn fact. Not only the Jewish religion in the Old Testament, but heathen religions of the past and the present, give evidence of this profound fact and great need. The only adequate answer to the question is to be found in God's revelation of himself in Scripture. Faint hints are given in the Old Testament (Gen. 15: 1; Hab. 2: 4); but for the full, definite teaching it is necessary to look to the New Testament, especially to the teaching of the Apostle Paul (Acts 13: 38, 39; Rom. 3; Gal. 3). The recent celebration of the Luther quadri-centenary is a fresh reminder of this great foundation truth, which, when proclaimed by Luther and his fellow Reformers in the sixteenth century, delivered men everywhere from spiritual bondage and introduced them into joyous liberty. Four questions cover most of the ground.

I. What is Its Meaning?—It is important to keep in mind the fact that justification always and only refers to our spiritual position in the sight of God, never to our spiritual state or condition. Sin has affected our relationship to God by bringing us under condemnation and guilt and involving us in separation. From the Garden of Eden onwards sin has always meant guilt and separation. The theme of the first three chapters of Romans has been rightly described as "guilty or not guilty." The Apostle first discusses the case of Gentiles (1: 17-31); then that of a particular class among them (2: 1-16); and lastly that of the Jews who had so many special privileges (2: 17 to 3: 9). The result of his inquiry

---

This address, and that which follows, What is "Sanctification"?, were two Bible studies given at the 1917 Conference at Princeton. They have been put into leaflet form and may be had from The Sunday School Times Co. at 3 cents each, 30 cents a dozen.

What is "Justification"?

was to bring in all the world guilty before God (3: 10-20). So that in the divine sight "shall no flesh be justified." This is in harmony with the words of David: "Enter not into judgment with thy servant; for in thy sight no man living is righteous" (Psa. 143: 2).

Justification is the act of God in which he declares the sinner free from condemnation and guilt, and reinstates him in a position of Divine favor. The condemnation is removed by forgiveness, the guilt is taken away by the sinner being regarded as righteous, and the separation is removed by restoration to and reinstatement in the original position of fellowship. Those who know the Greek for our English word "justify" (*dikaioo*) are aware that it means to reckon or account or regard as righteous. To justify a man is to reckon him righteous before God's throne. It is quite easy to reckon righteous one who is actually righteous, for any one could do that: it would be simply acquitting a man against whom no accusation could be made. But the Gospel speaks of the glory and wonder of God's grace in justifying "the ungodly," a very different matter (Rom. 4: 5).

When this is thoroughly understood, it is at once seen that justification is something far more than forgiveness. The two are intimately related, but they are not one and the same thing. The Apostle clearly distinguishes between them (Acts 13: 38, 39). Forgiveness is negative, but justification is positive. Forgiveness is like being stripped of old clothes. Justification is being clothed in new garments. It is possible for a man to forgive his fellow-man, pardoning the wrong-doing and refusing to take legal action against him; but it is beyond his power to justify him, to regard him as though he had never transgressed. There is an arrangement in England whereby the King can of his royal clemency pardon a criminal, but he cannot reinstate the man in the position of one who has never broken the law. To the end of his days the man will be a pardoned criminal. But the King of kings not only can forgive, but can clear the offender and reinstate him by regarding him as "right" in the eyes of law.

This shows that while forgiveness may be repeated day by day, according to need, justification is never repeated, because justification deals with our position or status in the sight of God, and this naturally covers the whole of our life, past, present, and future. After our justification, our need of forgiveness is then associated with our filial position, and we

Dr. Griffith Thomas

are then forgiven as children, not as unconverted sinners. This is seen in a well-known passage where God is said to be "faithful and righteous to forgive" (1 John 1: 9). This could not be said of the unconverted, because it is of God's mercy, not his faithfulness, that the sinner is forgiven. And so while forgiveness cancels the penalty of sin, justification provides a permanent standing before God.

It is also important to bear in mind the distinction between justification and sanctification. Although these two are connected in experience, they must be carefully distinguished in our thought. Justification, as we have seen, is concerned with our position, while sanctification is almost entirely connected with our condition. The one means relationship; the other, fellowship. Justification is never repeated, because it is an act; sanctification is repeated, because it is a process. The former is associated with Christ *for* us as our peace; the latter is connected with Christ *in* us as our power.

Thus justification, let it be repeated and clearly understood, is the gift of a new standing before God. Not only is the sinner pardoned, but he is received into the Divine favor. He is not only a forgiven criminal; he is a reinstated son.

II. WHAT IS ITS SOURCE?—There are only two main sources to be considered, the one human and the other divine. Human ways of justification need to be considered in order to show their impossibility and falsity. Sometimes justification is thought possible in connection with natural descent. The Jews of Christ's day made their boast of relationship with Abraham (John 8: 33), but this was of no power in relation to God, and John the Baptist shattered this false confidence when he told them that God was able of stones to raise up children unto Abraham (Matt. 3: 9). Christ himself gave a similar warning when he spoke of many coming from afar and sitting in the kingdom of heaven, while the children of the kingdom would be cast into outer darkness (Matt. 8: 11, 12). Paul had to face this problem in almost every place he visited, and the Epistles to the Galatians and Romans both deal specifically with this sad pride of descent (Rom. 2: 28). A similar confidence is apt to be shown to-day, when men think of their position as belonging to a professedly Christian nation, and even to be the descendant of generations of Christian men. But the Lord would never have said "ye must be born again," if the first birth had been sufficient.

What is "Justification"?

Closely associated with this, in connection with the Jews, was the desire to obtain justification by their own efforts, by what is known as "works of law" (Rom. 9: 31, 32). Saul of Tarsus was a striking example of this, and perhaps it was this fact that led him to emphasize the impossibility of it in his Christian preaching. Many to-day seem to take the same line, by regarding good resolutions and amendment of life as an adequate guarantee of their position before God. But the Apostle was easily able to show the hopelessness of such an attitude, because any one who wishes to be justified by his own work must keep the law perfectly, in thought, word, and deed, and this both negatively and positively. "Cursed is every one who continueth not in all things that are written in the book of the law, to do them" (Gal. 3: 10). Merely to mention this is to show the utter impossibility of any one being justified by his own efforts (Rom. 3: 20; Gal. 3: 11).

There is also the serious tendency of thinking that justification is somehow dependent upon ordinances. We know that circumcision was the ground of Israel's boasting, and against this the Apostle had to fight with all his power. He shows clearly that Abraham had righteousness reckoned to him before he was circumcised (Rom. 4: 10, 11), and that in Christ Jesus circumcision avails nothing (Gal. 5: 16). Bishop Moule, in an interesting treatment of Romans 2: 28, 29 suggests that the words "Jew" and "circumcision" might well be altered to "Christian" and "baptism" or "the Lord's Supper," because the same truth is applicable to-day in connection with Christian ordinances. As in the old rite of circumcision, so in the sacraments of to-day, there is a serious tendency to trust for justification. But while there is no desire or intention of derogating from the value and importance of these ordinances in their place and for their purpose, it must, nevertheless, be pointed out that the fact of baptism, or of Church membership, or of regular attendance at the Lord's Table is no necessary guarantee of a right relation to God. Justification is not by ordinances, however precious and divinely appointed they are.

There is only one way of justification, one ground, one basis, one foundation: the work of our Lord Jesus Christ. This is the heart of Paul's argument in Romans 3: 21-26. After showing that men have universally sinned, and thereby need a justification which they cannot themselves provide, he points out that God has set forth Christ to be a propitiation for our sins, and that on the ground of this work of our Saviour we are reckoned to be righteous in God's sight. This justifying act of God was due to his free grace, and was intended primarily to show to the world that he himself is righteous as well as the One who regards as righteous those who believe in Christ. Thus, as it has often been pointed out, the Gospel is God's arrangement or plan by which a sinner may enter into a new relationship to him. The Atonement of Christ forms the foundation of this acceptance of the sinner, and thereby God bestows what man cannot himself produce. The very God against whom we have sinned, and whose righteous anger we might well fear, has himself found a way whereby in perfect harmony with his righteousness he can justify even the most ungodly sinner (Rom. 4: 5). This is the meaning of Calvary, where "mercy and truth met together; righteousness and peace kissed each other" (Psa. 85: 10).

It is also deeply interesting to observe the various aspects of the work of Christ on our behalf with special reference to justification. From one point of view God is the source (Rom. 4: 5); from another, grace is the spring (Rom. 3: 24); from another, the atoning sacrifice of Christ is the basis (Rom 5: 9); and from yet another, the resurrection is the proof (Rom. 4: 25).

All this gives special point to the wonderful words of Paul: "Him who knew no sin he made to be sin on our behalf; that we might become the righteousness of God in him" (2 Cor. 5: 21). The finest commentary on these words is found in the magnificent paradox of Luther, which needs to be pondered and proclaimed again and again: "Thou, Lord Jesus, art my righteousness; I am thy sin. Thou hast taken what was mine; and hast given me what was Thine. What Thou wast not Thou didst become; that I might become what I was not." To the same effect are the equally splendid words of the great English theologian, Hooker, who, speaking of justification, said: "Such we are in the sight of God the Father as is the very Son of God himself. Let it be counted folly or frenzy or fury or whatsoever; it is our wisdom and our comfort. We care for no knowledge in the world but this, that man hath sinned and God hath suffered; that God hath made himself the sin of men, and that men are made the righteousness of God."

III. WHAT IS ITS METHOD?—The act of God whereby he

What is "Justification"?

declares the sinner righteous is on the one simple yet all important condition of *faith*. This principle is constantly and emphatically taught in the New Testament, especially by the Apostle Paul. "We reckon therefore that a man is justified by faith apart from the works of the law" (Rom. 3: 28). In the same way the faith of Abraham is used as the outstanding illustration of faith; "Abraham believed God, and it was reckoned unto him for righteousness" (Rom. 5: 3). The Apostle also illustrates this faith from the words of the Psalmist (Rom. 4: 6-8). There are several other passages, both in the Old Testament and in the New Testament, where this emphasis on faith is found, showing that from first to last, from the commencement of the Christian life to the close, "the righteous shall live by his faith" (Hab. 2: 4).

If it be asked why this emphasis is placed on faith, there are several answers. First, it is the only adequate response that man can give to the divine revelation. Second, it is the acknowledgment of our dependence on Another and of the cessation of our dependence on ourselves. It is this that makes the contrast between faith and works so important. This was the error of the Jews of old and it is the error found in several quarters to-day, for there seems to be something inherent in human nature that makes it cling to its own works. It has always been found most difficult for people to accept a salvation which is by grace through faith (Eph. 2: 8). If a man endeavors to work for his own salvation, the Apostle plainly states that the vital and essential truth of the Gospel is destroyed, while to him who believes in Christ and renounces his own works God's message of salvation comes, assuring him of righteousness (Rom. 4: 4, 5).

When this is properly understood, faith is at once seen to be entirely without merit, and is in no sense the basis, but only the condition, of our justification. We acknowledge by our trust that we do not and cannot rest any longer in our own efforts.

Besides, faith links us to Christ and constitutes the means of our spiritual union with him, and, as such, it is the foundation of all Christian life and experience, covering the whole of our career from beginning to end. Everything in the New Testament is in one way or another "by faith," and justification is only one of the blessings of the Christian life which come to us in Christ through faith. It is, therefore, not surprising that Paul said to Peter before the Christians in Antioch

Dr. Griffith Thomas

that a man is not justified by works of law, but by faith in Christ, because "by the works of the law shall no flesh be justified" (Gal. 2: 16).

IV. WHAT IS ITS POWER?—The value and importance of justification through faith in Christ touches the Christian life at every point, and it is of supreme importance that it should be considered in relation to all the necessities of spiritual experience.

It is the secret of *peace with God*. Justification gives to the penitent and believing soul a new relationship to God. He is forgiven and restored to the Divine favor, and, resting on the assured Word of God, he knows that all is well. Some of these immediate blessings of justification are stated by the Apostle Paul, when he speaks of our being justified by faith, having peace, and being introduced into the Divine presence and favor (Rom. 5: 1, 2). All this has been helpfully stated in some words that are frequently quoted: "God said it; Jesus did it; I believe it; that settles it. Amen."

This truth is also the secret of *spiritual liberty*. It has been well pointed out that the Christian life requires at least two elements: it must be free, and it must be filial. Bondage must be removed and the assurance of our sonship be experienced. This is possible only through justification by faith in Christ, which both destroys the bondage and reinstates us in our position as children of God. It is not surprising, therefore, that Luther should speak of this doctrine as "the article of a standing or falling Church"; and a modern writer has gone further with equal truth, saying that it is "the article of a standing or a falling soul."

This blessed truth of justification by faith is also the spring and guarantee of *holiness*, for in uniting us to God in Christ it at once brings into the soul the Holy Spirit of God and all the blessings of sanctification. Thus, it is impossible to be transformed into the image and likeness of Christ until and unless the penalty of sin is removed, the power of sin broken, and the grace of God thereby permitted to flow into every part of our life.

Further, this doctrine is the source and power of all true *Christian service*. The heart is "at leisure from itself" in order to work for others, and, because it is firmly fixed on the Rock of Ages itself, it is able to labor without fear or hesitation on behalf of those who are still in the mire and bog of sin. The fact that justification is a complete act of

What is "Justification"?

God and is never repeated, but covers the whole of our life, past, present, and future, is the basis and spring of our assurance of a new relation to God which enables us to live and work without any thought of ourselves in self-sacrificing effort on behalf of others. It is not too much to say that no work for God worthy of the name is possible until and unless we have the "blessed assurance" that all is well through justification between God and ourselves.

Not least of all, and in special relation to some of the greatest problems of to-day, this doctrine of justification through faith in Christ is really the only answer to the moral perplexities raised by the fact of what is known as Original Sin. It vindicates God's righteousness, while manifesting his mercy (Acts 17: 30; Rom. 3: 25). Our deepest need is a right idea of the divine character, and above everything else it is essential to know how God can at once be righteous and yet justify the ungodly. This problem is insoluble apart from Jesus Christ, who is the proof of God's capacity to justify, while himself remaining just (Rom. 3: 26). This is the message of Paul in teaching that the Cross is the manifestation of God's righteousness rather than of his mercy (Rom. 3: 21, 26). So that, as has been aptly said, while mercy can bring man to God, only righteousness can bring God to man.

WHAT IS "SANCTIFICATION"?

Professor W. H. Griffith Thomas, D. D.

ONE of the greatest words of the New Testament is Salvation, because it covers the whole of our life, past, present, and future. In regard to the past, it can be summed up in the word Justification, or "in Christ." In regard to the present, it can be expressed in the term Sanctification, or "like Christ." In regard to the future, it can be described as Glorification, or "with Christ." Justification is entirely concerned with the Christian position, and, while it commences in the past, includes the whole life. Sanctification has to do almost entirely with the present.

Few doctrines of the New Testament need more careful consideration than Sanctification, because of the different aspects of presentation. Thus, Sanctification is found both in Romans and Hebrews, but with a very decided difference. In Romans the main thought is concerned with our relation to the divine throne, and how we can approach it without fear. In Hebrews the thought is connected with the divine sanctuary, and how we may be morally and spiritually fitted for this place of worship. On this account it has been well pointed out that Justification deals with the righteousness of God, and Sanctification connects itself with the holiness of God. It is certainly interesting to realize that in Hebrews the term "the sanctified" is descriptive of the whole company of believers, and is almost equivalent to the Justification of Romans. This emphasizes the necessity of the clearest possible conception of what is meant by Sanctification.

I. The Divine Revelation.—It is important to start with the thought of Sanctification as God's requirement. "This is the will of God, even your sanctification" (1 Thess. 4: 3). But what is the meaning of the word? The root-idea is that of "separation," and this is clear both from the Hebrew and Greek terms. Very often the first place in which a word occurs is helpful as a guide to its meaning elsewhere, and this seems to be true of Sanctification. It is found for the first time in connection with the primal institution of the Sabbath,

---

One of the Bible studies given at the 1917 Conference at Princeton. See note on page 61.

What is "Sanctification"?

when it is said that "God blessed the seventh day, and hallowed it," or "sanctified" it (Gen. 2: 3). As this took place before the entrance of sin, it is clear that no reference is possible to the thought of cleansing or purification. It means that God set apart or separated the Sabbath as a special day. For the same reason, we read of things and places being "sanctified," that is, "separated," as specially belonging to God. This, too, is the fundamental idea of persons being "sanctified," that is, "set apart," for God's possession and service (Exod. 13: 2; 19: 14; Lev. 8: 30).

When this is understood, the reference to Christ's Sanctification becomes perfectly clear and luminous. It is obvious that he had no sin from which to be cleansed, so that when he said, "I sanctify myself" (John 17: 19), he meant "I set apart" myself, "separate" myself, meaning that he thus devoted himself to the work that God gave him to do. This view, also sheds great light on a well-known passage referring to Christians: "The God of peace himself sanctify you wholly" (1 Thess. 5: 23), meaning that we are to be wholly set apart, entirely separated for God as belonging to him. It is of the utmost importance that this thought of the believer's complete sanctification in the sense of complete separation for God should be grasped at the outset, because it means that our life is claimed as altogether belonging to him.

This work of Sanctification is associated with each Person of the Trinity. Thus, we are said to be "sanctified in God the Father" (Jude 1, King James Version), and this corresponds with the reference of the Apostle Paul to "the God of peace himself" (1 Thess. 5: 23). Then, too, Sanctification is associated with Christ, and it is here that the importance of Hebrews is seen. Christ is the Sanctifier, and Christians are the sanctified; and this is the force of the words, "both he that sanctifieth and they that are sanctified are all of one" (Heb. 2: 11). Then in Hebrews 10 we learn the ground of our Sanctification through Christ's perfect sacrifice, in contrast with the imperfect sacrifices of the old dispensation. "By which will we have been sanctified through the offering of the body of Jesus Christ once for all" (Heb. 10: 10). "For by one offering he hath perfected for ever them that are sanctified" (Heb. 10: 14). We are thus set apart by the will of God, because of Christ's one perfect sacrifice. This is absolute and complete, and cannot possibly refer to that progressive work in the soul which we often think of as Sanctifi-

Dr. Griffith Thomas

cation, for in Hebrews it is not the work of the Spirit, but the work of Christ, which is under discussion. To the same effect are the Apostle Paul's words: "Of him are ye in Christ Jesus, who was made unto us wisdom from God, and righteousness and sanctification, and redemption" (1 Cor. 1: 30). Every believer is thus God's sanctified, or separated, man, being set apart by God for himself in and through the sacrifice of Christ.

Then the work of the Spirit is to be distinguished by regarding it in a twofold way. First, it is due to him that we have been set apart; then, it is the result of this that we are being continually purified by the same Spirit, so as to become in reality what we already are in the mind and purpose of God. Thus, the Word is clear that the work of the Spirit in Sanctification is, first of all, to be regarded as absolutely complete. "Ye were sanctified . . . in the Spirit of our God" (1 Cor. 6: 11). Yet, as we know, the actual moral and spiritual state of the Corinthian Christians was by no means what it ought to have been (1 Cor. 5: 1). The name of our Lord was being sadly dishonored; but this deplorable condition, terrible as it was, did not affect their position "in Christ," and the apostle seems to lay all the greater stress on this in order to touch their conscience and make them utterly ashamed of their ways. So also when it is said, "in sanctification of the Spirit," the reference is clearly to the setting apart or separation of us for God (1 Pet. 1: 2). The same thought seems to be true of the Apostle Paul's words, "In sanctification of the Spirit" (2 Thess. 2: 13). The position of the Christian is shown to be marked off for God by means of the work of the Holy Spirit.

It is of vital importance to recognize this primary and fundamental idea of Sanctification as meaning separation, for it shows that in this respect there is no difference between one Christian and another, the youngest being as truly sanctified (as in Heb. 10: 10, 14) as the oldest and most experienced. It is only, as we shall see, when this position is *realized in experience* that there comes a difference between Christians in regard to progress; but the position itself is absolutely and permanently the same in every case. It is inspiring to realize that the terms "sanctified" and "perfected" describe the present position of every believer by reason of the sacrificial work of the Lord Jesus.

When all this is fully perceived, it becomes clear that the

What is "Sanctification"?

primary and fundamental idea of Sanctification is neither an achievement nor a process, but a gift, a Divine bestowal of a position in Christ. So that while Justification may be considered to refer to position leading to condition, Sanctification includes both position and condition. The link of connection between them is Regeneration, or the gift of a new life. Both Justification and Sanctification are, therefore, complete from God's standpoint, but while Justification needs immediate and complete acceptance, Sanctification calls for thorough recognition followed by constant realization.

II. THE HUMAN REALIZATION.—At this point comes in the attitude of the believer in response to God's separation of him. The divine Sanctification or setting apart is intended for practical use, just as the apostle says, "sanctified, meet for the Master's *use*" (2 Tim. 2: 21). It will help us to understand and distinguish the divine act and the human attitude, if we think of the former as Sanctification and the latter as either Consecration or Dedication.

A vivid illustration of this is seen in the history of Israel. They had been redeemed from Egypt and had arrived at Sinai, where they received instructions from God for their life. While there, they were taught about the various offerings, and the first of these mentioned in Leviticus is the burnt offering, which meant, beyond all else, whole-hearted consecration to God. On the basis of the redemptive sacrifice of the Passover, the people were to regard themselves as wholly belonging to God, and the complete consumption of the offering by fire was an outward and visible symbol of the people's perfect dedication to God. The same thought of consecration was taught in connection with the priesthood and, indeed, in many other aspects of their life. God separated them for the purpose of their being used in his service, and the divine sanctification was to be met by perfect and continual human dedication.

The same truth is taught immediately on the arrival of Israel in Canaan. A significant episode makes this clear. Just before the capture of Jericho, Joshua was out, perhaps reconnoitering, and seeing a stranger, went up boldly and asked whether he was "for" Israel or the Canaanites. The mysterious stranger replied that he had come in neither capacity, but actually intended to supersede Joshua in the command of Israel. "As prince of the host of Jehovah am I now come"

Dr. Griffith Thomas

(Josh. 5: 14). The point of this message is seen in the word "now." God had come to them in Egypt as Redeemer, and at Sinai as Teacher, but in Canaan he was to be their Lord, Master, Prince, Captain, and Leader. This was to be the secret of Israel's blessing and power; God as their Captain, and Joshua as only an instrument in God's hands. It is not surprising, therefore, that Joshua recognized this at once, and both in word and deed signified his readiness to take the place of subjection and to do as he was told (Josh. 5: 14, 15; 6: 1, 2).

This thought of Divine Lordship, as following Sanctification, marks the true life of the believer. The prophet Isaiah suggests this in the significant order of the two words: "government" and "peace" (9: 7). First government, and then peace; for, of course, it is only as there is government that there can be peace, and only as Christ is our Lord can there be any true life for the believer. The same thing is taught in the New Testament, where, beyond all else, Christ is shown to be Lord. "To this end Christ died and lived again, that he might be Lord" (Rom. 14: 9).

This is the meaning of the well-known phrase: "I believe; I belong." We are to accept the fact that, when Christ died and rose again, he did his work for the purpose of our life being wholly given to God; and then the Holy Spirit marks us off for God by the bestowal of a new life and nature, which enable us to be what God intends.

III. THE HUMAN RESPONSE.—From this thought of divine separation and human realization comes the natural enquiry as to how all this may be made real and true in our experience. The answer is found in the word *Faith*.

Practically everything in the Christian life is associated with faith. We are *justified* by faith (Rom. 5: 1); we *stand* by faith (2 Cor. 1: 24); we are *purified* by faith (Acts 15: 9); we *live* by faith (Gal. 2: 20); *Christ dwells in us* by faith (Eph. 3: 17); we *walk* by faith (2 Cor. 5: 7); and it is, therefore, not surprising to read that we are "*sanctified* by faith" (Acts 26: 18).

How, then, does faith work in Sanctification? We know how it works in Justification, when we have to accept as God's free gift his provision of the position of Justification in Christ. But it is sometimes overlooked that our Sanctification comes in exactly the same way, by the acceptance, through sim-

What is "Sanctification"?

ple faith, of God's gift. "As therefore ye received Christ Jesus the Lord, so walk in him" (Col. 2: 6). It is for us to accept God's revelation of Sanctification in Christ by the Spirit, and then to appropriate, appreciate, and apply it, so that every faculty of our being may be the Lord's.

But let us go more into detail, and see how faith works in Sanctification,—what is its proper response.

1. *Faith realises.* Several times in Scripture are the words found, "Know ye not"; and the first act of our Christian life is to recognize the blessed facts and realities of God's work for us in Christ by the Spirit. There are several things we ought to know, and the knowledge of which will enable us to see what God has provided for us (Rom. 6: 3, 6; 7: 1; 1 Cor. 3: 16; 6: 15, 16, 19). Faith realizes these facts and accepts them as divinely true. This is the meaning of our Lord's words: "Sanctify them through thy truth: thy word is truth." The heart and life are to be continually informed by the revelation of the Divine truth of Scripture.

2. *Faith then reckons* (Rom. 6: 11). The Apostle seems to use the illustration of two columns of figures, debit and credit, and reminds us that in the one column is everything we need because of sin, and in the other everything that has been supplied in Christ. We are to reckon that everything he was and did belongs to us; that when he died, we died; when he was buried, we were buried; when he rose, we rose; when he ascended, we ascended. This "reckoning" is in the present tense, implying a continuous act by faith of the believer. It is not feeling or emotion, or imagination, but fact made real by faith. We are to reckon ourselves dead unto sin, but alive unto God. This does not mean that self is dead. We are, therefore, not to reckon it dead, and still less to reckon sin dead, but to reckon ourselves "dead unto sin, but alive unto God." Then as faith keeps on reckoning, God sees that the reckoning becomes true in our personal experience. Every fact in Christ accepted by faith is to become a factor in our life.

3. *Faith responds.* This suggests the attitude set forth in various places in the New Testament. Thus, we are to "present" ourselves unto God, as alive from the dead (Rom. 6: 13); we are to "present" our bodies a living sacrifice (Rom. 12: 1); we are to "commit" ourselves to him that

Dr. Griffith Thomas

judgeth righteously (1 Peter 2: 23). It means that we are to place ourselves alongside of God, so to speak, putting ourselves at his disposal. This is the true idea of the word used of Paul and Barnabas, men that have "handed over their lives" (Acts 15: 26). This response is, of course, made by an initial act of surrender and then maintained by a constant attitude, whereby we realize that everything we are and have belongs to God.

4. *Faith receives.* This is another of the acts of faith, whereby it appropriates from God what it needs. Just as faith receives Christ for salvation (John 1: 12), so it continues to receive of his fulness (John 1: 16), his grace (2 Cor. 6: 1), and his Spirit (Gal. 3: 3). In this connection it is important to distinguish between the faith that *asks* and the faith that *takes.* Perhaps this is the meaning of the close association so often found in Paul's Epistles between prayer and thanksgiving: prayer being the faith that asks, and thanksgiving the faith that appropriates. It is only too possible for us to go on asking without receiving, but faith is seen as much in appropriating as in appealing to God.

In the same way, it is equally important to distinguish between God's *promises* and his *facts.* A promise is something to be pleaded and expected, but a fact is something to be believed and accepted. Promises are to be fulfilled in the future, and we wait as we expect God to be true to his word; but a fact is something to be accepted, used, and enjoyed here and now. Christ drew this distinction when he said: "Whatsoever ye pray and ask for, believe that ye *receive* them and ye *shall have* them." Promises are always worded in the future tense, God saying either "will" or "shall"; but facts are always in the present tense like "the Lord is my shepherd" (Psa. 23: 1), and "my grace *is* sufficient" (2 Cor. 12: 9). This is why Dr. Meyer is able to speak in one of his books of "the present tenses of the blessed life."

5. *Faith resists.* In the great passage on the Christian armor the Apostle Paul says that we are to "be strong in the Lord, and in the strength of his might" (Eph. 6: 10). It is often asked whether the Christian is not to fight, in the conflict with personal sin. The answer is that of course he must fight, but it is necessary to remember that it is the "good fight of *faith*" (1 Tim. 6: 12), and it is particularly important to realize that the fight is not to *obtain* but to *maintain.* It is

What is "Sanctification"?

not a struggle *for* a position, but *from* a position. As has been well said, the Christian is not like a man in the valley struggling to reach the top of the hill, but like a man on the top of the hill fighting to maintain his position there against enemies who are trying to drag him down. And so the apostle is able to say, "Put on the whole armor of God, that ye may be able to stand against the wiles of the devil," and, "take up the whole armor of God, that ye may be able to withstand in the evil day, and, having done all, to stand" (Eph. 6: 11, 13). "This is the victory that overcometh the world, even our faith" (1 John 5: 4).

6. Faith rests. This is the meaning of the great word "Abide" (John 15: 4). It means "stay where you are." We are to abide in Christ (John 15: 4), in his love (John 15: 9), in his Word (John 8: 31), and in prayer (Col. 4: 2). This attitude of restfulness is one of the prime secrets of true sanctification. When Canon Harford-Battersby of Keswick came back in 1874 from the Oxford Conference, he was asked what he had learned there that was new; and he replied, "I learned the difference between a struggling and a resting faith."

And so, as we contemplate this necessity of faith and what it means, we recognize that, to use familiar words, faith first "submits," then "admits," then "commits," then "permits," and then "transmits." The great aim of Satan is to get the believer to become occupied with himself and by means of introspection to fight in his own strength, instead of appropriating the One who is stronger than he is. If only this lesson of faith is learned, first will come the act, then the habit, then the character, and we shall be "more than conquerors *through him that loved us*" (Rom. 8: 37). Everything depends upon our clear recognition of the two facts; first, that God has marked us off as his own, for his complete possession and his continual use; and then, upon our ready, prompt, full and constant recognition and realization of this truth, as we yield ourselves to him to work in us both to will and to do of his good pleasure (Phil. 2: 13).

It is said that once Mendelssohn came to see the great Freiburg organ. The old custodian refused him permission to play upon the instrument, not knowing who he was. At length, however, he reluctantly granted him leave to play a few notes. Mendelssohn took his seat, and soon the most won-

Dr. Griffith Thomas

derful music was breaking forth from the organ. The custodian was spellbound. He came up beside the great musician and asked his name. Learning it, he stood humiliated, self-condemned, saying, "And I refused Mendelssohn permission to play upon my organ!" There comes One to us, who desires to take our lives and play upon them. But we withhold ourselves from him, and refuse him permission, when, if we would yield ourselves to him, he would bring from our souls heavenly music.

PRAYER IN THE CHRISTIAN LIFE

Professor W. H. Griffith Thomas, D. D.

I HAVE very little doubt that there is one question beyond all others that is being asked by many of us at this time. It is asked at every conference towards the closing days,—"After the Conference, how?" People feel that the Christian life at the time of a conference is not altogether difficult, in some respects it is easy, in the atmosphere of fellowship, in meditation on the Word of God, in the singing of praises; and generally speaking, throughout the conference the Christian life seems quite simple, and easy, and obvious. But it does not seem quite so easy, and simple, and obvious, when we go down from our conference to—it may be a home, or an office, or some similar establishment where there are people who are not God's people, and with whom we have little or no fellowship. And so the question is, "How may we retain the influence of the conference? How may we retain that attitude and experience of victory of which we have been hearing so much?"

Now the one word beyond all others is, of course, one which you all know; but I am going to tell you, whether you know it or not,—it is the word "abide." Our Lord Jesus Christ's relation to us may be summed up, as I said to the ministers the other day, in these four words: "Come unto me," "Learn of me," "Follow me," "Abide in me." "Come unto me," as Saviour; "Learn of me," as teacher; "Follow me," as Master; "Abide in me," as life. That word "abide" is rendered sometimes "continue," "dwell," "remain," but if you will look at the Revised Version of John 15 it is always "abide."

There are two men of whom it is written that "they continued." In the Old Testament, "So Daniel continued," and in the New Testament Paul said, "Wherefore I continue." What we need to learn is the secret of continuance. Now I

This address was delivered at the Friday morning Bible period at Cedar Lake, and together with the address that follows, was given at Whittier. See note on page 101. At Princeton Dr. Griffith Thomas gave four addresses on prayer, some of the main points of which are summarized in this article.

Dr. Griffith Thomas

want to suggest that there are two prime secrets of continuance, and on these two we are going to dwell to-day and to-morrow,—prayer and the Bible. This morning we shall take prayer.

A great deal could be said about prayer, its philosophy and all the rest of it, about the Bible, its authority, inspiration, and the rest of it, but we are going to concentrate attention upon these two subjects as they relate to our own life.

I. THE FOUNDATION OF PRAYER. You will never find any argument about prayer in Scripture. People often argue to-day on what may be called the philosophy of prayer,—why we should pray, but Scripture takes it for granted that we will pray. Just as it never argues for God, but starts with the proposition, "In the beginning God," so it always takes it for granted that people will pray. The basis of prayer is the revelation of God. Unless God had revealed himself we could not pray. Prayer is not so much natural, as supernatural, and we want to think of God's personality, God's character, God's truth, God's will, and God's work. God and His Word are the basis, the foundation of our prayer.

He *can* hear; if one may say with reverence, He *must* hear; and we are also certain that He *will* hear, and that He *does* hear. So we want to settle it beyond all question that everything we know of God warrants our prayer.

II. THE EFFECTS OF PRAYER. What will prayer do for us in our Christian life? First, it will *make the presence of God real to us*. There will be in our souls a consciousness of God's peace calming us in our difficulties, a sense of joy cheering us in our service, and a sense of God's glory illuminating every doubt. It will make the presence of God real.

Prayer will also *make the power of God felt*. We become conscious of the power of God in our daily life.

Prayer will *make the will of God clear to us*. It is marvelous, and yet not marvelous, that before we pray we are often in doubt and perplexed as to what to do, and after we have prayed our perceptions have become purified, our moral balance has been put right, and we are prevented from doing what is wrong, and enabled to see what is right. In familiar old words, "We perceive and know what things we ought to do."

Prayer *makes the service of God easy*. How often in our

Prayer in the Christian Life

Christian life we find things hard and difficult, and after prayer comes the very opposite; things become easy. Someone has said, "We often pray, 'Lord help me to do my work;' as we learn more of the Gospel we pray, 'Lord help me to do Thy work;' but as we come closer to Christ we see that the prayer we need to pray is, 'Lord do Thy work through me.'" That is prayer. We find God's service perfect freedom. One of the prayers translated into English in the Episcopal prayerbook is this: "O God, in knowledge of whom standeth our eternal life, whose service is perfect freedom." The terse Latin of it is, literally translated, "Whom to know is to live; whom to serve is to reign." And thus God's service is made easy through prayer.

> "Lord, what a change within us one short hour
>   Spent in Thy presence will avail to make!
>   What heavy burdens from our bosom take!
> What parched grounds refresh as with a shower!
> We kneel, and all around us seems to lower;
>   We rise, and all the distant and the near
>   Stand forth in sunny outline, brave and clear;
> We kneel—how weak! We rise, how full of power!
> Why, therefore, should we do ourselves this wrong,
> Or others,—that we are not always strong;
>   That we are ever overborne with care;
>   That we should ever weak or heartless be,
> Anxious or troubled, when with us is prayer,
>   And joy, and strength, and courage, are with Thee?"

In this great Sonnet on Prayer, by Archibshop Trench, we see a little of what prayer will do. Prayer *makes God's blessings available for others*. It not only blesses our life, but through us it blesses others. Our life becomes a channel, and prayer—because it means contact with God—enables us to set up contact with other lives, and the outcome is grace.

III. THE PROMINENCE OF PRAYER. So, dear friends, at this point I want to pause for a moment and emphasize the prominence that prayer should have. You remember Dr. Johnston on Tuesday evening referred to a point in the history of the apostolic Church, which needs to be continually mentioned. The apostles said, "It is not suitable for us to serve tables. We will give ourselves continually to prayer and the ministry of the Word." It has always been so in the Christian Church. Every advance has been associated with prayer. Every crisis, every revival, has always been connected with prayer; and for this reason we must make prayer as prominent as possible in our spiritual life.

One who was greatly used of God years ago in the Welsh revival, said these three things as the divine order connected with prayer: "First, God wants a thing done; second, God moves a believer to pray that it may be done; third, God does it in answer to prayer." Now that is the vital and essential place and power of prayer. Dr. Andrew Murray once said, "Christ actually meant prayer to be the great power by which His Church should do His work in this world, and nothing avails without it." So let us go from this place this morning convinced above all else of the absolute necessity of prayer.

IV. THE SUBJECTS OF PRAYER. I am concerned now only with those topics of prayer that have to do with Scripture. There are many things outside of the Bible for which we are permitted to pray according to God's will, but we ought to make sure of these topics that are, in Scripture, clearly the will of God for us.

First, we should pray with regard to *our own spiritual life*. You will find again and again in the New Testament, prayer on behalf of spiritual realities in our own lives and in the lives of others,—adjustment and progress. You get the principle in Colossians 4: 12, where we are told that Epaphras prayed for those people in Colossæ, that they might stand perfect and complete in all the will of God. That was a prayer on their behalf, for their spiritual life.

Another aspect of this is *intercession*. I want to suggest to you that our spiritual life will be at its very best if we give a very large place to intercession, and I want to come down to very particular matters and ask you, as I have asked myself, this question, "How much of our private prayer time do we give to other people?" Suppose we have a quarter of an hour for prayer, how much of that quarter of an hour do we give to others? Among the various sins that are stated in God's Word, there is one sin that is sometimes overlooked, the sin of ceasing to pray for other people: "God forbid that I should sin against the Lord in ceasing to pray for

Prayer in the Christian Life

you" (I Sam. 12: 23). Samuel had been put to one side, and if his own feelings had been the criterion he might have said, "Well, let them alone. They have put me on one side; let them find out the mistake and the sin they have committed." But instead of that, he said, "God forbid that I should sin against the Lord in ceasing to pray for you." So I say again, how much of that time that we have for ourselves in private devotion, do we give to others? In our prayer-meetings in our church how much of the hour do we give to intercession on behalf of others? If we call ourselves priests of the Most High God, priests in union with the Lord Jesus Christ, we ought to exercise our priesthood in this ministry of intercession. In James 5: 16 we are urged to pray for one another, and are reminded of the power of intercession: "The supplication of a righteous man availeth much in its working."

Another element in connection with intercession is *prayer for the ministry*. Spurgeon was once asked why so much blessing came to his church, and he said, "My people pray for me." We had a prayer-meeting in our Church in London, and in Oxford, and I was asked not to go to that meeting, held a quarter of an hour before the service commenced, so that the people might feel freer to pray for me and my preaching. That evening, as I looked around the church I could see the people whom I knew had been at that meeting, and it was a wonderful inspiration. When I went back to my church in London years afterwards, where Dr. Stuart Holden is now, they still had the meeting, and we joined together in prayer for him and for the sermon he was to preach that night. There is power in the ministry when there is the consciousness that the people pray. You remember how Paul again and again said, Brethren, pray for us, that the Word of the Lord may have free course and be glorified.

I need hardly remind you of our day text for to-day, "Pray ye the Lord of the harvest,"—*prayer for missions*, and again and again this is brought before us in one way or another in the Word. We ought to pray for the whole world, but there should be a definite prayer cycle, intelligent and detailed. It is only too great a temptation to lump all the countries together and pray for the whole world instead of praying in detail, definitely, for missions.

Some years ago there was a province in China that had

Dr. Griffith Thomas

been occupied by missions, but had become closed, and there were no missionaries in that province. It was laid upon the hearts of several in South Africa to pray; a clergyman and four or five of his people used to meet every week in his study to pray that God would open again that province in China. They prayed, and by the end of a year some of the people from that prayer-meeting were working in that province. God often calls us to answer our own prayers. When He said, "Pray ye the Lord of the harvest," He sent them out two and two to work; and perhaps the reason why many of us do not pray for missions is that we are afraid that God may want us to answer our own prayers; and if we take that attitude, depend upon it, we shall suffer thereby.

Intercession is not easy. I do not think for a moment we are ever justified in being impatient, but it is a temptation to some of us to be impatient, when we hear a man say with regard to missions, "Well, if you cannot do anything else you can pray," as though prayer were the easiest thing in the world. Prayer is the hardest thing in the world. My impression is, that if you and I can pray for missions, we are doing that which is not only the hardest, but in some respects the most effectual.

There are other subjects that I cannot mention individually this morning, but I would call attention to this: *"Whatsoever ye shall ask in My name."* Asking in Christ's name does not mean using His name, and closing our prayers by saying, "We ask in Christ's name." Asking in Christ's name is asking in union with what you know of Him. The name of Christ is always the revelation of the revealed character of Christ, and it means that you and I are so to study God's Word, and so to realize what He has revealed of Himself, that we are enabled to ask and feel sure that we are asking according to His will.

We can ask for all sorts of things when they are revealed in God's Word, and what is not revealed in God's Word we always ask subject to His will. You know in the earliest days of this terrible war there was, as there still is, a great deal of prayer. I was in England just the week of the battle of the Marne, when the Germans were driven back. At that time there were two British Generals, Lord Roberts and Lord Kitchener together, and when the telegram came that the Germans had been driven back, Lord Roberts said, "This is God's doing;" and Lord Kitchener said, "Somebody has been

Prayer in the Christian Life

praying." Lord Kitchener used to turn into a church every morning on his way down to the war office for quiet prayer, and in the British War Office to-day, in the vestibule, put there no one knows by whom, are these words on a card: "This war will be won by prayer." There it is, a testimony to everybody who passes in and out during these busy days. Dr. Dixon of the Metropolitan Tabernacle, formerly of the Moody Church, says that a member of his congregation told him that he had been praying all that night before the Germans were driven back, with scarcely a break for sleep, and in the morning he found out that the Germans had had to fall back thirty-five miles in two days. We are aware from other authority of the marvelous results, even to-day, of that first battle of the Marne. So we can pray for everything and anything which we feel is according to God's Word and God's will.

V. THE HINDRANCES TO PRAYER. "What various hindrances we meet in coming to the mercy seat," says the old hymn, and there is the great problem of hindrances, and of unanswered prayer. Sometimes hindrances are *the work of the devil*. We were talking a little about this yesterday in our question hour, that the devil will delay prayer. You remember what the apostle said, "I want you to know how great a conflict I have." Why the conflict? Because the devil was trying to prevent him from praying; and you and I are often prevented in the same way from praying. Prayer is not easy, because there is truth in the old hymn, that "Satan trembles when he sees the weakest saint upon his knees." If only he can keep us from prayer, he knows that he will have gained a great victory.

Sometimes our hindrances are due to the fact that God cannot answer. It may be there is *sin in our life,* or it may be what we ask is not according to God's will. Moses asked, "Lord, let me go over to Canaan;" and God said, "Don't ask me again about that." Oh, how touching is the story of Moses. Through one sin he was prevented from entering into the Promised Land, and yet you know how marvelously God answered. He did get there at last, didn't he, on the Mount of Transfiguration? That was the way God answered his prayer thousands of years afterwards, and God no doubt will answer many prayers in ways that we hardly think possible.

Dr. Griffith Thomas

Sometimes our hindrances are due to *difficulties*. Paul had a thorn in his flesh, about which he prayed. Our Lord had a cup in Gethsemane about which He prayed, and the prayer was not answered in the way in which either the Lord or Paul expected.

Sometimes it is the revelation of *differences between us and God*,—we want one thing, and God wants us to have another. Says John Newton,

> "I asked the Lord that I might grow,
> In faith and love and ev'ry grace,
> Might more of His salvation know,
> And seek more earnestly His face.
>
> "'Twas He who taught me thus to pray,
> And He I know has answered prayer,
> But it has been in such a way
> As almost drove me to despair."

God often answers our prayer for growth in grace by revealing our black heart all the more, until we are depressed and discouraged beyond measure, and all the while that is God's way of answering us. So let us think of these things.

Once more, hindrance is *due to delay*,—not denial, but delay. Prayer is not always answered at once. When the message came about Lazarus, the Lord abode in the place where He was. He did not go, even at the request of the sisters, because he had something still better before them. Abraham was promised a son, but had to wait for twenty-five years before the son came; and so we are told in Hebrews 6 about those who through faith *and patience* inherit the promises. Promise your child a nickel and it believes you absolutely, but would like to see the color of that money, or would like to know when it is coming. There is no difficulty about the faith, but just a little difficulty about the patience. We are often child-like,—we believe God's Word, but still we would like to know that he is going to fulfil it. George Muller prayed for fifty-one years for the conversion of two men, and he died before either of them was converted; but they were both converted within a year of his death. That was not denial, but it was delay. So let us believe in the power of prayer, and let us use its power.

A writer very helpfully said a little while ago, "All of us cannot be great preachers or teachers, but there is no reason

Prayer in the Christian Life

why the humblest should not be a great intercessor." "How often," said he, "we ask for power from God that we might do great things, and He needs to give us weakness that we might do better things."

VI. CONDITIONS OF PRAYER. I am only going to mention two general conditions of prayer this morning, and I believe that these two sum up practically everything. The first is *acquaintance with the Word of God*. Prayer and the Word are connected in more than one passage: "We will give ourselves to prayer and the ministry of the Word," and "sanctified by the Word of God and prayer." Prayer is our speaking to God, and the Bible, the Word of God, is God speaking to us; prayer, because it is based on revelation, must always be closely associated with the Word of God. "If ye abide in me, and my words abide in you, ask whatsoever ye will" (John 15:7).

It is impossible, dear friends, to exaggerate the importance of the Bible in connection with prayer. Here again, coming to a very practical matter, what do you do in your quiet time? Do you commence with prayer and then go to your Bible, or do you commence with your Bible and go to prayer? There was a time when I commenced with prayer and then went to my Bible, but I learned to start with the Bible and then go to prayer. George Muller said for a long time in his Christian life he prayed and then went to the Bible, but that he had found a better way,—he lifted up his soul to God in prayer for illumination, and then went to the Bible, and the Bible gave him examples of prayer, promises about prayer, incitements to prayer, encouragements to prayer. He said the Bible became the very food of his prayer, and he was enabled thereby to pray all the more effectively and effectually because he had already had a time with his Bible. Those that know God know how to pray, and you cannot know God unless you study his Word.

The second condition of prayer is to be *"full of the Holy Ghost."* About eighteen months ago a Y. M. C. A. Secretary showed me a book on prayer, and said, "What do you think of that book?" "Well," I said, "it is full of very good things, much that is very suggestive, but from first to last there is not a reference to the Holy Ghost in relation to prayer. Any book that does not include a reference to the Holy Ghost in prayer, fails at a very vital point."

Dr. Griffith Thomas

No one can pray unless he sees very definitely that the Holy Ghost is the sphere and the atmosphere of our prayer. We have the Holy Ghost in Zechariah 12: 10, "The Spirit of grace and of supplications;" in Romans 8: 26, "the Spirit also helpeth our infirmities;" in Ephesians 6: 18, "with all prayer and supplication, praying at all seasons in the Spirit;" Jude 20, "Praying in the Holy Spirit."

So I want to emphasize the Word of God and the Spirit. Though there are many detailed conditions, these two practically cover everything. The more we know of the Word, and the more we know of the Holy Spirit, the more powerful our prayers will be.

An old Lancashire woman was listening to the reasons her neighbors gave for their minister's success, one speaking of his gifts, another of his delivery, still another of his grammar. "No," she said, "I'll tell you what it is; your mon is very thick with the Almighty." That was her Lancashire way of putting it, but without any irreverence, surely you and I ought to covet this beyond all else, of being very thick with the Almighty, having such fellowship with Him that through His Word and Spirit we may just lift up our hearts in prayer.

VII. METHODS OF PRAYER. I want now to suggest very practically the methods of using our "Quiet Hour." I can only give certain suggestions for your comparison, because perhaps one method may not suit another; but I always like to read how other people do this or that, so that I can compare and contrast. I was very thankful for that word Mr. Trumbull gave us in the vespers last evening, that we are not to be tied down, in thinking that because other people have had a certain experience we are wrong if we do not get the same experience. I heard a man once preach about the Gospel in such a way as to give the impression that if you did not know the text by means of which you were led to Christ you might very seriously doubt your conversion. I went to an old friend and said, "I do not know any text connected with my conversion." He said, "Never mind, so long as you are sure you were converted." So with regard to the victorious life, so with regard to these methods, just compare them with that which you find essential in your Christian life.

But there are certain things of which we ought to be absolutely certain. First of all there must be *time for prayer;*

Prayer in the Christian Life

I Corinthians 7: 5: "that ye may have leisure for prayer." It is a wonderful phrase,—leisure for prayer. "How much time do you spend every day in prayer?" is the title of a very helpful little booklet.[1] Some years ago at a conference of ministers in New York, the chairman of the meeting propounded this question to his hearers. He began by saying that as they had met for a practical heart-to-heart talk, he would like to begin by asking how many of them spent half an hour a day in prayer. Only one, in response to the invitation for a show of hands, put up his hand. He then asked how many could say they prayed fifteen minutes a day. Not half the number present put up their hands in the affirmative. At last he said, "How many can say they pray for five minutes each day?" This time all held up their hands, but one afterwards said he did not know whether he was really honest in doing it. It was a revelation to that man, and to others, of how little time even ministers can spend in prayer to God. Dr. Truett of Dallas, Texas, said something similar when he was meeting with a group of ministers, as they discussed the perils and the problems of the preacher, and as one after the other had his say, and as they searched their hearts, every man was convicted, when the question was raised, "How much time do you pray?"

The next thing I want to suggest is that *there must be system*. I believe that we ought to have a carefully arranged plan for prayer and intercession. It is simply impossible in these days to pray for everything and everybody every day of our life. I have here a little book called "Pray Without Ceasing—Helps to Intercession,"[1] by Dr. Andrew Murray. It spreads over a month, and there is a topic for each day, "What to Pray," and then there is a suggestion "How to Pray." At the bottom there are blank spaces for special petitions. I bought two of these some years ago when it came out, cut them up and pasted them into a little loose-leaf book, and that is the basis of my own plan, covering four weeks. You will find if you use it, or some similar book, that it will systematize your prayer and give you great blessing.

There should be not only time, but *definite occasions for prayer*. These definite occasions are like reservoirs that store

---

[1] See page 379.

Dr. Griffith Thomas

up water for emergencies. I believe that the morning is the best, but if you feel that the middle of the day or the twilight or evening is more convenient, by all means let it be so. The busy mother will probably find her best time when the children have gone to school, and when breakfast is over she can have her quiet time. Others may find it useful to have it at midday, as a certain business man who eats his mid-day meal in fifteen or twenty minutes, then goes into his office and shuts the door, and all the clerks know that unless it is a matter of life and death he is not to be disturbed. But whenever it may be, there should be these occasions, and prayer will thus become the habit of the Christian life, and we shall find it part of ourselves. You know the word "habit" is worth while remembering. Take off the letter H, and have "a bit" left. Take off the letter A, and there is still a "bit" left. Take off the letter B, and still "it" is left. So you see the habit of prayer is simply a part of ourselves.

How shall we use the time? What means shall we employ? I think it is well for us to start our quiet time with *praise*, linking on what we have had in the past, with what we are now going to expect in the present. Second, we might spend a moment in the realization of *God's presence,* as the presence of God is a fact, not a promise.

Third, there should be the element of *confession,* clearing away every cobweb, and removing everything that would hinder God speaking to us and blessing us. Then will come *petition,* and we ask God for things. Do not let us be afraid to ask God definitely for things, for petition is an essential, vital part of prayer. Fifth, will come *adoration,* as we occupy our thought and our heart with God and His character, and after this will come *thanksgiving.* There comes a time when we are to stop asking and commence taking. I believe that is the reason why prayer and thanksgiving are so often associated by the apostle Paul, just like the bird with two wings,— not one wing, but two wings, by means of which it rises into the air; so the Christian should have the faith that asks, and the faith that takes,—prayer and thanksgiving. Seventh, there should be *surrender,* yielding ourselves afresh to God. So you have praise, the presence of God, conviction, petition, adoration, thanksgiving, and surrender, and this, day by day, will be the secret of blessing.

I quote from the book, "Preacher and Prayer:" "The Church is looking for better methods; God is looking for

Prayer in the Christian Life

better men. The Holy Ghost does not flow through methods, but through men; He does not come on machinery, but on men; He does not annoint plans, but men. Talking to men for God is a good thing, but talking to God for men is greater still."[1]

More than once in our Conference those words in Isaiah 59: 16 have been mentioned: "He . . . wondered that there was no intercessor;" and therefore, using the words of Isaiah 62: 7, 8, which we had as one of our day verses at Princeton in July, we are to take "no rest, and give Him no rest until He establish, and till he make Jerusalem a praise in the earth." Take time to pray.

> "Take time to pray!
> When fears and foes distress you,
> And tiresome toils oppress you,
> Then the Master waits to bless you,
>   If you take time to pray.
>
> "Take time to pray!
> When little things annoy you,
> And worry would destroy you,
> Nothing better can employ you,
>   Than to take time to pray.
>
> "Take time to pray!
> When fickle friends forsake you,
> Disasters overtake you,
> Repine it will not make you,
>   If you take time to pray.
>
> "Take time to pray!
> When emotions have subsided,
> And the enemy derided,
> If in God you have confided,
>   Always take time to pray.
>
> "Take time to pray!
> Would you speak or preach with power,
> Keep the Pentecostal shower,
> Have the Spirit every hour?
>   You must take time to pray."

---

[1] See page 379.

THE BIBLE IN THE CHRISTIAN LIFE

Professor W. H. Griffith Thomas, D. D.

ALTHOUGH a conference is often concerned with a *crisis* in our life, the crisis is intended, as we know, to lead on to a *process*. The crisis by means of which we may have entered into the life of victory, develops into the process, which is intended to cover the whole of the Christian life, and it is this process with which we are to be concerned to-day in various ways, so that we, by the grace of God, may avoid any other such crisis in our life as we may have had to face this week.

Now the two things beyond all others, which will be the guarantee of that process being normal and satisfactory all through our days, are Prayer and the Bible. Yesterday morning we were considering prayer. This morning we shall think about the Bible, and first of all, of what the Bible is.

I. What the Bible Is. You will notice there are five things in Hebrews 4: 12, 13, which answer that question, what the Bible is.

(1) First, it is *living*,—the Word of God is alive. That is to say, it has life and it gives life. You remember in I Peter 1: 23, "the Word of God, which liveth." It is living because it comes from the living God.

(2) Secondly, the Word of God is *powerful*. The word in the original is that from which our word "energetic" comes,—"the Word of God is living and energetic." It is always energetic. It is energetic in our conversion; we are born again by the Word. It is energetic in our consecration; we are sanctified by the Word. It is energetic in our correction; the Word of God is intended for correction. And it is energetic in our cleansing: "Ye are clean through the Word."

(3) Then it is *sharp*, "Sharper than any two-edged sword." I rather think the idea should be "knife" there, not sword. I believe this refers to the knife of the priest, by which he dissected and tested the sacrifice. This is a Jewish epistle,

---

This message was given at the Bible hour Saturday morning at Cedar Lake and was also one of the Bible studies at Whittier. See note at close of the address.

The Bible in the Christian Life

and I am rather inclined to think that it is "knife" rather than "sword," the priest rather than the soldier. The priest had the duty of cutting the animals, of dissecting and testing the animals offered for sacrifice; but whether that be the case or not, you will notice that the Word of God is sharper than any two-edged knife or sword. Sharp? Yes, we perhaps have found that. Someone has said, "It wounds the sinner, it convicts the hypocrite, it rebukes the saint." That is the sharpness of God's Word as we know it day by day.

(4) Then you notice it is *penetrating,* piercing even to the dividing asunder of the joints and marrow, distinguishing between soul and spirit. Now the Word of God is able to do what you and I cannot do. We cannot distinguish between soul and spirit, except in a very doubtful way. I have never yet been able to find anyone who can tell me the distinction between spirit and soul, except that the spirit is that part of our nature which enables us to have fellowship with God, and the soul is that non-material part which animals also have in some degree. But the Word of God can cut between even soul and spirit, so clear and definite is its penetrating power.

The Word of God makes no allowance for sin. That is one reason why we think of it as penetrating. It attacks, it lays bare everything about which we are doubtful. You know in that particular, some people fail to distinguish the difference between a "cross" and a sin. People say, "Yes, I am very frank; I am in the habit of speaking my mind. Unfortunately that is my cross." No, that is your sin. Other people say, "I have a very difficult temper,—that is my cross." No, that is your sin. "I do not feel that I can get up in the morning; I am rather lazy, that is my cross." No it is not; that is your sin. John Wesley once was talking to one of his workers, and he said, "Mr. Wesley, I do not hesitate to tell people my mind. I tell them frankly. I say what I think of them,—that is my talent." "Well," said Wesley, "the Lord won't trouble if you bury that talent; there will be no sin in that."

Yes, that is where the Word of God distinguishes; when you and I come face to face with the Word of God, all these subterfuges have to go, and it penetrates into the deepest recesses of our spiritual being.

(5) The fifth thing is, the Word of God is a *judge.* Now that is the meaning of the word "discerner," and I would like to ask attention to the fact that it is the only place where

Dr. Griffith Thomas

the word "critic" is found in the Bible. The word "discerner" in the Greek is "critic" and it is a most interesting thing to notice. We hear a great deal to-day about criticism, especially the criticism of the Bible, but here is the only place where it is mentioned in the Bible, and the Bible is shown to be *our* critic. I often think, that if we allowed the Bible to criticize us more, we should criticize the Bible less.

Now that is what the Bible is,—living, powerful, sharp, penetrating and judging.

II. WHAT THE BIBLE DOES. Here comes the vital question in regard to our spiritual life: What does the Bible do for our spiritual life?

(1) *It brings peace.* In the year 1914, just before the war broke out, I was in England at the Keswick Convention, and on a Saturday morning, after the convention closed on Friday night, at seven-thirty we had a thanksgiving and testimony meeting. As there are so many people, twenty-five hundred or three thousand, it is obvious that in three-quarters of an hour you cannot have very many testimonies. So they give a testimony by means of a text, and everyone is invited as far as time permits, to give a testimony. The Chairman starts, the speakers on the platform follow, and over the tent as far as possible one after another gives a text that has been blessed or in some way prominent through that week. When it came to my turn I gave this, "Great peace have they that love thy law, and nothing shall upset them." I saw the chairman and one or two people smile at that rendering, and afterwards I had a talk with one or two, and I said I believed that to be the literal meaning of the word in Psalm 119: 165, "Great peace have they that love thy law; and nothing shall offend them,"—cause them to stumble, trip them up, upset them,—"nothing shall trip them up."

Oh, is it not true that the Word of God does bring peace? The Word of God brings peace to the sinner; when the sinner accepts salvation, that Word is the ground of peace. So it is all through the Christian life, we heard from Mr. Trumbull yesterday morning, the Word of God is the basis; not our feelings, our emotions, but the Word of God and faith. By faith we accept God's Word, and the result is peace.

(2) The Bible will *provide the fuel for prayer.* George Muller of Bristol, that wonderful man of God, with his un-

The Bible in the Christian Life

erring insight, suggests that the Bible should be the first in our Quiet Hour, because the Bible will suggest prayer. The Bible will be an encouragement to prayer, and there will be examples of prayer, incitements to prayer, warnings, precepts and promises, everything that we can turn into prayer. The Bible therefore is like the fuel of prayer, and the food of prayer.

(3) Then the third thing is *purity*. Oh, how the Bible purifies our thoughts, our motives, our desires. "The washing of water by the Word" has a good deal to do with the purity of our inner life, cleansing the thoughts of our hearts by the inspiration of the Holy Spirit, by means of the Word.

It is an old story, but I think it is worth repeating. There was a woman who lived in a cottage by the side of which ran a little stream. One morning she was leaning over the stream with a sieve, a sort of rough framework of wood, with wires across. Fastened on this sieve was some wool, and she was holding it in the stream, letting the water run through it to wash the wool. As she was doing this, a clergyman came along, and not knowing what it was, stopped to see. When the woman saw him she turned around and said, "O Sir, I am so glad to see you."

"Why, I am a stranger here," he replied, "I didn't know anyone knew me."

"I heard a sermon from you twenty years ago, and it was a great blessing to my soul."

"I am very glad to hear that," he said, "what was the text?"

"I cannot remember the text," she answered.

"Well, it is rather curious that that sermon should have done you so much good and you cannot remember the text," he said.

"Well, you see," she replied, "my mind is very much like this sieve, very full of holes; and just as the water does not stop in the sieve, but runs through it and washes the wool, so that sermon ran through my mind, full of holes as it is, and washed it, and I have been a different woman ever since."

If you go to the House of God on Sunday once, you are what Mr. Gladstone used to call "oncers," and if you go twice you are "twicers." You cannot remember fifty-two sermons. I would like to know how many of you remember the sermon you heard the last time you went to church. You may be like the old lady who said she did not understand much after the text was given out; but dear friends, every sermon, if it is a proper sermon, will do its work of cleansing and purifying. We cannot possibly remember fifty-two, still less can we remember one hundred and four; but every sermon, if it is a true sermon, will do for our minds what that water was doing for the wool in that old woman's sieve, it will cleanse as it goes through,—the washing of water. "Ye are clean through the word that I have spoken unto you."

(4) The Bible is *the secret of perception*, and I mean by that, spiritual insight, knowledge. There is nothing like the Bible to open the eyes of the mind, of the heart, of the soul; and I believe that the reason why there are so many people to-day in error, is that they do not have their time with the Bible to get that spiritual perception which is the mark of the ripening and the growing Christian. You know people tell us that defective sight is often due to enfeebled health, and if our health were stronger our sight would be better. Certainly spiritually we should have better judgment if we were better people. A sick soul always involves an uncertain and untrue judgment. Spiritual eyesight and health invariably go together. I believe that very very many people are led astray into error because, through the neglect of the Bible, they do not get that spiritual insight.

I was talking along these lines at Keswick in 1914, and after I had given the address a gentleman came on the platform and said, "I want to tell you something that you can use in that address, and I hope you will tell it wherever you get the chance," and I have been doing it ever since. He said, "This is almost first-hand. There was a young gentleman in the West of Ireland, a landed proprietor. He found Christ as his Saviour, and fed his soul on the Bible, and was greatly blessed in his soul for several months. After a while a gentleman came from London, who had rented the shooting over this man's property in the shooting season, and had come there to shoot birds, or rabbits, or both. He was deeply interested in the landed proprietor in Ireland, and he said in the course of conversation one day, 'I know something in London that would be the very thing for you, and you would be able to profit by it, and would just add immeasurably to what you have got.'

" 'Well,' said the young Irishman, 'if there is anything good that will help me in my spiritual life I am ready to take it.'

"It was arranged that when the Londoner went back to

The Bible in the Christian Life

London the Irishman should go with him. When he got to London he was introduced to the gentleman, a Christian Science practitioner and teacher. It was arranged that the young Irishman should have six lessons, one lesson every morning on Christian Science. On Monday morning he went for the first lesson, on Tuesday for the second, on Wednesday for the third, and on Thursday for the fourth. On Friday morning he had only been there a few minutes when the Christian Science teacher burst out into a torrent of anger, a towering rage, and rather surprised, the Irishman looked at him. Then the man said, 'Here you have been for four mornings, and you have not learned a single thing.' 'No,' said the Irishman, 'that is true. I was so thoroughly grounded in the Word of God before I came that you have not taught me anything.' He got up and left, and of course did not have the remainder of that course."

That is the point. I am perfectly certain, whether it is Christian Science, "which is neither Christian nor Science," or what is called Millennial Dawn, which ought to be called "Murky Darkness," theosophy, which is "theo-sophistry," or spiritualism, or any of the rest, that the trouble with people who go astray along these or similar lines is that they do not know the Word of God.

Not very long ago an Englishman was traveling in Palestine, and got to Nazareth in the evening, when the shepherds were bringing their flocks to water them at the well. Three shepherds brought their flocks into Nazareth, and there were about twenty-five or thirty sheep in each flock. Soon all three flocks got together and had their water, and then the shepherd who first went away just made a call, and thirty sheep, his own sheep, separated themselves from the rest and followed him. The second shepherd made his call, and another thirty sheep followed him; and the third one with his call, took his sheep away.

The Englishman said through an interpreter, to one of the shepherds, "That is very interesting to see all those sheep mixed together, and all of them coming separately when they were called. Do the sheep always do that?"

"Yes," said the shepherd, "except in one condition."

"What is that?"

"The sheep that do not follow the voice of the shepherd are the sick sheep. If a sheep is healthy it will always follow

Dr. Griffith Thomas

the shepherd; but if it is not healthy, if there is something wrong with the sheep, it will follow anybody."

The mature, ripening, deepening Christian is the one who knows; not the one who has intellect. God does not give any increase of brains when a man becomes a Christian, but He does give wonderful spiritual insight; and it is the power of the Word of God that will be our protection, not only against error, but in recognizing everything that is right and true, as we allow the Word of God its proper place in our life.

(5) The next thing is *power*. Oh, the power that comes through the Word of God. You remember how our Lord met the temptation of the devil three times over by the Bible, "It is written;" and you remember in Psalm 37: 31, "The law of his God in his heart; none of his steps shall slide," and in Psalm 119: 11, "Thy Word have I hid in my heart, that I might not sin against thee."

The reason of our weakness is undoubtedly due to our neglect of the Word of God. Look at Psalm 1: 2-4: "In his law doth he meditate day and night. And he shall be like a tree planted by the rivers of water." Look at the contrast between the tree with its leaves and the chaff that the wind driveth away. O dear friends, if you and I want power, we must have the Word of God in our hearts and lives.

I dare say you remember the story of the evangelist who went to have supper one evening with a young couple who had just one boy. In the middle of the meal they heard a great thud on the floor upstairs, and found that the little fellow had fallen out of bed. The next morning the evangelist, Gypsy Smith, chaffed the boy, saying, "What was the matter? Why did you fall out?" "Because I went to sleep too near where I went in," said the lad. Ah, it is easy to laugh, but you and I do the same thing every time we fall,—we do not go far enough into the Christian life, and we fall out; too near where we got in. The power of the Word of God is such that we may be strong and be protected from harm.

(6) Then I must mention *progress*. Joshua 1: 8, 9 says, "This book of the law shall not depart out of thy mouth; but thou shalt meditate therein day and night . . . then thou shalt make thy way prosperous, and then thou shalt have good success." This is the only place in the Bible where

The Bible in the Christian Life

the word "success" occurs. So if you want to know what the secret of success is, it is the Word of God. I know that the Hebrew means "Thou shalt do wisely," but it is an interesting point that that is the only place where the word "success" is found, and it is associated with the Word of the living God.

(7) The last point to be mentioned under what the Bible does, is *permanence*. "If ye continue in my word, then are ye my disciples indeed" (John 8: 31).

And so this is what the Bible will do for our lives: it will bring peace, it will provide fuel for prayer, it is the secret of purity, it is the guarantee of perception, it is the source of power, it is the spring of progress, it is the absolute assurance of permanence.

III. WHAT THE BIBLE NEEDS. Here is that which is very definite and practical in our spiritual life. (1) First of all the Bible needs *daily use*. Our use of the Bible must be regular and methodical. The Bible for our spiritual life is as essential day by day as our food, or our cleansing, or our clothing is for the body. There must be daily use.

(2) Secondly, it must be *direct use;* it must be what may be called a first-hand use; and I want to suggest that for our devotional purposes, there must be no helps. I want to suggest (no doubt you will think this very serious, and perhaps a little heretical) when you have your devotional time you put aside your Scofield Bible. Have a Bible without any helps at all, and do not look at any other books.

What is more, I want to suggest this for your devotional hour: have an unmarked Bible. We are all fond of marking our Bibles, underlining words, making railroads, and other marks in the margin; but it is only a very strong and independent mind that can read a marked passage and get something new out of it. The trouble is that when you have a marked Bible your thoughts go along the old lines, and that is something like eating stale manna. You want something fresh from the most familiar passage, from Psalm 23, John 14, or Isaiah 53. By all means put any marks you want to in another Bible, score and underline and do what you want to, but for devotional purposes I recommend very strongly that you use an unmarked Bible.

(3) The Bible must be used *definitely*. By "definite" I mean this: "What does the Bible say to *me?*"

Dr. Griffith Thomas

The great temptation of ministers or Christian workers is to read the Bible for other people. When I read the Bible and come to some thought I say, "Ah, that will do for my sermon next Sunday, for my Bible class." Oh no, "What is this to *me?*" Not my class, not my friends, but what is it to me?

Two Sunday School teachers were walking along the road one day, and one said to the other, "What is your point for next Sunday's lesson?"

"I do not know what you mean," said the other.

"What is the particular point you are going to teach next Sunday?"

"I don't know that I have anything particular; why do you ask?"

"As the lessons are arranged, I know what is coming, and I go into my room on Monday with my Bible, open it to the passage where we teach next Sunday, and say, 'Lord, Thou knowest the pupils better than I do. Wilt Thou show me something in this lesson that Thou desirest me to teach?' I read and I pray, and sometimes at once, sometimes in ten or twenty minutes, a word or a phrase stands out and grips my soul from that passage, and I know that is God's message for the boys, and I do not leave that out."

As I read that, I thought to myself, why shouldn't I do that for my own life? I have gotten into the habit of saying, "Lord, show me something in this passage for myself." That is my prayer every day, and I do my best to try to get away from other people, my sermon, my Bible class, my anything else, and say, "Lord, speak for thy servant heareth."

Of course if God gives you any thoughts and ideas you can mark them in a book or put them in the Bible you have marked. I have a book near at hand in which I record everything that God teaches me, and have in it any number of discoveries from the Greek Testament that I have not found in any book. I do not know that these notes will ever see the light, but they have been a wonderful help to me, and I jot down anything that occurs.

(4) The use of the Bible should not only be daily, and direct, and definite, but *detailed*. You know we hear a great deal to-day about quick lunches. Ah, you must not be too quick over the lunch that you have with the Bible. There is no need of any Hooverism about the Bible. You can eat

The Bible in the Christian Life

as much as you like. If you want to spoil your appetite I know nothing that will spoil it more quickly than a pound of tenderloin steak. But the remarkable thing about the Bible is that the more you eat the more you want to eat. There can be no Hooverism here, because you go on eating, and eating, and eating. You cannot do any quick lunches in connection with this work of meditating on the Bible; there should be a detailed use. In the Gospel of Mark, where our Lord is the pattern worker, ten times we are told of His going aside in solitude, in fellowship with the Father. I like to quote Tennyson's words, "Solitude, the mother country of the strong."

When we have the Bible for our daily, direct, definite, and detailed use, we may with profit, adopt this plan for our quiet hour: open the Bible with prayer, and say, "Lord, show me something for myself." Then I think we should dwell upon the Word. Is it a promise? Let us plead it. Is it a command? Let us seek to obey it. Is it a precept? Let us follow it. Is it a warning? Let us heed it. Is it an example? Let us keep it. Is it a fact? Let us accept it. Is it an experience? Let us try to reproduce it. That is the meaning of meditation. Meditation has been well defined as "attention with intention." Attention—I give my mind to it,—but I *intend,* as well, to carry it out. Then we turn it all into prayer, and we seek for grace to realize what God has taught us as a result of our meditation. Then we surrender ourselves to God, that He may work in our faith, to will and to do according to that word. Then we link it on with what we have learned yesterday, or the day before, and we find that God's truth is vital, and we trust God to reproduce it in our lives.

(5) And so, if the use of the Bible is daily, and direct, and definite, and detailed, it will be *delightful.* "How sweet are Thy words to my taste." "Thy words were found and I did eat them. They were to me the joy and rejoicing of my heart. I rejoice in Thy Word as one that findeth great spoil." And so the Bible will be everything in our Christian life.

Dear friends, as we draw these meditations to a conclusion, let me say if I may, that so far as the Christian life is concerned it is absolutely impossible to exaggerate the importance of the quiet hour. It is the absolutely universal and unqualified secret and condition of spiritual health and progress.

Dr. Griffith Thomas

I spoke the other evening in my little testimony, about failures, and I believe if I could understand them all, and look over all my failures, I should find that every failure was due to neglect of prayer and the Bible. The day is never the same to me, if, through some reason or other, I fail to have my quiet time in the morning. I am not laying down the law for you, but for me the morning is the time, and if I am at home I find it an immense help to have that quiet time before going down to breakfast. As McCheyne says, "See the face of God before you see the face of man." Two or three times since I have left home, on the train or elsewhere, I have not found it easy to get my quiet time before breakfast, and it is never quite the same, even though I have it afterwards. But whether it is morning, afternoon or evening, it is absolutely essential, if we are to go and grow, and never recede and backslide: it is the quiet hour we need beyond all else in our Christian life.[1]

> "The Master came to the fig tree,
> And saw the foliage there
> Of thick and shady branches,
> To hungry eyes so fair.
> But He found that it was barren,
> And bore no luscious fruit,
> For life was gone, and even
> 'Twas withered from its root.
>
> "The Master came to the temple,
> And saw the worship there,
> The ritual and the customs,
> To Jewish eyes so fair;
> But to Him 'twas all corruption,
> His house a den of thieves,
> And all its boasted glory,
> Was fruitless, only leaves.

---

[1] Dr. Griffith Thomas' studies on prayer and the Bible are included in a little book entitled, "Life Abiding and Abounding," where some of these topics are treated more fully. The story of the Christian woman who questioned the statement that all backsliding was due to the neglect of the Bible (which has been omitted here) is included in the book, and may also be found on page 143 of "Victory in Christ at Princeton Conference." See page 379 for information on books.

The Bible in the Christian Life

"The Master comes to the churches,
  And sees our service here,
The busy nightly meetings,
  To worldly hearts so dear.
And still He probes the motive,
  And still His Spirit grieves,
To find our modern methods
  So fruitless,—mostly leaves.

"Lord Jesus, quicken our vision,
  That we may see our state;
Show us where we are guilty
  Of doing what Thou dost hate.
Help us to bring true worship,
  And give Thy Word its place;
And henceforth live to witness
  To Thine unbounded grace."

OUR LORD'S SECOND COMING

By the Rev. Professor W. H. Griffith Thomas, D.D.

EVERY part of the Bible has an outlook towards the future. In the Old Testament no fewer than seventeen out of thirty-nine books are prophetic, while in several of the others there are references to the future that may almost be called prophetic. Each section of the New Testament similarly looks forward, as may be seen from a careful study of the Gospels, the Acts, the Epistles, and Revelation. Dr. Sandy not long ago admitted that he had not realized until lately how far the "center of gravity" of our Lord's ministry and mission lay beyond the grave. Another New Testament scholar, speaking of the element of the future in the Gospels, remarks that it is "fundamental and pervasive to an extent which has not been appreciated." The apostle Paul, in speaking of the Christian life, frequently refers to the three graces in their completeness, Faith, Love, and Hope; Faith looking upwards, Love looking outwards, and Hope looking onwards (1 Thess. 1 : 3, 9, 10).

It has been computed that there are over three hundred references in the New Testament to the coming of the Lord, an average of one in every twenty-five verses. This prominence clearly shows the importance of the subject, and the contrast with such comparatively infrequent references to Baptism, the Lord's Supper, and even the Church and the Ministry, is significant. Some one has described the Second Coming as *the one converging event of prophecy and the future.*

Yet this subject is neglected by very many Christian people. Some say that they have no time for it in the pressure of everyday affairs; others do not regard it as practical enough for ordinary life; while still more point to the difficulties of the subject and the differences between students as the warrant for their neglect or ignoring of the subject. But it ought to be pointed out that the believer should find, or, if necessary, make time for anything found in the Bible. Further, the subject, as stated in the New Testament, is one of the most

---

Dr. Griffith Thomas' address on the Second Coming was given at Cedar Lake on Sunday morning, and the same message was given at Whittier.

Our Lord's Second Coming

practical and vital for daily living; and in regard to difficulties and differences, it should be made clear that these are in great measure concerned with details, and do not affect what may be called the "beaten track" of prophetic teaching. There is only one really fundamental difference between true Christians, as will be seen.

All this and much more that could be said constitutes a special reason for giving attention to what the New Testament calls "that Blessed Hope."

I. THE LORD'S COMING IS PERSONAL

In reference to his *spiritual* presence, our Lord has never left his Church; and when he said, "Lo, I am with you always" (Matt. 28:20), he emphasized what every Christian knows as the spiritual reality of the Lord's perpetual presence. He lives in the believer and abides in the Church (Gal. 2:20).

But his personal coming also is recorded as a fact. This was first stated by himself (John 14:3), then by an angel (Acts 1:11), and then by the apostle Paul (1 Thess. 4:15-17). It is impossible that anything could be plainer than these statements.

For this reason it is wholly inaccurate to think that the Lord's coming is to be identified with death. Many millions have died since the Lord's ascension, and we know that Christians are dying day by day, but all this is not a coming of Christ; it is a going to be with Christ, in the words of the apostle, "to depart and be with Christ" (Phil. 1:23). When Stephen died, he did not say, "Come, Lord Jesus," but "Lord Jesus, receive my spirit" (Acts 7:59).

In the same way, the coming of the Lord to the heart moment by moment (John 14:23) is to be clearly distinguished from that personal coming which the New Testament reveals as at once literal and future.

There are some who would identify the Lord's coming with the Day of Pentecost. But this is impossible, because long after Pentecost statements were made that the Lord would come (Acts 3:20, 21; 1 Thess. 4:16). Besides, the coming of the Holy Spirit was definitely stated as dependent upon the *departure* of Christ (John 16:7), and the New Testament clearly teaches that the presence of the Holy Spirit is due to the absence of our Lord.

Some think that the coming of Christ is to be identified with the destruction of Jerusalem in A. D. 70. But here, again, there is no trace in history of anything at that time except judgment on sin, and certainly there was no personal coming of Christ.

Then it is suggested that the coming of Christ is to be understood as meaning the diffusion of Christianity. But, once more, it should be pointed out that the coming mentioned in the New Testament is personal, not spiritual; literal, not symbolical.

Perhaps the most important and obvious proof of this personal coming of Christ is its analogy with the First Coming, which was undoubtedly personal, and the two are closely associated, with one used as an argument for the other (Acts 1:11). In the same way the doctrinal teaching of the First Coming for redemption is closely connected with the Second Coming for complete salvation (Heb. 9:24, 26, 28). So that, as at the First Advent a certain part of Old Testament prophecy was fulfilled, at the Second Advent New Testament prophecy is to be fulfilled. A careful reading of the New Testament in its obvious meaning shows beyond all question that the coming of Christ will be personal.

II. The Lord's Coming is Premillennial

The word "millennium" is the Latin term for the period of a "thousand years," mentioned in Revelation 20:7; and while it is, of course, true that this is the only passage where the actual duration is mentioned, the proof of a period which may be described as "millennial" is altogether independent of this statement about its precise length. There are many passages descriptive of a period of universal peace which, whether we call it millennial or not, demand an interpretation which points to a future time of unmistakable blessing. Such passages as Psalm 72:7-11; Isaiah 2:2-4; 11:1-10; 65; 66, and many more to the same effect indicate a period which millennialism holds is to be associated with what in Revelation is described as a definite time of a "thousand years." It is at this point that the fundamental difference occurs between Christians on the subject of the Lord's coming. All agree that Christ is to rule the world, but there is a difference on one point, as to when this will take place.

Those who consider that the coming will be after the millennium, called Postmillennialists, think that the world is gradually to get better, that evil will thus be eliminated, and all this is to lead up to Christ's coming.

Our Lord's Second Coming

Those who cannot accept this view and are called Premillennialists consider that Scripture gives no proof of the universal acceptance of the Gospel before Christ comes, or of the gradual improvement of the world until everything is good. On the contrary, there is much to show that the condition of the earth when the Lord comes will be one of awful wickedness, and that Satanic agencies will be in operation right up to Christ's appearance. A modern writer has pointed out that our Lord nowhere predicts a glorious future before the end of the age; and this view is supported by the state of the world today, for, while the Gospel is ever extending among the heathen, so-called Christian nations are exceedingly far from what the Christian ideal requires, as the present war only too plainly indicates.

Postmillennialism tends towards an erroneous view of human nature and pays too much regard to man's power and ability to accomplish things. In 1915 I heard the late Dr. B. Fay Mills speak of his experiences on the Pacific Coast. He said that up to the time of the war he thought things were going on so well that the kingdom of God was almost at hand, but that the war had dashed all his hopes to the ground and made him realize that "this is a lost world." Another preacher has given expression to the same view in saying: "My Postmillennial dreams of the age becoming better and better seem to be awfully shattered by the corruption and worldliness of the church and by the downward plunge of society and civil government." A few months before the war broke out, a preacher, speaking of the three Divine judgments of war, famine, and pestilence (Ezek. 5:12), remarked that through the modern wonderful strides in hygiene pestilence was almost impossible, that the splendid facilities of communication between various countries almost entirely removed the likelihood of famine, while as to war, he read a letter from a German officer (of all people!) to show that any conflict in the future was practically impossible. It would be interesting to learn what the preacher thinks of his sermon today. We all know what a rude awakening arbitration has had through the war and with what feelings The Hague Palace of Peace is regarded at the present moment. The truth is that modern civilization is a superficial veneer and only tends to cover for a while the essential depravity of human nature.

If it be said that the leaven of Christ's parable, "till the whole was leavened" (Matt. 13), is descriptive of this gener-

Dr. Griffith Thomas

ation and refers to the steady assimilative influences of the Gospel in human lives, it can be said without contradiction that after nineteen centuries of Christianity we are nowhere near any such process of universal leavening. On this point it should be noted that Christ does not simply say that the kingdom is like leaven, but that the kingdom is like leaven which a woman hid in three measures of meal; and when this is thoroughly understood, there does not seem any valid reason to believe that the parable is an exception to the invariable teaching of Scripture about leaven as evil (Matt. 16:11, 12).

In harmony with all this, it is clearly taught that the present dispensation is one of election and selection (Acts 15:14-16) and is not intended for universal salvation. Then, too, the rule of Christ, according to the New Testament, is to be direct and personal, not indirect and spiritual, as it is to-day. It is significant that Christ is never described as King in the present dispensation, that term never being used of him in relation to his Church. In his earthly ministry he came to be "King of the Jews," and in the great future depicted in the Revelation he will be "King of kings." But, meanwhile, in between, he is the "Lord" or "Head" of his Church, and Hebrews significantly speaks of him as not yet on his own throne, but seated at the "right hand of the Majesty on high" (Heb. 1:3; 8:1).

Postmillennialism is also incorrect, because it robs the Christian life of any true ideal and power of the coming of Christ. For if the millennium is to be reached by the gradual progress and improvement of the world, Christ's coming must be an event of a very remote future, and this makes it absolutely impossible for us to watch and wait (1 Cor. 1:7), an attitude which is so frequently emphasized in the New Testament as an essential feature of the Christian life.

For all these reasons it is, therefore, concluded that the New Testament teaching indicates Christ's coming as before the millennium. By some writers this coming is regarded as marked by two stages: his coming *for* his people (1 Thess. 4), and his coming *with* his people. Others prefer to think of the coming as characterized by two phases rather than stages: the former indicating the joy of his coming for his people, and the latter expressing the judgment associated with the non-Christian world. But on the whole, while it does not perhaps matter much whether we favor stages or phases, it seems best and clearest to think of two separate,

Our Lord's Second Coming

though connected, stages or periods of his coming. His coming "for" his people is often called the Rapture, because of their (the Church) being "caught up to meet him in the air." Then may follow a period between the first and second stages. The exact duration is not known, though some think that it will last for seven years, representing the seventieth week of Daniel. During this period the marriage supper of the Lamb will be celebrated (Rev. 19: 9), with the reward of Christians for faithfulness since their conversion (Phil. 2: 16). During this time, too, will take place "the great tribulation" (2 Thess. 1: 4, 5; 2: 8-12). This tribulation will be Jewish and is called "Jacob's trouble" (Jer. 30: 7), and does not refer to the Church, which will have already been "caught up to be with the Lord." Then will follow our Lord's coming with his people to judgment and to usher in the millennial period. This is seen to be "immediately after the tribulation" (Matt. 24: 29-31).

The millennium will then follow, with the judgment of the living Gentiles (Matt. 25: 31-46), who will be dealt with in regard to their treatment of our Lord's brethren, the Jews (Matt. 25: 40). During this time it would seem that Israel's national salvation will take place, because the Jews will have been able for the first time to look on him whom they pierced (Rev. 1: 7; Rom. 11: 26).

The millennium will be followed by the end of all things, as recorded in Revelation 21 and 22, when "God will be all in all" (1 Cor. 15:28).

This summary of the outstanding events is purposely and strictly limited to what may be called the "beaten track" of New Testament prophecy, and it is important that for the purpose of thorough study we should avoid all unnecessary detail and concentrate attention on the main elements alone. Those who wish to give special consideration to this subject can be confidently recommended to several books like "Jesus is Coming," by W. E. Blackstone; "The Lord's Return," by J. F. Silver; "The Return of the Lord Jesus," by Torrey; "What Do the Prophets Say?" by C. I. Scofield.[1]

III. THE LORD'S COMING IS PRACTICAL

It is sometimes contended, but with manifest inaccuracy, that all consideration of Christ's coming must necessarily be

---
[1] See page 379.

Dr. Griffith Thomas

speculative and out of touch with ordinary everyday life. But the very opposite of this is true. The coming is associated with several of the most vital issues affecting Christian character and conduct.

The resurrection of those who have passed away in Christ is always associated with the Lord's coming (1 Thess. 4: 14; 1 Cor. 15: 54). The redemption of the living saints is also connected with this event, for not only will the dead be raised, but the living will be changed. It is sometimes forgotten that the Apostle has two classes in view when he speaks of "this corruptible" (the dead) and "this mortal" (the living) (1 Cor. 15:53). Those who will be on the earth when the Lord comes will be changed and will be like Christ, for they will see him face to face (1 John 3: 2).

Then will naturally follow the reunion of both classes of saints in the presence of Christ, and this blessed thought is intended to inspire with real comfort and cheer those who sorrow and yet sorrow with hope (1 Thess. 4: 13, 18).

Another aspect of the Lord's coming is associated with the reward of God's people for their service since the commencement of their Christian life. While sin has already been judged and thereby dealt with, it is still essential for the believer to receive the reward of grace according to his works. This solemn and yet blessed thought is often found in the New Testament, and it emphasizes the call to faithfulness (1 Cor. 3: 13; Phil. 1: 6; 2: 16).

At this time, too, will be realized the unspeakable joy of meeting those whom we have been permitted to lead to Christ. This cheered and encouraged the Apostle in the midst of persecution and suffering, for he knew that, notwithstanding every difficulty, the day would come when he and those whom he had led to Christ would rejoice in the presence of the Master (1 Thess. 2: 18-20).

IV. THE LORD'S COMING IS POWER-GIVING

In opposition to those who think that any contemplation of Christ's coming is merely a matter of what may be called spiritual luxury, the New Testament shows beyond all question its spiritual power for daily life.

It is the inspiration of hope. When the apostle Paul speaks of "the Lord Jesus Christ, our hope" (1 Tim. 1: 1), he shows that the object of Christian expectation is not death, but the Lord's coming. "The sky, not the grave, is our goal." It is

Our Lord's Second Coming

impossible for any one who is spiritually healthy to look forward to physical death without a certain fear and even dread, because death is invariably regarded in the New Testament as "the last enemy" (1 Cor. 15: 28). But the coming of Christ is described as "that blessed hope," and, as such, is intended to be the inspiration and joy of the Christian's contemplation of the future (Phil. 3: 10, 11, 20, 21).

It is also the inspiration of Christian service. Not long ago the charge was made against Premillennialism of bringing a "blight upon the most aggressive and significant work of the kingdom of Christ in our own day." It is marvelous that any one could make so sweeping and obviously erroneous a charge, because thought at once goes out to Moody and others like him who have been connected with some of the greatest evangelistic work of the last fifty years. Then, too, think of men like Spurgeon, Hudson Taylor, George Muller, Arthur T. Pierson, and very many more, whose work for world-wide missions is known everywhere. The lives of living exponents of Premillennialism testify to their remarkable interest, success, and blessing in evangelistic and missionary work.

It is also an incentive to courage. The Premillennialist is often charged with pessimism, but in reality he is the only true optimist. This does not mean the cheap and easy optimism of ignoring facts, but that spirit of courage which comes from looking even the most dark problems in the face, and then rejoicing to know that "the Lord God Omnipotent reigneth." The present awful conflict in Europe is no indication that Christianity has failed, but only that education and civilization have been engulfed in the spirit of militarism. There was a civilization long before Christianity, and in the same way civilization can exist to-day quite apart from the Gospel. If only men had tried regeneration instead of civilization, we should have seen the difference in corporate and national life. Meanwhile, those who are influenced by the great truth of the Lord's coming rejoice to know that, notwithstanding everything, as old Charles Simeon once said, "he must reign, he shall reign, he will reign." And they are able to anticipate the day of Christ's perfect victory, in the words of Frances Ridley Havergal, "Oh, the joy to see thee reigning, thee, my own beloved Lord."

It is also, and not least of all, an incentive to holiness. In the light of the coming great day, the apostle John says that "every one that hath this hope set on him purifieth himself, even as he is pure" (1 John 3: 3); and another apostle, referring to the same great and glorious event, says, "seeing that ye look for these things, give diligence that ye may be found in peace, without spot and blameless in his sight" (2 Pet. 3: 14). Christ himself urged his servants to do business till he himself should come (Luke 19: 13). And the apostle Paul, while pointing out the appearing of Christ, urges us to "live soberly and righteously and godly in this present world," as we contemplate the coming of our Master (Tit. 2: 12).

Four words are used by the apostle Paul in connection with the coming of Christ. (1) We are to *wait* (1 Thess. 1: 10), as we live our life day by day. (2) We are to *watch* (1 Thess. 5: 10), keeping alive the flame of hope as well as exercising faith and love. (3) We are to *expect* (Rom. 8: 19, 23, Greek), eagerly anticipating the coming and looking out for the first indications of it. (4) We are to *love* (2 Tim. 4: 8), our heart's affections being centered on his "glorious appearing."

Thus in occupation with Christ as a present Saviour and Lord and in constant expectation of him as our coming Master and King, we shall realize everything that God intends for us in connection with the teaching of the coming. "Christ in you the hope of glory."

VICTORY'S FIRST STEP: SALVATION

Charles Gallaudet Trumbull

AT THE conference at Princeton a couple of summers ago a young fellow became deeply interested in the victorious life. He went to one of the leaders for a personal interview. As the two talked together, the leader asked him whether it was all right as to his relation to Jesus Christ as his Saviour, and the young man, eager for victory over the power of sin, showed that he did not know. It soon came out that he did not know what the plan of salvation was at all.

He had been brought up in a community, and in a home, and in a denomination which in some ways leads away from the Gospel rather than to it,—not one of the so-called evangelical denominations. So the leader said, "Let us settle this before we go any farther in the matter of the victorious life." The boy was perfectly ready, and said he would like to do so. They got down on their knees together, and the older man told the young fellow about the death of Jesus Christ, about Christ as his Saviour, and with eagerness the young man accepted Jesus Christ as his Saviour then and there for the first time in his life,—at least for the first time in his own consciousness.

If we have come to this conference with an interest in the victorious life, it is very important for us to be perfectly clear on Jesus Christ as Saviour, first of all.

Not long ago a friend of mine asked twenty-five Sunday-school teachers in Philadelphia whether they were saved. Of that twenty-five, twenty-three said they did not know. Sunday-school teachers these were, teaching their pupils about the Gospel of Jesus Christ in Christian Sunday-schools; and yet when they were asked whether they were saved, twenty-three of the twenty-five *did not know*.

Suppose you were walking along a road in the hope of getting to a certain place, and you were not quite sure of the way. Suppose you met another person, who asked you where you were going; and when you said you wanted to go to a

---

The first of Mr. Trumbull's six messages on the Victorious Life, given at Princeton and also at Cedar Lake.

Mr. Trumbull

certain destination, he answered, "Come with me." "You want to go there too, do you?" you ask, and upon receiving an affirmative answer, you reply, "Well, do you know whether you *are* going there?" If that person should say "No, I do not, but you come with me," would you feel particularly safe with such a guide? Twenty-three of those twenty-five Sunday-school teachers were in just that position. They did not know, whether they were going there or not. They hoped they were, of course; they wanted to go there; but they did not know whether they were.

So at the very beginning of this Victorious Life Conference, let us be clear, under God, what salvation is, so that we can say that we *know* where we are going, we *know* that we are saved.

It is true, that for a person to say he does not know, does not necessarily mean that he is not saved. Some of those twenty-three uncertain Sunday-school teachers may have been saved, and may not have had what is called a clear assurance of their salvation. A striking illustration of this came to my notice a few weeks ago at a series of evangelistic meetings in New York City, when the young people's societies came together to study the message and the method of evangelism.

The message of evangelism was given night after night for seven weeks, making simple and plain the plan of salvation as God reveals it in his Word. A middle-aged man surprised some of us by saying, after he had been there three or four weeks: "The message on the plan of salvation that was given here tonight has marked a new epoch in my life." Now that man had already been a true convert to Jesus Christ. He had accepted Christ some time before, and since then he had thrown his whole life into the service of the Lord. He had been holding evangelistic meetings and telling people about Jesus, and souls had been saved; but he now testified that until that night he *never knew what the plan of salvation was.* He had been telling people about Jesus, but he could not with clearness, with definiteness, with any ringing certainty declare to his hearers, "If you do this you may know, and you must know, that you are saved." Now, said he, a great burden of uncertainty had rolled from him, and he had a clearness of conviction about his own salvation, and a message to give to others, that he had never given before. And yet there was a real Christian worker, a soul-winner, who had not *known*.

Victory's First Step: Salvation

May God help us to be crystal clear on what he makes so clear in his Word.

To begin with, in the plan of salvation, let us look first at the sin question. The sin question is the central question of the *victorious* life; and the sin question is also the central question in the matter of salvation.

Suppose you went into a great hospital full of incurables in body and mind,—some incurably insane, some incurably diseased in body; and you asked, "How did these people become diseased in this way?" And suppose you were told that they were born so, every one of them. Congenital disease, the doctors call that,—diseased at birth and therefore from birth. It would seem like a dreary place, an unspeakably tragic place, a great hospital filled with only those incurably diseased in body and mind, and all of them *born* so.

As God looks down on this world, we realize that he sees the whole world as a hospital of those incurably diseased; and all *born* so. That is why we are all sinners; we are congenital sinners, every human being in the world. Romans 5: 12-15, you will remember, states that for us: "Wherefore, as by one man sin entered into the world, and death by sin; and so death passed upon all men, for that all have sinned . . . through the offense of one many be dead." That settles it. The whole human race, since Adam, has been born dead, born incurably diseased by nature. That is the result of sin as Adam brought it into this world.

And do you recall how God describes this congenital nature of man in the eighth chapter of Romans? Of this nature of the unsaved man God says: "To be carnally minded is death, . . . because the carnal mind is enmity against God. It is not subject to the law of God, neither indeed can it be." That is God's Word about this disease that the whole human race has by nature.

Looking at it another way, suppose you should see a man step to the curb of the street, roll up his sleeve, take a knife, open an artery in his arm, and let the blood gush out. What would happen? The answer is simple enough,—he would be unconscious in a very few minutes; and in a very few minutes after that he would be dead.

Well, any one who has ever sinned has done just that, so far as his spiritual life is concerned; or rather, it was done for him by Adam. The moment sin entered the human race, the result was exactly the same as with the man who has

Mr. Trumbull

let the life-blood of his body pour out. The spiritual life of a man goes the moment a sin is committed. He is not physically dead, but he is spiritually dead. Ephesians 2:1 tells us that; "And you . . . were dead in trespasses and sins." The life is the blood, the blood is the life; and spiritually all sin lets the God-life out, so that there is only death left there.

There is no "divine spark" in every man today, although a great many people want us to think that. There is no divine spark in a dead man, there is just death there. God said to Adam before Adam had sinned, warning him against the sin of eating the fruit of the tree, "In the day that thou eatest thereof thou shalt surely die." When God says "surely" he means it; and in the day that Adam did eat thereof, Adam died,—he died spiritually, and later he died physically as a result of that sin. Again in Romans 6:23 God tells us that "the wages of sin is death." So the Word of God leaves no doubt whatsoever as to the sin question in relation to salvation, and the congenital condition of the whole human race. And sin, you know, never cures itself.

There have been some modern writers and preachers who are unfolding what they call a new religion, who have said that sin is a stumble upward. No, God says that sin is a fall downward, down to the pit, down to death, down to hell. Sin never cures itself. The man who has sinned cannot do right in his own nature; and the end is hell.

"But," men say, "we ought not to talk about hell, anyway. Men are not going to be frightened into the kingdom of heaven." Now that is the devil's lie, that men are not going to be frightened into the kingdom of heaven. It sounds very plausible, but it does not happen to be true.

For *God* seems to think that it is a very good thing to frighten men wholesomely, terribly, by telling them the truth about the end of sin. God does this all through his Word. Jesus did it. John the Baptist did it in preparing for the coming of Christ, speaking of one who was coming to burn up the chaff with unquenchable fire (Matt. 3:12). Our Lord speaks of how much better it is for one to lose an eye, or a foot, or a hand than to enter into the place where the fire never ceases; and goes on in a description of the unending torment and torture of Gehenna (Mark 9:43, 44). The apostle Paul, under the inspiration of the Holy Spirit, speaks of that everlasting destruction from the face of the Lord

Victory's First Step: Salvation

which awaits those who, at Christ's coming, have rejected Him (2 Thess. 1:9). And in the last book of the Bible (Rev. 20:10-15) we read of the awful fate of the final world-ruler and the false prophet in the lake of fire; and then of those at the great white throne judgment, whose names are not found written in the Book of Life, being cast into the same lake of fire.

We Christians ought to make perfectly sure that we know what God says about hell, and then tell the way of escape. But what is the way of escape? What is there to do about it?

May I mention first some things that it is *not* man's place to "do about it" in order to be saved? For there are so many things that are being told people in these days as the way of salvation which are directly contrary to the Word of God. In the first place, *service* is not man's part in salvation.

You remember the old story of the man who was lost in a snowstorm in the mountains. The snow was coming down more and more fiercely, and the cold was increasing, and he felt himself freezing to death. He pushed on almost hopelessly, and, when about to drop down from exhaustion, he stumbled over something, and looking, found another man helpless. He was not dead, and he resuscitated him and got him to his knees, and then to his feet, got him to take a step, and with his arm around him he made him walk for his life. They went on together until they saw a light, and then a house, and entered into it, and both were saved. The lesson is,—if you want to be saved, save somebody else; get busy and do something for somebody, and your salvation will take care of itself.

Don't any of you ever tell that story as an illustration of the way of salvation! It is a lie. That is *not* the way of salvation. It is a good thing to save people in a snowstorm; but you are not going to heaven because you do it, and *you are not going to heaven because of anything that you can do.* Service is not the secret of salvation,—it is not man's part in salvation, although the saved man will serve as the unsaved man never can.

Turning over a new leaf is not man's part in salvation: saying, "Well, I will just turn away from my sins, leave them behind, and start in all over again." That is not the way to be saved, although we are turned away from our sins when we are saved.

Asserting our manhood is not our part in salvation; yet

Mr. Trumbull

it is often urged that that is the way to be a Christian. "Be a man, assert your manhood, do your best, and enlist for Christ." Enlisting in Christ's service does not save anyone; coming over on to Christ's side, that is, stepping over on to the side of righteousness instead of being on the side of sin, in order to live right and do right, does not save anyone. Even the question of "deciding for Christ," while it may be meant correctly, is misleading. You do not find it in the Bible as the way of salvation.

In this matter of asserting our manhood in order to be saved, think back for a moment to the dead man lying in the gutter,—that man who opened his arteries until his life-blood had all poured out. How much good would it do him to step up and say, "My dear fellow, be a man; assert your manhood now, and you will be all right." A dead man hasn't anything to assert! It does not help a dead man to tell him to *do* anything,—he cannot.

Of course, it appeals to the pride of the natural man to tell him to "be a man." He is sure he has lots of manhood, and he will gladly show everybody what a man he is! He would far rather be told to "be a man," as the way of salvation, than anything else; but the offense of the cross does not tell him any such thing. The offense of the cross makes no appeal to our manhood, our womanhood. We have none,— "there is none righteous, no, not one." The cross exposes the degradation of every human being. It appeals to nothing in them except their awful need, their desire to live—for a spiritually dead man can desire to live. A spiritually dead man, after the Spirit of God has begun to work on him and has convicted him of his sin, can want to be saved; but he cannot do anything about it.

Right thinking is not the way of salvation. Some people talk as though it were, "Oh, just think lovely thoughts, right thoughts, good thoughts, pure thoughts; put a lovely picture on your dressing stand, where you will see it every morning. That picture will uplift you; and so in thinking good thoughts, and looking at beautiful pictures, your divine life will come out and you will be saved. Keep a picture of your mother, or your sweetheart, or your wife, in your watch; surround yourself with uplifting influences." That is New Thought,— new thought as old as Satan! You will not find anything in the Scriptures about right thinking in order to be saved.

"But," says some one, does not the Bible say, "whatsoever

Victory's First Step: Salvation

things are pure, whatsoever things are lovely, whatsoever things are of good report; . . . think on those things"?

Yes, the Bible says that, but to whom does it say it? To the unsaved? No, that passage is written to believers. After you are saved you can "think on those things,"—whatsoever things are of good report. But you never can do it while you are unsaved, with any effectiveness or saving power at all.

Denying the existence of sin is not man's part in salvation. Yet there are those who tell us that if we will simply deny the existence of sin, sin won't bother us, because there is no sin anyway. That is Christian Science: deny the existence of sin, and evil, and error of every sort, and you will be free.

I wonder what would happen if the Allied lines in the trenches "over there" just denied the existence of the German armies for a few weeks, and said, "They do not exist!" Even the Christian Science chaplains do not recommend that! But the German armies are a trifle, they are friendly, as compared with the armies of Satan and of sin that are assaulting us and assaulting all mankind every day. To deny their existence is just as foolish, just as suicidal as it would be for the armies of the Allies to deny the existence of the Central Powers. God does not deny the existence of sin; God says that sin put his Son to death.

Denying self,—is that the way of salvation? Some tell us that it is. No; asceticism is only another word for this, and it never saves any one. Some think that by doing the hard things they may be saved and have victory. But God never says so. God wants people to have an easy life. Did you ever know that? He wants them to have the easiest life in the world. It is the way of the transgressor that is hard; it is the yoke of Christ that is easy. The only easy life is the saved, victorious life; every other life is hard. Doing hard things, denying self, is not the way of salvation; although after we have taken Christ as Saviour we are to deny the sinful self and let Christ live our life for us; but as a *result* of our salvation, not as the *condition* of it.

Last of all, is *sacrifice* the way of salvation? Sacrifice is on the very highest plane, is it not? If we carry it to the laying down of our lives, won't that save us? Why, Jesus himself said, "Greater love hath no man than this, that a man lay down his life for his friends." Isn't that enough?

It is true that Jesus said that, but he was not talking about salvation when he said it. He was talking about love,

Mr. Trumbull

and the supreme expression of love; but he did not say that the man who lays down his life for his friends gets saved by it. In the context you will find that Jesus was not referring to the way of salvation at all; yet it is the peculiar peril of today, in these war times, that the emphasis on sacrifice shall mislead people into thinking that this is the way of salvation. You have read soldiers' articles in the magazines, saying that a man who has gone to the front and accepted "the baptism of blood," as they call it, offered up his life, whether he loses it or not, has atoned for whatever past life he has led, and is right with God. And one of the generals at the front is quoted in the *London Times,* as saying, "My faith in the Almighty is such that I am perfectly sure he takes to himself, and looks after, men . . ., whatever their past lives have been, who, doing their duty nobly, have died fighting for their country."

Yet sacrifice is not the way of salvation. As someone has said, the soldiers themselves, most of them, know better, because this would be giving more efficacy for salvation to a German bullet than to the cross of Christ.

Well, if none of these things is our part in salvation, if none is the way of salvation, then what is the way? What can we do about salvation? My friends, that dead man lying out in the gutter cannot do anything about it. If he is to be brought to life, it will have to be done for him. And if the unsaved person is going to be saved, something must be done for him. God must do something for him; and God has done something for him; and that is the Gospel, that is the Good News—that God *has done* all that is needed.

What is it that God has done?

Let us think of it in this way for a moment. When God the Father, the Son, and the Holy Spirit, way back in the far reaches of eternity, before ever any creation had been wrought, knew that when man was created he was going to sin, and when they knew that the wages of sin was death, and that man could not stop sinning after he had once sinned, but that sin would go on through all eternity with all the punishment that that requires,—we can think of just three possibilities that the Godhead could consider.

The Father might have said: "Well, we shall have created man, and man will have sinned. We know that he is going to sin; therefore we will just forgive him, we will ignore his sin, and say, after millions upon billions of the human race

Victory's First Step: Salvation

have been born, and have sinned, and have died, 'Now, sin-saturated though you are, in the bondage of sin though you are and always will be, we will take you into eternal fellowship with ourselves in heaven,' and the holy and sinless God will fellowship through all eternity with sinful human beings."

That is one possibility—but can we think of that as a possibility? No, a holy, sinless God could not do that. He could not condone sin; he could not ignore sin. That is where the forgiveness of God has to be utterly different from the forgiveness of any human being. We can ignore the sin of another human being,—God cannot.

Then there is a second possible alternative that we can think of. God might have said: "We cannot ignore sin. We cannot take sinners into fellowship with ourselves, the sinners with the sinless and the holy. We shall have to condemn to eternal punishment, to hell, all of the human race, every man, woman or child that shall ever be created or born."

But does that seem possible? Does it seem thinkable, that God would create an entire race for that end? It does not, so we shall have to set that aside.

Then there is a third possibility. We can believe that, in accordance with the Father's will, God the Son said, "Father, I will pay the whole penalty of all mankind's sin myself. I know what it means, you know what it means; but if you will let me,—for we cannot ignore the sin, and we cannot let them all go,—I will pay the whole penalty myself."

May we not believe that then, way back in the far reaches of eternity, the heart of the Father broke, as he accepted the Son's offer? We must remember that it was in the will of the Father from the very beginning, and in the will of the Son, and in the will of the Holy Spirit. But the fulness of time came, aeons later, when, as we read in the second chapter of Philippians, the Son of God became man, and took those seven downward steps in his humiliation, rendering his willing obedience even unto death, the death of the cross.

Do we know what that meant? For just here is the unthinkable wonder of the Gospel. Look at 2 Corinthians 5:21, and we see the marvelous statement "Him [Christ] who knew no sin he made to be sin on our behalf." Christ, the Son of God, was made sin, in some mystery that we cannot fathom. He took into himself the sin of all mankind. Then, as we read in Galatians 3:13, "Christ hath redeemed us from

Mr. Trumbull

the curse of the law, *being made a curse for us.*" Jesus Christ was made a curse for us, "for it is written, Cursed is every one that hangeth on a tree." There on the cross, having taken our sins, bearing them in his own body on the tree, Jesus Christ became a curse; and God the Father could not look upon him, and had to turn his face away from him. Then came the heart-broken cry on the cross, "My God, my God, why hast thou forsaken me?" And for the first time in all eternity, the Father and the Son were separated, as Jesus paid to the full the death-penalty of man's sin,—separation from the Father, the very pains of hell in body, mind, and spirit. And it was finished; the sin-debt was fully paid.

Nineteen centuries before that dark day, the blackest day in all time or eternity, to a place near that very same spot outside Jerusalem, came another father and his son, his only son. The father came to offer up his son, his only son, unto death. He bound the boy and laid him on the altar. He took the knife in his hand, raised it, and was about to plunge it into the heart of his son, his only son; and then he heard a voice speaking his name, "Abraham!" The father's hand was stayed just as it was about to strike into the body of his boy, and God told him that he saw now that Abraham was willing to make that sacrifice, but that he need not, and an animal was provided as a substitute for the sacrifice.

But oh, dear friends, nineteen centuries after that time, at that same place, when God's Son, his only Son, hung on the cross, and the hand of God the Father was raised to strike, as a holy God must against sin which God cannot ignore or condone or tolerate, *there was no one to stay the Father's hand;* and the blow fell; and the Son died. There was no substitute for Christ, because Christ was the substitute for all mankind. God the Father suffered what Abraham the father was not permitted to suffer. And now the penalty of sin was paid, fully paid.

The Father raised the Son from the dead to show that he accepted the sacrifice, and that he was satisfied with the offering that Jesus Christ had made. And from that day to this God has been telling the whole world, or trying to as best he could through his imperfect messengers, that it is *done;* that back there on Calvary the whole penalty for all the sins of mankind was paid, paid so perfectly that nothing can ever add to the finished payment in time or eternity. "For God so loved the world, that he gave his only begotten Son, that

Victory's First Step: Salvation

whosoever believeth in him should not perish, but have everlasting life."

Yes; for that man lying dead in the gutter, with no life in him, something has to be done if he is to live. He cannot do it for himself. But God *has* done it: that is the Gospel; and now God only waits for men to believe, has been waiting all these centuries, lovingly, patiently postponing the coming time of judgment. He is longsuffering, not willing that any should be lost who are willing to believe. What does God ask us to do? Assert our manhood? Deny the existence of sin? No. Deny self? No, we cannot. Sacrifice everything? No, we have nothing worth sacrificing. *Just believe!* Just look up into his face and say, "Father, if you have made that sacrifice for me, I do believe. And you say that if I believe in Jesus and what he has done for me, I shall have everlasting life. I *do* believe; and I thank thee now."

Are any of us taking any risk in this matter? Are we letting our friends take any risk? Church membership does not save us. It is only within the last few years that, as I looked back over my life, I realized how thoughtlessly I had become a church member. I felt that I did not dare take any risk myself; and so I told the Lord Jesus, as though I had never heard of it before, that whatever I might or might not have done before, I wanted him to know right now that I believed that Jesus Christ had died for my sins, and that I now accepted him as my Saviour. And do you know, it was a joy to look up into his face then! This was not many years ago; and, while I have little doubt that I was saved many years ago, I did not want to take any risk, and so I made sure of this simple transaction with him.

I have an officer friend who is in France; he has been there since last summer in one of the most dangerous branches of the service. He has been for many years a church member, and probably a Christian. But last summer I got to thinking about him, and I knew that in recent years he had not been particularly close to evangelical Christian influence. So I wrote him a letter, over there in France, and in a simple, definite way I ran over the necessary steps of salvation,—the fact that we are sinners, and that Jesus Christ died on the cross and paid the penalty of our sin, and that the moment we believe on him for ourselves he saves us. I asked my friend, "Have you ever done that? And if you have not, won't you do it now?"

Mr. Trumbull

I did not hear from him for some months; and I wrote again. Then I had a letter from France, and my friend said he had now done exactly what I had said in my letter, and he knew it was settled.

I wonder whether every one of us here has settled it in just that same directness, simplicity, and clearness? I do not care whether we are church members,—so many of us joined the church thoughtlessly, or not thoughtlessly, and yet are not absolutely clear today on our salvation. Is every man and woman here absolutely clear? Are we seeing our Lord Jesus there on the cross, as the children of Israel saw the serpent lifted up in the wilderness, when all they had to do was to look, and believe, and they were healed from the death sting? "And as Moses lifted up the serpent in the wilderness, even so must the Son of man be lifted up," that we might look unto him and be saved.

This message on salvation is given in fuller form in Mr. Trumbull's new book, "What is the Gospel?", which includes also several other chapters on the Gospel and one chapter giving a simple presentation of the Victorious Life. See page 379.

II. SOME VICTORY TESTS

Charles Gallaudet Trumbull

MRS. JONATHAN GOFORTH of China wrote some time ago to Mr. Borton, chairman of our Board of Managers, a letter in which she said, "Isn't it wonderful to find in the fifth verse of the twentieth Psalm the secret of victory?" and she called attention to the margin of the Revision, *"We will triumph in Thy victory."*

There is our key-note for these studies in the Victorious Life,—and, bless God, for the rest of our lives: "We will triumph in Thy victory." And we will ask God to unfold more and more to us this week what it really means for us to triumph in his victory.

An epitaph was found on a tombstone in a little Kentish graveyard, reading:

> "Here lies a soldier
>   And brave was he;
> He fought many battles
>   By land and by sea;
> But the fiercest engagement
>   He ever was in,
> Was the conquest of self
>   In the battle of sin."

Ought "the fiercest engagement" we ever are in to be "the conquest of self in the battle of sin"? No; for we shall never have victory in that way, by wresting our victory from Satan with the most terrific, prodigious struggles and efforts of will-power "in the conquest of self and the battle of sin." We are going to learn something better than that, as some of you already have done. "The conquest of self in the battle of sin" is not to be won by any fierce engagement of ours. The only way is to "triumph in *His* victory."

I wonder if every member of this conference is not in one or another of half a dozen classifications, or groups, as God sees us.

Suppose we say that the first class or group consists of those who have not surrendered everything to the Lord Jesus Christ, but who do not know that they have not. They are

Mr. Trumbull

not having any struggle, they have no uneasiness of conscience. They are Christians perhaps, or perhaps not,—God knows. For they may really be Christians and be practically free even from any consciousness or struggle in the matter of not having surrendered everything to the Lord Jesus Christ. There are some who say that this matter of "surrender" does not interest them, and that so far as they are concerned they do not need to do what the folks here talk about,—such people are "fanatics," they say. That is the first group: those who have not made a clean sweep of it with the Lord, who have not gone the whole way and said, "Lord, you can have all there is of me." They have not done this, and apparently they do not know that they need to.

I think it is Dr. Scofield who has said that not every one, by any means, has had the experience of the seventh chapter of Romans, that agony of conflict, of desire to do what we cannot do, of longing to do the right that we find we cannot do. It is a great blessing, he has said, when a person gets into the seventh chapter of Romans and begins to realize the awful conflict of its struggle and defeat; because the first step toward getting out of the struggle of the seventh chapter and into the victory of the eighth, is to get into the seventh. Of all needy classes of people, the neediest on this earth are, not those who are having a heart-breaking, agonizing struggle for victory, but those who are having no struggle at all, and no victory, and who do not know it, and who are satisfied and jogging along in a pitiable absence of almost all the possessions that belong to them in Christ.

A man once said to me, commenting on the victorious life: "I have no desire for any mountain-top experiences. I know a good many people think of them, and want them, but I have no desire for anything of the sort." That man is not having any mountain-top experiences, and is not likely to have, until he at least begins to have some desire for them. May God speak to every one who has not surrendered and who does not know that he has not, and who does not know that he needs to.

The second group is of those who have not surrendered, who know that they need to surrender, and who intend not to. That is a hard group to deal with. Some of us who have been at these conferences know how person after person of that sort has come here. I remember one athletic young fellow who was here several years ago, and who came to "have

Some Victory Tests.

a good time." He certainly did not come for the "religious stuff" that was here, and he wanted to keep on with the games, tennis and everything else, while the meetings were going on. At the suggestion that he should go the whole way with the Lord he was indignant and rebellious. He had not surrendered, and probably knew that he had not, but he certainly did not intend to. More than one person is in that attitude of conscious rebellion against the mastery of the Lord Jesus Christ.

But there is more hope for that group than for the first. There is plenty of hope for *all*, in the sufficiency of our Lord Jesus Christ; but the second group is a step ahead of the first. Mr. Moody used to say that there was hope for a man if you could get him mad! When there is a conscious rebellion and determination not to surrender, it shows that at least the Holy Spirit's work is being recognized. If any such are here at this meeting, I am just going to tell you that you are going to "come across" in the Lord's own time, because he does not "let up." Praise him for that!

The third group is of those who have not surrendered, but who are now about ready to do so. They do not intend *not* to; they intend to surrender; and they are about ready, but are believing the devil's lie that the surrendered life is an awfully hard life. Oh, yes, they are going to surrender,— that is what they came here for, to step out into the surrendered life; but my, how they dread it! It is like standing on the brink of a cold pool of water, which you intend to plunge into. You are there for that purpose, and some other folks are already in, and are calling out, "Come on in, the water's fine!" You say, "Yes, I know, but I do hate the first plunge." After a while, with great nerve, you make the plunge and go in. It is a shock for a second, but after you have been there a moment you are mighty glad you got in, for then comes the exhilaration and the tingling joy of it. Well, that is not a circumstance to the exhilaration and tingling joy of the surrendered and victorious life. And if there should be anyone here who has not surrendered, who knows he ought to, and who intends to, but who is shivering and holding back, do not believe that lie of the devil any longer, that it is hard after you get in. The victorious life is the easiest life in the world,—and it is the only easy life.

The fourth group is of those who have surrendered, but who are still defeated. The first three groups consist of those

Mr. Trumbull

who for various reasons have not surrendered; now we come to this fourth: those who have surrendered, who have taken the plunge, thrown up their hands and said, "Lord, I'm through trying to run my life; you can have all there is of me, forever; I am glad to turn the job over to you, Lord, so here goes." They have surrendered and have experienced (as one instantly does on making a complete surrender) something of the joy of it, the relief, the release, the peace and power of the life that has "let go."

But here is a strange thing,—this fourth class consists of those who, although they have yielded everything to the Lord, are still defeated, are not having the victory that they confidently counted on as coming to them after they should have let everything go. And they *have* let everything go; they are not deceiving themselves. Satan may be trying to deceive them by telling them they have not surrendered everything; that is probably a lie, because many a real Christian who has let everything go, has had that experience of more or less habitual defeat, even in the surrendered life; that is possible, and it is very usual. Wholly surrendered, yet often defeated, almost never having the experience of utter freedom and victory in the power and joy that they long for! And those in this fourth group, who have surrendered everything yet are having defeat, do not know what the trouble is; they are baffled and discouraged as to the secret of victory.

In the fifth group are those who have surrendered everything, and who know that they must add to their surrender *faith*. But they do not know how to get that faith; and so they too are defeated. They have not gone back on their surrender. "Oh, if I could only have the radiant faith of Mrs. Goforth [or of this, that, or the other victorious Christian, they say], it would be all right. I have asked the Lord for such faith; I have tried to believe; but I have never succeeded in having this faith. It is a wonderful thing to have perfect faith, but I am afraid it is not for me." The persons in this fifth group know that they need more faith, long for it, but do not know how to get it.

The last group, the sixth, is of those who have surrendered everything, and are actually "foolish" enough to believe that God's Word is true, and who therefore are having victory! In their lives may be found the whole fruit of the Spirit, with its nine parts, love, joy, peace, longsuffering, gentleness, goodness, faith, meekness, self-control (Gal. 5: 22, 23). All those

Some Victory Tests

nine parts of that wonderful fruit of the Holy Spirit are being produced in their lives, and are all being produced at once, all at the same time. Not some of them in the morning, and some in the afternoon, and some the next day,—no, all nine growing there now. They have all that the Lord Jesus offers them so far as victory is concerned, and "the life that is Christ." From the light on the faces of some of you, I know that you are praising God that he *is* working this miracle in your lives, that he is *able* to work it, is *faithful* to work it, and he is working it now. You do not know how he does it,—no one does; but you know that he is true to his word.

That is the last group of the half dozen, and, praise God! every one of us belongs there. And every one of us is going to be there, just as soon as we are ready to step out on him and believe in him for it all.

As we think of the victorious life, let us ask ourselves whether we are perfectly clear on what *sin* is. We cannot have much desire for victory until we know what it is that we need to be victorious over. We cannot have any intelligent desire for freedom if we do not know what it is we need to be free from. Satan has so dulled our natures, and our standards, and our minds, as to what sin is, and the practise of sin itself has dulled us so terribly, that many a real Christian honestly believes that some sinful things are not sin. Let us test ourselves for a moment.

Some of us have come here to the conference, and have found to our great surprise that this Victorious Life Conference was subject to human imperfections, and that perhaps the room we have is not as perfectly appointed as some room at the Bellevue-Stratford in Philadelphia or the Waldorf-Astoria in New York; we may have to put up with a roommate who is really the last person we would have chosen if we could have chosen; or some of the meals have not been exactly what we would have ordered had we been ordering; and I have a lurking idea that some of us, in these circumstances, have been just a little irritated. We have been saying: "Well, I did not suppose *this* sort of thing was going to happen." Or we may not have said a word about it to any human being; we may even have been smiling at that room-mate the whole time, telling folks how we were enjoying everything; but way down inside we have been irritated.

Mr. Trumbull

Now, irritation is *sin*. It is the kind of sin that put the Lord Jesus Christ on the cross. Not irritation that is spoken out snappishly (that is sin too, irritation that shows itself in the clouded face, or the sharp word); but the inner irritation that never shows itself to any human being, but only to God, who looketh not at the outward appearance, but at the heart. That is a sin, dear friends; and there is only one kind of sin—not two kinds, nor twenty: all sin is the same kind, black, murderous, God-resisting, God-defying, Christ-crucifying. So when we have felt that passing flash of irritation,—if any of us have since we came here to the conference,—we have sinned. And the victorious life means that we can be free from that innermost irritation. Yes, *free*.

What about worry? The next step from irritation is worry. A Christian woman came to this conference some years ago, and at the first Vesper service Mr. McQuilkin gave a radiant message on the fact that the Lord Jesus Christ is able to keep us from worry and anxiety. Mr. McQuilkin seemed to believe that when God said, "In nothing be anxious," God really meant it, and that the Christian who "lets go and lets God" can really be kept from anxiety. As this woman heard him talking about freedom from worry she was saying to herself: "Hm, if some of those speakers and the Board of Managers would worry a little *more*, some of us delegates would have a more comfortable time." She was worried because things did not suit her, and the message made her indignant. Praise God—there was hope for her! And at the end of the week, when the testimonies came, I shall never forget the testimony that Christian woman gave. She told how that week she had learned that worry is a sin, and therefore a conquerable sin,—conquerable not by her, but by her Lord Jesus Christ; and now she had stopped worrying and had had the most wonderful experience of freedom from worry she had ever known. She said she was going back to her home, in the grace and strength of the Lord Jesus Christ, free from the sin of worry.

Have we all realized that worry is a sin, a black, murderous, God-defying, Christ-rejecting sin,—worrying about anything at any time? This does not mean that we are to be indifferent, or careless,—that we may not be concerned for this, that, or the other need; it does not mean that we may not have a longing desire to see things different, to see things changed that God wants to have changed. But this is the

Some Victory Tests

miracle: while we are more sensitively conscious of what is going wrong around us than ever, there is no worrying, but there is thanksgiving as we look at Jesus and praise God for His sufficiency; that this thing that is going wrong, and that is worse than unpleasant, the Lord Jesus Christ can change, and in the meantime can keep us happy and joyous and praising him even while it is going wrong.

Again, have we peace in our lives? Suppose we are waiting for a letter to come, and that letter is going to give us information without which we cannot go ahead in plans that we must make. Perhaps it is a letter regarding the most important piece of work that we ever undertook in our lives. We have written about the matter, and prayed about it, and now this letter is due us, and it ought to have come to-day, or even last week; but it did not come. The days go by, and still the letter does not come. Have we peace, undisturbed, undisturbable peace every day, or are we nervously waiting, chafing and restless? The victorious life is a life of peace, peace no matter how long we have to wait, peace under all circumstances. Have we the peace of God which passeth all understanding, garrisoning our hearts and our thoughts in Christ Jesus? If we have, we have victory. If we have not, we are sinning. That is the point: it is not that we are not as high up as we might be, or as low down as we might be; the lack of peace is as real a sin as any other kind of sin. The Christian who lacks peace is a defeated Christian.

Are our lives cleansed from impurity? Perhaps some of us men have been congratulating ourselves that impurity of act, or even of word, has been taken out of our lives. I wonder if any of us are finding that, so far as our hearts are concerned, or our thoughts, or the look of the eye, we are constantly being exposed to sights that stir up in our innermost hearts genuine impurity. We may allow it to stay only for a second, and then come to our senses, as with a blush inwardly we ask the Lord to forgive us; but we have enjoyed it the moment it was there. That is not victory. The Lord Jesus Christ has no such feelings in *his* heart. It is good to have the impure act, the impure word, forever gone; but it is still better to have the briefest impure desire of the innermost unspoken thought gone. That is victory. And anything less than that is *sin*.

Another suggestion by which we may test ourselves whether we need victory,—what about unlove? Have we that?

Mr. Trumbull

Have we love? Yes, we have lots of love. We love most people. But do we love *everybody?* An old man who had gone the whole way with the Lord, and whose heart was flooded with the victory and joy of the Lord Jesus Christ, sprang up in prayer-meeting and said, "I just love everybody," and sat down. Love was the one big thing in his life,—there wasn't a human being on the face of the globe of whom he could think that he did not love. Is that true of all of us? Or can any of us think this moment of some person of whom we would a little rather *not* think, of whom it is not pleasant to think; some one whom, if we should go out from this chapel and meet on the campus, we would get away from as quickly as possible? Perhaps that one has done or said something bitterly unjust, cruelly unfair, utterly untrue, about you or about some one you love far better than yourself. Never mind; do you love that person who has done it, right now? Could you go to him and put out your hands and look in his face and say, "I love you,"—say it with the supernatural love of God flooding your heart and your face? If not, if there is any one of whom you can think to whom you could not thus go and of whom you cannot now think with real love, it is sin, the kind of sin that crucified Jesus. Do we need victory here? We do if we have not the very love of God shed abroad in our hearts by the Holy Spirit.

Perhaps you are thinking: "I might have this wonderful victory, might have freedom from all these sins, if only I had known about it earlier; but I have gone too far. I am a Christian, and I am going to keep on serving the Lord, but only God knows how habitually I have yielded to some of these sins in my life."

Or again: "I am of a nervous temperament, and am not particularly strong physically, and the things that do not irritate everybody do irritate me,—the doctors have told me so. So this matter of the victorious life I believe is perfectly possible for some people, but it is not for me."

I wonder if any of us are thinking such thoughts? Oh, what a liar the devil is, and how he comes to us as an angel of light! How he loves to tell us that our bodies prevent us from having victory; how we have been nursing that thought, holding on to it because it is such a comfort to think it is the body all the while, and that we are not responsible; or that it is our "broken pinions," those terrible failures we have made, that are keeping us down.

Some Victory Tests

I remember a flash of righteous indignation that swept over Dr. Scofield's face once as he said, "People talk about the bird with the broken wing,—'The bird with the broken pinion never soars as high again.' As though we did not all have a broken wing! For most of us both our wings are broken, and both legs, and our necks!" So let us just give up this notion that it is the "broken pinion" that is going to keep us from soaring as high as some victorious life Christians can soar. One thing is certain: the bird *without* a broken pinion is never going to know victory. One qualification you must have for the victorious life is the broken pinion, the broken nature, uttermost weakness. God makes no offer of victory to strong people, people who have not failed, and failed utterly. But for *sinners* he has a Gospel. The foolish, the weak, the base, the despised, "yea and the things that are not" did God choose, "that he might bring to nought the things that are: that no flesh should glory before God . . . that, according as it is written, He that glorieth, let him glory [not in his own record, but] in the *Lord*" (1 Cor. 1: 26-31).

Oh, do not let us listen to the devil when he talks to us about our past, about our weaknesses, about our physical failures, about the weaknesses of the body. Let us tell the Lord Jesus Christ that we haven't anything but weakness to offer him; and let us praise him for what he says about our weakness as being our qualification for his strength resting upon us (2 Cor. 12: 9).

One last suggestion, for now, as to the victorious life,—are you rejoicing always? Is joy a fact in your life? Not a feeling—our feelings are very variable; but joy, as Dr. Griffith Thomas has pointed out, is not a feeling but a fact. Have you that fact, rooted and grounded in the Rock of Ages, the fact of joy in your life?

Do you remember the story of the old Scotch woman who was such a joyous Christian that when her pastor was preaching and would come anywhere near the heart of the Gospel she would have to shout, "Hallelujah! Praise the Lord!" One day he went to her and said: "Betty, I wish you wouldn't shout that way when I get to the best part of my sermon, because it throws me off the track and makes me forget what I am going to say. Now, I'll tell you what I will do. If you will keep quiet for a year while I am preaching, I will give you a pair of woolen blankets." The winters

Mr. Trumbull

were severe where Betty lived, and woolen blankets looked pretty good to her, so she said she would keep still. Weeks passed by, and poor Betty had to choke her joy down when her pastor was talking. But one day another preacher came to the church in her pastor's absence. This preacher was preaching wonderfully about the Gospel and what the Lord Jesus has done for us. Poor Betty stood it as long as she could. Finally she couldn't stand it any longer, and springing to her feet she cried out, "Blankets or no blankets, Hallelujah!"

I rather think Betty had something worth more than a pair of wool blankets, and that she was warmer without the blankets but with her joy than she could have been in any other way.

Have *you* the joy that will make you say, "Blankets or no blankets, Hallelujah"?

III. GOD'S THREEFOLD WORK OF GRACE

Charles Gallaudet Trumbull

YESTERDAY morning I was seeking for the right Scripture to bring here as the particular key-note for our studies in the victorious life. I had been praying, of course, for guidance. There are so many blessed Scriptures that give the truth of victory that it was hard to choose, and I had thought of two 1: 21's, Matthew 1: 21 and Philippians 1: 21. One tells why Jesus was named "Jesus,"—"thou shalt call his name Jesus; for it is he that shall save his people from their sins"; and the other tells that we may have him as our life,—"to me to live is Christ." But somehow I was led to set those aside and take up the passage in Psalm 20: 5 that Mrs. Goforth had sent all the way from China to Mr. Borton, which he passed on to me months ago: "We will triumph in thy victory." Only six words, but they tell the whole thing. They are talking about *us*, they are talking about *Christ*. It is *his* victory that we triumph in. He makes it ours, but it is his first, last, and always; we never have to win the victory, he has won it for us. Surely here is our key-verse for the victorious life.

Now here is the interesting confirmation of God's leading. This very morning Mr. Borton received a letter from Mrs. Goforth sent from China, forwarded to him from home, reaching here this Tuesday morning; and this is what she says: "My message is concerning the first clause of Psalm 20: 5, Revised Version, marginal rendering: 'We will triumph in thy victory.' Oh, praise his glorious name, the victory is not ours,—that is, we do not have to work it out for ourselves, or win it for ourselves."

That is just an earnest of God's leading in details that may seem small, but that may become blessedly large in our own lives if we will keep right on praising him in absolute confidence that he will do what he says.

Let us also keep plainly before us this great fact about the victorious life, that God wants us always to remember: the victorious life is a life of ease, not of effort. Life becomes an utterly different thing for the Christian who is taking Christ as victor. I say "is taking" rather than "has taken," because it is a moment by moment relationship of faith to

Mr. Trumbull

the victorious life of our Lord Jesus Christ. When we remember that the victorious life is a life of ease, not of effort, it will simplify the truth for us, and will enable us instantly to detect whether we are on the right or the wrong track.

If we find there is something we need to *do* in the matter of victory, or find that victory is becoming hard, a matter of effort or struggle, we are on the wrong track; we are not on God's basis; and we are to heed the danger signal just as the railroad engineer, seeing red, knows it is a sign to stop. The moment our life becomes a matter of effort in having victory over sin, we are heading the wrong way, we are looking the wrong way. The Lord says, "My yoke is easy"; and it is the easiest yoke in the world.

Over a subway entrance on Market street in Philadelphia is a sign reading, "Live the simple life till victory is won." That is a good slogan for winning the war. But for victory over sin let us change it to, "Live the simple life *and* victory is won." Because the simple life is letting Christ live our life for us,—not attempting to live it of ourselves. Or we can change that sign again, to read, "Live the simple life and victory goes on,"—remembering that by "the simple life" we mean the life of quiet trust in the complete sufficiency of our Lord Jesus Christ,—letting him live our life for us. That indeed makes life easy instead of hard.

Another point God wants us to remember as to the victorious life is this: it is the life in which we are kept from sin *in our hearts.* Of course if we are kept from sin in our hearts we shall also be kept from outward expressions of sin; but so many of us have felt that being kept merely from outward expressions of sin was the victorious life. Many of us have thought that so long as we kept the sin in our hearts and did not let it express itself at all we were having victory. We have already seen that that is a mistake.

The victorious life is a life in which we are so kept from sin in our hearts that we not only do not say irritable things, but we do not feel irritable. What a difference there is here! Anybody can keep from saying irritable things if he has inducement enough. If a man owes you ten dollars that you are hoping to get this morning, and you realize that if you say something sharp to him he might not pay you, you can keep from saying anything irritable in order to get the

God's Threefold Work of Grace

money. It is not Christianity to do that; it is mere selfishness! But not to feel irritation in our heart is supernatural. And that is the wonder of the victorious life; that in victory, somehow, we do not know how, the Lord Jesus Christ and the Holy Spirit deal with our innermost heart in the matter of sin, and keep us from sin even there.

I know a man who naturally has one of the most irritable dispositions of any one I ever have known, and who has said as sharp things as any one I have ever known. After he took Christ as his victory, he had this amazing experience. He had occasion to step into a room where there was someone who, over and over again, had "gotten on his nerves" terribly, and over and over again had said things that "sent him up in the air," and at such times he did not keep the irritation in his heart either, but let it right out in some sharp word. This time that man with that natural disposition, and with that record of past failures with this person who had so often irritated him beyond control, was greeted as he entered the room with a word that was like a slap in the face. In the old days it would have caused him to fairly "hit the ceiling"; this time he stayed right on the floor, and he not only did not say anything sharp in reply, but he did not even feel any irritation in his heart! On the contrary, he was just bubbling over with the sheer joy and gladness of the fullness of the Lord Jesus Christ in his heart at that moment, so that he made a sunshiny reply,—because he felt sunshiny inside.

Suppose you were fighting with the Allies, and the Germans were pouring the bullets into you with machine guns, while you had some utterly supernatural, miraculous protection, so that not a bullet could touch you—would you be glad? So it is, as you see the darts, the bayonets, the bullets, whatever they are ("every fiery dart of the adversary," God says) drop before you, and you safe and untouched, you feel like shouting for joy. It is an actual fact that Christ so deals with sin in our hearts, in the victorious life, that with ease, without struggle, without effort the innermost heart-sin that we have experienced somehow, by a mystery that we shall never explain in this life, ceases to operate. Never mind about any theological explanation of what happens in our hearts; God knows, and it is his business, not ours. But he offers to do it, he promises to do it, and thousands of Christians will testify with joyous thanksgiving that he *does* it.

Mr. Trumbull

Look at Romans 6:11 and see what God says about the condition we can be in in our relation to sin: "Even so reckon ye also yourselves to be dead indeed unto sin, but alive unto God in Christ Jesus." Well now, a dead man, one who is dead unto sin, unto those attacks of sin, does not have to struggle in the matter! If you have not made a special study of the way in which God uses the word "dead" and "death" in relation to ourselves and our attitude toward sin, you will get a great blessing in studying such a chapter as the sixth of Romans.

It is the *grace* of God that does these things, that gives us a life of ease instead of a life of effort in victory over sin, that deals with our hearts and somehow cleans them up and prevents the inner struggle, the inner sin; for, as we saw yesterday, even to feel irritated in our innermost heart, though we never let anyone know it, is sin,—the same black kind of sin as murder.

And grace, you know, does not mean merely God's *attitude* toward us,—it means God's *activity* in our behalf. The grace of God means that God's attitude toward us is loving and not unloving, that it is helpful and not vengeful, that he wants to save and not to punish. That is his attitude. As we look toward God we can see him looking toward a sinful world in grace, his very face (if we could see it) shining forth with love toward us. That is his attitude; but what a hopeless thing it would be if the grace of God meant only that his attitude toward us was loving! The grace of God means also his activity for us. I might have a very loving attitude toward some one and not be able to do anything for that one; but God's attitude is not only favorable toward us, but it is *able*. So his grace includes not only his smile in our direction, but his omnipotent activity at work all the time in our behalf. *That means victory.* The grace of God is the dynamo of heaven, working night and day, all the time, to accomplish things for us and in us that we never can accomplish for ourselves.

1. There are three great things that the grace of God does for us. Let us put the third first, for a moment; it is mentioned in many Bible passages. Turn to Romans 8:21 and you find that "the creation itself also shall be delivered from the bondage of corruption into the liberty of the glory of the children of God." That is, not only men, not only the saved

God's Threefold Work of Grace

are going to be delivered into the liberty of the glory of the children of God, but all creation, the animal world, the vegetable world, the earth under our feet which was cursed because of sin—there is going to be a deliverance through the entire natural world. "Behold, I tell you a mystery; we all shall not sleep, but we shall all be changed, in a moment, in the twinkling of an eye, at the last trump: for the trumpet shall sound, and the dead shall be raised incorruptible, and we shall be changed" (1 Cor. 15: 51, 52). "For the Lord himself shall descend from heaven, with a shout, with the voice of the archangel, and with the trump of God: and the dead in Christ shall arise first; then we that are alive, that are left, shall together with them be caught up in the clouds, to meet the Lord in the air: and so shall we ever be with the Lord" (1 Thess. 4: 16, 17).

These are wonderful facts, and they are going to occur at the same time. Creation shall be *delivered*, the dead shall be *raised*, and the living shall be *caught up*. Do you realize that all three of those verbs are in the passive voice? God does not say that creation shall deliver itself; he does not say that the dead shall raise themselves; he does not say that we that are alive shall leap up to meet the Lord in the air. The verbs are passive; all three of those things have to be done for those who are affected by them.

When I was a youngster in school, and later in college, I was fond of track athletics, and in a small way went into the running high jump. I succeeded in jumping high enough to win some prizes at school, and in the freshman games at Yale. I remember how proud I was of the college copper cup that I won and still have, and that Mrs. Trumbull uses to put flowers in. I was able to jump within four inches of my own height,—not much of a feat for high jumping, but it pleased me. There are other men who can jump much higher than their height, men who have broken world's records. Now I want to ask you something. Was my very slight accomplishment in the running high jump, or is the accomplishment of the man who holds the world's record for the running high jump to-day (if he happens to be a Christian), going to give us jumpers a slight advantage over the rest of the Christians at the day of the Lord's coming, when believers are to be caught up to meet him in the air? Are those who jump going to have a bit of advantage over those who cannot jump at all? Is the Rapture, the catching up

Mr. Trumbull

of the church in the air, going to depend somewhat on the strength of our leg muscles?

Perhaps you wonder why I ask such a foolish question,— for it is foolish, absurd; but wait a moment, it is not a bit more foolish or absurd than a mistake I made for the first twenty-five years of my Christian life, and a mistake some of you dear people are making here this morning. We all know enough to know that when the time comes for the church to be caught up into the air to meet the Lord, the Lord is going to do that catching up exclusively, and no lifting power of ours is going to have any bearing on it whatsoever. Yet some of us Christians have not realized that there is another work which the Lord also must do for us exclusively, a work in which we can have no share whatsoever (except to let him do it); and that not to realize this is to make the same foolish mistake that a high jumper would make if he supposed he would have an advantage over his fellow-Christians in the day of the Rapture. We shall see in a moment what it is.

2. Now let us look at the second of the three great things that God's grace accomplishes for us. You will find it in Ephesians 2: 1-6. "And you did he make alive, when ye were dead through your trespasses and sins. . . . God, being rich in mercy, for his great love wherewith he loved us, even when we were dead through our trespasses, made us alive together with Christ (by grace have ye been saved)." There is another thing that you notice was done *for* us.

You notice that so far in what we have seen of the grace of God in these two great works,—first, delivering creation and raising both the dead and the living; and second, raising to spiritual life the man dead in trespasses and sins,—*grace does it all*. Let us be always clear on the fact that grace does not mean God's offer to share a work with us. Grace is the work of a jealous God, who must do his work alone if it is ever to be done; and if we foolishly insist on having a share in that which is exclusively God's work, we not only do not help, but we hinder and prevent. Suppose an unsaved man came to Jesus in prayer and said: "Lord, I know you died for me, and you have done a great work, a wonderful work for me, and now I am ready to come alongside and work with you in accomplishing my salvation, and together you and I will make my salvation secure." Christ could not

God's Threefold Work of Grace

save that man while he continued in his mistake. Christ's saving work is finished, it never can be added to or improved in all time or eternity. "Will you accept my grace, the finished work that I have done for you?" our Lord asks the unsaved man. If the answer is, "Yes, Lord," he is saved; if he insists on having a part in it himself, he is lost. Romans 4: 5 says about as flatly as any passage in the Bible that our salvation is all wrought for us by God: "To him that worketh not, but believeth on him that justifieth the ungodly, his faith is reckoned for righteousness." That settles it. Grace shuts out our works; but grace results in other works of ours, of course. *After* we are saved, then the Christian life, the victorious life, is a working life of constant activity.

3. And now what of the third of the three great things that God's grace accomplishes for us? We have seen that it glorifies believers, raising up the dead and bringing dead and living into the liberty of the glory of the children of God; while before that time it has justified them, saved them. What about the between time, the time for us here to-day who have believed on the Lord Jesus Christ, have therefore been saved and made alive, and who are looking for his coming when we shall be glorified? In the meantime we have to live, it may be, an hour before his coming, or perhaps ten years. It may be we shall live through our life-time and pass by death into his presence; only he knows. But we must live on between the time of being justified and the time of being glorified; and what message has the grace of God for us in this meantime?

Well, it has been a pretty "mean time" for some of us, hasn't it! It has been a time of defeat, of mean defeat, and we are wondering whether this "mean time" can ever be changed. Praise God! it can be. God wants it to be a golden mean between the first part of his work of grace and the last part. He wants it to be golden every step of the way.

Romans 5: 10 gives us the confidence that this may be so. "For if, while we were enemies, we were reconciled to God through the death of his Son, much more, being reconciled [after we have been saved], shall we be saved by his life." Or as Bishop Moule renders it, "shall we be kept safe in his life." If his death saved us from the penalty of our sins, his life, the living Christ *now*, can keep us safe, if we will

Mr. Trumbull

let him, from the power of our sin. "If, by the trespass of the one, death reigned through the one [that is, Adam]; much more shall they that receive the abundance of grace . . . reign in life through the one, even Jesus Christ" (Rom. 5: 17).

Then we have that wonderful word in Romans 6: 14, "For sin shall not have dominion over you: for ye are . . . under grace." Grace again. Colossians 2: 6 is the secret of it all: "As therefore ye received Christ Jesus the Lord [when ye took him by faith as your Saviour], so walk in him"—from the beginning to the end of your Christian life. "As ye received" him. How did you receive him? By faith. Walk then by faith every step of the way, kept safe in his life.

In other words, to use theological or Bible terms for just a moment, the first part of God's threefold work of grace is our justification, and the last part is our glorification; and the meantime, the time between in our daily life, is our sanctification. All three are perfect as God sees them; it is simply a question whether we are willing to take all three by simple faith without trying to add our works. If we cannot, by muscular power, help Christ to catch us up to meet him at his coming, neither can we while we await his coming help him to set us free or keep us free from the power of sin. It is *all* his work, and exclusively his. To work or struggle or fight for our victory is as foolish as to expect to help in our glorification at Christ's coming.

I was talking with a minister a few weeks ago who was tempted to discouragement because of the uncertainty of a call he was hoping to have. He was humble and in conscious need, and wanted to learn, if anybody could tell him, how he might have peace and victory in his uncertainty while waiting to know the Lord's will. We talked it over quietly together, and he saw that he might now trust the Lord for complete victory, letting the Lord do everything in him and for him. And then he made this clear-sighted comment: "I see that I have always been thinking that it was my duty to do things and then trust God. Now I see that it is my duty to trust God to do things." It makes a big difference, putting God first!

We are going on in further studies in the victorious life, especially with reference to what it is to surrender our wills

God's Threefold Work of Grace

utterly to the Lord and let him be Master as well as Saviour; and what it is to believe on him for victory and for everything else; but in the meantime I believe there are some of us who do not want to wait for any further study, any further meetings, not a single session more of this conference, but who, not yet having been satisfied with the sufficiency of Christ, want all that he has for us now. May I pass on to such the experience that a young woman had a few summers ago just before she sailed for Egypt as a missionary?

She came to a conference late in the week, where various messages had been given on the Lord's sufficiency for power and victory; and she had problems in her own life that were unsettled, and defeats, and wanted to know the way out. She heard some of the messages, but said frankly that she could not understand. I was talking with her one day, and was trying to run over the points of the victorious life. Finally I made some suggestions as to passages in the Bible that she could take up for study, to satisfy herself as to just what God's Word said and not take any man's word. She noted those passages and said she would study them. Then I said: "In the meantime, why not tell the Lord right now that you do not understand this thing, that you are going to find out all you can about it through the study of his Word, but that you want all that he is ready to give you now, and you will take the whole thing at once as a sealed package, as it were, from the Lord, and trust him later through your Bible study and in any way he will to open up that sealed package and show you just what is in it." She said she would do that; and then she told the Lord quietly, in a word of prayer, that she took all he had for her now as a sealed package, and trusted him to open the contents to her later on. "It may be weeks or months later," I suggested, "as you go on in your Bible study; but that is the Lord's work to show you, as it is your duty to read and study and believe."

The next morning I saw her in the crowded hallway. I thought I would step across and ask how things were going, but she caught sight of me and stepped in my direction with a shining face. Before I could say a word she had said, "The Lord has opened the package!" She had it all, and not only had it all, but *knew* that she had it all. She went on with her Bible study, of course, rejoicing to find that the Lord had ever more to tell her about rejoicing in Jesus Christ;

Mr. Trumbull

but that girl had within twenty-four hours become as radiantly clear on victory in Christ and what it meant to her, and what it was going to mean to her, as she could have after long study. She had the fruit of the Spirit in all its nine parts (Gal. 5: 22, 23); she had victory over sin in her innermost heart. She was rejoicing indeed,—though perhaps she had not yet seen in her Bible reading our key-verse, Psalm 20: 5, "We will triumph in thy victory."

Prayer

Lord Jesus, we do thank thee for thy threefold work of grace. We thank thee that thou wast willing to pay the unspeakable price of becoming sin for us and receiving into thine own body the righteous wrath of our holy God against sin, and there dying under the stroke of death, that we might be saved.

We thank thee that this work is finished, and that we who believe on thee as Saviour, though we were dead in trespasses and sins, have been made alive. And we thank thee, dear Lord, that thou art coming to change all creation, and to raise our loved dead who are with thee even now in spirit,—to raise their loved bodies from the dead, and to give us that wonderful reunion with them, as thou dost change our bodies if we are alive at thy coming, and catch us all up into the glory to meet thee and our loved ones in the air.

We thank thee for this, Lord Jesus, and we thank thee that thou dost not ask us to help thee in it, for we could not. And now we thank thee that right now and here, in our still corruptible bodies, with the temptations of Satan and the flesh and the world hammering at us, perhaps even in this moment of prayer the fiery darts being hurled at us as we leave this church and go about our life, nevertheless thy work is as perfect for us now as it will be at thy coming, and as it was at thy death and in thy resurrection.

O Christ Jesus, what a Saviour thou art, and how sinful we have been, and how foolish we have been to doubt thee or try to help thee in this work which is thine for us! We want to help thee in every way that thou dost direct, if only we may keep our hands off thy work and rest as tired little children, on thy everlasting arms, and in thy very bosom. Lord Jesus, we are tired of trying, and we want to start trusting in thine own grace. We do trust thee now, and we praise thy dear name. Amen.

IV. UNCONDITIONAL SURRENDER

Charles Gallaudet Trumbull

A MISSIONARY from China, Mr. Merriam, who is with us in this conference, was reading the Psalms this week in his morning reading, according to his regular custom, and on Monday he had come to the twentieth Psalm. He was using the Authorized Version, and when he came to the fifth verse, "We will rejoice in thy salvation," God spoke specially to him through it, and he stopped and marked two parts in the verse. Then he came over here that morning to the eleven o'clock session, and found that a fellow missionary from China, Mrs. Goforth, had sent that same verse months ago to Mr. Borton, who had passed it on to me, calling attention to the margin of the Revised Version, "We will triumph in thy victory." And yesterday came the new letter from Mrs. Goforth, sending the same verse as her suggestion for the Victorious Life Conference this year. It looks as if God wanted us to hear this word of his when two missionaries from China, thousands of miles apart, not knowing each other, have both been especially blessed through it. "We *will* triumph in *thy* victory." The Authorized Version, "We will rejoice in thy salvation," says the same thing, but the different rendering of the Greek brings it home to us,— we will not only rejoice because we are saved, but rejoice because we are conquerors and more than conquerors, not in our victory, but in *his* victory.

An old colored woman wanted to learn to read. She had been accustomed only to working in the field, but at sixty started to learn the alphabet. She was used to big things like hoes and spades, and the tiny letters of the alphabet bothered her a good deal. But she was a devout Christian, and her chief desire in learning to read was to read the Bible. One day she said to her teacher, "I wish you would teach me to spell 'Jesus.'"

The teacher answered that she would be glad to; "but Auntie," she said, "why do you want to learn to spell 'Jesus'?"

"Why," was the reply, "I think if I could learn to spell 'Jesus,' all the rest would come easy."

Yes, praise God, and everything else, including victory! If we learn to "spell Jesus" all the rest of the victorious life

Mr. Trumbull

will come easy, because victory is nothing but Jesus. Victory is not "an experience," it is not "a blessing" (though it is, of course, both); it is Jesus Christ himself; he is our victory, in himself as a person. Seeing Jesus only is victory. That means putting him first and letting him have the whole place, letting him be our actual life. The life we have thus with him and in him will be an easy life as compared with the hard life we have without him.

His yoke is easy; he said so himself. One thing we must remember is that the victorious life is a life of ease rather than effort, so far as the sin question is concerned. I do not mean to say that victorious life Christians do not work hard—all those that I know do; I do not mean we shall never have difficulties, or heart-breaking sorrows and tribulations. Of course we shall—the Lord declared that we would, in this world. Nevertheless, through it all, Christ is rest, peace, joy, gladness in the midst of sadness. There is never any Scriptural reason for having a hard time with the sin question in your own life.

But when it is urged that the victorious life is an effortless life, some ask, "Is that safe? Is it true? Doesn't the Bible tell us to fight? Doesn't it tell about struggle, effort, strife, fighting, contending earnestly?"

Yes, the Bible does; but we must be careful to get the *whole* message of the Bible on this. The Bible tells us to fight, and how to fight. Now there is a fighting with ease, and a fighting by effort. The one is a victorious fight, the other is a losing fight. People ask, "What about the definite injunction of Paul to 'fight the good fight'?" They always stop there. But what is "the good fight"? The fight of *faith*, as the rest of the verse shows (1 Tim. 6: 12). Fight the good fight of effort? No. Fight the good fight because you are under the law? No; fight the good fight of faith because you are under grace. What does "the good fight of faith" mean? It means fighting by proxy, fighting by the proxy of our Lord Jesus Christ,—he is our substitute. Not merely was Christ our substitute nineteeen hundred years ago on the cross, but he is our substitute to-day just as truly. "I have been crucified with Christ," Paul says, "and it is no longer I that live, but Christ liveth in me." It is Christ in you that is to do the fighting. "Greater is He that is in you" than any adversary you ever had (1 John 4: 4).

It is true that the victorious life is a fighting life, but it is

Unconditional Surrender

an effortless fighting life because it is always the fight of faith. I one time took a Concordance and went through every passage in the New Testament I could locate that brought in the words "fight," "strive," "contend," or anything with that suggestion. I found that every passage I could discover, with the thought of fight in it, either directly stated that it meant, or could be understood from the context as meaning, the fight of faith. And "faith does nothing, faith lets God do it all."

What about the injunction to "Resist the devil," in James 4: 7? Yes, the Word does tell us to resist the devil, but wait a minute—how? With your bare hands? I hope not. With your will power? I am sorry for you if you try it. By your own efforts? You are defeated before you start if you do. You are never safe in taking any verse in the Bible to settle any question unless you interpret that verse by the other verses in the Bible that bear on the same truth. The Bible is the best help to Bible study that there is. Turn over, if you are interested in the business of resisting the devil, to 1 Peter 5: 8, 9, and what do we see there? "Be sober, be vigilant; because your adversary the devil, as a roaring lion, walketh about, seeking whom he may devour: whom resist *stedfast in the faith*." Now you have it,—that is the way and the only way to resist the devil, "resist stedfast in the faith," resist him by proxy, let the Lord Jesus Christ resist the devil for you, and the devil will be defeated. It is only by "taking up the shield of faith" that we "shall be able to quench all the fiery darts of the evil one" (Eph. 6: 16).

Of course, what is said here as to effortless fighting has to do only with the matter of the individual believer's victory over sin within himself. There is a fighting, a striving, a contending, a struggling which, by no means effortless, has a large place in the Christian life: it is in connection with the intercessory prayer-life against the attacks that Satan may make upon the work of the church, against others for whom we have a prayer responsibility, against the body of Christ anywhere or everywhere. But it will be recognized that that kind of struggle and contending and striving, in intercessory prayer for others, is fundamentally different from the mistaken struggle and striving that most of us have thought we must have in getting freedom from our own sinning. Here effort and struggle have no Scriptural place.

Mr. Trumbull

So do not let us be troubled about this matter of the effortless life. It is a very delightful and effortless thing to do, to let somebody else "do it for you"; and that is exactly what the Lord Jesus Christ offers us in this matter of victory over sin. He will always do it for us if only we will let him.

This morning we want to take up especially the matter of surrender in the victorious life, or yieldedness, because there is no victory for us if we are resisting Christ. We may have believed on Christ as our own personal Saviour, and if we have we are saved, and Satan shall never pluck us out of our Saviour's hand; but even after that we can resist the Holy Spirit, we can grieve Him, and we can resist the Lord Jesus Christ, our Saviour. Some of us know too much about that, the tragedy of resisting Christ even though we belong to him.

So the first thing in the victorious life, for the Christian, is yielding. Romans 6: 12-19 is the great passage in the New Testament on this yielding if we would have victory. Paul begins the chapter by saying, "Well, shall we continue in sin? God forbid." Then he goes on and tells how we need not continue in sin, because when Christ died, was crucified and died, every believer was crucified and died in him. We do not know how, but it is true because God says it. Then he says: "If you all died that way, just recognize the fact that from that day your sinful nature is dead unto sin. Just reckon on that *fact*." He goes on: "Do not let sin reign in your bodies, to obey the lusts of sin, do not present your bodies unto sin, but present [or yield] yourselves unto God."

The surrendered life is as life from the dead. A person who died because of his sinful nature, in the death of Christ, and who has been raised from the dead as Christ was, is to offer that resurrection self to God, so that He may use it, and his members as instruments of righteousness unto God.

Every one of us here is a surrendered person, by the way. We are surrendered either to Satan, to sin, doing the works of unrighteousness, or we are surrendered to the Lord Jesus Christ so that God can do the works of righteousness in us.

Did you see that poster at the time of the last Liberty Bond issue, with the letters U. S. A. very prominent? "Have you bought your liberty bond?" was the heading, then "U. S. A." And the poster explained, "U. S. A." means "You subscribe at once." Let us change one word and say, "If you really

Unconditional Surrender

want your liberty bond, *you surrender at once."* You will never have the victory Christ wants you to have unless you surrender wholly to him; and if you want it now, do it now; if you want it at once, surrender at once. The Lord has got to have all there is of us if we would have victory.

Another wonderful passage on yielding is Romans 12: 1, "Yield your bodies [or, present your very beings] a living sacrifice, holy, acceptable unto God." The Revised Version uses the word "present," and the Authorized Version, "yield." "I beseech you therefore, brethren, by the mercies of God, to present your bodies a living sacrifice, holy, acceptable unto God, which is your spiritual service." Dr. Scofield has said of that, that we can properly change the word "holy" to "wholly." If you want to be holy in God's sight you must be wholly in God's hands. There is no holiness without wholeness and full surrender. May God show every one of us here whether we have surrendered entirely to him!

We are likely to get hurt if we do not surrender. If we are Christians we are going to suffer and have a hard time of it as long as we continue unsurrendered.

You remember Faraday, the great scientist, who even as a small boy was of a scientific turn of mind. As a youngster ten years old he was once looking through an iron gate while waiting for some one. Looking up through the bars of the gate, he put his head and arms through the railing. Born metaphysician that he was, he began to speculate as to whether he was on one side of the gate or the other side. Said he to himself, "My head and arms are on one side, but my heart and body are on the other side. Which side of the gate am *I* on?" Just then some one opened the gate, and he got a bad wrench while debating the philosophical question; he learned the lesson, too, that he had better be entirely on one side or the other.

We had better go clear through, or we shall get a bad wrench from Satan over and over again, or even lovingly from our Lord himself, who will not hesitate to let us suffer if that is the only way he can bring us to see the blessing of going the whole way with him.

What does our surrender include? What does it mean to surrender? Of course, it means letting everything go. Sometimes we do not realize that everything means "everything." Surrender means letting the wrong things go out of our life,—everybody knows that, that the wrong things, the

Mr. Trumbull

things that we know are wrong, or that we are doubtful about, must be abandoned wholly. If there is anything that any one of us here is holding on to, and that we are conscious is not wholly pleasing to the Lord Jesus Christ, in the midst of doing which we could not turn easily to a friend and say, "Are you a Christian, are you rejoicing in Jesus?" why not surrender that thing *now?*

Perhaps you say, "I wish I could give it up, but I cannot." Well, that is honest. It is far better to face it honestly than superficially and then go back. But are you willing to say to the Lord: "Lord, I cannot give this thing up. I could not trust myself twenty-four hours to keep away from it if I had a good opportunity to do it. But, Lord, I will let you take it from me if you will do it." Will you say that to him? Are you "willing to be made willing"? If you are, Christ will make you willing.

But we must surrender not only the wrong things in our lives, but the right things, the best things in our lives. "Everything" means everything, and "wholly" means wholly, and "yielding our very beings" unto God means our very beings; and if there is anything right or good in our beings it means yielding that. Have we done it, turned over to Jesus the things that are praiseworthy, that are not wrong at all?

There is a fellow in this conference who just two summers ago saw Christ as his victory, and went the whole way with the Lord, letting go of everything. Six months before in High School, where he was finishing his studies preparing to enter college, he had made up his mind that he was going to win such a high standing as to be exempt from all examinations at the end of the year. Not a bad thing for a High School boy to determine to do. He set his teeth and went at it, determined to do that thing no matter what happened. So far as I know he did it; but do you know what the Lord said to him that summer, when he found Christ as his victory? This is the way the boy told it to me: "I saw that my dogged determination to do that particular thing in my High School work, no matter what happened, and at any cost, was just an assertion of my self-will. The Lord Jesus Christ might not have wanted me to do it; he might have wanted me to do other things that I could not do if I did that. At any rate, I saw that I had no business to make up my mind to anything by myself and say 'I am going to do it,' no matter

Unconditional Surrender

how worth while it might be." That High School boy was right; the Lord had been speaking to him.

It may be that you and I have fairly set our teeth into a piece of work which is fine, which is praiseworthy, but if we have done it simply because we *want* to do it, we have something to surrender. It must go and everything else, our life-ambitions, our purpose to do this, that, or the other thing that is praiseworthy. The Lord wants to run your life for you; he does not want you to run it for him.

We must surrender (and this is hard for some of us) our loved ones. Christ said this very definitely when he called for the letting go of father, mother, husband, wife, children, brothers, sisters, and taking up the cross and following him. We must surrender our loved ones, and I do not know anything harder in the world to surrender than that. Some of us are letting our loved ones stand between us and Jesus Christ. We are Christians and we love the Lord, but we love them better. We have not realized it, for we really love him, but in some way unrecognized by ourselves they are between us and our Lord; and we must surrender them.

I remember a woman in my Bible Class some years ago in Philadelphia, who had lost her husband. She was heartbroken, as a wife ought to be when a loved one is called home in that way; but she was also very bitter about it. As I talked with her and tried to comfort her, "Oh," she said, "Mr. Trumbull, you cannot understand this." I knew I could not understand it (only those who pass through a certain sorrow can sympathize to the uttermost with others who have had that sorrow); but I was trying to tell her that the Lord Jesus Christ could be sufficient even in her sorrow, and give her peace, and even joy in the midst of her sorrow. She replied that no one could give up a loved one in any such spirit as that.

I was telling a friend about it later, who had been recently married. He and his wife were living as devoted a life to each other and to the Lord Jesus Christ as I have ever known. I knew that he had gone the whole way with the Lord, and I said to him, "Suppose the Lord should ask you to let So-and-so go (calling his wife by name). Would you give her up?"

I shall never forget his answer, as he said quietly, "I *have* given her up."

Now she has not died; the Lord has let those two dear ones stay together, and probably will keep them together for

Mr. Trumbull

service; but the surrendered husband had let the wife go; he had wholly surrendered his dearest one. It is really not a matter of death or life at all; it is the complete surrender of the most precious possessions we have *while we still have them*. On the other hand, some of us may have to surrender the loved one who has already been taken. We may have unconsciously been letting even the one who has gone keep us from the fullest fellowship with our Lord,—and so from the victory he wants us to have.

Did this young bridegroom friend of mine love his wife the less because they had let each other go in the Lord's sight? No, they loved each other ten thousand times more. Oh, that poor woman who was so bitter because the Lord had given and the Lord had taken the one she loved! For surrendering our best, surrendering our loved ones, does not decrease, it marvelously increases, our love for that loved one, because God's love for them is greater than our love for them; and by surrender we ourselves may have God's own love for them.

We must surrender our past. Some of you are feeling that your past, the failures you have had, necessarily prevent the victory you would like to have. Satan is lying to us about our past. I have seen the tragedy of that. A few years ago at a conference I heard one of the most wonderful testimonies I have ever listened to from a missionary, a young woman who had gone out to the foreign field. She told how she praised God for sending her to the foreign field, because there she had found Christ as she had never found him in the homeland, and she came back radiant. Two or three years later I met that same young woman at that same conference, and I shall never forget the change in her face, in her look, in her tone, in her life. She had had failures. Why, of course one who has known the victorious life may have failures,—not must have, but *may* have; and John tells us the remedy: "If we confess our sins, he is faithful and righteous to forgive us our sins, and to cleanse us from all unrighteousness" (1 John 1: 9), and then there is instantaneous restoration. She had had failures, and the devil had used those failures and told that girl she could not have victory again. The thing had gone for months. I asked her if the Lord Jesus Christ was not sufficient now, and she tried to believe it, but somehow she could not. And so far as I know that girl is still in the bondage of defeat, because

151

Unconditional Surrender

she could not see that Jesus Christ is more than equal to taking care of her past. I do not imagine that the failures she has had have been anything like what some people call sins at all; but they have been departures from what she knew the Lord's highest will for her life was. We must utterly surrender our past. Have you done it?

A minister at this conference was telling me the other day of his interest in Victorious Life literature, and how he had been reading and distributing it for several years. I asked him whether victory was clear in his own personal experience.

"No," said he, "it is not yet. I am going to take it up some day for myself. I have too much to do, I have a great many obligations, I am on a lot of committees, and I believe I ought to get out of some of these obligations later. Then, some day, when I get where I believe God wants me to be with regard to my work and duties, I am going to settle this matter."

"Do you mean," said I, "that you think you will have to resign from certain obligations before you can have victory?"

"I have been imagining so," he said. "I took a day off a while ago and thought through my life; I saw things there that I had forgotten were there, things I had to clean up. And I have now cleaned up most of them. There are one or two matters, however, that I have not yet cleaned up; and when I have taken care of those, I expect to take up seriously this matter of the Victorious Life."

"And do you really think," I asked, "that you have to get anything 'cleaned up' for yourself before you can take Christ as your Victory?"

"I imagine so," the minister answered.

Well, I began to see that he had a pretty lively imagination! We went into my room, and then he told me about one of the things that he had not, as he believed, yet cleaned up. It was not anything very dreadful, though it was a failure he had made years ago, when, as a preacher conducting certain meetings, he had publicly lost his temper. And he believed that he ought now to go back to the place where he had held the meetings, call the people together, and make a public confession of that sin. Until he had done this, he believed he could not have victory.

"What about those committees and other lines of work to which you are committed?" I asked. Some of these positions

Mr. Trumbull

n Christian service were of considerable prominence; he was treasurer of an evangelistic committee, and the like. "Would you be willing to let any of these responsibilities go, or all of them, if God wants you to?"

He hesitated, and said he was not sure about that. And we got down on our knees together and settled that first; and that man, perhaps for the first time, made a definite surrender of those various important responsibilities in Christian service,—good things, every one of them, but things on which he had set his own heart and will, and things that he wanted to do. He surrendered them all. Have we made a clean sweep of it, surrendering our best ambitions?

Then it was only a very few minutes before this man confessed to God the folly and sin of supposing that he himself had to do, or could do, anything for his own victory,—except surrender everything and trust Jesus for all. He saw that he could not "clean up" anything in his life. He saw that, whatever God might later tell him to do or not to do in the way of a public confession before those people who had known of his loss of temper, he must trust the Lord at once for complete victory at every point. That he did; and then and there he took Christ as his Victory.

I wish you could have seen the joy and the radiance in his face as we rose from our knees, and as he went away, not waiting to "do" anything except to surrender everything and believe. He was free now. He knew something of what he had in Christ. He was rejoicing in His victory. Do not misunderstand me when I say that the question of making confession of the loss of temper was, as compared with what this minister had now done in surrendering and trusting, a minor matter. God might ask him to make a confession, when a suitable opportunity offered; or God might ask him to trust that wholly to the all-forgiving, all-cleansing grace of God through Jesus Christ without any further reference to the matter. Satan has tortured some of us about "confessions" that God did not want made to any but himself.

How is it that Christ can take care of our past? It is not Christian Science,—we are not to think that our past was not, that it never existed. No, our past is a reality, and we are not denying the existence of sin. How then can Christ really lift us out of our past and enable us to live as though there had been no past sin in our life? Here is the answer: Christ makes himself our life, literally our life. Christ's

Unconditional Surrender

life is from everlasting to everlasting; it has no beginning and it has no ending. He has no past nor future, he lives in a timeless eternity. Then when you let the Lord Jesus Christ make himself wholly your life, so that it is no longer you that live but Christ liveth in you, he is as completely your past as he is your present and future; he is from everlasting to everlasting, and you have the life that is not a matter of mere eternal duration, but an absolutely new *kind* of life, filling your whole being. So Christ enters right into your past himself, making himself the only past you have, and you have a life filled with the fullness of God from everlasting to everlasting. If you can keep from shouting Hallelujah I am sorry for you. That is the joy of the Spirit-filled, Christ-consisting life. (Rom. 4: 17.)

We must surrender our unlove. Christian people so often keep a little corner of unlove for somebody in their hearts. They say, "Oh, I have forgiven that person. But I never can forget." Well, then, they never have forgiven. Forgiving as God forgives—which is the only forgiveness—forgets. God, when he forgives, remembers our sins no more; and if we are really willing to forgive, we forget. I do not mean that our minds must be a blank about something that has happened, but I do mean that we can so completely forget a wrong that another has done us that we can think of that one and love that one as completely as if that one had never done anything but love us. Let us forgive, and let us forget.

You remember the experience I told of yesterday?—the missionary who took the whole thing as a sealed package, and the Lord opened the package within twenty-four hours in most wonderful victory. I want to give you the sequel. She told me that there had been a woman in her prayer-group that she "just did not like." Frankly she explained, "I was glad I did not have to live with that woman." You may know somebody that you do not like, and would not like to live with. She had the feeling of unlove in a mild form, perhaps. But she knew the feeling was sinful; and after she had taken Christ as her victory, the next time she and that woman were together in the prayer circle she slipped her hand into the other's hand, and the Lord took every particle of that feeling of dislike out of her heart. Now she loved the woman as God loves, with the love of Christ which passeth knowledge. She had surrendered everything, including her unlove, and God created in her a new love for an unattractive person.

Mr. Trumbull

The bitterest feelings that we may have in our hearts, dear friends,—will you surrender them? You cannot change your unlove into love,—no human being can. You cannot say, "I will stop feeling unpleasantly toward that one." But you can say, "Lord, I surrender my unlove; take it away, kill the vile thing, and replace it with love"; and God will do this.

All this means that we must simply surrender *ourselves;* for all these things are tied up in the bundle of self,—unlove, the worst, the best, the past, even our loved ones. If we have any sins of selfish love (and a very pure, beautiful love can be at the root selfish love), we must simply surrender self, yield our very being, and turn it all over to God.

"Surrender" does not mean your promising God that you will never do wrong again. Some people have supposed it did. Nobody ought to dare make such a promise to God, never to do wrong again. God does not ask it; that is not surrender. Surrender does not even mean promising God always to do his will. He will see to that; it will be a miracle, and he will work the miracle. But a definite, legalistic promise to do the will of God is not surrender. What then is surrender? Just what the Word says: turning yourself over and putting yourself into God's hands, letting go of yourself, saying, "Lord, here I am. I am a poor specimen, a worthless, defeated, failing Christian. I am through running my life; you can run it as you like; you can take away from me anything I have, assign me to any position you want. Lord, I am yours, take all there is of me." It is very simple; and when you do this he does the rest.

A girl at this conference came to one of the older girls yesterday; she had been hearing and watching the older girl, and said with tears in her eyes: "I want what you have. I want Jesus in the way you have him, and you must show me how." The two knelt together, and the younger girl let everything go, surrendered herself wholly, and arose from her knees happy and victorious. Then an awful fear smote her (Satan was there), and she said in fear, "Oh, but suppose when I get away from here I find myself wondering whether I really *did* surrender to the Lord; what am I going to do?"

The other very wisely answered: "Well, we will just settle that." She took her friend's Bible and wrote in it, "On July 23, 1918, at Princeton, N. J., I surrendered [and there is an italic line under the *"ed"* at the end of the word surrendered,- emphasizing the past tense] my life to the Lord

Unconditional Surrender

Jesus Christ, for him to work in me his good will and pleasure. I know him, he is able. (Signed)———." And then in the lower left-hand corner, "Witness: ———," [the name of the older girl]; and under that, "But best of all, in the presence of the Lord Jesus Christ." Later, if the devil comes to this girl and says, "You did not surrender at all," she can quietly turn to that writing in her Bible. Not that it is necessary to have this in writing, but every surrender can be just as definite as that.

If God wants you to make a covenant here in this meeting, will you say, "Yes, here at Princeton I surrender all." You do it safely, because it is surrendering to your great heavenly Lover. Oh, how Satan has lied to us about the "hardship" of surrendering,—surrendering to One who loves you more than anyone in this universe, the Lord Jesus Christ, who died for you on the cross, and would have died just for you alone, if for no other human being in the universe; and would do it again if it were necessary, but, praise God, he does not have to! Christ's work is finished, and it included *you*, not only for salvation but for victory.

So, dear friends, may God forbid that any one of us should leave this meeting this morning if we have not let everything go. God forbid that we should leave here still holding on to any part of self. May we now, in quietness, tell him that we surrender all!

> "Saviour, 'tis a full surrender,
> All I leave to follow thee.
> Thou my leader and defender
> From this hour shalt ever be.
>
> "I surrender all. I surrender all.
> All I have I give to Jesus,
> I surrender all."

V. VICTORY BY FAITH

Charles Gallaudet Trumbull

IN 1901 I had the privilege of attending the World Missionary Conference in Edinburgh. I went hoping for a very special spiritual blessing. While I had a wonderful time there, as did all who attended, I did not get the blessing I had hoped for. Failures and defeats in my Christian life went on, the conference was over, and I took steamer for the homeward voyage.

One morning I knelt down in my stateroom alone, to have a quiet time with God and his Word; and I was utterly discouraged as there swept over me a realization of what a failure I had made of that trip as compared with the blessings I had looked for. And not only that trip, but my whole life as I looked back on it—how the failures loomed up all along the way!

I got down on my knees and poured out my heart to God; but it seemed as though, whatever others might have, I had gone too far and too long in failure ever to have the complete deliverance I longed for. Without any hope I rose from my knees and glanced out of the port-hole of that steamer cabin. There was nothing in sight except water and sky, as far as the eye could see. I kept on looking,—just the measureless ocean stretching on, and on, clear to the horizon, and, I knew, way beyond. And suddenly there flashed to my mind, "There's a wideness in God's mercy like the wideness of the sea." I dropped to my knees again, and told the Lord I believed he could take care even of a failure like myself. For he could; and that was the summer, a few weeks later, when he patiently succeeded in showing me the truth of victory by simple faith in Jesus Christ.

If there are any at this conference feeling that they cannot get the blessing that others seem to have, and *do* have, won't you remember that "There's a wideness in God's mercy like the wideness of the sea,"—only, praise God, his mercy goes way beyond the wideness of the sea, for it is limitless and infinite.

Before leaving the matter of surrender that we discussed yesterday, may I pass on an incident that helps to make plain just what it is God wants of us.

Victory by Faith

"A miser lived in his little shack on a costly piece of land: a large corner lot in a section of the city where the millionaires had their homes. Many offers had been made to him for his property, but with each offer he simply raised his price and lived on in his little shack. The roof of the little shack leaked at times. The floors had many broken boards. The windows—some of them had rags stuffed in them where the glass had been shattered. There was no joyful look about it, and the paint had faded to the color of the bark on the nearby scraggy trees.

"Sitting in a doze one afternoon on the porch of his little shack, the miser was roused by the agent of a man newly come into possession of large wealth. The agent had been instructed by the wealthy individual who wanted to buy the lot, to get it at any price. He asked the miser his price for the lot.

"'One hundred thousand dollars,' replied the miser.

"'Sign this paper then,' said the agent, filling in the amount asked.

"'Here is a check for $10,000 to bind the contract,' said the agent, 'and I will be here in ten days with a check for the remainder, and you can sign the deed. Good-by until then.'

"'Good-by,' said the miser, and was rather dazed at the quickness of the transaction.

"The old miser's conscience hurt him a little in asking so much for his lot, and he set about to fix up the shack and make it presentable. In ten days a small group of men were before his door. He entertained them on the porch and signed the deed in the presence of the attorney, the witnesses, and the future owner. The party turned to go when the deed was signed, but the miser caught at the owner's coat, saying, 'Don't you think you have gotten a fine piece of property, sir?'

"'Yes, I do,' answered the owner. 'There are great possibilities here.'

"'But what about what's here already?' the miser asked with a pained expression as he turned and pointed to the little shack.

"'What do you mean? I do not follow you,' replied the owner.

"'Ah,' sighed the miser. 'Have you failed to see how well I have painted the little shack? I have put new boards in

Mr. Trumbull

the floor, new glass where the rags were before; I have patched the roof, and it's a dear little place you have bought now. You should be proud of it and thank me for fixing it up.'

"'Stop,' said the new owner, 'and listen to me. In a few days I will tear that little shack down.'

"'Oh, don't,—why—' cried the miser, greatly distressed.

"'But,' answered the new owner, 'isn't it all mine now? May I not do with my own what I please?'

"'Yes, but I spent money and time fixing it up.' The miser sighed, looking longingly back at his little shack.

"'Listen,' said the new owner, 'I do not want your shack, good as you think it is. It must all come down. This lot must be cleared. But there is something here which I want very much, and have paid this tremendous price for it. The thing I want here is the situation, and on it, out of my wealth, I am going to erect a new structure: a beautiful mansion. Do you see? I wanted the situation—*only the situation.*'"

That is exactly what the Lord Jesus Christ says to us when he asks us to surrender. We have a miserable little shack on our property; and perhaps some of us have made the mistake of thinking that if we got a pot of paint and some panes of glass, we could put it into pretty good shape for the new millionaire owner, Jesus Christ. But as he looks at our pitiable little building, painted and patched up by ourselves, he shakes his head lovingly and patiently, and says: "Why, my dear child, I cannot do anything with that. All I want is the situation. *Only the situation.*"

And if we say in reply, "All right, Lord Jesus, I want you to have only your own way here," and then let him clear away that little tumble-down shack that we have been in charge of, he can put up a wonderful building there; and it will be such that people will admire the situation, and the building, and all connected with it, *provided it is all of the Lord.* That is why he asks for our *surrender;* that is why he asks us to yield ourselves a living sacrifice, that he may do all the rest. It is a good exchange, is it not?—his building for ours.

Commenting on the fact that the Victorious Life is a life without struggle, one of the delegates at this conference has asked, "Is it not possible that we may have to struggle in order to surrender?"

Victory by Faith

Yes, of course it is. Many a Christian has had a terrific struggle before coming to the point of yielding wholly to Christ. But such a struggle always *precedes* the Victorious Life; only when, perhaps through struggle, one comes to the point of surrender, and then makes complete surrender, can victory begin. Victory begins after struggle ceases; and let us remember that, while we may have a struggle if we insist upon it, it is not necessary to struggle. The more clearly and quietly we think who God is, that he is Love, and what it is our Saviour wants to do for us, bear every burden for us, and lavish upon us all the riches of his possessions, the sooner shall we see how foolish is any struggling *against* that and against him. Seeing this, some do come easily, without struggle, into surrender and victory.

When one is asked whether he has surrendered everything to the Lord, how often we hear the answer, "Yes, I think so." But one ought never to say he *thinks* he has surrendered. Suppose you hand me a book, and I ask you whether you have handed it to me or not; would you answer, "I think so"? Or would you say, with some surprise, "Of course I handed you that book"?

Surrender is as simple as that. Have we handed our life over to the Lord, or have we not? Either we have or we have not. If we have, we can know it; if we have not, we can know it.

If we can honestly say that we know of nothing we are wilfully, rebelliously holding on to against God's will, know of nothing we are deliberately doing or intending to do which we believe God would not have us do, and if we can say, "Lord, I am ready to have thy whole will done in my entire life, at every point, no matter what it costs," then the surrender question is settled.

Surrender is not making a promise to God to be good, nor even making a promise to God always to do his will; God does not ask any such promise as that, which would be living under the law, not under grace. But surrender is simply turning over all that we are and all that we have to the Lord for him to do with whatever he wishes. That we can do at any time that we will. And we can *know* that we have done it.

One of the girls of this conference lost her purse on the way here, containing the money for all her expenses. How would you have felt if it had been your purse? It was not

Mr. Trumbull

easy for her, but after a little she prayed something like this: "Lord, if you want to have that purse come back to me, I want it, and I will trust you to do that if it is best. But if it is not best, Lord, I believe you are going to let that money fall into the hands of some one who needs it more than I do; and that will be all right, Lord." There was a real surrender of the matter; she turned it over wholly to the Lord, and did not worry. Did she find the purse? No. But a little later a Christian man at the conference, who learned of her loss, handed her the amount of money that had gone. It looks as though the Lord answered her prayer both "coming and going"!

A southern man wrote to a friend of mine about a Christian woman who was hungry for victory but was afraid she could never do personal work; she was not entirely clear whether she could surrender that fear, that bugbear of personal work. And this is what the southern man wrote: "I think I know just where she is. Satan has put up in her cornfield that fierce-looking scarecrow, personal work. It sure looks terrifying, but on close examination it will be found unable either to bite or to scratch. The devil makes me tired." And so will the devil make any of us when we see through his scarecrows, which cannot bite or scratch or do us any harm while we are trusting Christ Jesus. Don't let Satan keep you out of the Victorious Life by any scarecrow.

And now, dear friends, although it is absolutely essential that we surrender wholly to the Lord if we are going to have his victory, does it surprise any of us to know that, even after we have surrendered wholly, we may have defeat? Yes; the surrendered life may be a defeated life. The Victorious Life is always the surrendered life; but the surrendered life is not always the Victorious Life. Unless we see this clearly, and understand why, we may be sadly confused as we go on.

"Well, my surrender could not have been complete," says some Christian who, after surrendering, meets with defeat. No, that was probably *not* the trouble at all, that your surrender was not complete. For your surrender may be as complete as God himself would have it, and yet defeat may follow. What is the trouble? Simply this: you have done *your* part, which is surrender, but you are not trusting Christ to do *his* part. You have not added to your surrender, faith.

There are the two conditions of the Victorious Life, Surrender and Faith. "Let go, and let God." Our part is to let

Victory by Faith

go; all the rest is God's part. When we "Let God," we are believing that he *is* doing his part. Unless we thus believe, our surrender will not give us victory. For it is Christ, not our surrender, that accomplishes our victory.

Can we have victory at once after surrender? Must it be instantaneous?

A young man was asking some questions yesterday about the Victorious Life, and finally he said: "I suppose that people are not all the same in this, and that with some persons the victory may come gradually, after surrender, until after a while that one has entire victory."

I happened to know that this young fellow was an expert wireless operator, and that he knew a great deal about electricity, far more than I did. So I said: "When you bring two electric wires together and complete a circuit, I suppose the electricity begins to come in gradually, until, after a while, the flow of current is complete?"

The boy smiled,—he did not answer; he knew he did not need to. The question was too absurd for anyone who knew the simplest facts of electricity.

"Well," said I, "when the circuit is completed, does the current start at once?" He smiled his assent.

"And the moment the circuit is completed in the Victorious Life, the victory is instant and complete," said I. He saw the point. It is no more possible for a Christian *not* to have instantaneous and complete victory, after meeting the conditions, than for the electric current not to flow instantly and completely when the circuit is closed. When we do our part, by surrender, and believe that God is doing his part, victory is complete and instant.

That young fellow and I kneeled down and prayed together. He had already surrendered his life completely to the Lord, and this came out very clearly in his prayer, as he reaffirmed his surrender in simplicity and directness, and dedicated his life wholly to the Lord. He went on to ask the Lord now to give him victory.

I interrupted him as he was praying, and suggested that I would not do that. "You have settled the surrender question," I said; "that is the negative pole in this matter." (Most of us know that in a closed or completed electric circuit there is a negative and a positive pole. Every time you turn a switch or press a button to light an electric light, you complete the circuit by bringing together the negative pole and

Mr. Trumbull

the positive pole; the instant they touch, the electricity flows.) "The best we can do is only negative, in our surrender. We simply give up, and let God have the whole situation. We haven't anything positive, worthy the name, to offer to the Lord. Now you have brought the negative pole up to position by your surrender. And it is the Lord Jesus Christ's responsibility to bring the positive pole up and complete the circuit,—that is his part. He has promised to do his part, when he says, 'My grace is sufficient for thee.' Do you believe that Christ delays in meeting his responsibility?"

"No," the boy answered.

"Does Christ *always* meet his responsibilities?"

"Yes, he does," he replied earnestly.

"The Lord Jesus is right here now," I went on. "You have brought up the negative pole, and the Lord Jesus has brought up the positive pole, and is completing this circuit. You cannot complete it; he must do so. If he is true to his responsibility, then the circuit is completed now. You need not ask him to do what he pledges himself to do. There is only one thing that can prevent the flow of this current of electricity, and that is the insulation of your unbelief. If you insist upon inserting your unbelief between the negative and the positive pole, the electricity cannot flow, can it?"

"No," the boy answered.

"Well," I said, "as you have furnished the negative pole and Jesus is furnishing the positive pole, won't you just thank him for it all now?"

The thanksgiving was earnestly offered. That was all that was needed. To thank Christ Jesus for the perfection and the sufficiency of his work is to believe on him.

Of course it is not meant, when we say that through surrender and faith our victory is instantaneous and complete, that we can take victory now for the rest of our lives. Nor can any Christian ever say, "I never can sin again." If we trust our Lord wholly we do have complete victory for *now*, for the present moment while we are trusting. But our victory is continued moment by moment, as we continue to trust him moment by moment. We cannot take victory to-day for tomorrow. We cannot take victory this morning for this afternoon. We can take victory now for now. And we are never asked to live more than a moment at a time.

But we can easily trust Christ for complete victory all the time, when we remember that Christ is doing his whole work

Victory by Faith

perfectly, for and in the life of the Christian, all the time. The trouble is, so many of us have not known this *fact*. It is a fact all the time; yet if we do not know what the facts are, we prevent their efficacy in our actual experience.

Dr. Scofield tells of a lady in Mississippi who told him that when the news of the surrender at Appomattox came she knew the war was over. Her husband and two sons had been slain. They had a large plantation and a great many negro slaves, and when that news came she called her slaves together and she said, "You are free. The North has conquered, and the Proclamation of Emancipation has been issued by the President, and you are all free." And she said it took a week to get any of them to believe it. Finally it got about from other sources, and they began to believe it was so, that they really were free.

Were those slaves any freer at the end of the week, when they finally came to believe in their freedom, than they were at the first moment when they were told, or even the very moment when the ink had been placed on the Emancipation Proclamation by President Lincoln? Not a bit. They were as free as the President of the United States could make them when he first signed the proclamation. But they had to hear, and then to believe, before they could get the benefits of their freedom.

It is the same of the Victorious Life. Every Christian on the face of the earth has the Victorious Life in its completeness at this present moment. We are all free, if we have taken Jesus Christ as Saviour; our Emancipation Proclamation has been signed, the work has been done, and every true Christian is so free from the law and the power of sin that *in all time or eternity God can add nothing to that freedom.* But some of us have taken a week to believe it, and some of us years, and some of us do not believe it yet. Yet we are *free*, FREE, FREE!

As Dr. Scofield has said, "Remember that God can give nothing more to the Christian, except realization." *All things are ours,* because we are Christ's, and Christ is God's (1 Cor. 3:21, 22). We have victory, we have freedom, we have every spiritual blessing in the heavenlies in Christ Jesus (Eph. 1:3).

Think for another moment about those slaves in Civil War times that were free. Suppose we think of them as in two groups. Some shiftless, low down, lazy Negroes, always trying to dodge their work, and living badly in many ways; the other group made up of faithful, active workers, devoted, tireless. Now after the Emancipation Proclamation was signed, were those in the second group, the faithful, devoted workers, freer than the shiftless, lazy Negroes? Not a bit; all were equally free. For both groups had been freed, not upon the basis of what they had been doing, but upon the basis of what the United States Government was doing for them. Their past record had absolutely nothing to do with it.

How true that is of us! The Christian whose past record has been the worst is just as free from the law and the power of sin, if he has taken Jesus Christ as Saviour, as the Christian whose record has been of the best. The freedom of each is "freedom indeed" (John 8: 36) because it is the result, not of what he has done for Christ, but of what Christ has done for him. That freedom is so perfect that God himself cannot add to it. Are we going to believe God? Do we believe God now? That is the only question upon which our victory depends.

We see now why we cannot have victory in personal experience without faith. Faith does not accomplish our victory; faith accepts our victory *because it has already been accomplished*. Our victory is true, whether we believe it or not. Our belief does not bring it into being; we believe it because it has already been brought into being. If we wish to say that God is a liar, as the Bible declares some men do (1 John 5: 10), we can live on in slavery, and wretchedness, and poverty, and defeat. If we say that God is the Truth, as he says he is, we can "possess our possessions," and know in personal experience the joy and peace and power and victory of Christ himself.

The Victorious Life is the life that *knows*, not that *hopes*, about victory. Do not say, "I hope so," about any of these things that Jesus Christ tells you are true. It is an insult to him, after he has told us what he has done, to say that we hope it is so. Quietly, gladly, joyously, let us say "I *know*." "For I *know* him whom I have believed, and am persuaded that he is able to guard that which I have committed unto him against that day" (2 Tim. 1: 12). That is victory.

We shall not have victory if we say, "Yes, I take it all, and I am now ready to see whether it will work." "It" never will "work" on those conditions. Victory is not an "it," it is a "He," even Christ Jesus. And he has finished the work of our victory; and he and the Holy Spirit are working now in

Victory by Faith

the fulness of omnipotence. Christ awaits our saying that we *know* that he *is* working in perfect victory; and that that is all we ever need to know. Then, in his own time and way, he will show us whatever he would have us see, as to the results of victory. But we are never to wait to see anything before we believe him fully.* Faith is not sight; we shall see only after we believe.

And faith is not feeling. Oh, let us not make the mistake of saying that because we have no new feeling in this matter, we have not victory. Victory is a fact, not a feeling. Our feelings are as uncertain as the waves of the sea; our victory, which is Christ, has no variableness nor shadow of turning, but is the same, yesterday, to-day and forever.

One of the women at this conference said to me a few days ago that she knew that faith was the secret of victory; she had surrendered everything, and she knew that her only trouble now was her lack of faith. She believed that faith was the last step and the only step she needed to take. "But," she added sadly, "I haven't got that faith, I cannot exercise that faith."

I asked her whether she was saved. "Why, yes," she said, "of course I am." There was not a trace of uncertainty in her voice.

"What makes you think you are saved?" I asked.

"I know that on God's Word," she answered.

"Then you have all the faith you need for victory," said I. "You have that faith right now, because the faith for victory is the same faith that you already have for salvation."

We talked together quietly about this, and little by little she came to see that her trouble was that she had been examining her faith, instead of "examining" Jesus Christ.

You remember that illustration of the traveler going on a journey and coming to a bridge that he must cross in order to pass over a dangerous river? Suppose you came to such a bridge, a new bridge that you had never been over, but you must get to the other side. And suppose you were not entirely sure about the bridge. Would you examine your faith in that bridge, or would you examine the bridge? If you had common sense, you would examine the bridge. If you had an engineer with you, you would say to him, "Look here, you know about bridges, and I don't. Make an investigation, and tell me whether that bridge is safe." Then if upon reliable evidence you are led to believe that the bridge is

Mr. Trumbull

absolutely safe and sound, you will go over it without the slightest anxiety or uncertainty,—and not only you, but thousands of others like you.

And it would not even occur to you to think about your *faith* in that bridge as you were crossing over; you would only be glad that the *bridge* was trustworthy.

In this matter of victory, if you have been troubled as that Christian woman here was a few days ago, fearing that she did not have the faith that is needed for victory, get your eyes off your faith, stop examining your faith, and *examine Jesus Christ*. Have you got the Saviour that is needed for victory? Put him through the severest cross examination you can! Find out just where Christ is weak. See whether he has failed to meet the test in times past, has gone back on those who trusted in him, has proved unfaithful to his responsibilities. And if your mind and heart revolt at even the asking of these questions, then drop down on your knees and thank God that you have a Saviour who is a *Saviour*, a Christ who has never been unfaithful from all eternity, a Christ who is omnipotent and all-sufficient and perfect beyond the mind of man to conceive. *That* Christ is your present Victory. Do you need more?

VI. GOING ON IN VICTORY

Charles Gallaudet Trumbull

A CHRISTMAS sermon by the Rev. Daniel H. Martin last year called attention to something in Luke's account of the birth of Jesus that has blessed me greatly. You remember that, after the angel of the Lord and the glory of the Lord had appeared to the shepherds in the field, and the angel had brought them the good tidings of great joy, that there was born that day in the city of David a Saviour, Christ the Lord, the shepherds then talked it over together. But here is the point: They did not say one to another, "Let us now go even unto Bethlehem, and see *whether this thing is come to pass*, which the Lord hath made known unto us." No; that is the way some of us would have talked about it, I am afraid. This is what the shepherds said: "Let us now go even unto Bethlehem, and see this thing, *that is come to pass, which the Lord hath made known unto us*" (Luke 2: 15).

Had they seen it yet? No. Had they found the babe? No. How did they know, then, that it had come to pass? *Because God had told them so.*

We do not need to see what God says is so, in order to know that it is so. His Word is better than our sight. And his Word is better than any evidence of his Word. So when God tells us that a thing is so, let us not say, "I will go and see whether it is so." But let us, by simple faith in his inviolable Word, say, "I will go and see this thing that *is so*, which the Lord hath made known unto me." In his own good time and way we shall see it. But we do not need to wait until we see it before we know it. There is the whole secret of the Victorious Life. If we are going out from this Conference to see *whether* this Victorious Life is "going to work" in our lives, we may be sure before we go that it will not work. But if we say, "Let us now go even unto our homes and see this thing that is come to pass, which the Lord hath made known unto us," we shall see more than we ever dreamed of seeing. Don't forget that word of James McConkey, "Believing is seeing." The natural man thinks that seeing is believing; the spiritual man knows that believing is seeing. Praise God for the faith of those shepherds!

Mr. Trumbull

Remember, the Victorious Life is Christ Jesus himself; and every Christian has Christ; and therefore every Christian has the Victorious Life. All God wants us to do, and asks us to do, is to recognize the fact that he declares unto us. Restfully we are to abide in the Fact, Christ.

The day I reached this conference I went to the office to get the key to my room. The key was not on the hook bearing my room number, and I thought it likely that a man who had been doing some work for me in my room earlier in the day had it with him, and that I could get it from him later. I noticed a key on another hook bearing the number of the room of a friend of mine, and I said, "I will take that key along with me, and turn it over to my friend." Now I carried that other key around with me for quite a while; and later on I found to my surprise that that very key, which I had had in my pocket for several hours, was the key to my own room. It had been misplaced and put on the wrong number. Here it is in my hand now, and I have been using it all the week at this conference.

Do you see? I had the key to my room all the time, and did not know it. And every one of you here, from the moment you first took Jesus Christ as your Saviour, has had the key to victory all the time. You have had it every instant of the time, the key that would unlock and open to you the palace of the glory and the beauty of the Lord Jesus Christ; and you have it still, if you have Christ as Saviour. You can never lose him, because he will never lose you. Would it not be well to use the Key that you have?

Mr. Galt, the Business Manager of this Conference, has announced, as you recall, that a bunch of master keys has been lost here. I have not heard whether it has been found; but I do know that a lot of Christians here have found the Master keys of their lives,—keys that will open up everything, every problem, every need, day by day for the rest of lifetime. We have all of us had all these "keys" from the moment we took Jesus as Saviour. Oh, let none of us have the idea that the Victorious Life is a peculiar doctrine or a special blessing. True, it is a special blessing,—that is, it brings folks special blessings, of untold richness and number and variety; but it is not "special" to any one Christian apart from another: it is what every Christian has, and always has had, in Jesus Christ. The only thing God is waiting for with some of us is that we will believe him as he has been

Going on in Victory

telling us through these nineteen centuries and on every page of the New Covenant of Jesus Christ, the New Testament, that all things are ours, for we are Christ's.

At the beginning of this conference week a Christian woman came up to me and said, in a tone of quietness and peace, "I found the Victorious Life just by seeking Jesus." Why, of course she did, and nobody ever found it in any other way. "And," she added, "by praising him." Yes, she had the heart of the whole thing: after we have sought Jesus, we are to praise him, in quiet faith, whether we have any feeling about it or not.

What about the "witness of the Spirit," which so many earnest Christians think they lack Remember Mr. McQuilkin's clear word on this given in his book, "Victorious Life Studies":

"As to the 'witness of the Spirit,' there is no suggestion in the Word of God that this 'witness' has any connection with a great flood-tide of feeling. 'He that believeth on the Son of God *hath the witness in him*: he that believeth not God hath made him a liar; because he hath not believed in the witness that God hath borne concerning his Son. And the witness is this, that God gave unto us eternal life, and this life is in his Son' (1 John 5: 10, 11). The witness is God's record, or God's eternal Word to us, that he has done something, that he has given us a gift. He does not want us to *feel* this word, or witness of his. He wants us to *believe* it. When we believe this word, and the wonder of the gift breaks upon us more and more, we shall have feelings, of course, and they will find expression according to our different temperaments and environments.

"(Dr. Griffith Thomas notes that the often abused passage on the witness of the Spirit in Romans eight does not say that the Spirit beareth witness *to* our spirit, but *with* our spirit, that we are children of God. That is, our spirit says 'Father,' and the Holy Spirit says 'Father' with us.)"

We have been wanting so many things that we do not need to have in connection with victory. And, not having the things we wanted, and thought we needed, then we thought we did not have and could not have victory. One of the young ministers at this conference made a great surrender the other day. I did not know, at first, that he needed to make this surrender, and neither did he. We were talking together, and he said he did not have victory, and he was

170

Mr. Trumbull

longing for it. So far as he knew he had surrendered everything to the mastery of the Lord Jesus Christ. As we talked on, he said, "I have no realization of Christ; I have no conscious communion with him; I do not feel as though he were here with me at all; that is my trouble."

Plainly he showed that he had set his heart on having a realization of Christ, a consciousness of Christ's presence. I asked him whether he believed that Christ was with him or was far away.

"Why, Christ is with me, I know that," the young minister answered.

"How do you know?" I asked.

"Because the Bible says so," said he.

"That is true," I answered; "and now will you tell the Lord Jesus that, if he asks it, you will surrender to him forever your desire, your longing for a realization of his presence, for a consciousness of his fellowship?"

It was a hard step to take. The young fellow put his head down in his hands, and seemed dazed, as he thought it over. Finally, in a very simple and direct prayer he said: "Yes, Lord Jesus, I will let it all go, my desire for a realization of your presence, and for this consciousness of fellowship with you that I have been hungering for. I will let it all go."

"Will you praise him now," I suggested, "not only that he is here, but that he is working in your life the whole work that is necessary."

"Yes," he answered, "I will," and very quietly, in cold, blind faith, with no emotion, no feeling, and no sight, just resting on what the Bible says and not on any consciousness or realization whatever, he then praised the Lord for the answer.

Later that afternoon I saw him again. "I have been thinking," said he, "ever since we were together, what a big fool I have been. I had been looking all this time for something I did not need to have; and all the time that which I had been needing I already had." This young minister was now so filled with the realization of the presence of the Lord Jesus Christ, the consciousness of his fellowship, that he could not keep still about it! He had been looking for something that he did not need,—the consciousness of Christ's presence; and all the time he had all that he did need,—Christ himself. When he trusted Christ without any

Going on in Victory

such consciousness, the consciousness came. And when later, as he told me, the consciousness left him, he still kept on trusting Christ.

Dear friends, it is not the *consciousness* of Christ's presence that gives us victory: it is *Christ*. Our consciousness of his presence may vary; he never varies. Is Christ any weaker when our consciousness of his presence is less keen? Is he made stronger when our consciousness of his presence is very strong? No; he is the same yesterday, today, and forever; and if we have him, we have all the victory that any human being ever can have.

Do you notice how surrender and faith seem to be pretty nearly the same thing, perhaps entirely so? As we surrender everything, even our desire for a consciousness of Christ, we are by that very surrender expressing our faith in him. We are to surrender our desire for an "experience" of victory, and trust, not in an experience, but in Jesus only. You know the old sentence attributed to Mr. Spurgeon: "I looked at Jesus, and the dove of peace flew into my heart. I looked at the dove of peace, and she flew away." When we look for or at peace, or joy, or consciousness of fellowship, or manifestations of Christ's presence in any way, we are turning our eyes away from himself.

As I suggested this one time to a Christian woman, she asked, "Suppose my vision of Jesus should grow dim?"

"His vision of you will never grow dim," I answered. After all, it is Jesus' looking unto us that enables us to keep looking unto him.

Let us utterly reject the idea that it is anything that we do, even our looking unto Jesus, or our faith in him, that is the secret of victory. *Christ* is the secret of victory, and he only. God's faithfulness is infinitely better than our faith.

So it is not my believing that makes the victory; it is the victory that makes my believing. We get the thing turned right around, and then wonder why we are defeated! Let us always remember: I do not believe in order to bring a fact into existence; the fact is there, and I believe *because* it is in existence. It is there whether I believe it or not. My belief does not strengthen the fact; but the fact does strengthen my belief.

This, you see, is the difference between the Victorious Life and Christian Science. Christian Science believes a thing

Mr. Trumbull

that is not so in order to make it so. Christian Science says, "Act as though the thing were so, and it will be so." But the Victorious Life says, "Believe, not in order to make it so, but because it is so." I am not to live and think and act *as though* I had victory; I am to live and act and think *because* I have victory. I have victory because I have Christ; he is a Fact; and I do not need to go ahead as though he were here, and as though he were my life, but, praise God, because he is here, and because he is my life.

Yet, strange to say, some people have sincerely supposed that the teaching of the Victorious Life is practically the same as the teaching of Christian Science. We have had letters in the office of The Sunday School Times asking if this were not so. They mistakenly identify the false teachings that Christian Science gives about quiet, and peace, and freedom from sin, with the fundamentally different teachings of the New Testament. Oh, the tragedy of the multitudes of members of evangelical Christian churches who are snared by the falsehoods of Christian Science. Saved Christians can be and are being deluded and led astray by it. The unsaved persons who are snared by Christian Science are going to hell by that pathway, unless they are brought out of it and led to Jesus Christ, not Science, as their Saviour.

May I ask how many of you who are here in this meeting have friends or members of your family circle who are either interested in, or actually believing or thinking they are believing in, Christian Science? [Almost every hand in the chapel went up.] That shows what Christian Science is trying to do in our midst. Have you ever intelligently studied its positions? So many Christian people who think they are interested in Christian Science would be horrified if they knew what Mrs. Eddy's book teaches. I have had to make it a point to know, from her text book itself, because we have so many letters and inquiries about it. And I know at first-hand that Christian Science denies every fundamental of the Christian faith.

Christian Science starts with the fundamental premise that God is all,—and this is false to begin with: the Bible nowhere says that God is all. Then Christian Science goes on to say that, because God is all (which he is not), there is no sin; and this too is a lie. God never denies the existence of sin; the Bible never denies it. God declares that sin is such a desperate, tragic reality that it cost the life of his Son.

Going on in Victory

Denying the existence of sin, which put Jesus on the cross, Christian Science denies the death of Jesus; it denies the resurrection of Jesus, saying that Jesus was not dead when he was in the tomb, but his disciples mistakenly thought he was dead. And if there was no death of Jesus, there was of course no resurrection of the body of Jesus. Christian Science denies the very existence of the body of Jesus. It denies the Holy Spirit, calling itself the Holy Spirit. It denies the shed blood of Christ and the need of the shed blood of Christ.

At the midwinter Victorious Life Conference held in Philadelphia last January two or three women, friends of each other, came to one of the meetings. At the close of the meeting the speaker gave an opportunity for all who wished to express their simple faith in Christ as their life and victory to rise to their feet. One of these women was a Christian Scientist, who had been talking to her friends about Science and how much it had done for her. At the invitation, she arose with the others, and said to them, "You are surprised to see me standing? I am glad to stand. The teaching given here at this meeting is what I have been trying to tell you about. This is Christian Science."

They sat down, and a little later, before closing the meeting, the same speaker spoke of the blood of Jesus Christ, and said that there was no remission of sins without it. And the Christian Scientist arose and left the building. She could not tolerate the message about the *blood* of Jesus. For Christian Science denies the blood, the sinner's need of the blood, the all-sufficient efficacy of the blood. Thus Christian Science, which is the denial of Christ, and the Victorious Life, which is Christ himself, are fundamentally, eternally different, as different as midnight and noonday, as hell and heaven, as Satan and Christ. Let us lovingly pray,—not argue or criticize or condemn,—for any friends of ours who are being snared in this awful delusion.

At the close of one of the sessions here I was asked this question: "When we are tempted, is not the way of deliverance to ask Jesus instantly for deliverance and victory?"

"No," I suggested; "better than asking Jesus for deliverance in that instant of temptation is to thank Jesus that he *is* delivering us, just then, from the temptation."

A young college student, now working among the soldiers

Mr. Trumbull

in the camps, told me two or three days later that he had happened to overhear that question and the answer, and that he had been living since then in victory.

Later a letter was shown me by Mr. Culp, the Treasurer of these conferences, from a woman who had attended the conference a year ago, and had been tempted to disappointment because she could not come this summer. But she testified that she was having victory about the matter, in the Lord, and so she was remaining at home in quietness and peace and thanksgiving. Then she wrote this: "A glorious message that has made clearer all that Jesus is to me was brought back from the conference at Princeton by my friends. It is this, that when irritation or testing of various kinds comes to us, we are not to pray asking Jesus to be our victory, but, better still, we are to say, 'thou art right now my Victory.' We are not to ask him to be our Victory, but we are to thank him that he is our Victory."

And last spring I received a letter from a missionary in China; see what she says about this same truth: "The fight is getting more strenuous all the time. We are made to realize that we are in the enemy's country; but if we look up and thank the Lord, and go ahead singing, 'Victory for me through the blood of Christ, my Saviour,' victory is complete. Oh, such a glorious Saviour! Oh, the difference between asking God to give the victory, and trusting and praising him for the fact that he *is* the Victory."

How significant are these three testimonies, one from a young fellow in the full flush of life, not yet twenty-one; one from a Christian woman prevented from attending the conference; one from a missionary in China,—and all testifying how God has used for them this simple secret of victory: of not asking Jesus for deliverance, but thanking him that he is our deliverance. Better than praying for victory, you see, is praising for victory.

Grace does not say, "It is going to be done." Grace says, "It has been done."

May we never forget what Dr. Griffith Thomas has so helpfully pointed out, the difference between the facts and the promises of the Bible. Both are precious, both are from the Word of God and therefore true; but there is a difference between them, and they are to be used differently.

You know, for example, such a promise in God's Word as, "If ye abide in me, and my words abide in you, ask whatso-

Going on in Victory

ever ye will, and it shall be done unto you" (John 15: 7). That is a promise. Its conditions are to be met, and then we are to trust God for his answer in his own good time and way.

But when we come to those things which the Bible declares to be facts, we are to use them quite differently. The promises may refer to the future; the facts are of the present and the past.

One of the blessedest facts in the entire Bible is stated in the first verse of the 23rd Psalm: "The Lord is my Shepherd." The Bible says that is a fact. We do not need to ask God to make the Lord our shepherd. He *is* our Shepherd. The fact remains unaltered, the Rock of Ages.

We may properly ask God to fulfil a promise. But we must not ask him to fulfil a fact, but rather thank him that he is fulfilling it. The promises are to be pleaded; the facts are to be accepted.

In 2nd Corinthians 12: 9 we are told, "My grace is sufficient for thee." That is not a promise; it is a fact. Do you remember the revolutionizing experience that occurred in the life of the Rev. Prebendary Webb-Peploe of England, through that verse? Forty years or more ago, when he was a young minister, his little daughter had been taken home to heaven, and, heartbroken and crushed by the loss, he was in an agony of suffering and darkness, trying to pray his way through. One day he went into his study to prepare a sermon. He dropped down on his knees and cried out to God for help and comfort and deliverance. And he prayed something like this: "O Lord, make thy grace sufficient for me in this hour of sorrow and darkness."

Opening his eyes, he saw on the wall of his room a framed text, reading, "My grace *is* sufficient for thee." The word "is" was in different colored ink from the rest, and the glorious truth stood out! The young minister stopped praying, and commenced praising. He saw that he had been asking God to make a fact what God had already told him was a fact. He could now say, in joy and thanksgiving, "Lord, I do not need to ask thee to *make* thy grace sufficient for me; I praise thee that it *is* sufficient."

By that simple but wonderful fact, declared by God to be a fact, Prebendary Webb-Peploe's life was revolutionized. He arose from his knees a changed man. And for forty years, living in the fact that Christ's grace is sufficient for him, he has been a speaker of untold blessing to thousands at the great Victorious Life Convention in England meeting every year at Keswick.

So far as I have been able to see, you will not find anywhere in the New Testament a passage telling Christian believers to pray for deliverance from the power of sin in their own lives. Why? Read Romans 6 and you will find out. The New Testament constantly brings before the believer the wonderful *facts* of the deliverance which has been completely wrought for him in the death and the resurrection of Jesus Christ, and the gift of the Holy Spirit. God says the work is done, *done*, DONE! Shall we not thank him for it?

We are, of course, to pray for a great many things. God's Word is very clear on this. We are to pray against the power of Satan and the works of Satan as these are directed against the work and the body of Christ in this world. But such prayer is intercessory: praying in behalf of others. And we may properly offer many prayers in connection with ourselves, for guidance, for the meeting of our needs in many directions, as God has promised to supply them if we ask him. But let us be clear between the privilege and duty of praying for such matters, both in petition and in intercession, and the privilege and duty on the other hand of praising for what God tells us are the facts of the finished work wrought by Jesus Christ nineteen centuries before were born.

It may startle us, but it is none the less true, that we are not to pray for deliverance from the power of sin in our own life, for the simple reason that *we cannot be delivered as long as we keep on praying for this*: *we can be delivered only when we stop praying and commence praising for the completely wrought deliverance.*

Remember, "We are not fighting to win a victory; we are celebrating *the* victory that has been won." "We will triumph in Thy victory" (Ps. 20: 5).

Suppose, after praising and trusting the Lord Jesus for complete victory, and after enjoying the miracle-experience of Christ's own victory, there should be a slip, a break, an outright sin?

Satan will be quick to say, "There is nothing in 'victory.' You never had the blessing you thought." God forbid!

Going on in Victory

Satan's great weapon is the lie. He can keep us out of the personal experience of victory only by lying to us about Christ.

They say at Keswick, "If you should fail, shout Victory!" Not on any Christian Science basis, not in denial of the fact that you did fail; but simply recognizing that you may now have, through the cleansing blood of Christ, instantaneous restoration and victory again.

The temptation will come to dig into our failure and see just how it happened. The temptation will come to feel that we must get away somewhere and have a time of special prayer before we can hope to be "on the heights" where we were before we failed. Do not yield to that temptation for an instant. Do not feel that you need even to understand how you failed, before you can have entire restoration and victory. Turn utterly, instantly away from the past, even the past of the last five seconds, and, looking unto Jesus only, praise him that he is your cleansing and your keeping and your victory. Of course, he would have us learn any lessons out of any failure that we ought to learn in order to be safeguarded for the future; but if we find ourselves unable to explain just why we did fail, let us not waste time over trying to find out, but let us praise God for the present sufficiency of our Lord Jesus Christ for perfect victory. We may be kept in a maze of doubt and confusion and then discouragement by trying to understand our past failures. God does not want us to face that way. God may be testing our faith to see whether we are willing to trust Christ now for entire victory without even understanding how or why we failed.

"But, of course," Satan is whispering in the ear of the one who has failed, "you cannot now expect to have quite the same victory as you might have had if you had not failed." That is another lie of Satan's. Has our failure weakened Christ? No; our failure does not make it harder for Christ to give us victory now; and an unbroken record of ten years of complete victory does not make Christ any stronger to give us victory now. Our present victory is not in any way conditioned upon our past of either victory or defeat. A long record of victory does not insure present victory: Christ, not our record, is our victory. A long record of defeats does not prevent or hinder present victory; Christ is not weakened or hindered by our past defeats if we simply

Mr. Trumbull

trust him now. Do you see how gloriously simple and easy it is, as we put it all into terms of "Jesus only?"

There are special perils in the Victorious Life. Those who are trusting Christ for victory are certain to be tempted as they never were before. They are in a front line trench now, with all the deadliest darts of the enemy sure to be directed against them. The Victorious Life is a life of victory without struggle or effort on our part; but it is not a life without temptation. The Victorious Life is the most tempted of any life possible to man.

As we trust Christ for victory we shall be tempted in new ways, in subtle ways, in horrible ways, tempted by refined, scarcely recognizable sins, tempted by gross sins. We shall be left untempted, apparently, for hours or even days; then temptation will sweep in upon us in hellish storm of power that seems as though it would break our hearts. But, "When the enemy shall come in like a flood, the Spirit of the Lord shall lift up a standard against him" (Isa. 59: 19).

One of the subtle temptations and perils of the Victorious Life is the temptation to feel that we are now on a higher plane than most Christians, we know truth that they do not know,—and then comes the "pious,'" priggish, "holier than thou" attitude. We may not have meant it at all; we might be shocked at the suggestion; but it has happened over and over again in the Victorious Life.

Young people have gone back from these conferences to their churches, have seen other good Christian people, even the minister perhaps, not recognizing and claiming Christ as Victory, and have started in criticising! Oh, how Satan has used this temptation and this failure of those who believe in the Victorious Life to discredit this precious teaching. So may we clearly recognize this peril, and, asking God to keep us in the dust, abide there under the cross, kept safe from the awful sin of pride and Pharisaism which discredits our Christ and wounds his eager, loving heart.

May God keep us, in the Victorious Life, from the sin of criticism in any and every form. Love, not criticism, ought to be the great, outshining glory and characteristic of the Victorious Life.

"When you go home from this conference," said a speaker some years ago to the young people at a summer gathering, "may I make one suggestion as to what to do first? Before

Going on in Victory

you have told any one in the home circle about the wonderful spiritual blessings you have had, just do something kind for somebody." Shall we all try to remember this? Pick up a book some one has dropped, open a door, get a glass of water,— just a little act of common, ordinary kindness will help people to believe, a great deal more than much talking about it, that there *is* something in the Victorious Life. God wants us to tell, simply and humbly, about the sufficiency of our Lord Jesus; but he wants us to let Christ reveal himself in our unspoken actions even more.

There are the two perils of being driven beyond the will of God, and of lagging behind the will of God.

In the joy of the new blessings that come to one who has wholly surrendered to the mastery of Christ, who has given up everything to God, there is likely to come the temptation to believe that God would have us do this, that, or the other "hard" thing which perhaps God is not asking us to do at all. It has been well said that, when the devil finds he cannot prevent one from doing the whole will of God, he tries to drive that one beyond the will of God. So the devil may bring us imaginary duties, things good in themselves, things on a very high plane, in the line perhaps of renunciation or difficulty, and, as an angel of light (2 Cor. 11: 14) tell us that this is God's will for us. We may do these things, and find no blessing in result. We have been driven beyond the will of God. Asceticism is one form of this: denying ourselves things that God wants us to have; deliberately becoming careless about our person or our dress in the mistaken idea that God does not want Victorious Life Christians to be attractive! May God deliver us from the peril of being driven beyond his will into imaginary duties or hardships.

Then, when we have come to see this temptation as from Satan, there is danger of a reaction the other way, lagging below or lagging behind the will of God. We are in danger of letting Christian liberty become license; of letting faith become presumption. Because it is God's grace, not our works, that is the great thing, we mistakenly think we need not do this or that duty. And we fall below the standard that God would have us live by.

May we be delivered from the peril of thinking that we can get along with less prayer, or less Bible study, now that we have "all things in Christ."

Mr. Trumbull

Other speakers at this conference are urging upon us, as God wants us to realize, the absolutely vital place of the daily quiet time of prayer and feeding upon God's Word. There is no sustained life of victory in Christ without this.

As we go out from this conference trusting in the Lord Jesus for victory, let us remember the beautiful illustration that Dr. Griffith Thomas gave us the other morning, from the life of the great missionary, John G. Paton. Dr. Paton, you remember, as he was translating the Scriptures, had almost despaired of finding a word for "faith," or "believe." Then, as he was working in his study one day, a native helper, very tired after a long walk, came in and threw himself down on a chair, resting his feet on another chair, and, leaning back, used a word meaning that he was leaning his whole weight on those chairs.

Like a flash the Holy Spirit said to the missionary, "That is the word you want." He asked the man for the word which meant "leaning the whole weight," and then took it and used it in translating the idea of "faith" or "believe" wherever this occurred. We see, as we try it ourselves in New Testament passages, how wonderfully it illuminates. "God so loved the world, that he gave his only begotten Son, that whosoever leans his whole weight on him should not perish, but have everlasting life" (John 3: 16). "What must I do to be saved? And they said, Lean thy whole weight on the Lord Jesus Christ, and thou shalt be saved" (Acts 16: 30, 31).

And Dr. Thomas reminded us that there is not a single passage in the New Testament where "faith" does not mean the leaning of our whole weight on Christ; and that that is the Christian life,—not merely the act by means of which we commence the Christian life, but the attitude by means of which, moment by moment leaning our whole weight on Christ, we live the life of faith.

Dear friends, are you not tired of trying to carry any of your weight yourself? I am. Will you thank the Lord Jesus, now, for his wonderful sufficiency in bearing all our burdens, and in carrying us in victory, for time and eternity?

PRAYER

Lord Jesus, when those nail holes were made in thy hands and thy feet, thou didst bear thy whole weight on those

Going on in Victory

tearing wounds. Then there was put on thee the awful weight of the sins of the world, with my sins, and thou didst bear them all, the Lamb of God which taketh away the sins of the world, bearing all this in thine own body on the tree.

Oh, Lord Jesus, this cost thee the awful price of separation from the Father, crushed and dying, under the agony of the burden of our sin. And that is how we can be free from that awful burden, Lord Jesus. We thank thee and we praise thee for this; and we praise the Father that he raised thee from the dead with joy and triumph in his heart and thine, and that thou wilt never have to die again.

Lord Jesus, may we lean our whole weight on thee now! If we have not been doing so, wilt thou forgive us. We thank thee that thou dost forgive us, as we confess our sin of unbelief, our sin of even making God a liar, our Saviour, Jesus Christ who died for us,—and we have wondered whether it could be possible that thy grace was sufficient for us, though thou didst say it was, and art saying it is now!

Holy Spirit of God, wilt thou at this time enable every child of God here who has been trying to carry some of his own weight to lean that whole weight now on Jesus, and now and henceforth to be free from the weight, the burden, the power, and the bondage of sin.

Resting everything on thee, Lord Jesus, we thank thee, we praise thee, we trust thee that thy grace is sufficient for us. In thy dear name, Amen.

THE SPIRIT'S FIRE IN KOREA

Jonathan Goforth, D. D.

I SPEAK of the revival in Korea because it has done so much for me. I cannot even consider the attainments and sacrifices of the Korean Christians without feeling ashamed of the little I have ever done for the Master. I have often seen Chinese Christian audiences break down and weep when I told them the story. If you realize that you have been "bought with a price" you will surely be ashamed and humbled, too, if you give this tale of Gospel triumph in Korea a fair hearing.

It was in the year of the great revival, 1907, that I visited eight of the chief mission centers of Korea. On returning to China I told the facts to the Chinese Christians at Mukden, and they seemed deeply moved. I went to Pei Tai Ho, and told the missionaries there how the Lord had blessed Korea; and I heard some in tears vow that they would pray until a like blessing came to China. Afterwards I was invited to go to Chi Kung Shan, another health resort, to tell about Korea. I told the story on a Sunday evening. As I finished it occurred to me that I had been too long, and immediately I closed with the benediction. But no one moved. The stillness of death reigned. This lasted six or seven minutes, and then suppressed weeping broke out over the audience. Sins were confessed; forgiveness was asked for bad temper and quarrels, and the like. It was late when the meeting broke up, but all felt that the Holy Spirit had been among us, refining as by fire. Then we had four days of conference and prayer. It was the most wonderful time I have ever seen among missionaries. We resolved that we would pray every afternoon at four o'clock until the church of China was revived. That autumn we began to see the power of God manifested among the people, but increased in mighty measure after the beginning of 1908 in Manchuria and elsewhere.

The beginnings of revival were first seen in Korea in 1903. Dr. Hardie, of Gensan, on the east coast, had been asked to

---

This message and that which follows were given at the 1917 Conference at Princeton. This article, which here has been somewhat reduced in length, has been published in its complete form in a leaflet, "When the Spirit's Fire Swept Korea." See page 379.

The Spirit's Fire in Korea

prepare some addresses on prayer for a little conference the missionaries proposed to hold. As he was preparing his subjects, from John fourteen and elsewhere, the Holy Spirit taught him many things. When he delivered his talks on prayer all the missionaries were moved. Afterward the Korean Christians met in conference and were very manifestly moved. Then Dr. Hardie visited ten mission centers throughout Korea and gave his prayer talks; and during 1904 ten thousand Koreans turned to God. The revival thus begun continued in power and spiritual result until 1906.

In June, 1907, Mr. Swallen, of Ping Yang, told me how they came to see greater things in Korea. Said he, "I personally didn't expect to see greater blessings in Korea than we had seen up to the middle of 1906. When we compared our results in Korea with those in China, Japan, and elsewhere, we saw that our ingatherings far exceeded anything in those lands, and we came to the conclusion that probably God did not intend to grant us greater blessings than we had already seen. But we got our eyes opened at Seoul, in September, 1906, when Dr. Howard Agnew Johnston, of New York, told us of the revival in the Kassia Hills, India, in 1905-6, where they had baptized 8,200 converts during the two years.

"We missionaries returned home to Ping Yang humbled. There were over twenty of us in the Methodist and Presbyterian missions at Ping Yang. We reasoned that since our God was not a respecter of persons, he did not wish to give greater blessing in the Kassia Hills than in Ping Yang, so we decided to pray at the noon hour until greater blessing came.

"After we had prayed about a month, a brother proposed that we stop the prayer-meeting, saying, 'We have prayed about a month, and nothing unusual has come of it. We are spending a lot of time. I don't think we are justified. Let us go on with our work as usual, and each pray at home as we find it convenient.' The proposal seemed plausible. However, the majority decided to continue the prayer-meeting, believing that the Lord would not deny Ping Yang what he had granted to Kassia."

They decided to give more time to prayer instead of less. With that view they changed the hour from twelve to four o'clock; then they were free to pray until supper time if they wished. There was little else than prayer. If any one had

Dr. Goforth

an encouraging item to relate, it was given as they continued in prayer. They prayed about four months, and they said the result was that all forgot about being Methodists and Presbyterians; they only realized that they were all one in the Lord Jesus Christ. That was true church union; it was brought about on the knees; it would last; it would glorify the Most High.

About that time Mr. Swallen, along with Mr. Blair, visited one of the country out-stations. While conducting the service in the usual way many commenced weeping and confessing their sins. Mr. Swallen said he had never met with anything so strange, and he announced a hymn, hoping to check the wave of emotion which was sweeping over the audience. He tried several times but in vain, and in awe he realized that Another was managing that meeting; and he got as far out of sight as possible. Next morning he and Mr. Blair returned to the city rejoicing, and told how God had come to the outstation. All praised God and believed that the time to favor Ping Yang was close at hand.

It had now come to the first week of January, 1907. They all expected that God would signally bless them during the week of universal prayer. But they came to the last day, the eighth day, and yet no special manifestation of the power of God. That Sabbath evening about fifteen hundred people were assembled in the Central Presbyterian Church. The heavens over them seemed as brass. Was it possible that God was going to deny them the prayed-for outpouring? Then all were startled as Elder Keel, the leading man in the church, stood up and said, "I am an Achan. God can't bless because of me. About a year ago a friend of mine, when dying, called me to his home and said, 'Elder, I am about to pass away; I want you to manage my affairs; my wife is unable.' I said, 'Rest your heart; I will do it.' I did manage that widow's estate, but I managed to put one hundred dollars of her money into my own pocket. I have hindered God. I am going to give that one hundred dollars back to that widow to-morrow morning."

Instantly it was realized that the barriers had fallen and that God the Holy One had come. Conviction of sin swept the audience. The service commenced at seven o'clock Sunday evening, and did not end until two o'clock Monday morning, yet during all that time dozens were standing weeping, awaiting their turn to confess. Day after day the people

The Spirit's Fire in Korea

assembled now, and always it was manifest that the Refiner was in His temple. Let man say what he will, these confessions were controlled by a power not human. Either the Devil or the Holy Spirit caused them. No divinely enlightened mind can for one instant believe that the Devil caused that chief man in the church to confess such a sin. It hindered the Almighty God while it remained covered, and it glorified Him as soon as it was uncovered; and so with rare exceptions did all the confessions in Korea that year.

Let me give a few samples.

A doctor had boasted that he had one of the most honest cooks in Korea (in the East cooks do all the marketing); but when that cook got convicted he said, "I have been cheating the doctor all the time; my house and lot have been secured by cheating the doctor." The cook sold his home and paid all back to the doctor.

A teacher had been entrusted to buy some land for the mission. He secured it, and said the price was $500. The missionary paid the bill, though objecting to so big a price. In the revival that teacher confessed he had secured the land for $80. He now sold out all he had and paid back the $420 out of which he had cheated the mission.

Mr. Mackenzie, the war correspondent, had a boy who cheated him out of less than four dollars. That boy, when convicted, walked eighty miles and had a missionary send that money to Mr. Mackenzie. Is it any wonder that Mr. Mackenzie became a strong believer in the kind of Christianity they have in Korea?

A man who had a wife and one son in We Ju left them and became rich in another city. There he married another woman, and by her had two daughters. When his soul was revived he arranged for the support of this woman and her daughters, and went back to We Ju and was reconciled to his lawful wife. If the Korean kind of revival ever reaches some Christian lands, where divorce prevails, there will be some startling social upheavals.

A deacon, who was looked upon as almost perfect, seemed to get very uneasy as the revival progressed, and he confessed to the stealing of some charity funds. All were astonished, but expected him to get peace; however, he descended into deeper distress and then confessed to a breach of the seventh commandment.

Dr. Goforth

A woman, who for days seemed to pass through the agonies of hell, confessed one evening in a public meeting to the sin of adultery. The missionary in charge of the meeting was greatly alarmed, for he knew that her husband was present, and knew that if that husband killed her he would be in accord with Korean law. That husband, in tears, went over and knelt beside his sinning wife and forgave her. How the Lord Jesus was glorified as he said to that Korean woman, "Sin no more"!

Such extraordinary happenings could not but move the multitude, and the churches became crowded. Many came to mock, but in fear began to pray. The leader of a robber band, who came out of idle curiosity, was convicted and converted, and went straight to the magistrate and gave himself up. The astonished official said, "You have no accuser; you accuse yourself; we have no law in Korea to meet your case"; and so dismissed him.

A Japanese officer at the time of the revival was quartered in Ping Yang. He had imbibed the agnostic ideas of the West, therefore to him spiritual things were beneath contempt. Still, the strange transformations which were taking place, not only among great numbers of Koreans, but even among some Japanese, who could not possibly understand the language, so puzzled him that he attended the meetings to investigate. The final result was that all his unbelief was swept away, and he became a follower of the Lord Jesus.

As Mr. Swallen said, "It paid well to have spent the several months in prayer, for when God the Holy Spirit came he accomplished more in half a day than all of us missionaries could have accomplished in half a year. In less than two months more than two thousand heathen were converted." It is always so as soon as God gets first place; but as a rule the church, which professes to be Christ's, will not cease her busy round of activities and give God a chance by *waiting upon him in prayer*.

The revival, which began in 1903 and had gone on increasing, now flowed on in increasing volume, from the Ping Yang center, all over Korea. By the middle of 1907 there were 30,000 converts connected with the Ping Yang center. In the city there were four or five churches. The Central Presbyterian Church could hold 2,000 if the people sat close. Korean churches have no seats. The people sit on mats

The Spirit's Fire in Korea

spread on the floor. They said in the Central church that if you packed 2,000 in they would be so close that if any one had to stand up a bit to ease his cramped legs he never could sit down again, for the space would just fill in. But the utmost packing could not meet the need of Central Church, for its membership was 3,000. The way they did was for the women to come first and fill the church, and when their service was ended, the men came and took their places. It was clear that the revival had not died down by 1910, for in October of that year 4,000 were baptized in one week, and thousands besides sent in their names, saying they had decided to become Christians.

. . . .

Some one may say, "But numbers don't count; on one occasion the Master discouraged the multitude from following." True. The point is well taken. Well, then, what standard shall we apply? Let us go to the early chapters of the Acts. We can readily agree to apply that standard to the Korean Church, even though we prefer not to have it in its entirety applied to ourselves. Now, let us see how the Korean Church measures up to the Pentecostal standard.

The early Church did great honor to God the Holy Spirit by dropping everything and spending ten days in prayer to prepare for his coming. I have told how the missionaries spent one to several hours each day for months, preparing a way in their hearts for the Holy Spirit. These missionaries heard from Dr. Howard Agnew Johnston how the Holy Spirit was poured out upon the Kassians in India. At the same time and place a Bible colporteur from Kang Kai, away up among the pine forests along the Yalu, also heard Dr. Johnston. He went home and told the Kang Kai Church of 250 believers that the Holy Spirit alone could make effective the finished work of the Lord Jesus Christ, and that he was promised them as freely as any other gift of God. They honored God and appreciated the gift of the Holy Spirit by meeting in the church for prayer at five o'clock; not five o'clock every evening, but every morning, through the fall and winter of 1906-7. They honored God the Holy Spirit by six months of prayer; and *then he came as a flood.* Since then their numbers have increased manyfold. Do we really believe in God the Holy Spirit? Let us be honest. Not to

Dr. Goforth

the extent of getting up at five o'clock through six months of cold weather to seek him!

A burning zeal to make known the merits of the Saviour was a special mark of the church at Pentecost. The same is not less true of the Korean Church. It was said that the heathen complained that they couldn't endure the persecution of the Christians. They were evermore telling of the strong points of their Saviour. Some declared they would have to sell out and move to some district where there were no Christians in order to get rest.

The missionaries at Ping Yang honored God the Holy Spirit in their high school. They had a school of 318 students, and that Monday morning of the opening in February, 1907, the two missionaries in charge were early at prayer in the principal's room. They wanted the Holy Spirit to control the school from the start. They knew that if he did not control, the school would only turn out educated rascals who would be a menace to Korea.

Before nine o'clock had struck that Monday morning, in the Ping Yang high school, the Spirit of the Lord was smiting those boys with conviction. Agonized cries were heard upstairs and down. Soon the principal's room was filled with boys agonized over sin. School could not be opened that day, nor the next, and Friday still found it unopened. By Friday evening the Presbyterian boys had all come through to victory, but it was clear that something held the Methodist boys back.

It all came out that evening, when about a dozen of the Methodist boys went and pleaded with their native pastor to free them from their promise to him. It seems that this Korean pastor had got jealous because the revival had not started in the Methodist church. He got the high school boys to oppose it, and to resist all public confession as from the Devil. But by Friday night their agony of mind was unbearable, hence their pleading to be set free from their promise.

With that, the pastor went and flung himself at the missionaries' feet and confessed that the Devil had filled him with envy because the revival had commenced among the Presbyterians. A missionary told me that it was dreadful to hear the confessions wrung from those students that week. That it was as if the lid of hell had been pulled off, and every

The Spirit's Fire in Korea

imaginable sin laid bare. By the following Monday the students were right with God, with their teachers, and with one another, and the school commenced under the Spirit's control.

Just then about one hundred preachers and colporteurs of the Methodist mission arrived in the city to study a month. The missionaries in united prayer committed this important class to the control of the Holy Spirit. They realized that it was not by might, nor by power, but by the Spirit of the Lord of hosts. They honored God, and he rewarded them by a manifestation of his presence and power at the very first meeting. In a few days crooked things were made straight. The Divine One took control. They studied with effect, and at the end of a month they went out to do exploits.

. . . .

Let us apply the *prayer test* to the Korean Church. Prayer was a very conspicuous trait of the Church in the Acts.

Some years after Elder Keel had been made pastor of the Central Church at Ping Yang, he noticed that the love of many had grown cold. He proposed to one of his most spiritually-minded elders that they two meet in the church for prayer every morning at half past four. As they met each morning during that month others noticed and came too, so that by the end of a month about twenty were meeting each morning at 4.30 o'clock. The time now seemed ripe to announce a public prayer-meeting. On the Sabbath the pastor announced a prayer-meeting for each morning at 4.30. He told them that the church bell would be rung at that hour. At two o'clock the next morning 400 people were waiting outside the church for the prayer-meeting to begin, and at 4.30 fully 600 were there. By the end of a week 700 were meeting each morning, and then the Holy Spirit flooded their hearts with divine love. Blessed people to have a pastor so clear-sighted. Oh, how low have we fallen! Where two or three meet together in His name, he is there, but imagine us getting up at 4.30 in the morning, even to meet the Lord of glory.

The biggest prayer-meeting in the world is at Seoul, Korea. The average weekly attendance for one year was 1,100. One Wednesday evening I went to prayer-meeting at one of the flourishing Presbyterian churches in Toronto. It was a special occasion, for a Korean missionary was going to speak. I sat

Dr. Goforth

alone in my seat for a time, then a fine-looking old gentleman came and sat with me. The meeting was soon to begin, but in the by no means large room many empty seats were still visible. The old gentleman looking around the room remarked, "I can't understand why people don't attend prayer-meeting." When I replied, "Because they don't believe in prayer," he looked me all over, not knowing what to make of me, for he didn't know me, and I added, "Do you suppose if they really believed the words of the Lord Jesus, 'Where two or three meet in my name there am I,' they could keep away?" The Master cannot help but take note of our prayer condition.

* * * *

Abounding liberality was another very striking characteristic of the early church. The Korean Christians abound in that, too. At one place a missionary told me that he dared not mention money to his people for they were giving too much now. I should like to meet the pastor in favored Christendom who could truly say that of his people. The year I was at that center the people were supporting 139 workers, male and female, teachers and preachers, and that year alone they increased the workers by fifty-seven. That missionary said, "When we found our church was too small, we met to plan for the erection of one that would hold 1,500. The people present gave all the money they had. The men gave their watches and the women stripped off their jewelry. Others gave title deeds for portions of land. They gave all they had and wept because they couldn't give more, and they built their church free of debt."

At another place the missionary was present at the dedication of a new church. It was found that there was still $50 owing on the church. A member present arose and said, "Pastor, I will next Sunday bring $50 to pay off that debt." The missionary, knowing the man was very poor, said, "Don't think of doing it yourself. We will all join together and can soon pay it off." There are churches in the homeland that are not ashamed nor afraid to carry a $50,000 debt. Next Sunday arrived and this poor Christian brought the $50. The missionary astonished asked, "Where did you get the money?" The Christian replied, "Pastor, don't mind. It is all clean money." Some weeks later the missionary, touring in that region, came to this man's home. On asking the man's wife where her husband was she said, "Out in the field plowing."

The Spirit's Fire in Korea

The missionary on going out to the field found the old father holding the plow handles while his son was pulling the plow. The missionary in amazement said, "Why, what have you done with your mule?" "Now, Pastor," said the Christian, "I couldn't bear to have the Church of Jesus owing a $50 debt to a heathen, so I sold my mule to wipe it out." I fancy some time, when we see these Korean Christians standing very near the Lord while we are afar off, we will be too ashamed to look up or get jealous. These Korean Christians say, "We don't run our business or our farms to make us rich, but to pay expenses. Our business is to extend the Kingdom of God." The Korean religion has got control of the pocketbook and makes near approach to the Pentecostal standard.

Another proof that the Korean Church is guided by the same Spirit that guided the early church is their zeal for God's Word. At the time of the revival they could not get the Bible printed fast enough. In one year at Ping Yang 6,000 Bibles were sold. Every one learns it, even the dullest women. Christians traveling on business always carry the Bible along. By the way, and at the inns, they open up and read, and many are attracted and saved. The Christianity of this continent does not make such open use of the Bible.

The Koreans have a proverb or saying that the elders have the right to criticize the juniors, then when they get through if there is anything left of the juniors they may in turn criticize the elders. In Christian lands that practice is not followed very well. In our time the juniors largely monopolize the right of criticism. Now the Koreans admit that the oldest criticism of man is in the Bible; therefore they always let the Bible criticize them first, and they never find anything of themselves left so as to venture to criticize God's Book. I believe in that kind of Biblical criticism. We can't have too much of it. If men were all humble enough to approach the Bible in the Korean spirit, there would be more books burned around some seminaries than ever were burned on the streets of Ephesus when Paul preached there. It would cause world-wide revival.

When Korean pastors and evangelists and elders were flung into prison wrongfully by the Japanese they didn't waste time by idle repining, but set to work at their Bibles. One of them read the Bible through seven times while in prison, and then exclaimed, "I never imagined my Saviour was so won-

Dr. Goforth

derful!" Another thought the Japanese might take the Bible away and destroy it, so he memorized Romans and was hard at work at John when liberated. If real persecution ever arose in Christian lands the Bible would meet with more appreciation than at present.

. . . .

The early church rejoiced in that they were deemed worthy to suffer for that blessed Name. The same spirit characterizes the Korean Church. It is not unlikely that the demon of jealousy prompted the Japanese to persecute the Korean Church. That absurd charge that the Christians of Shun Chun had conspired to assassinate Governor-General Terauchi! There never was anything more unlikely, but it served as a pretext to fling the Christian leaders there into prison. It is notorious how cruelly they were tortured in the police cells to terrify them into saying just what the Japanese wanted them to say. They were hung up by the thumbs, they were burned with hot irons. One man fainted away seven times, but through all they remained faithful, and the courts had to dismiss them as innocent.

There was a man who confessed his Saviour in his native village only to find that his clan turned him out of house and home. He did not go to law, but by the grace of God remained sweet. He meekly bore with insult and wrong and lived and preached Christ, until *the whole clan was converted,* and his possessions restored.

There was a man who while visiting the city was converted and confessed the Lord Jesus Christ in baptism. Then he went home to tell his wonderful story. His clan received it in anger, and soon the enraged relatives fell upon him and beat him almost to death. When he was brought to the hospital his life hung by a thread. At the end of many weeks the doctor told him he might go home, but told him that his life might end with a hemorrhage any day. That Christian bought a great quantity of books and went home. For three years he went about his home district, giving away his books and telling of his Saviour. Then there came a day when his blood flowed out and his soul ascended to his God. But in that heathen county, where they had tried to murder him, he left eleven churches.

Surely God the Holy Spirit has been glorifying our ascended Lord in Korea, as certainly as he did in Palestine in the first

The Spirit's Fire in Korea

century. It is a challenge to our easy-going Christianity to awake and seek God as these children of the East have done. They have given ample proof that it is not by might, nor by power, that the Kingdom of God is made manifest among men. In all humility they yielded themselves to the Lord Jesus Christ, and the very fulness of God flowed through them. God waits to visit us with the same fulness of salvation. But we must pay the price, or merely have a name to live and be open to the condemnation of those who despise the Giver of so great salvation.

GOD'S OVERFLOW IN KOREA

Jonathan Goforth, D. D.

IT WAS at the feast of tabernacles that our Lord gave a promise for overflow. That feast commemorated the overflow of God's goodness to Israel during the wilderness journey. Now the Fulfilment of all type and symbol stood amid the crowd on the last day, the great day of the feast. That Rock which followed them, even the Lord Jesus Christ, now stood and cried, "If any man thirst, let him come unto me and drink. He that believeth on me, as the Scripture hath said, from within him shall flow rivers of living water." Our Saviour means *overflow through every saved and sanctified channel*. It is his promise, which can be relied upon, up to the full one hundred per cent., at any time in any land.

He knew the world's need was divine overflow. The Nile's overflow is Egypt's salvation; Egypt would starve if the Nile kept within its banks. If the church of Jesus fails to overflow, earth's millions will perish. The Master planned that every believer, through the Holy Spirit, should overflow. No one without eternal loss can shirk this privilege. Have we the proof of overflow? It is said that thirty rivers take their rise in the vicinity of Damascus, and yet not one of them reaches the ocean; they are all lost in the desert sands. How like this are many churches and many Christians! At the start, flowing so full of promise, then swallowed up in the world.

Let no one say, "The time is not yet." Before Pentecost they could say it, but not since. Since Pentecost the promise is an eternal present. The hindrances are all on man's side.

If we joyfully accept this promise in all its fulness the following proofs of overflow will follow:

There will be an *overflow of prayer*. This was the outstanding proof of Spirit-filled men at Pentecost, and has been ever since.

The most wonderful proof of intercessory prayer I know of is that of the Kuang Chow station in South Honan. Mr.

This is the second of Dr. Goforth's messages at the 1917 Conference at Princeton. See note on page 183.

God's Overflow in Korea

Argento, of the China Inland Mission, began work there about twenty-five years ago. In 1900 the Boxers seized him, poured kerosene over him and set him on fire. He was rescued by the Christians, but not before his eyes were ruined. Since then he has lived in Europe; but it is said he only lives to pray for Kuang Chow.

For years no resident missionary lived there. During the last four or five years Mr. and Mrs. Mason have been in charge. When I visited the place in December, 1915, they were just putting the last tiles on a church, which when completed would hold 1,400. The money was almost all subscribed by the Chinese Christians. There were twenty-one outstations, and about 2,000 believers.

When Mr. Wen, the leading elder, was introduced, I asked him his honorable age. "Just eighteen years of age," he replied. It was plain he was a man of sixty. With a twinkle in his eyes he said, "Yes, I am only eighteen. Before that I was dead in sin. I was so low down with opium and drink that when a friend met me on the street one day he said, 'If you don't go over there to that Jesus hall and have that missionary pray for you, you will soon die off.' I took the hint and went that day; and the missionary prayed for me, and opium and drink dropped out of my life. That was eighteen years ago."

Next day, Sunday, I commenced meetings in that church. The galleries were not in, but fully a thousand were packed into the body of that church, and hundreds of others were listening outside the doors and windows. Again and again, during the nine days of the meetings, the convicting power of the Holy Spirit broke down hundreds. As many as six or eight hundred would come to a daylight prayer-meeting. During those days 144 persons were baptized, and more than one hundred others whose time was up for baptism were put off, because there was no time to examine them. The chief banker and his head clerk, with some of the chief business men of the city, came and asked for baptism, saying, "We have been baptized by the Holy Spirit these days, and believe we ought to receive water baptism." Many heathen who attended the meetings said in awe, "The living God is among you."

Demons, too, were in evidence. When the Holy Spirit was moving the people mightily, two demon-possessed persons would blaspheme and cry in fiendish fashion. Once when one

Dr. Goforth

of them, an evangelist's wife, was acting thus a Bible woman pulled her down. In a rage she spat all over the Bible woman. When Mrs. Mason wiped the spittle off, the demon-possessed woman wept with her head on Mrs. Mason's shoulder. On the last day, the demon-possessed man was brought to the guest room to be prayed for. I, being tired out, took no part except to look on.

Mr. Mason prayed first, and then Elder Wen. I noticed when either of them used the name "Jesus Christ of Nazareth," the man became awfully agitated. The third who prayed was Mr. Changan, evangelist. Putting his hand on the man's head, he said, "In the name of Jesus Christ of Nazareth, foul fiend, I command you to come out of him." With that the demon-possessed man, uttering fiendish cries, flung himself on the floor. With the long-skirted Chinese standing close around I could not see, but the sound was as though he wallowed, foaming. Then he vomited. At least it sounded like it; something seemed to have gone out of him. He was raised up on to a chair, limp and pale and trembling. I looked carefully on the ground, but there was no sign of vomit. Later on, the evangelist's wife was prayed for, and her demon was cast out. Both have since been serving the Lord in their right mind.

I heard a year later that the twenty-one outstations of that mission had increased to thirty-one. The gallery is in now, and at the Christian Endeavor Convention fourteen hundred were packed into the church; and as many as eight hundred were out each morning at the daylight prayer-meeting. The key to such splendid results is just this: *one disabled missionary in Europe praying in the Holy Ghost for Kuang Chow.* At the judgment seat of Christ many will be startled over the way they have sinned against God, by restraining prayer.

In my own case I got to praying for China, and would have been a hopeless hypocrite if I had not gone to China. It is a dangerous thing to get praying for any heathen land. You will either have to go or send. But it is more dangerous still not to overflow in prayer for lands for which the Saviour died.

Another proof will be our *overflow of love.* At Pentecost the love of God was so shed abroad in the hearts of believers that they could not but proclaim the matchless graces of their King. The Holy Spirit in them did not glorify himself but

God's Overflow in Korea

so testified to the Lord Jesus Christ that He became all glorious. They did not keep still. They could not.

A Lushai schoolboy became filled with divine love through hearing of the Kassia revival. He went home, and within a week led forty of his family and clan to God. In 1907 a turnkey in one of the great Japanese prisons was converted, and in a month he was the means of turning forty other turnkeys to trust in the Lord Jesus. God has planned that we overflow in love so that the unsaved may know it. Rivers of living water flowing through a sin-cursed earth is what our Saviour means by the promise of the Holy Spirit. It is sin to clog the channel.

The *overflow of sacrifice* is assured in any Spirit-filled believer. The spirit of Jesus is the spirit of sacrifice. All true sacrifice is the free outflow of his life. If you want to know what sacrifice is read of Paul in 2 Corinthians 11. Whenever inclined to laziness I just read that chapter. It shames me. If any one imagines he has suffered much in the service of his Saviour, let him read that chapter.

We saw this spirit in China. In 1902 we recorded a man named Hu Chwang. We called him Shakespeare, because before conversion he had written over one hundred plays for Chinese theaters. To direct his training I kept him with me for a year. In a few years Hu became mighty in the Word. He became a marvelous preacher, and was called the Spurgeon of China. At his own charges he went around his county preaching Jesus. I asked Mr. Hu to come and help us at Changtefu with the several thousand students who were coming up for examinations. I found that he had pawned his overcoat, though it was bitterly cold, so that he could get the money needed for his traveling expenses. Mr. Hu died with cancer early in 1916, but he left a self-supporting congregation in his district, with its pastor and assistant pastor, and a self-supporting boys' school and girls' school.

At the city of Huang Hsien, Shantung province, in December of 1910, some of the Chinese leaders with Dr. Ayers came some distance out of the city to meet me. After greetings had been exchanged, one of the Chinese evangelists asked if I believed the Holy Spirit would visit them in great power as he had done in Manchuria and elsewhere. I replied that that did not depend upon the Holy Spirit, but on themselves. That if they truly valued the gift of the Holy Spirit, and had got

Dr. Goforth

rid of every offensive thing, there was no reason why they might not be filled with all the fulness of God. Two days later I heard that evangelist weeping in prayer, saying, "O Lord, the Doctor has turned twenty-seven men and women over to me that I might get them ready for baptism, but you know I am only an empty vessel; unless I am filled with the Spirit of God I can do nothing." At breakfast on the sixth day Dr. Ayers told me that after midnight the previous night that same evangelist, with one of the medical assistants, had wakened him saying, "Dr. Ayers, we can't sleep. Mr. Goforth has been here for five days, and we are not revived. Won't you join us in prayer?"

When the spirit of prayer is upon men so that they can't sleep, God's time to favor Zion is at hand.

On that sixth day, after the afternoon address, as usual I left the meeting open for prayer. Sometimes one or two or three were praying. This continued for about fifteen minutes. Then for many minutes there was an absolute hush. To me God seemed to fill the building. I was humbled to the utmost, and ready to fall at his feet. My only thought was, "Of ten million parts of glory I claim none. Pour floods upon the parched ground." The stillness was broken by the evangelist who was so eager for blessing. His first sentence was a burst of praise, "God is here!" Instantly, others all over the assembly voiced the same thought. Some were praising God in prayer or song, but the majority were confessing to God, and seeking forgiveness. In the seeming disorder there was absolute order, for no one seemed hindered by his neighbor. I allowed it to go on for about an hour, then, fearing they would become exhausted, I closed the service by pronouncing the benediction with a loud voice; but the people paid no heed to me, and went on for an hour and a half longer.

It was during that time that intercessory prayer rose to such a height of intensity as I have never known before or since. Even little schoolboys of eight and ten with tears streaming, and trembling in every limb, would pray for their unsaved friends at home. It came out that there was an infidel club among the high school boys. The missionaries did not know of it. The boys had got books on Darwinism, etc., and had concluded that there was no God. But now the living God was supreme. Boy after boy would fall down on his knees, with face on the ground, confess his sin and plead for mercy. The ringleader, one of the largest boys, passed

God's Overflow in Korea

through a time of judgment. He was agonized to the utmost, and cried out, "O Lord Jesus! make a whip and put lots of knots in it, and whip this devil of unbelief out of me. I now believe there is one living and true God." There was not one unsaved one left in that audience, all were saved.

Though it was in December, and no fire in the church, those revived men, women, and children were back in the church at three o'clock next morning, singing praise unto God and praying until sunrise. Their faces fairly shone. They had seen a vision. This early meeting was their idea, not mine.

I have again and again seen all in an audience convicted and saved; but it was only *after the followers of the Lord had got right with one another and with God.* The three thousand never would have been saved that day at Pentecost unless the one hundred and twenty had first got right with God and man and had been Spirit-filled. The Lord Jesus Christ is hindered in the house of his friends. Judgment must first commence in the house of God. It is a sin, equivalent to murder, to hinder the salvation of souls by our non-victorious lives. It defrauds the Son of God, for it keeps him from seeing of the travail of his soul, even unto Divine satisfaction.

In the terrible war now being waged the Allied commanders are under the strongest obligation to make use of all the resources of the lands they represent. If any disaster came to the Allied cause as a consequence of their failure to do so, it would be justly blamed on them. In the promise, "He that believeth on me, as the scripture hath said, out of his inmost being shall flow rivers of living water," *all the resources of heaven are pledged to us for the war against Satan.* Who among us with any spiritual discernment can claim that we have hitherto made use to the utmost of all Divine resources? In consequence great has been the disaster to many souls. Have we no guilt? May the King of kings open our eyes to our need of His promised power!

PHILIPPINE TROPHIES

E. J. Pace

"THESE waters shall go down into the east country," was said of the stream that issued from the Sanctuary in Ezekiel's wonderful vision. And these living waters have gone down into the east country, and I have seen the bitter waters sweetened, and regions of desolation and death changed into veritable gardens of the Lord,—over in the Philippine gardens, where it was my privilege to go as a missionary some twelve or thirteen years ago, on the island of Luzon.

Luzon, as you know, is one of a group, of which there are a thousand or fifteen hundred islands, most of them very small, eleven quite large. Luzon is about one hundred and seventy-five miles north of Manila, and it is about the size of Ohio. I lived at Tagudin, on the west coast of the island. There is a wide range of mountains about two hundred miles long, paralleling the coast. A narrow coastal plain separates these mountains from the sea, in some places not more than two miles wide.

Along this coastal plain, an old Spanish road, now greatly improved by American thrift, threads its way, and along this old Spanish road, strung like beads upon a thread, are the rough pueblos or towns of the Igarot people the so-called Christians (Roman Catholics), three quarters of a million living along this coastal plain.

It was my privilege to live in the province of Sigay, on the sea-coast. I used to go out on the old Spanish road many times to enjoy the vista, and to worship God, especially in the afternoon, when the sun's rays were lighting up those mountains to the east of us, five thousand feet above the sea, all lit up with gold, and blue, and purple, and amethyst, and great billows of cumulus clouds up above. I have gone out there many a time and worshiped God, and said, "O Lord, if heaven can be more beautiful than this, I will have to have an enlarged capacity, for I have reached the limit; I do not see how anything could be more beautiful."

This message was given on the opening Sunday morning at Princeton, and the substance of it was given also in a Vesper service at Cedar Lake.

Philippine Trophies

Way to the northeast of us, low on the horizon, and yet on the top of this mountain range, one can descry on a clear day a mountain crag shaped like a hound's tooth, protruding out of the summit of the mountain, a natural landmark that can be seen many miles out to sea,—the northern limit of the province of Amburayan. I had a circuit of five hundred miles, most of it set up on edge, and that was the northern limit of my responsibility.

Way up there, they told me, was a little town almost at the top of this mountain range, where the Igarots live, the primitive mountain peoples, scantily clad, yet splendid chaps, vigorous and strong of body. Really I loved them a little more than the folks on the lowlands, because they were so unsophisticated, and child-like, and simple-hearted, and they looked you clearly in the eye and told you what they thought of you, characteristics which you do not often meet on the coast.

I fell in love with them, the whole province of them. I had been there two years before I had the privilege of visiting the town of Sigay, at the base of that Hound's Tooth on the mountain crag. One day in May I got on my little horse and went up into the mountains. That horse was so little that I had to lift my feet up for fear I would strike the boulders in the way. It was an extremely hot day. It gets extremely hot on the Philippine Islands. When June comes, the rain comes, and it rains more, and more, and more, until in August it is raining all the time, and in September come the great typhoons, and then it begins to let up a little. There are just two seasons there, wet and dry, hot and not quite so hot.

It was a fearfully hot May day when I climbed the mountains and made my way up there, tired and weary. When I reached that village, a stranger, they immediately began to conjecture who I was. They are very suspicious at first, and it was not very long until somebody suggested that I must be the Protestant missionary, and that was the signal for an exodus. They had been told all sorts of awful things about us, until the people had the impression that about the worst possible creature outside of the infernal pit must be a Protestant missionary. I had come into a little village again and again, where I had not been before, but folks had known me, somebody had seen me in another town, and whispered that I was a Protestant missionary, and they would get out

Mr. Pace

as quickly as they could, except those that had rheumatism and couldn't get away, and were at my mercy.

I used to be a newspaper cartoonist, and found that to be a marvelous help in my work. I would say to a fellow, "Do you want me to draw your picture?" He would look at me and say, "What are you going to do with it?" "If you behave yourself," I would rejoin, "I will give it to you. If you don't, I will send it to the United States of America." He had great fears of what might follow if I sent that picture to America, and being child-like, and full of curiosity, he would let me draw his picture, and the others could not stand it very long, they must see what I was doing. I would get the fellow to hold still, and then somebody else would want his picture drawn. They would gather around, and then I would begin to hear them pass remarks. "Why, there goes his nose! Why there is his ear! There is his other ear. Well, if it don't look like him!" They would have a great time, and I would pay no attention, but go on drawing, and pretty soon someone would say, "He isn't such a bad devil after all, is he?" And so, by one device and another, we seek to make ourselves as pleasing as possible to the inhabitants.

About the time evening came, they invited me to the Men's Club, a little grass thatched house, seven feet at the top, four feet at the edge, sided with reeds, and, in this case, by rough-hewn pine planks; but on the inside one color,—one solid black, and a shiny black, too. When they burn pitch pine it gives off a shiny smoke that produces a shiny interior, a deep black. I said to those fellows, "If you please, we will have our little seance on the outside; I do not believe I can stand it in here."

They had a courtyard about twenty-five feet across, with a little depression in the center, paved with flag stones, with a little wall about a foot high about the edge. I sat there talking to those Iggarotes, and the moon was full. Oh, how the moon does shine in the tropics, about half again as bright, it seemed to me, as in these northern countries. I said to the Iggarotes, "Did you ever see the mountains on the moon?"

"Mountains on the moon! Who ever heard of mountains on the moon?" they exclaimed.

"Yes," I said, "I can see them through my field glasses, see the crater and the hills."

"Mountains on the moon? Let us see."

Philippine Trophies

That was what I wanted them to ask, and I handed one my glass. The fellow looked up and said, "That's right, there are mountains up there." He brought the glass down and saw his house across the valley, and then they all wanted to see. Each one took his turn, and by that time we were quite chummy, and I thought it was time to get down to business, and said, "I would like to have you tell me who your god is up here. Who is your god?"

"Our god? Our god is Lumawig."

"Who is that?" I asked.

"He is our god. He makes the rains to come, and the crops to grow, and he loves the Igarots, and takes care of them. He is our particular god. And furthermore, he came down to earth once on a time, and we will show you where he put his spear in the ground, in a great hole in the rock yonder. He gave laws and customs to men, and he is our god."

I said, "He is my God too."

"What? Lumawig your God?"

"Most assuredly. Didn't you say that he loves the Igarots?"

"Yes."

"That is my God. Didn't you say he makes the rains to come, and the crops to grow? That is my God. Didn't you say he came down and gave laws and customs to men? That is my God, only I do not call him Lumawig. What have I in front of me?" They told me their word for "hat." "No," I said, "it is a *hat,* and the German would call it a *'hut,'* and the French a *'chapeau,'* and the Spaniard something else. Well, there can only be one God, just one God, and 'He whom ye ignorantly worship I have come to tell you of.' You call him Lumawig, and I call him by another name, but there is only one God. I know more about him than you do."

"How do you know?" they asked.

"I have his book, and you have not."

They have the strangest belief over there, that if anything is printed, it is true,—it is true because it is printed. I knew they did not have any book, and I said, "I have his book, and you haven't."

"Where is it?" they asked.

I pulled out of my hip pocket the Gospels translated into the language of the Filipinos, and began to read. I shall

Mr. Pace

never forget those Igarots, seated around the fire in the moonlight; in the light of the fire I read from the precious stories in the Gospels, and I shall never forget their faces, and the interest and the eagerness with which they listened. They said, "Say, have you any more of those books?"

"Yes, I have lots of them," I said. "I will give you this, and get another on the coast."

"There is one man here that can read," they said, "and we would like one of those books."

"I will not only give you this book, but will send you a man to teach you this book. Would you like to have him?"

"We would," they said.

"Will you promise to obey and follow his teachings?" I asked.

"Yes, we would like to see him," they said. "Will he teach our children?"

"Yes."

About two and one-half months after that, we discovered a man. We had prayed about it, and sent out a call for volunteers. Nobody volunteered excepting one fellow. I wish you could see him. You would say, "Mr. Pace, is he a sample of your Filipino preachers?" "I would to God they were all like him. What is the matter?" I would ask. "He is so long, and lean, and lanky, and awkward, and homely. He shambles as he goes."

He married the prettiest girl over there, but when I summed up his unsightly defects I think I completed the list. He went up into the mountains, a missionary, and settled down in the midst of those people and began to work. I heard not a word from him for eight months, and then I got a letter, and he said, "Pastor, I wish you would come up. There is one man to be baptized."

I went forty-five miles on my little horse to baptize that one man, about a year after my first visit, in the month of April. I got to the top of the mountains, tired and weary. I had proved by experience that it is a mighty ticklish proposition to speak in a foreign language when you are tired,—difficult enough when you are fresh, and I said, "I will have to rest." They gave me such a cordial welcome when I came that time,—so different from the first. I said, "Excuse me, folks, I cannot talk to you now, I must sleep a little while. I will be here a number of days, and we will have plenty of time to talk, and sing, and preach."

Philippine Trophies

I went to the building where this young native missionary had been living, and with my saddle as a pillow, lay on the hard pine planks and slept soundly, until away into the night I was awakened by the murmur of voices in a corner of the room. There I saw this Filipino brother with twenty-five or thirty little boys in front of him, and in a very low tone of voice he kept up a running fire of questions. I do not know when he began on Genesis, but he was over in Joshua when I awoke. They would answer in a very low tone of voice, as one boy. He went on through the Old Testament with one question after another, and just as rapidly as he could ask questions they would answer. I lay there as long as I could, and stood it, and then I scrambled to my feet, and walked over, and said, "Look here man, what have you been doing here?"

He looked abashed, and I said, "How on earth did you get those boys to know so much of the Bible in eight months' time?"

"I taught them," he answered.

"Well, how did you do it?"

"I had Sunday School every day in the week, and some days I would have two sessions, and when night would come the older fellows who had been working in the fields came in, and wanted to hear about this."

Need I say to you that I awoke to discover a marvelous work of God's grace in that community? I was almost speechless with the joy of it all. To make a long story short, I had the great privilege the following Sunday, after thoroughly investigating and catechizing, and hearing the confession of faith of Jesus, and seeing their faces radiant at the singing of those songs, which were utterly new to them, of taking those Igarotes, men, women and children, to the cold crystal stream, tumbling out of the rocks at the top of the range, and there baptizing forty-four of them, and planting another church.

I want to say to you that it is jolly good fun to preach the Gospel where it has never been preached before, if for no other reason than to feel the tingle of joy that surges all through you, and the consciousness that you have planted one more beacon-light in the world!

Oh, I went down the trail that day singing to the top of my voice, "His loving kindness, O how free!" and the mountains over yonder would echo back, "O how free!" "His loving kindness, O how good!"—"O how good!"

I got a letter from that country eight years afterwards, and am going to read a portion of it. It was written by a Filipino brother, not the one I have spoken of, but a man who gave his heart to Jesus Christ about a year before I reached the Philippines. He had the highest salaried position in the government of the United States held by a Filipino, save one, in the province of Luzon. He gave it up to preach the Gospel, and Oh, such a preacher of the Gospel as he is! I know of no preacher of the Gospel on the face of this earth, that I can put my arms around and hug quite so tightly as this brother. He knows God just about as well as a human being can know Him. He is quiet, modest, humble, a deep thinker, his English is almost perfect, and rarely does he make any mistakes in the order of his English; he can use colons and semi-colons, which I cannot use to save me. He knows just when to begin a paragraph, and when to end it, and that is something I do not know. Let me read you a portion of his letter, written several years after my departure, from a mountain province four miles South of my district:

"My dear brother Pace:

"When we arrived in this place this morning, and after an enjoyable swim in the river to wash off the mud we had gathered on the way, I said to myself, 'I shall have time to write to Mr. Pace,' and I took my pen to write.

"We have just come from Sigay, where I held a ten days' institute, and we baptized thirty-five, and very many children.

"You ought to see the contrast between the old Sigay and the new, and to hear the testimonies of the brethren, of how the Gospel got hold of their lives. Surely the Gospel is the power of God that saves men. No more sacrifices of pigs and chickens, no more worship of evil spirits, no more strong drink. [I know of several communions in the United States of America where the churches could not say that.] Only three or four of the old men are any longer practicing the old superstitions, and practically all the people are faithfully following the teachings of Jesus. I thought this might make your heart happy, when you remember the hardships you suffered in climbing up these mountains."

Philippine Trophies

Maybe you think it did not make my heart happy! There was a spontaneous combustion within me, and I could scarcely refrain from shouting on the street as I read that letter.

I shall never forget the first of those forty-four that were baptized. They sat in every posture around the pool, and I preached on the subject of Baptism. I saw a fellow sitting on a ledge of rock three or four feet above where I was sitting, and I said to myself, "If I get you I think I will get all the rest around here, because anybody can see you are the leader of this group,"—a big, stalwart fellow with a perennial grin on his face.

After I had been preaching for twenty or twenty-five minutes, I stopped and said, "Now who is the first one to be baptized?" And bless me, if he didn't jump down, the first one, and I baptized him. He began to preach right off. He didn't have any license to preach, but he did it nevertheless. That is the wonderful thing about the Gospel in a new country. They instinctively *tell it*, and keep on, and that is the way it was in the beginning. We have things mixed in these days, setting aside fellows, and saying, "These are the ones to preach the Gospel. The rest of us will pay the bills and go about our own business." In the beginning, it was the members of the Church that told it, and whenever the members of the Church get their hearts and lives full they cannot keep their mouths shut; Goforth told about certain Koreans who had to move out of a community, because the Christians kept telling about Jesus' glory and loveliness, until they could not stand it, and had to move out of the community or else become one of them. Would that God would put upon the laymen of America the same passion for telling the Story.

This Filipino preacher said, "You have no business to sacrifice pigs and chickens, for one sacrifice was offered for sins forever."

I do not know how many churches and missions we have in that country largely through the preaching of this one man. When we found he *would* preach, we gave him a license to preach, for he preached anyway. The last I heard of this preacher he was in the penitentiary.

Imagine my great sorrow and chagrin when I got a letter from up-country, when I was teaching on the faculty of a seminary, saying, "Ciriaco is arrested." It was about as crushing a blow as I had received all the time I lived there.

Mr. Pace

! groaned, and said, "O God, is it possible that after three or four years of such beautiful testimony this man should fall? What on earth has he done?"

I could scarcely wait for another letter. It came two weeks later, telling me all about it. In that letter I learned that Ciriaco had been, years and years before, a soldier in the Philippine constabulary, and being a hot-headed, adventurous chap, he got into trouble, fled to the mountains, and hid his identity for more than ten years. In the meantime he was converted, and did not hide his light under a bushel, but went out preaching. Someone recognized him, and he was brought before the tribunal and the old charge brought up against him.

We wondered what Ciriaco would do, whether he would lie out of it like so many others. How I praised God, that he stood up and manfully said, "I did it, but I want to bring my fellow townsmen to witness that I have been living a different life the last four or five years. I plead guilty." The Judge gave him half the sentence he gave the other fellows that did the same thing, and recommended to the Governor General a pardon as soon as he thought it wise to give it. A few months afterward, I had the privilege of going to the penitentiary to preach to my fellow Americans at Thanksgiving time. As I passed through the gate and into the yard, I passed by a dormitory. In the prisons there they have dormitories, no cells. The windows are barred, but as I passed by one of those dormitories I noticed forty or fifty Filipino prisoners listening to somebody speaking, and as I passed I saw on the front seat, at the end, my friend Ciriaco. I could have put my hand on the window, and reached him and shaken hands with him, if I had dared; but I grinned, and he grinned, and Oh, such a grin as it was!

I went on to the next building where the Americans had gathered. Five or six had been convicted of murder, and I never appreciated in my life quite so much as then, how a man is shut up to one message, when preaching to murderers whose hearts are tortured day and night with "the worm that dieth not." I remember, as I preached to those murderers, one big fellow sitting back there, with eyes as black as night, and with a look of hatred in his face. I was led to point my finger at him and say, "My dear fellow, if you will come back He will never mention it,—He will never mention it." He understood me, and tears started into his eyes, his great

Philippine Trophies

big frame just shaking; I shall never forget the grasp of his hand that day.

While I was speaking, in came my friend Ciriaco with twelve or fifteen Filipino prisoners and sat down behind the Americans. He had gotten permission to come. I asked the privilege of speaking in the language of the Filipinos for about ten minutes, to give them the gist of what I had been saying in English. When I went back to shake hands, I came to Ciriaco, and said, "Ciriaco, I am very glad to see you, but am sorry to see you here."

He kept on grinning, and said, "Oh, that's all right," and bless me, he quoted Philippians 1: 12, "The things which happened unto me have fallen out rather unto the furtherance of the Gospel." "I am going to stay as long as the government says I can, rejoicing in the privilege of preaching the Gospel. Look how many I have already. They give me lots of privilege, and I am going to stay here." I heard an echo from the Philippian jail coming down through the centuries, and I could have hugged him.

I said, "Ciriaco, you have got it; you are the kind of a fellow we have been wanting to be multiplied over here a hundred thousand-fold."

But Ciriaco is not the only one. There are many others who have caught the vision of our Christ, and our message is to you to-day, that the same Jesus who delivers us Americans, with all our peculiarities of mentality, is able to adapt his truth and his saving grace to them. The miracle of regeneration is the same the world over,—black, white, yellow, or whatever it may be,—this Gospel that we love, that has freed us from the penalty and the power of sin, is the only thing that this world really and vitally needs.

Going across the Pacific Ocean, on one of the biggest steamships on the Pacific, we found there were on board a number of distinguished individuals, among them a millionaire and his wife, and the Captain of one of the battleships of the United States Navy. The Captain was dressed in civilian clothes, a modest, unassuming fellow; but his wife was on board, and that was another matter. I am persuaded that no one on board that ship after three days was in ignorance of the fact that her husband was the Captain of a battleship of the United States. I began to make the acquaintance of my fellow-passengers by sketching them, and she came up

Mr. Pace

and said, "Will you draw my husband's picture?" I told her I would, and he came, all dressed up, and suffered me to draw his picture. (I got seven dollars for it, too.) While I was drawing the picture, in came the elegantly dressed wife of the Captain of one of the battleships of the United States Navy. She said, "What a perfectly talented young man you are,—drawing my husband's picture in this wonderful fashion! You must make barrels and barrels of money! What a perfectly charming vocation yours is! You must be a newspaper man going out to write for the newspapers and magazines"—and on, and on, and on.

When I got a chance to get a word in edgewise, I said, "I am not that, madam. I am a missionary."

"Ohh!!" And then she began, and such a fusilade as I did receive the next few minutes! I am persuaded that nobody ever received such a broadside of projectiles from her husband's battleship as I received. If she didn't tell me what she thought of me! "The idea of a young man so talented as you are, able to make a great name for yourself, and a lot of money,—the idea of your burying yourself in the midst of a good-for-nothing, low-down, degraded people! You can't do anything with people in the tropics anyway; they are naturally immoral. You cannot do anything with them. The idea of wasting your life when you might be doing so much for yourself!!" and on, and on, and on she went.

There wasn't anything I could answer, but, "Just a difference of view-point, madam, just a difference of view-point." But those words have never left me, "Will you bury yourself in the midst of a degraded, low-down, good-for-nothing people, immoral, licentious, drunken, so lacking in worthiness, so lacking in ideals! Will you bury yourself in the midst of a people like that, when you could be doing so much for yourself?"

Those words came back to me many times over in the Philippines, when they would throw stones at our buildings, and cast our name out as evil,—when the work went so slowly at first, and they seemed to be so ungrateful, when they so misunderstood us; and I used to say, "Well, I wonder if it is worth while to bury myself here? I think I could have a pretty good church in the United States, at least a comfortable parish, and enjoy it all. What is the use of my staying here?" And then many a time would come that awful tug downward that nobody knows who hasn't lived

Philippine Trophies

in the midst of pagan surroundings, that intangible, and yet very real power of sin, with all its insidious suggestions,—sin rampant, brazen, unblushing round about you. It gets one—unless,—Oh, unless he is kept by the power of God, he is gone.

I have fallen on my face many a time on the sands of the river trail, or the mountain trails, and groaned, and groaned, and groaned, and God knew what I was groaning about. I almost lost my soul over there, but "this poor man cried and the Lord heard him, and delivered him out of all his distresses," for there I found Jesus as my life, and the life of victory unspeakably sweet and precious. Life can never be the same again since the day He illuminated my eyes to see the vision of His glorious loveliness.

I think about those words, "Will you bury yourself in the midst of a low-down, good-for-nothing people, when you could do so much for yourself?" I think of them to-day, and I thank God for the burial! No one ever yet buried himself for Jesus Christ and His saints, that did not have a resurrection immediately thereafter, a resurrection to new life, a more glorious life than he ever dreamed possible. There is no such thing as Life, in its truest sense, until there is death with Jesus Christ. It pays! It pays!! to bury yourself for Jesus.

AFRICA FROM THE WATCH TOWER

Dr. H. Virginia Blakeslee

GOD is calling in this conference—Oh, how he has called!—for eleventh hour laborers. That great missionary seer, Dr. Samuel Zwemer, has said that the reason so much of the world is still unevangelized to-day is because Christian men and women never had a vision of *a lost world*. I wonder if, in this audience tonight, there are men and women who have not been doing the thing the Lord Jesus Christ wants them to do because they have not had a vision. I wonder if there are those here who should be out there on the firing line, out there where the battle is fierce and the fighting is strong, where men and women are trying to bear the burdens of ten men and ten women, where they are falling for lack of help.

Yesterday, as I was speaking over at the Inn, a woman physician told me of a friend who came home from missionary work in China a few years ago. She was a physician; her husband died during their furlough, and she had something of a struggle to know whether she should go back to China. Finally she decided to take her children and go back to that land, and those people whom she loved and who so needed her. But before she went, remembering the great need and how she had been bearing burdens that were too heavy, she went from medical college to medical college and told of the awful need. And not a single physician in any of those colleges volunteered to go with her. Then as with heavy heart she faced the return to those problems and burdens, she thought "Well, a nurse would help greatly." So she went to the hospitals, and wherever she could find a door she entered and made known the need. Not a single nurse volunteered. And that Christian woman sailed back to China with her children to face the needs alone.

In our mission study group the other morning Mr. and Mrs. Neipp, who brought us a little message from their field of work in Africa, told of one woman over there whose furlough is very much overdue. The Board has ordered her

---

A missionary message on the call of Africa and the world given on the closing Saturday evening at Princeton.

Africa from the Watch Tower

home, and she has written back and said, "I cannot go home and leave these people without any shepherd. I am going to stay until I get some help." Mr. Neipp has just had a letter saying that that woman, because of her run-down condition has been attacked with African fever, and her life is despaired of.

A man from another field, another day, not knowing anything of these previous accounts, had been in touch with Mr. Bailey, working under the South Africa General Mission, and told how they had been begging him to come home, and he has been refusing, saying, "I cannot come until one young man at least comes out to hold the fort."

Just the other day I received a letter from Dr. Henderson, of British East Africa. He and his wife have charge of two heart-trying stations about fourteen miles apart, and he is going back and forth, bearing burdens enough for four men, and his life is simply ebbing away. His furlough is three years over-due, and he is a man that has had twenty-five years' experience in Africa. He knows the language, he knows the people, he knows the diseases, he knows that country and that people as no other man in British East Africa knows it, and if that man has to lay down his life there for the lack of help, there isn't one man in this United States or any other part of this world who is qualified to go out and take Dr. Henderson's place.

If it is true that there are men and women in this very audience who have never done the thing that He wanted you to do because you never had the vision, will you climb with me to the watch-tower this evening hour, and look with me on the harvest that is white to the reaping?

Shall we look out across the waters to Japan, that land whose material awakening has been one of the marvels of the present day,—that land which with all her intellectual and material awakening is not Christian? The doors are open.

If you look with me into the heart of China, you will see there vast regions with fifty millions of people that no missionary society is touching, and which, under the present program, no missionary society is planning to touch. And most of the doors in that section are open.

Will you look with me into the heart of South America, that wonderful land that my heart just yearns for, with her fifty million people, and but a small handful of soldiers of the Cross? In February, 1916, at the Panama Conference,

Dr. Blakeslee

representatives from every republic in Latin America told of the open doors and the unparalleled opportunity.

Will you look with me into the heart of Korea, and India, where whole villages are turning aside from their idols, and from the old religions, and are asking for Christian teachers?

Will you look with me to those Bible lands that have been so recently released from Turkish tyranny and allowed religious freedom; and the land is open from Dan to Beersheba for the preaching of the Christ whose feet trod the streets of Jerusalem?

Then there is Africa, gigantic, awful, treacherous; but pathetic, fascinating, and alluring, she waits there. That land that makes every true soldier of the cross of the Lord Jesus Christ, once he has seen her, bow his head and his heart with that great soul who bowed on the banks of the Congo, by that flickering candle, as the light of his life flickered out, and prayed for God's richest blessing on the men and women who helped to heal the world's awful sore; a land that puts an ache in your heart and a sob in your throat that never can be relieved until the Balm of Gilead has been applied to every last waiting tribe; a land that makes you sorry you have not a thousand lives to live, and could lay every one of them at the feet of the Lord Jesus Christ to live out in those untouched tribes.

There she stands, and there she waits, and as we stand in the watch-tower together to-night, and look out into the depths of that land, we cry, "What of the night, watchman, what of the night?" "Well, the morning cometh out there, the morning cometh. But Oh, the darkness, also." I speak of this land because it is the land I am familiar with, but what I say of Africa can be said of all these other lands we are looking upon to-night.

I am thinking of that ridge just over to the right of Kinyona station, in the heart of the Kikuyu tribe in British East Africa, and of the day when suddenly, outside our house, I heard a raging, mob-like noise. We went out to see what was going on, and they were calling to us, and beckoning to us to come out. We stepped outside the little cabin door, elbowed our way through the crowd to where the center of excitement seemed to be, and saw in the midst a man. He had his yard of unbleached American muslin, soaked in castor oil and red clay, thrown around his shoulders, but his face was ashen (for they do change color over there when

Africa from the Watch Tower

they have excruciating pain). The blood was running down his side; his collar-bone had been severed and one piece was projecting one way, and the other the other way. They were talking excitedly, and we thought the life of the man was soon to go out.

They told us that a man on their ridge had been working for a settler, and some of that settler's sheep had disappeared when the man finished his work. It was reported to the government officials, who had sent a native as a government messenger to find out who had stolen those sheep. He went to the man's village, and as he approached the village (knowing what he was after), they gave the African war cry, that echoes from hill to hill. All the members of that clan shot out with their arrows, spears and swords, and began to cut right and left. It was a frenzied mob, in its hatred and savagery, and full of all the characteristics of heathenism.

They brought him up to the house that day and asked us to fix him up. The leaders who participated in that uprising were taken to the court and put in chain gangs for six months or a year. In the meantime, the people of that hill, a few of them, had asked that we send a Christian teacher over there to teach them to read and write.

So we sent Mucai, that young native Kikuyu warrior who had lived for the fun he could have, dressed in his castor oil and red clay, with dancing and immorality of all sorts and description, in all of its hideousness over in that tribe. He had lived for that, but when his mother died, and the Christian boys went out to bury her, they persuaded him to come to the village school. He heard the story of the Cross of Calvary, and he received Christ as his own Saviour. If you should come to the chapel some Sabbath morning, as the missionary stands up to tell about the Cross of Christ, that story to Mucai is so wonderful, you will see the tear drops roll down his cheek; and if he heard the story every day in the week, you would see his head resting upon his knee, his whole frame shaking with emotion. It is so wonderful to Mucai that the Lord Jesus Christ should leave his eternal throne in the Glory-land and come to the Cross of Calvary for *him*.

After Mucai had been in the school a considerable time, and had learned to read and write, he was sent out to the hillside to take charge of that school. He went out on the

Dr. Blakeslee

hillside and began to tell the wonderful Story there day after day along with their lessons. When those boys were released from the chain gang and came back, they went into that school, and there Mucai showed them what a man or a woman had to do to receive eternal life. They believed on the Lord Jesus Christ, He changed those wild savage hearts and made new creatures of them. Just the other day I received a letter from the station which said that of the natives in their class of catechumens the largest percent. are from that ridge and that school.

The light has come to that ridge, the morning is there. But Oh, my friends, I am thinking of the ridge upon ridge, and ridge upon ridge in that Dark Continent where there is not a single Mucai to tell them about the Lord Jesus Christ. And I am thinking of the lives in this very audience, out of which, if they fall into the ground as a corn of wheat and die, there would spring forth abundant fruit. Some of you would go over there before another Conference at Princeton, equipped, prepared and anointed by the Lord, to bring the light of the Gospel of the Lord Jesus Christ to some of those ridges.

It may be, as we are on the watch tower to-night, thinking of these things, and these lands, and these people, that some are saying, as I suppose hundreds have said to me, and to other missionaries, "Oh, I wish I had had this vision when I was young. I wish I had had a vision of these needs before I became entangled with things which bound me hand and foot, making it utterly impossible for me to ever go. I wish I had known about these things. I wish I could go." Many men and women who are bound by physical weakness say, "I wish I could go." My friends, there is a glad word for you to-night. You have been hearing in this conference something about intercession,—intercessory prayer, and prayer warriors, and you have been saying, "I would like to be a prayer warrior, but it costs so much." It costs more to be a prayer warrior than it does to go to the field. I know it, and have seen it proved in this conference. The other evening a lady made her way over to the prayer room, a woman whom all her friends think has lived the surrendered life for years; a woman of faith, and prayer, and fruit-bearing. She thought there was nothing in her life that she would not give to the Lord Jesus Christ, that she was utterly surrendered. She went into that prayer room on one of those nights when the power

Africa from the Watch Tower

of the living God was manifest over there, and He searched and cut deep. The Lord Jesus Christ asked her to lay on his altar one of the dearest, most sacred treasures of her life, and she was surprised when she saw herself begin to quail under it. She prayed all night, and struggled all night, and finally, by the grace of God she laid this sacred, precious treasure of hers right over into the hands of the Lord Jesus, and the power of the living God has come into her life, and as she prays she looks into the face of the Lord Jesus and speaks face to face with him. As she prays her God answers, and she knows things have been done, and as she prays now, it seems she is able to remove mountains of difficulty in those hard heathen lands.

Yes, it costs; but when we think of the Lord Jesus Christ and what he has done for you and for me,—how he has saved us from sin! Did you ever have a picture of sin? Someone said to me the other day, "I wish we could understand what sin is, and see sin, and what the Lord Jesus Christ has really saved us from." I saw a picture of sin in Africa one day. I was riding down one of the roads towards a village, with the Bread of Life in my hand. As I made my way into some of the villages far away from the mission station, where white people scarcely ever were, the people scattered in all directions, because they were afraid. But this one village I made my way into, among the rubber trees in a tiny little forest, where there were grass huts and grain huts in a semi-circle. I was looking for people, and was about to turn away, thinking they had all gone, when suddenly I discovered a form lying in the middle of the village with his face upturned to the sun. He was a boy about twelve years of age. As I made my way over to him I saw his hair was all matted, and knew that meant that he had been sick for many days; for to shave or cut the hair of a sick person in my tribe brings devils, and a sheep must be killed for purifying; no one cuts the hair of a sick person because of the fear of devils.

As I drew near this boy he looked up into my face with large brown eyes full of pathos, and there were lines of suffering in his face. I saw that he was clothed in what had been a yard of unbleached American muslin, ragged and torn, hardly enough threads holding together to keep it over his shoulders. It was black and filthy, and covered with dried pus, and he had a great, awful ulcer from his

Dr. Blakeslee

hip down below his knee; the muscles were all eaten away, and I could see the bone, and pus all around the remaining muscles, oozing out and running down on the ground. The only thing he had to occupy himself with that day, and all the days and the nights, was a little bunch of leaves he held in his hands, which he kept going from one side to the other to keep the flies away.

I knew that disease, and there is not a living soul in the world that knows a cure for it, not a single ointment known that will heal that disease. There wasn't a soul to bind up the wound, to wash it or help him to get out of the bright sun away from the flies, into the shade of a tree. He was utterly helpless.

Every time I think of that picture I think of that sixth verse in the first chapter of Isaiah, "From the sole of the foot, even unto the head, there is no soundness in it; but wounds, and bruises, and putrifying sores: they have not been closed, neither bound up, neither mollified with ointment'.' As I think of that poor boy, I have a picture of just what I looked like when the Lord Jesus Christ found me; and when he saw me in that condition, and when he saw you in that condition, do you know he did not do what the men and women are doing as they are asked to look on the harvest fields and told of the sin, the ignorance and filthiness, and need over there; he did not shed a few tears and then go away and say, "I am sorry, I wish someone would help," go away and allow the vision to fade. Do you know, it cost him something when he saw me in that condition? Do you know, as he found me there, nothing but a great eternal love would ever have induced him to leave that place of Glory and come down to the sight of putrifying sores, and odors, and filthiness that he found me in. But he stooped down, he had the ointment that could heal, he poured in the ointment, the Balm of Gilead, and closed up my wounds, and bound up my sores, he washed me, and made me every whit whole, and perfectly white. He clothed me in his robe of righteousness, and with his garments of salvation; he lifted me up, and adopted me into his family, and made me a joint heir with himself to all the possessions of God.

I cannot think of being unwilling to do a single thing the Lord Jesus Christ asks me. Can you? No matter what it costs. Can you? It may cost some of you to obey him and do the thing that he is asking you to do; he may cut deep.

Africa from the Watch Tower

It may cost you terrific suffering, to be an intercessory warrior. Are you willing to do it for his sake?

You have been told of the Christian business man who a few weeks ago caught a vision of the mission field as he sat in a service, and the Holy Ghost brought the needs before him, and it cost him an automobile. The other day I was visiting an old man and an old woman, saints of God, who love their Lord, and have never ceased to work that his name might be proclaimed to every last waiting man and woman. They had saved through the years seventy-five dollars, putting aside a nickle or dime or quarter when they could, so they might have a little vacation. Just as they were making their plans for this trip, the mail man came, and the letter which he left presented a need in Korea. The need was very great and pressing, and it would take just seventy-five dollars to meet it. That dear old saint of God read the letter, and then handed it to his wife and she read it, and laid it down in his lap. And he said, "Well?" She said, "Well, I think we can stay home this year, can't we?"

He was only waiting for that word, and he tripped up the stairs like a man of twenty-one and wrote out a check, and with shining, glistening faces they told me that was the happiest vacation they had ever had. It cost.

It may mean to some of you that you will have to support a missionary in every land in the world. He might ask you to do it. Oh, "Whatsoever he saith unto you, do it." Be sure you do not miss the blessing and reward, and joy unspeakable and full of glory, that comes to the men and women who obey him.

As I am standing in the watch-tower to-night, my heart going way out across the waters, I am thinking of that last charge that I received before I left Africa and set my face toward America. It was a native Christian who gave me that charge, Kihugu a Kikuyu man of about forty-five years of age. He had gone into the little schoolhouse in charge of Mucai, there on the hillside, and as he wandered into that village schoolhouse with just his red blanket thrown around his shoulder, tied over the left shoulder with a string made from the bark of a vine, he wondered if, at his age, he could go there morning after morning and learn to read and write. He worked away with the letters and syllables, until he was able to put two of them together and say a word. As they sat in that village school, Mucai explained to them the plan

Dr. Blakeslee

of salvation, for over in Africa, education and religion go hand in hand.

Kihugu heard for the first time about the village of God, where there was no sickness, no tears, and no sorrow, and no sighing. He heard that the streets of that village were paved with pure gold, and he said, "Why, we have never heard of a village like that. The only thing we know to believe is that our spirits leave the body and go out to rove around in the bushes among the animals, and come back to the village and bring curses. Our fathers' and mothers' spirits come back to our village, and the witch doctor tells us to kill a sheep or goat and put the meat under a tree, and get some sugar cane and beat it and make some beer, and take it out to the forest so the spirits of the dead can come and feed on it and be appeased, and remove the curse. We have never heard that there was a village like that.",

He was charmed by the description of that wonderful village of God, and said in his heart, as he listened morning after morning, "If there is a village like that I would like to live in that village." He heard about a path leading up to the village, and that the Lord Jesus Christ was the path, and he said in child-like simplicity, "I would like to know the Lord Jesus Christ."

You know what happens to the man or woman who wants to know the Lord Jesus Christ just like a little child, how He stretches out his wounded, pierced hand and takes them into the path that leads to the eternal city. That is what he did for Kihugu. He touched his life, and all the superstition, and darkness, and fear, and bondage that had bound him those many years, fell away, and he became a new creature in Christ Jesus, and oh, what an inspiration that man was to those of us who knew him.

We were living forty-five miles from food supplies of any kind, and there were narrow trails leading to our station, wide enough for a man or a mule to pass in single file. All the supplies had to be carried on the backs of natives those forty-five miles. Sometimes when the rains were on, and the paths were impassable, the food supplies would give out. Then we had to go from school to school and ask for natives who would volunteer to go and bring us food supplies.

They would say, "Bibi, haven't you ever traveled over these plains in the rainy season, and don't you know how the water is so deep that as you ride through on a mule it

Africa from the Watch Tower

splashes over your back? And don't you know how cold the winds are out there, for there are no trees to break the wind, and the blankets are thin, and the rain soaks us, and our hands and feet become stiff with cold?"

I knew it was true, and then I would go to the next school, and they would say, "Bibi, haven't you ever traveled through that forest yourself, and know how the mud is so deep it comes up to a man's knees, and he has to travel for hours and hours?" "Yes, I know it is true," I would answer, "but the food is gone, and we must have supplies." "Well, Bibi, if you will just wait until the sun shines we will all go out and bring a sixty pound load, but Bibi, you cannot expect us to go through the rains."

Then in distress, we always wended our way over to Kihugu's village, and as I would tell him of the trouble we were in, he would make his way to his grass hut, come out with his cow-hide strap that they use to carry their loads, making a rope of it to put across his forehead; and taking a little bucket of food that would last four days, he would say, "Why should we not help the people who have come across the seas to tell us about the path that leads up to the village where there is no sickness, and no death?"

Kihugu would make his way two days' journey through the mud up to his knees, and over the plains where the water was deep, never stopping until he had traveled two days out and two days back and dropped his load at our door. I wonder if we know something about that kind of victory in our own lives over here, that kind of victory that makes us willing to do the unpleasant things that no one else is willing to do?

There came a day when they came from Kihugu's village to tell us that he wanted some medicine. When we found that he had been sick for many days, we said, "Go back and tell Kihugu we will come out to see him as soon as we have finished our work." We took the little stretcher from the grass hospital (two poles we had cut from a nearby forest, to which we had tacked a red blanket), and made our way to Kihugu's village. We found his wife pounding corn, and said, "Is Kihugu very sick?" "Oh yes, Bibi, he is very sick." "What has he been eating?" "Oh, he has not been eating, he cannot eat." "He cannot eat?" "You know, Bibi, when a man cannot eat, and cannot talk, he will die." And so she had just left him in his hut.

Dr. Blakeslee

I made my way to Kihugu's hut and peered through that low door. There were some dying embers in the middle of the mud floor, and I called to him. He replied in a weak voice, and I said, "Kihugu, could you come to the outside and sit in the sunlight where I can see you?" He tottered out through the low grass door, and almost fell in a heap at my feet. I saw that his throat was swollen with a bad attack of quinzy. I said, "Would you like to come to the mission station and stay in the hospital where I can take care of you every hour or so?" "Yes, Bibi, but the mission station is far away and I cannot walk." "Oh, but we have brought the stretcher, and will ask the school-boys to carry you up."

We carried him up and took care of him day after day, until his throat was ready to lance. I lanced it, and he seemed to be getting along very well. Then there came a morning when I had to make my way out to that little grass dispensary and say goodbye to those native patients of mine. Kihugu was well enough to sit in the sunlight outside the house. His wife had brought his day's supply of food. I said to her, "Goodbye, Wanjiru."

"Why, Bibi, where are you going?"

"I have to go back to America."

"But you are not going until Kihugu is well are you?"

"Well, Wanjiru, he is almost better, and the other missionaries are here, and they will take care of him until he gets well."

"Oh, Bibi," she said, "you are cruel to go away and leave Kihugu before he is well."

She began to rebuke me severely. But Kihugu looked up and said, "Wanjiru, don't you think that Bibi wants to go back to her land? Don't you think she wants to go back and see her father and mother, and sisters and brothers?"

Then he looked up into my face in his manly way and said, "Bibi, you go back to your land and greet your father and mother, and greet your brothers and sisters, and greet all your friends, but (Oh, I can hear him say it now) but Bibi, tell them to let you come back and tell the other people about the words of God, those wonderful words of God that tell about that path of life eternal that leads up to the village where there is no death, and no sorrow, and no sighing."

I had to leave that day, and a few months after I reached

Africa from the Watch Tower

America there came a letter with this word: "I am sorry to have to tell you, but you made us promise to tell you about the hard things that happen, as well as the good things. Shortly after you left, Kihugu went back to his village, and we thought he was well. Then we had to bring him back. We took the best care of him that we knew how to, but one day he left us. He went out triumphantly. If you could have seen the peace that passeth all understanding that filled and thrilled his heart as he passed out and up!" I am glad to-night that Kihugu is in the Glory land, and that he will stand through the ages and eternities, to prove to the principalities and powers what it is possible for the Lord Jesus Christ to do through His abundant grace and marvelous power and love.

As I stand in the watch-tower, many times that call comes ringing to my heart, "Bibi, tell them to let you come back and tell the other Kikuyu people about the Word of God." Then it seems to me, as he looks from the Glory of that land, looks down on the millions of brothers and sisters without a single provision for them to know about that Christ, that One who can change and transform, and lead up to the glorious city, it seems to me he is saying to me: "Bibi, those men and women in America, clinging to their sons and daughters, tell them to let them go; and all those men and women that are clinging to ambitions, and plans, and purposes, and things that are preventing them from going, Bibi, tell them to let them go; and those men and women that are clinging to their dollars, and their possessions, and their things, and are not willing to invest them in men and women that shall go out and show the men and women, those seventy millions, the path that leads up to the city of eternal glory, Bibi, tell them to *let them go.*"

But far more than the appeal of Kihugu to-night, I hear the voice of God. I am thinking of that place just to the north of where Kihugu lived, and of that time when He bowed his head, your Lord and mine, and said, "It is finished." What was finished? The redemption price of the world was paid. I am thinking how he went down to the lowest depths of hell, and led captivity captive, of how he rose, and sent out that victorious message, "I am he that liveth, and was dead, and behold I am alive forever more, and have the keys of hell and of death. All power is given unto me in heaven and in earth. Go ye, and make disciples

Dr. Blakeslee

of all nations, teaching them to observe all things, whatsover I have commanded you. And lo, I am with you."

"Master," some of you are saying to-night, "I want to go, but there are so many diff.culties, so many doors before me that won't open, and I cannot get through." "All power is given unto me, and I have the keys."

"But the way is so lonely, and I have so many friends, and it is so hard to leave my mother, and my father, and my brothers and sisters and all my friends." "Lo, I am with you. And I can be more than mother, or brother, or wife, or husband, or sister, or any earthly friend."

"But it is a dangerous way, and I am so afraid." "All power is given unto me. And lo, I am with you."

The day is nearly over, the harvest is almost ended, the summer is almost gone. I am thinking how soon, it may be this very night, you and I shall step into the presence and see the face of our lovely Lord, that face that was so marred more than the visage of any man, not by the thorns, and not by the sword, but by your sins and mine, and the sorrows of them. Can you mar His face to-night by being disobedient to him in a single thing he should tell you to do?

He is calling to-night for eleventh hour laborers. Will you go?

MISSIONS' WAR CHALLENGE

Mrs. Alice E. McClure

WE Christians in America have such an opportunity now as we have never had in all the world before. I think it would not be wresting Scripture if we should change that passage in Esther which reads, "Who knoweth whether thou art come to the kingdom for such a time as this?" to this, "Who knoweth if *we* are come to the kingdom for this time. We *know* that we are come to the kingdom for this time." And may we lay a bit of emphasis upon the individual, and the American, "*Thou* art come to the kingdom for this time." For the great task that God has given us, to carry the news of Jesus Christ to the ends of the earth, is placed upon the young men and the young women of America.

A French Lieutenant was to speak in one of our Western towns, and I expected to see a beardless youth, like our lieutenants. When he came he was a man perhaps fifty or sixty years of age, and then I remembered that the young men of France were dead. A friend of mine who returned from France told me as they approached Verdun they saw a number of white crosses in a large plain. As they came a little nearer to Verdun they saw a large mound, and upon it a large cross, bearing the words, "One hundred men lie buried here." As they drew nearer to Verdun, they found a very large mound, and upon it a large cross was placed, on which was written, "Ten thousand men lie buried here." The young men of France are dead, and the young men of Britain are dead.

This same Lieutenant told us, and it is true, we know, although these last terrific assaults may change the estimate somewhat, that probably less than two per cent of our men who are sent to bear arms will be killed. That does not, of course, include those who will be wounded, and perhaps incapacitated for service of any kind when they return. But probably 98 per cent. of our young men will return. We thank God for that. We in America will have the young men and

---

This missionary message was given Friday evening at Cedar Lake and in briefer form at Princeton on Friday evening.

Mrs. McClure

the young women. And we will have the trained men and the trained women who can undertake this great task that must be undertaken.

The thought may come to us, "Why press this missionary program just now at this time of crisis in our nation? Let us do this other task first, and then turn our attention to the other great task that we realize is necessary." I need only quote President Wilson, who is more interested in the war, perhaps, than any of us. In reply to a letter from a personal friend of mine, he said that it seemed to him that it would be most disastrous if we should for one moment take away any of the emphasis that we had been placing upon foreign missions; that he believed that that battle line out there was most important.

The sympathy that has been aroused by the war I believe is not sentimental; I believe it is something that is within every one of us, and God has aroused it. But if we would truly let that sympathy outflow, it must go out to the ends of the earth,—not simply to the wounded soldier, but to those who are suffering in non-Christian lands, whose needs are just as great, yea very much greater than the needs of our soldiers in France; for the needs in non-Christian lands are not being supplied at all. We are startled when we realize that five million men were killed in the first two years of the war; but are we startled when we realize that *every year* in India five million people die through diseases that are preventable? Now if our sympathy is more than just sentimental twaddle, we will take to the suffering world that sympathy, that life, that will bind up and heal.

So we need to consider today the whole need of the whole world, and the pressure that it ought to bring upon us, as intelligently co-operating with God in hastening the coming of Christ himself. He is the Prince of Peace, and shall bring in the true peace towards which we are all looking.

Let us consider for a moment the crucial time, and its special call to us. I remember hearing a student pray about the "new age" that was to come, and as we talked it over afterwards, they admitted that the new age was already here. It is a time when space is being annihilated. The world is near and the whole world is open. The countries that are supposed to be closed, Tibet, Natal, and parts of Africa, no doubt before this war is over will also be wide open, so that there will not be a single place on the face of the

Missions' War Challenge

earth where we cannot freely take the Gospel of Christ. When the call went out at the beginning of this war for the Mohammedans to rise up, the Mohammedans of India refused. Mecca, the holy city, has been photographed, and the pictures were published in the Geographical Magazine, a thing that would not have been possible ten years ago. The power of Mohammedanism is broken, and the whole world, when the war is over, will undoubtedly be accessible.

We have an open world. And we have a world that is in political upheaval, a world in chaos. We cannot say anything else about it. We missionaries have been trying to get the people of the United States to realize that the far East has been in political upheaval. A few years ago we were studying "Students of Asia." When Mr. Sherwood Eddy wrote that book China was a republic; when we began to study it in February (it was written in the fall), China had become a monarchy. Two weeks later she was again a republic. Who can say what Russia is to-day? We do not know. In my own city in India we have had riots. In 1906 seditions aroused the people and we had to get the troops out to quell the uprising. India is in upheaval, and has been for years. Now we are feeling the convulsions of Europe, and feel them drawing nearer to ourselves here in the United States. It is a chaotic world, a world in upheaval, as well as a world running with rivers of blood and sorrow.

Not only is there this political upheaval, but there is intellectual upheaval. We have recognized that also in the Far East. The intellects of men are being turned upside down, so that the intellectual premises they held ten years ago they have had to let go. A few years ago in China the "literati" were absolutely impregnable. It was like butting your head against a stone wall to try to touch them. But five years ago when Dr. Mott and Sherwood Eddy made their trip around the world, 18,000 of the literati of China signed a card declaring their intention to study the Life of Christ. And of the 18,000, eight thousand accepted the Lord Jesus Christ as their Saviour. Then came the war, and all that war means and has meant in the stopping of missionary operations in China. I met a Moslem student in the University of Ohio. He came there ostensibly to get his M. A. degree, but he told me he came over to study the religion of Christ. And he is going back a Moslem, *because he said*

Mrs. McClure

the people of America did not live their religion. There is an open mind, there is spiritual upheaval, and there is spiritual hunger.

The spiritual hunger of our students in North America is tremendous; but ah, it is as nothing in comparison with the spiritual hunger in non-Christian lands!

In Cashmere there is a fire that has burned for many years. We Americans would say it is gas, and we would investigate and find some gas wells. But the poor deluded Indian people have built a golden umbrella over it, and multitudes go up every year to worship. An old woman was going up one day, throwing herself headlong, her whole body on the road, then drawing herself up and throwing herself again. Her arms were bleeding, her knees, and she was in a pitiable condition. A Canadian missionary said, "Mother, why are you doing this?" Here is her reply: "I want to see Him! I want to see Him!"

What is true in India, is true in all the other nations of the earth. There is a longing in the heart to see Christ, a great spiritual hunger, and a great spiritual upheaval.

This war has added to the sorrow and the suffering in all our non-Christian lands. Ten years ago one woman in six was a widow in India. Today one woman in five is a widow.

In one of our Student Conferences in Niagara a year ago, a young Canadian Secretary stood up and told this incident: His brother had been an unbeliever when he went to France. He went early in the war with the first Canadian troops. A few weeks after he arrived in France he met a Y. M. C. A. Secretary, and this Secretary was interested in him, and led him to accept the Lord Jesus Christ as his Saviour. How the heart of the mother rejoiced that her son had found Christ! It was only a few weeks later when the news came of that terrific attack that was made early in the war. The Canadians and Americans are alike in one thing,—we are a bit reckless. The Canadians rushed in in those days without much thought. As they rushed into the attack and realized their danger, they looked back to see if anyone was following them, and on the first glance saw no one. They rushed on. To go back was death, to go on was death, and they rushed on. Again they looked back, and who do you suppose were following? The Hindu troops! On they rushed, and they fell together. In those early days, of a thousand men who would go in,

Missions' War Challenge

often less than two hundred would return. Mr. George Innes tells of an officer he met on a ship on the Mediterranean who was one of eleven men who returned, of one thousand who had gone in. He did not talk very much about the attack and the slaughter. He said that it was a miracle that he escaped.

The young Canadian of whom his brother told did not escape. He was killed. And his brother stood up there as straight as an arrow, and told what had happened when his mother got the word. She did not weep, although she felt real sorrow; she praised God for the Y. M. C. A. and for the Secretary who had brought her son to the Lord Jesus Christ, for she had hope of being with him in eternity.

And when I heard that story, I thought of the little card that King George sends back to every Hindu home whose son or brother is killed; the little card would enter a Hindu home, and they, unable to read, must rush about to find a letter-reader. Here is news from the boy! They rush to the reader, eager to find out what the news might be. And they come back with slow footsteps, because the letter-reader has told them that this has been written on the card, of their boy: "Killed in action, April 12th." Then there is sorrow that is without hope, and none of you here who have not been in non-Christian lands, know what it is, how they beat their breasts and tear their hair out by the handfuls, and weep, and weep, and weep, until I have met women who have been blind from their weeping, and from the intensity of their sorrow. For they have no hope, no hope! There is a spiritual hunger in the world to-day that can be satisfied only in the Lord Jesus Christ.

I was one of three missionaries among 900,000 people in our district. We were visiting a city of 10,000, the first time a white woman had ever visited it. As we were entering the city, we passed a woman who was sitting on the high city wall, and I said to the Bible woman, " I would like to find the home of that woman." We found the gate, and wended our way back, and entered the home where this woman had been sitting on the wall at the foot of the courtyard. The women began to pour in over the roof and from three sides. I said, "Won't you call that woman down from the wall?"

"Oh no," they said, "you won't want to talk with her."

"Yes," I said, "I want to talk with her."

Mrs. McClure

"But if you really knew why she is cursed of God, you would not want to talk with her."

"Please, I should like to talk with her. Won't you call her?"

She came and sat down in front of me, and as she looked into my face I saw that she was blind. Her hair was thin and her face wrinkled. They told me she was forty-five or fifty years old. As a very young woman she had married, and had children, which gave her great joy. Then her husband died. Cursed of God, of course she was! Her husband died, and I knew what had happened: She had been thrown into a dark room, food and drink kept from her in the hottest weather, three or four days and nights, stripped of all that she valued, and become the slave of the house,—worse than the slave of the house. She had gone on many weary pilgrimages, mile after mile, striving to be expiated from this sin of which she herself was unconscious.

Then they said, "She is doubly cursed of God," because her children died; all her sons died. And I knew what had happened each time, how she had beaten her breast and torn her hair, and how she had wailed, and wailed, and wailed, a piercing wail which we never hear in this country. She had wept until she was blind. Then I noticed what I had not noticed before. She could not understand a single thing I said. She was imbecile. I was too late, too late!

Men and women, I shall never forget the passion of sorrow that swept over me as I realized that I could bring no hope, no soothing, no comfort, to that woman. I thought of my own mother at home. She had written to me many times, "Alice, I am trying to be a good missionary mother, and we will have eternity together." It had been very difficult for her to let me go, but I realized the hope and the comfort that that hope had brought her. And this woman was without hope.

Then I must frankly say, a great anger possessed me, and I said, "The former generation should have sent someone to tell her the Good News of the One, and the only One who brings hope." I determined right there that I would do everything in my power to bring the glad tidings of Christ Jesus who brings hope to the hopeless, and that when I was at home I would do all in my power to get others to do so, too.

India's sorrow is now increased, oh, so many fold, because

Missions' War Challenge

of the increased number of widows. And their hearts are open. For, let me tell you a secret,—their men are away, a great many of them; they have very much more freedom, and we have much more access.

Let me tell you one more thing. Who was it who took Jerusalem and handed it over to us Christians? It was largely the Hindu troops. Of course under the generalship of General Allenby, who, as he entered the city, descended from his horse and walked in, because he said he could not ride where Christ had walked. And he led Hindu troops. Yes, God has allied the non-Christian world with us in this terrific battle for liberty. They are not fools, and they know that for which they are fighting. But the hunger of the hearts of the women who are behind, to me carries a tremendous appeal, and makes a great pressure upon my heart to get out as quickly as possible, to take to them the One and the One alone who gives hope.

Finally, may I remind you that this is a sacrificial age. A Hindu convert who took every opportunity to proclaim Christ, went up into Tibet, the forbidden land, to preach the Saviour. The men who followed him a little later found out the truth concerning his experience. The Tibetans told him when he began to preach the Lord Jesus Christ that he must stop preaching the Gospel, for it was contrary to government orders. There are missionaries on the borders of Tibet, but none of our missionaries are actually stationed within. He kept on preaching and they came to him and told him if he did not cease they would take his life. He went on preaching, and they carried him bodily to India. He went back, and they said, "Now we will put you to death." They killed and skinned a buffalo, wrapped that buffalo skin tightly around him, leaving only his head exposed, then put him out in the terrific eastern sun, where the buffalo skin would dry out and contract. Four days he lay without food or drink, and four nights he suffered the most terrible agony. Multitudes came to see him, and to hear what he had to say. He continued to tell them of the Lord Jesus Christ who loved them even unto death, and at the very end he prayed that God would forgive those who had put him to death, and died in agony.

A little band, seeing his death, accepted the Lord Jesus Christ, and now another native evangelist, Sunder Singh, comes summer by summer, to meet this little band and tell

Mrs. McClure

others of Jesus Christ, even though it is prohibited. He says he has his orders from a higher government.[1]

The Hindu troops in Europe are living a sacrificial life. It is the spirit of the age. An engineer who went over to France, "W. I. G.," wrote a little poem, published by the *New York Herald,* which took a prize of $250.00; it was one of the eight hundred submitted in the contest. It expresses so clearly the sacrificial spirit of the age that I want to read to you one of the two stanzas:

"Better in one ecstatic day
　To strike a blow for glory and for truth;
With ardent, singing heart to toss away
　In Freedom's holy cause, my eager youth;
Than bear, as weary years pass one by one,
The knowledge of a sacred task undone."

Fathers and mothers, I dare not close without bringing the appeal that young men and women in college have asked me to bring to you. *Let go of your children.* Keep your hands off when they decide their life work. You have thought they are yours. They are not. The government has stepped in and has shown you that your sons are not yours. They are here for a greater purpose than to live in ease with you in a luxurious home; they are here to serve their generation. So let us let go of our children; let us take hands off them, for they have this sacrificial spirit, and will go, being obedient even unto death.

And young people, when you hear the call of God, do not hesitate. It is not an easy way. I would not for one moment have you think that it is an easy way; it is not. But fellowship with Christ, one you love, and one who loves you, in that rugged stony path, will make the path appear even smooth, because you are walking with the one you love. For beyond the call of the world task, or the call of the world's need, is the constraint of the love of Christ, and the longing that his heart may be satisfied.

I said, "Let me walk in the fields;"
　He said, "Nay, walk in the town."
I said, "There are no flowers there;"
　He said, "No flowers, but a crown."

---

[1] Sunder Singh's remarkable story has been published. See page 379.

Missions' War Challenge

I said, "The skies are black,
  There is nothing but noise and din."
He wept as he sent me back,
  "There is more," he said; "there is sin."

I said, "The fogs are thick,
  And clouds are veiling the sun;"
He said, "Yet souls are sick,
  And souls in the dark, undone."

I said, "I shall miss the light,
  And friends will miss me, they say;"
He said, "Choose to-night,
  If I shall miss you, or they."

I pleaded for time to be given;
  He said, "Is it hard to decide?
It will not seem hard in heaven,
  To have followed the steps of your guide."

I cast one look at the fields,
  Then turned my face to the town.
He said, "My child, will you yield?
  Will you leave the flowers for the crown?"

Then into his hand went mine,
  And into my heart came he;
And I walked in a light divine,
  The path I had feared to see.

APOSTOLIC FAITH IN CHINA

Louisa Vaughan

"Wherefore I also, after I heard of your faith in the Lord Jesus Christ, and love unto all the saints . . ." (Eph. 1: 15).

I WANT to ask you a question tonight, and some of you, perhaps, will think it is a rather impertinent question; but I can assure you it is a very important question.

Paul had heard of the faith of these Ephesian Christians, he had heard of the faith of this church that was at Ephesus. Now what I want to ask you is this, "Who has heard of your faith? Who has heard of the faith of the church to which you belong? Has anyone heard of it?"

And I want to add to that question, a second question, because Paul not only speaks of the faith of these Christians in this Church at Ephesus, but he also speaks of their love. He said that he had not only heard of the faith of the Christians at Ephesus, but he had heard of their love to all saints, and the second question I would put to you tonight, is just this, "Who has heard of your love to all the saints?"

Have you ever heard of what occurred in 1900 in the Boxer massacres in China? Have you ever heard of the faith of the Chinese Christians during that time? Have you ever heard of their love? May I just tell you a few items that I am sure will interest you, and I hope and pray that God will use them as his two-edged sword to speak to your heart.

At the beginning of 1900 we had approximately 100,000 Christians in China. During the months of June, July and August of that year 25,000, one-fourth of the entire church, laid down their lives for love of Jesus Christ, because they loved him better than life, because they loved him better than gold, because they loved him better than anything on this earth. How does our love compare to that?

Hundreds of people, since I have been in this land, have said to me, "What kind of Christians do those Chinese people make?" This is the kind: Way out in Manchuria, during the first month of those massacres, there was a young woman. Her home was a heathen home. She was an only daughter,

---

A message given Monday evening at Cedar Lake. See note on page 243.

Apostolic Faith in China

and was the very apple of her parents' eyes. They loved her so that they broke all Chinese etiquette and sent her to school to be educated. Chinese women are not educated as a rule. They do not consider the girls in a Chinese home, but this girl was the only child in the family, and she was loved, and they sent her to school, and the only schools for girls in China, at that time were mission schools.

In that mission school she heard of Jesus, and she accepted him as her Saviour, and gave herself unreservedly to him. At the close of her education she was asked by the missionary in the school where she had been taught, if she would consent to do some teaching for the mission for a year or two, and she gladly said she would. She was sent, in the beginning of the year 1900, to a little village, and had a little primary school in the village, with ten or twelve pupils. The months and days flew by, until June came. Then one day that awful outbreak of passion and murder was poured upon the Christian Church, and her father came to her and said, "The Boxers have your name on their black-list. You are on their death-list. Now if you come with me I can put you in a place of safety, but you must come at once, and you must escape for your life, *now.*" She said, "You must wait a minute; you must give me time to think. I cannot go like that; I must ask my Master, I must pray to Jesus whether he wants me to go or not." So she knelt down and asked her Lord what he wanted her to do. She came back and said, "No father, I cannot go with you to a place of safety. These little girls here are all Christians (they were various ages from nine to twelve); I cannot go with you. I cannot leave these children. If I go away they will be frightened when those men come, and *perhaps they may deny the Lord.*"

He tried to persuade her; he used every argument to induce her to go with him. It was all of no use. She would not go, and she did not go. In but a few short hours those Boxers came and went into that schoolroom, and bound that young lady, and bound each one of those children, and carried them off to the town. They took them up before the great idol that is in all the temples in China, an immense idol made of clay, reaching almost to the ceiling, and they said, "If you bow down and worship this idol, if you burn this stick of incense, if you recant this Jesus-God, we won't injure one hair of your head. If you turn back again and worship your own Chinese gods we will do you no harm."

Miss Vaughan

What did she say? She said, "I will never recant my Jesus. He is my Saviour, and he is the Son of God, and I will never bow down and worship these idols; I will never burn incense." She had scarcely finished her refusal, when one of those men took his sword, and with one sweep of the sword, severed her head from her body. Then they took each one of those children in turn, and they said, "If you recant this Jesus-God, and if you bow down and worship this idol made of clay, we will not hurt you, and you can go home." Each child in turn refused.

My friends, that is love to Jesus. And that was the love of the Chinese Church to her Master, when she gave 25,000, a fourth of the entire Church, to die for him in 1900. That is love.

This love of God that dwells in our hearts, had two sides to it—it operates in our love to God, and then it operates in our love to our fellowmen. It is a two-edged affair, a two-sided thing, and you cannot have love to God without having love for your fellowmen; you cannot have love to God without having a care for the souls of those who are round about you; you cannot have love to God without being concerned about the spiritual condition of your fellow-Christians; you cannot have love to God without being concerned about the souls of your family and your relatives, and those people whom you know, with whom you are acquainted.

I remember one time when I was invited to come to the help of one of our Chinese pastors (I worked in a district where we had fifteen organized churches, and I had the great joy and pleasure of working with those Chinese people, some of whom were the third generation of Christians). Pastor Sun invited me to one of his churches. He had the oversight of three churches. When I arrived at this village, he said "Miss Vaughan, I do not know what is going to happen with this church. The people here seem to dislike each other; the Christians on the west side of the village will never come to church with the Christians on the east side of the village, and when the east side Christians come over and see any of the west side people there, they get up and go out. Now what am I to do with Christians like that?"

"Well," I said, "if I were in your place I would not take any responsibility about the matter; I would ask the Lord to deal with them, and I would ask the Lord to deal with them *very effectively.*"

Apostolic Faith in China

So we knelt down, and asked the Lord to deal with them very effectively. It happened that morning, when I was giving the message (in Chinese), at the close of the message, a woman sitting in the front, whom I had watched throughout the service, and had noticed she was crying, said to me, "O Miss Vaughan, if what you said this morning is true, I am afraid I never can get to heaven." I said, "That is very sad,—what is the matter with you? What was it that I said that made you feel that you could not get to heaven?"

"Oh, just the things you said. I feel that I can never get to heaven; but do you know, it is not altogether my fault, the trouble is with my daughter-in-law."

"That is very sad," I answered, and then she proceeded to tell me all about her daughter-in-law. Now, if what she told me was true about her daughter-in-law, her daughter-in-law was a very impossible proposition. She had a temper, and she had several other things in her disposition that were exceedingly trying. However, I listened until she finished the story, and then I said to her that I was sorry, and that we could see about her daughter-in-law later, but I said, "You know you told me that what I said had so convicted you that you realized that you could not get into heaven in the condition you were in. What is the matter with you?"

"I thought I told you," she said, *"my daughter-in-law."* Then she proceeded to tell me the entire story over again, and I listened with the patience that I had learned in the Orient. You have to learn patience in China. When she finished the second time, I said, "Now you have told me twice. You are not required to tell me again, I could tell you this time. Now tell me what is the matter with *you?*"

By this time she was very angry, and in a very indignant manner she said, "I would like to know what you think is the matter with me?"

"Well," I said, "I do not think about it at all; there is one thing that I see that is very much the matter with you,—you do not love your daughter-in-law."

"Love my daughter-in-law! Love my daughter-in-law!! I would like to know how anybody could love her?"

"I do not find in my New Testament," I answered, "that we have to except her. The Lord does not make any exception in the New Testament about your daughter-in-law. He says, 'This new commandment I give unto you, that ye love

238

Miss Vaughan

one another as I have loved you.'" I talked about this commandment, and insisted that this commandment had to be kept. Finally she began to realize that some of the things I was saying to her really had a meaning, and bursting into tears, she said, "Well, what shall I do? What shall I do?"

"It is very simple," I said, "you will just kneel down here with me, and we will confess this sin to God, and ask him to forgive you your lack of conformity to his standard, which is a sin, and then when we finish that we will do something else."

When we finished that she said, "What else is there?"

"Now," I said, "you have to go to your daughter-in-law and beg her pardon."

If a Zeppelin were floating over our heads and suddenly dropped a bomb amongst us we could not have had a greater explosion. "Beg my daughter-in-law's pardon? Beg my daughter-in-law's pardon! Why, have you lived in China for eight years and do not know China's etiquette any better than that? Why, I am surprised! How could a Chinese mother-in-law beg her daughter-in-law's pardon? Such a thing never was heard of. My neighbors would laugh at me, they would make fun of me, I would be the scorn of the whole village. I could not do that, I could not possibly do that!"

I waited until she quieted down a little bit, and then I said, "My friend, you said you were very much distressed because you could not get into heaven. Do you want to go there?"

"Of course I do."

"Well, if you want to go there you have to begin to observe the etiquette of the Kingdom of Heaven here and now, and let the etiquette of China alone. Now, you can take your choice about this matter. It is not a matter for me to decide at all. I came here to tell you these things; but this is a matter for you to decide what you are going to do."

I stood there and I saw a soul in actual conflict with Satan himself. My friends, have you ever passed through such an experience? As I stood there watching her, I prayed for her, that God would give her the victory through Christ Jesus. Presently she said, "Oh, I will go, on one condition. I will go on one condition. I cannot do this thing of myself, but I will go if you pray for me until I come back."

Apostolic Faith in China

I said, "Go quickly."

It was not long until she came back, and do you know, I did not recognize her when she came in at the door. Oh, my friends, as I look at some of your faces I realize that some such process has to go on in your lives. I did not recognize her as she came back with the very glory of God shining in her face. She threw her arms around my neck, and she said, "Fortunately you came to this village! Fortunately my heavenly Father sent you here. I have lost a thousand tons of a burden since I did that; I have lost a burden that weighed a thousand tons since I obeyed my heavenly Father." The burden of sin is not light, the burden of sin weighs us down, very often, down to the very grave itself, and especially with our polite, camouflage Christians in America,—our sins of omission weigh us down, to the very earth. You are not a bit different from the Christians in China. The same sins are paralyzing you people as paralyzed our Christians over there.

Do you know what happened that night? In the evening meeting the daughter-in-law was there. In the meantime we had prayed for her, and we had prayed for her in faith and love, and before I had spoken ten minutes, she came up and threw herself on the ground and said, "Stop talking, Miss Vaughan, stop talking. I have something to say."

I said, "All right, come along and say it."

She said, "I have to beg your pardon, my pastor," and she got down on her knees and begged the pastor's pardon. Then she said, "I have to beg my father-in-law's and mother-in-law's pardon. I have been a Christian girl, brought up in a Christian home, and I have come into this family, a Christian daughter-in-law, and I have acted like a devil. Now I want to beg your pardon."

Then she turned to me and the rest of the congregation, and she said, "Please forgive me, because I have been at the bottom of the entire quarrel in this church."

Then I saw a scene I have not witnessed since. The people over here began to stand up, and beg the pardon of the people over there, and those folks over there began to beg the pastor's pardon, and to beg the other people's pardon, and so we had a general reconciliation.

The next day those who were not at the meeting, came to the meeting to see what happened, and they began to do the same thing. When sin is put away from amongst the children

Miss Vaughan

of God, then His Spirit has a channel to work in, but oh, this lack of love amongst Christians is one of the most paralyzing things that can take a church and reduce it to the most helpless, and hopeless condition,—and yet they are Christians.

Paul not only says that he had heard of the Ephesian Christians' love, but he also speaks of the faith of those Christians. "Having heard of your faith." What does this faith include? This faith means that you believe that the Lord Jesus Christ is a living, risen, glorified Saviour, with all power in heaven and on earth, and that he has commanded you to be a witness bearer unto God's omnipotent power. In this passage which I have read to-night, it says "That ye may know . . . the exceeding greatness of his power to usward who believe," the same power which he wrought in Christ, when he raised him from the dead. Thousands of people will tell you to-day that the age of miracles is past. Well, it is past because you do not believe,—that is why it is past; it is past because your faith is a farce, that is the reason it is past; it is past because you are not a living witness unto the resurrection life of Jesus Christ in you,—that is the reason it is past. There is no other reason. The Lord is "the same yesterday, to-day and forever," and if he is the same yesterday, to-day and forever, the miracles that he performed all through the ages he can perform to-day, absolutely. He is not dead, he has not gone to sleep, he is still there; he doesn't even require to go to sleep. The same things that he did yesterday he is able to do to-day. In Hebrews the eleventh chapter it tells us that the Christians of that day subdued kingdoms, wrought righteousness, quenched the violence of fire, closed the mouths of lions. What sort of faith was that? I have seen none of it in this country,—I do not hear of it even. Where is it? Who is exercising it? Why is it not being exercised? Why are not the Christians in this land showing forth the power of God in their lives? What is the matter?

It is the sin of unbelief that is the matter. Wherever there is not this faith in the Christian, my friends, it is sin, for "without faith it is impossible to please God." "The just shall live by faith." Without faith, and without this kind of faith, it is impossible to please God. Now if we want to please God we have got to have it. How are we to get this living faith? There is only one process by which we can get it,

Apostolic Faith in China

absolutely only one process. It is by getting down on our knees and confessing these things as sin. That is the way to get it, and that is the only way to get it. "If we walk in the light as he is in the light, we have fellowship one with another, and the blood of Jesus his Son cleanseth us from all sin. If we say that we have no sin, we deceive ourselves, and the truth is not in us; but if we confess our sins, he is faithful and righteousness to forgive us our sins, and to cleanse us from all unrighteousness."

That is the only way to do this thing. Your faith and my faith are not sufficient for these things, and we have to have the faith of Christ. That is the only faith that will subdue kingdoms, work righteousness, close the mouths of lions, quench the violence of fire, faith that will honor our Lord and Master, and will glorify his name.

He wants to give us himself, he wants to come and let his very faith dwell in us, in the personality of the Holy Spirit. And yet we will not get down on our knees and confess that we haven't it, and we will not humble ourselves before God, and be cleansed in his precious blood so he can do it. Then he will answer our prayers, then he will teach us what to pray for, and teach us how to pray, and will teach us the things we are to ask for; then he will give us the things we have asked for. Oh, let us bow our heads, and let us do some confessing to-night!

Prayer

O loving and gracious Father in heaven, forgive me my sins of omission; forgive me my lack of love to thee; forgive me my lack of love to my fellow-men; forgive me my lack of trust and confidence in thee; my evil heart of unbelief. Cleanse me just now in the precious blood; and fill me with thy Holy Spirit, that he may reveal Jesus in me as the Son of God, and give me the faith of Christ. In Jesus' Name. Amen.

TESTING GOD'S METHOD

Louisa Vaughan

IN the spring of 1903 I was appointed by the Mission to take charge of the Bible teaching work for women in fifteen organized native churches, and was invited by a native pastor to take my first class in his church. I traveled by train, and then by wheel-barrow for two days, to get to my destination, a tumble-down hut that you would not keep a dog in. The corner of the room had fallen down, and the stars were plainly visible. There were twenty-five women in that first class, and I wish you could have seen the utter lack of interest, the utter indifference, the lack of intelligence, the deadness of those people. Most of you have seen in a museum idols of wood and stone, and it was just exactly the same as standing before so many idols,—there was just as much intelligence, just as much response to any remarks I might make.

As I asked them their names, one woman said, "My heart is just as hard as this table, and you cannot teach me anything!" and before very long I was convinced that I could do nothing, and I thought, "Ten days to teach these women! Teach them what? Teach them that the Son of God is their Saviour; teach them to go back to their homes and testify that they know Jesus Christ as the Lord of Glory!" Not one of them could read a single character, not one had ever been to school for a second, not one of them cared to know, and when I presented them with copies of the Lord's Prayer, suggesting that they might like to look at it, they said, "Oh no, Chinese women haven't any brains; we couldn't learn anyhow."

With this class I came to the end of myself. I had never in all my life met a problem that I hadn't some means of dealing with, until I saw those twenty-five Chinese women who came to study the Gospel with me, and could not find out any method by which to deal with them. I said to myself,

---

This message and that which follows, "Ding Li Mei—China's Moody," were given in the mission group on China conducted by Miss Vaughan at Cedar Lake. These prayer experiences and others related in the China group, are published in the little book "Answered or Unanswered?" which contains in all twelve of Miss Vaughan's experiences in China. See page 379.

Testing God's Method

"There is no use trying to deal with this proposition. It is a human impossibility. I will just tell them to go home, and pick up my things and go back, and tell the man who sent me what I think of the missionaries wasting their time and everybody else's." Then I thought, "These poor women have traveled from their homes to get something. I had better sit down and think a little while, if there is any possible way to help them."

As I sat there thinking, the blessed Spirit of God spoke to me and asked me this question, "Where is your faith? You came out here as a missionary, as a teacher of faith in God. Where is your faith?" I said, "What has faith to do with this proposition?" God had mercy on me, and upon those women, and said, "Where is your faith in God?" I knew where it was in the Gospels, I knew what it was connected with, I knew my Bible very well; I was equipped all right according to men's notions, and according to my own, but I was not equipped to do that work. As this question kept coming to me, a dozen times or more, at last I could not stand it any longer, went into the tumble down bedroom, got down on my knees, and said, "Lord, what is the meaning of this question that your Spirit is asking me?" I prayed, and the Spirit said to me, "With man it is impossible, but with God all things are possible."

I was still in darkness, and as I continued to pray, I said, "O God, forgive me for my spiritual ignorance and stupidity, and enlighten me." I hadn't any more than said that, when I got such a revelation of the faith, and power, and authority of the Lord Jesus Christ, and of my own helplessness, that the vision has gone with me down through the years since then. He said to me, "Whatsoever ye shall ask in my name, that will I do, that the Father may be glorified in the Son. If ye shall ask anything in my name, *I will do it*" (John 14: 13, 14). I said, "Oh how different, that I am not going to do this work for you, but you are going to work through me. Your mighty power is going to work through my faith. Lord, I am going to trust you to do it absolutely."

I prayed for those twenty-five women, and said, "Lord, forgive them as you have forgiven me; fill them with the blessed Holy Spirit, that they may go back to their homes to witness. I am going to wait until you do just exactly what I ask you to."

I went out and discarded all my literature, and haven't

Miss Vaughan

used anything but the Bible since. I said to the women, "I want to teach you how to pray," and I taught them a very simple prayer, "Heavenly Father, forgive me my sins; cleanse me in the precious blood of Christ, and fill me with thy Holy Spirit. I ask in Jesus' Name. Amen."

Some of those women were so stupid that it was four days before they could intelligently repeat that simple little prayer; some of them learned to say it that afternoon. But I did not see God's working. The day passed, and the next day, and still I did not see God's working. In the evening I was dismissing the women to go home and cook their supper, and said, "Just before we do so, we will kneel and pray." I led in prayer, and then said, "Let us pray this prayer, 'Heavenly Father, forgive me my sins.'" One of those women burst into tears and confessed all her sins from her childhood's days up to that moment, and asked the Lord to forgive her, and thanked the Lord for sending the light into her heart.

I thanked the Lord for sending the light into her heart, and pleaded with him to cleanse the exceeding filthiness in her life. She praised the Holy Ghost for coming in and giving her peace and joy, and when we got up from our knees she threw her arms around me and said, "Oh, the Heavenly Father sent you here just for me, just for me. He sent you here just for me!"

Do you believe it, when I tell you that before three more days had passed all the twenty-five women had the same experience? I could not teach them fast enough when they had Christ revealed in them as the Lord of Glory. I hadn't to tell them that Christ was coming again, for the Holy Spirit revealed it to them, and they went back to their homes and prayed for their sons and daughters-in-law, and multitudes of friends, until the native pastors came and said, "What did you do wth those women? How did you teach those women? We are Chinese and have never known how to teach these women. How did you teach them?" I said, "It is nothing that I did, it is the Lord's doing, and it is marvelous in our eyes."

There is sin, and crime, and vice, and ignorance of every kind on the mission field, and it is only God's Holy Spirit that can convert the soul and enlighten the mind. We have wasted the years on this method and that method, and have left untouched the weapon that God commanded us to use, "Pray ye therefore."

DING LI MEI—CHINA'S MOODY

Louisa Vaughan

DING LI MEI, the evangelist who was a pastor of five Chinese churches under our Mission, had been through the Boxer uprising, receiving three hundred blows to force him to recant. Three hundred blows with a bamboo are supposed to kill a man. They bind the victim for scourging, the back is bared, and one man stands on one side and one on the other. With both their hands they lift up the long rod and bring it down with all their strength, until with each blow it lifts the skin all the way along, leaving red gashes. After one hundred blows they asked if he would recant, and he said no; another hundred, and he still refused; when they finished the third hundred they got no answer out of him, and took him away as dead.

Pastor Ding, some months after my experience with the twenty-five women, wrote, "Miss Vaughan, will you come to my village and help me with some meetings? I am making the first effort for self-support, and am going to step out on faith, and am going to have all the Christians who can, come from my five churches for a conference of four or five days, and we will ask God for a great blessing. We need to have our spiritual life deepened."

I went to that village, and always where God is going to give a blessing, wherever God's Spirit is in power, the spirit of the Devil is there, and there on time, or before time, and we have the fight of faith told about in the sixth chapter of Ephesians. Satan had all his preparations made.

The richest man in that countryside had lived in this village. He had died sometime before, and his funeral was to take place that week, and they had made great plans for that celebration. They had hired one of the finest theatrical troops to come and have plays going all during the week of the funeral. A theatre in China is something everybody wants to go to. They go at dawn, and stay until sunset, and the play goes on all day, and for weeks at a time. They have it in the open, and it is part of their worship. This theatre was free to everybody, paid for by those rich people; and in a country where the people are as poor as in China, you can imagine what a crowd they would have. Thousands of people came

---

See note on page 243.

Miss Vaughan

from twenty miles around, walking, to see the play, and the streets on every side were lined with paper animals, paper carriages and paper money to be burned at the grave of this man. The people were all there to see them, going around like a flock of sheep.

There was our little tent at the end of the village, with a little flag up above it, and a cross on the flag. They thought this was part of the funeral celebration, and we had a great stream of heathen people, women with babies in their arms, and little children, and dogs barking. This great mass of people came in at one end of the tent and poured out of the other, and we never heard a single word of anybody's address. People had come to get a blessing, and at the close of that day there were a lot of angry, cross, irritated men,—and they were the leaders and deacons in those five churches where Ding was Pastor. They went to Pastor Ding and said, "What kind of a fool are you, that you appointed these meetings the same day as this man's funeral?"

Fourteen or fifteen of the men from those churches had means to help him financially, and he was looking to them for help. In despair he came to me and said, "Miss Vaughan, I was looking to these men for help, because I determined to learn something of the faith in Jesus Christ, and was not going to depend on the foreign mission any longer to finance our native Church. But you see it is all finished. These men say they are going home tomorrow at dawn, and are not going to waste their time here. What shall I do? Will you give me some advice?"

This man, who had endured three hundred blows of the scourge for Jesus Christ, was helpless before the onslaught that Satan brought because he was stepping out in faith in Jesus Christ. He expected me to say, "Don't worry about this, I will see about this money somehow, by writing to my friends, and in the meantime, do not worry about this, I will try to help you a little bit to pay the necessary bills here." To make you understand Pastor Ding's distress, he had $7.50 gold for a month's salary, to support himself, and wife and three children, one at boarding school, and it would take well up to a hundred dollars to finance our meetings for four or five days.

I said, "Pastor Ding Li Mei, Satan has made a breach upon us, and we have to hand this matter over to the Lord and ask God to rebuke him, and defeat him, and get to Himself

Ding Li Mei—China's Moody

the victory." There wasn't a word about finances in all my talk, much to Pastor Ding's dismay and grief. I said, "Let us pray about it." He had always prayed about everything, so we knelt down and prayed, and he prayed that God would give me a plan to give him, to deal with this difficulty. I did not see what I had got to do with it, but he asked God to change *my* heart, and make *me* obedient to the Lord. Then it came my time to pray, and very quietly, I handed the whole thing over to the Lord, and said, "Yes Lord, forgive us all, and cleanse us everyone, and rebuke Satan, and defeat him this day, and give us the victory, and show Pastor Ding how you do it."

I got up and sat down and was not burdened about the financial business at all, and began to talk about something else. He waited for an hour, and I thought, "Is the man ever going to go? What is the matter with him? If he does not go soon we won't be able to have our supper and go to the evening meeting." Still he waited, and finally my servant came, my Chinese cook, knocked at the door and put his head in. He was furiously angry—Satan had everybody angry. He put his head in the door and said, "Miss Vaughan, when are you going to get ready to eat? How do you expect me to get the dishes washed and get to the evening meeting, and not have your food by this time?"

"It doesn't make any difference whether I eat or not," I answered. "Go and eat your own."

Then four men came for Pastor Ding, saying, "Why don't you come and eat your food? It is waiting for you."

Pastor Ding did not go. There he sat. Then he got up and stood, and I stood. Finally I broke all the Chinese etiquette, and said, "Pastor Ding, would you eat with me?" He said, "No, thank you." He stood there, and I could not sit down while he was standing, for that was not Chinese etiquette. We stood, and we stood, and we stood, and we did not speak, and half an hour passed. He never said a word, and then his face got as red as a bed of coals, and he went out and slammed the door, and I thought he was going to take the door posts with him. He said to himself when he got outside, "That's what I get for asking a woman anything! What does she know?"

We were to meet at eight o'clock in the little church. The Chinese go home at sundown, afraid of evil spirits in the dark, and we were left, a little group of Christians by our-

Miss Vaughan

selves. Pastor Ding gave out the hymn, prayed, and came to where he was to announce his text. While he was finding it in the Bible, I stood up, and said, "I beg your pardon, Pastor Ding (I had no business to stand up in that company, it was not a woman's place), will you give us five minutes to pray before you preach, only five minutes?"

He said yes, and I turned to the people and said, "Oh, let us get to work at some confession of our sins. We have all fallen short of God's glory. Let us ask him to forgive us and cleanse us and fill us with his Holy Spirit. Pastor Ding said, "That is a good idea, let us kneel down and pray."

As we knelt down, our knees were scarcely on the floor when the Holy Spirit fell upon us, and the walls of that building were shaken, and everyone of those people were on their knees, with the tears running down their faces, crying to God for mercy, and for cleansing. The fourteen or fifteen men who were going to leave in the morning, were close beside me, down on their knees, and they were confessing, "Oh God, forgive me for my covetousness. I was not going away tomorrow because I was angry at Ding; I did not want to give him any money." In two seconds Pastor Ding's financial difficulty was wiped out of existence.

That meeting went on in praise and prayer, and Ding never preached that sermon to this day. At ten o'clock that night he got up and apologized to me, and told the whole story of the afternoon, with the tears streaming down his face on to his blue cotton garment. He stood and said, "O God, I want to make a covenant with you." He said to the people, "I want to take you and Miss Vaughan as witnesses to this covenant. Never in my life again shall I put any trust in the arm of flesh, and from this night henceforth I am going to use only one method in my work, and that is faith and prayer."

During the remaining days of the conference, we had the same great crowds from the theatre, but they sat or stood quietly throughout the service. A woman speaker could be heard distinctly. The Holy Spirit was in control.

For seven months Pastor Ding, Pastor Sun and I went around to all of those fifteen churches, and the same thing happened in each one of them.

Since then Pastor Ding Li Mei has gone on in faith, and he is called "The Moody of China." He has won more souls for the Lord in China than Moody did in this country, because he saw a vision of God's power.

THE JEWS AND THEIR KING

A. E. Thompson

I WISH to speak to you this evening on the fate of the Jews and their King, and I am going to give you a key verse for this fate, from the book of the prophet Hosea, "For the children of Israel shall abide many days without king, and without prince, and without sacrifice, and without pillar, and without ephod or teraphim: afterward shall the children of Israel return, and seek Jehovah their God, and David their king, and shall come with fear unto Jehovah, and to his goodness in the latter days" (Hos. 3: 4, 5).

This is a prediction of the divine judgment which would strip Israel of regal glory, of governmental forum, of priestly function, and of supernatural interference, until the nation would repent, would seek Jehovah their God, and David their king, and recognize that the One whom they had rejected and crucified had been crowned with glory and honor in highest heaven itself, and was now ready to recognize them as his nation, as his people.

It presents three phases of Israel,—first a kingless nation, second a nation seeking a king, third a nation and their king. When it was written the divided kingdom was at the zenith of its power. The greatest of the Northern kings, Jeroboam II, had extended his borders almost to the Euphrates. From Jerusalem, Uzziah subdued all the surrounding nations to the southeast. The territory under the sway of these two kings was quite as great as that which had been nominally under the kingship of David and Solomon. But this prophet knew that this was merely outward. He saw a row of tombstones of the kings of Israel, and on every one of them written this epitaph, "He walked in the ways of Jeroboam, the son of Nebat, who made Israel to sin," and he knew that that epitaph would be written on the tombstone of Jeroboam II. He saw the Assyrians, already threatening the very existence of his people. He saw Babylon, which soon would overthrow Jerusalem, and he told them that soon the nation would be kingless, and that it would abide kingless until the day when they would be ready to seek the son of David, and acknowledge him as their King.

Address given on Thursday evening at Princeton.

Mr. Thompson

It was but a little while, and the Northern Kingdom fell. It was but a little more than a century later, when Jerusalem itself was laid in ruins, the temple thrown to the ground, and the Jews carried into captivity. It is true that they returned, a remnant of them, but it is also true that never again did a son of David sit upon the throne in Jerusalem.

The years went on, and one day, perhaps one evening, three travel-stained men entered the city, asking of the people whom they met who seemed likely to be able to tell them, "Where is he that is born King of the Jews?" The word was carried to Herod, and the greatest rabbis of Jerusalem were called together. They turned to Micah and read, "But thou, Bethlehem Ephratah, though thou be little among the thousands of Judah, yet out of thee shall he come forth unto me that is to be ruler in Israel; whose goings forth have been from of old, from everlasting."

The men went, as they were directed, to Bethlehem, and found the baby King. Herod sent his men; Herod, the puppet king, sent to slay this baby King. A year or so and the puppet king died, and the infant King returned to his own land from his baby exile. He grew up, a normal boy, different from other boys, strangely different in some ways, but a real boy, lived to be a real man with toil-worn hands, among his brethren. Presently he was proclaimed a prophet among his people, and with the anointing of the Spirit of God upon him, he went about doing good; healing all that were oppressed of the devil, for God was with him.

Then one day this lowly man, who never exalted himself, entered Jerusalem, riding upon a humble little donkey, fulfilling the word of another prophet, "Rejoice greatly, O daughter of Zion; shout, O daughter of Jerusalem [and they did shout, "Hozanna, blessed is he who cometh in the name of Jehovah"]: behold, thy King cometh unto thee; he is just, and having salvation; lowly, and riding upon an ass, and upon a colt the foal of an ass" (Zech. 9: 9).

But you remember it was but a day or two, when he was arraigned as a criminal, charged with sedition, and the Roman governor asked him, "Art thou the King of the Jews?" He said, "I am." Around him were those Roman soldiers, scoffing at him, and crowning him with a crown of thorns, crying, "Behold the King of the Jews." Out yonder on the cross, he died, with a darkened heaven above, a reeling earth be-

The Jews and Their King

neath. There was written above his head in Hebrew, Greek and Latin, "This is Jesus, the King of the Jews."

But did you hear that cry? Did you hear that cry? That cry that came from the crowd, urged on by their leaders—"His blood be upon us, and upon our children!" The King had come, and they knew him not. Had they known him they would not have crucified the Lord of Glory; but they did not know him,—they crucified him, and they invoked upon themselves the most awful curse that men ever called upon themselves, or upon their fellows. There, under the shadow of that cross, the nation who had crucified their King went out to find the vengeance of their own curse in centuries that have been the darkest, blackest page of history. You remember how one of our poets has described it:

> "Tribe of the wandering foot, and weary breast—
> When shall you fly away and be at rest?
> The wild bird has his nest, the fox its cage,
> Nations their country,—Israel but a grave."

More than one of our greatest novelists has told their story as a tale of the Wandering Jew, a man who cursed Him on the streets of Jerusalem, as he passed, bearing his cross, and went out to live, and live, and live, and relive in every generation, to find death fleeing from him as he staggered on from land to land. That is the story of the Jews. In the Middle Ages, with the Spanish inquisition, they were given their choice of kissing the cross or quitting their country. When the swords of the crusaders were directed against them, the coffers of those princes who went to rescue Jerusalem from the Saracens were filled from the pockets of the Jews. The story of their persecution in Germany, in France, in England has been told and retold,—a long, long story of blood and of tears.

We boast that there has been freedom always in this country, and that here at least the Jew has always found a refuge, but I remind you that when Jews first landed on the shores of this land in the old days of the colonies, they were treated just as they were treated in Europe. That is history. It is not written in the school books, but it is history just the same. There has been no land, with the possible exception of Holland (and I am not at all sure that Holland is an exception), where the Jew has not been persecuted, and

Mr. Thompson

I want to remind you, my dear friends, that there is no city in this country where the Jew does not get some measure of persecution, even to-day.

I was told the other day of a county in New York State which has been flooded with Jews, and which has one little village in which no Jew has as yet bought property. In a ministers' meeting, a minister was boasting to his brethren, "Well, at any rate, they haven't got into our village." "How do you keep them out?" someone asked, "you cannot legislate against them."

"Oh no," was the rejoinder, "we have a better way than that. When a Jew comes to our town we give a boy a quarter to follow him around all day and torment him."

That is the old, old story of what the Jew is suffering in every land, and is suffering still. And will you look out today, out yonder where the battle surges? A German Jew is fighting for the Kaiser against his brother French Jew, who is fighting for the republic and for liberty. But a little while ago the Jew was fighting for the Czar against the Jew that was fighting for the Kaiser. A Jew who owed allegiance to the Bulgarian king was putting to death the Jew who owed allegiance to the Roumanian king. There a Russian Jew and a Turkish were struggling to the death, here an Austrian Jew and an Italian Jew gripped in battle. Saddest of all, Turkish Jews were compelled to bear arms against the British Jews liberating Jerusalem. Did you ever hear of such a thing, a nation without a king, calling the Kaiser, king; the Czar, king; our President, king,—calling the rulers of every nation under heaven their rulers, and all the while there is sitting up yonder on the throne of Glory, a Man, a son of David, crowned with glory and honor, who had worn a crown of thorns that had been placed upon his head in Jerusalem, and who was then, and still is, the King of the Jews! A nation without a king—a king without a nation.

That is the tragedy of the curse that they have invoked upon themselves. For two thousand years poor blinded Israel has been rejecting her King!

Hosea seemed to have seen it all. There is nothing so pathetic in all the Old Testament as Hosea's picture of these people and their king. I wish I had time to recall it to you, that wonderful story of Hosea, the prophet, who was commanded to marry a woman of the street, that he might be a sign unto this nation; and he did it.

The Jews and Their King

To her was born a little boy, and God said to Hosea, "Call his name Jezreel" (I will sow); "for I will sow Israel to the four winds of the earth." A little girl comes into the home, and he is told to call her name "Lo-ruhamah," which means "I will not have mercy." Then a little lad is added, and his name is Lo-ammi—"Not a people."

As the mother or the father called their children, running down the streets, in the old Jewish tongue they are calling for the first-born, "I-will-scatter, I-will-scatter, I-will-scatter!" They want the little girl and they are calling out, so that the whole town can hear, "No-mercy, No-mercy, No-mercy!" The little girl comes toddling home, and they want the little baby boy, and Oh, the heart-breaking word every time they call their little lad; it is "Not-my-people, Not-my-people, Not-my-people!"

One day the wife goes off and leaves the husband, and God says, "Change those names, and call the little girl Ruhamah," for "I will have mercy." Cut the "not" off, and call her "Ruhamah." And the father would call, "Mercy, Mercy, Mercy!" and the Jews would hear. And when he called the little boy it was no longer "Not-my-people," but Ammi, "My-people, My-people, My-people!" And the word of God went all through the town, that God had lifted the curse, and they would yet be his people, and he would yet have mercy upon them, and instead of scattering he would gather them and bring them from the four winds of the heavens.

Then he goes on to talk with his children, and tell them about their mother, and how, while she was wandering with strangers, he was sending her her food, and her clothing, and she knew it not; and how he was finally going to plead with her in the wilderness, and turn the Valley of Achor to the door of hope for her; and she would respond to him as in the days of her youth.

Then it goes on with that awful scene, where he finds her in the market, a slave, with her lovers all deserting her, and men wanting her no longer, will not bid for her, until her husband comes, and when the auctioneer cries, "How much am I offered?" Hosea makes a bid of half the price of a slave, and throws in a measure or two of grain, and the auctioneer "knocks down" his wife to him, and he takes her home.

Just here comes in my text, for he says, "The children of Israel will abide many days without a king, without any of

Mr. Thompson

those things that make a nation, but afterwards they will return and seek Jehovah their God, and David their king, and will fear his goodness in the latter days." Oh, to what fulness that has been fulfilled! Their cup of trembling has overflowed, their vial of sorrow has been drunk to the dregs—no, there remains the last awful bitterness of the dregs of that cup still, for their cup of sorrow, awful as it has been, is not yet drained. There remains for them the "day of Jacob's trouble," "a time such as never was," the Book says, and Oh, that they would get a glimpse of it!

But Hosea tells us that Israel will seek their King in the latter days. It has often seemed to me a strange coincidence that at just about the time God began to speak to my heart about the Jews (when he had convicted me of my sin of neglecting the Jew, and put a little of the love of their King for them into my heart, because he was dwelling in me),— that just about that time the Jews should have begun to seek their King. It was just after I became interested, that Herzl announced his program, which led to the Zionist movement. I think it was in that very year that he published his appeal to the Jews and sent it broadcast.

The next year, 1897, he called a great congress, and Zionism was born. I cannot tell you with what interest I have followed that wonderful movement among the Jews, the awakening of a nation,—a nation homeless, wandering, scattered,— already beginning to be a lion among the nations, already beginning to have a home in England, and France, and a bit of a home even in Germany, and something that could be called a home in America; and just at the time God was lifting his hand from the nation, and letting them have something of gladness, and joy, and pleasure, their hearts should begin to turn homeward, and their prayer, "This year here, next year in Jerusalem," became a real longing, a real heart-cry from the nation.

You know that story, a little of it, but I doubt if many of us have followed it closely enough to know how marvelous it has been. If I had been talking to you in a more studied way, I think I would have tried to open the Scriptures to you to show you the three-fold restoration of the Jew. Let me indicate briefly just what I think the Scriptures teach about that.

In the first place, it seems to me that the Jew will be brought back to his home in three stages. One of them is

The Jews and Their King

past. The Scripture says, "Behold I will gather them one by one." That has been done; I saw it with my own eyes. In spite of Turkish regulations (and if the Turks cannot make regulations then nobody else need try), every ship that came into Jaffa was loaded down with Jews, and when it weighed anchor it was freighted with a living load of Syrians. Wasn't that remarkable? I have seen whole villages board a train, men who did not know a word of English, who had never done anything but the work that their fathers did there four, five, six thousand years ago, holding a one-handled plow, driving oxen and donkeys around a heap of wheat, working as they did in the days of Abraham; yet these men were leaving for America. I have looked at them many a time, and said to myself, "What in the world will they do in America?" But presently the checks would be coming back home, and new houses would be going up in the village, and if it was a part where land could be bought, their people would be buying land. But while I saw the Syrian leaving home, enriching himself in America, and sending the money back to aid his friends in their poverty, I saw the Jews flooding our cities in Palestine, until Jerusalem was the most Jewish city in the world. It is quite true that New York is a Jewish city, with more Jews than in the whole of Palestine, twenty times more, and yet Jerusalem before the war was the most Jewish city in the world. Three out of every four men on the streets were Jews, and they had bought everything that could be purchased, and established forty colonies up and down the land, turning little pieces of the country into gardens of the Lord. They were doing all that could be done under a Turkish government, under a rule of oppression, to fulfill the prophecies. I could put my finger on prophecy after prophecy, in book after book, in the Old and in the New Testament, and I think, quite as confidently as Peter on the day of Pentecost, say, "This is that which was written by the prophets."

I saw Jeremiah's prophecy fulfilled. Jeremiah drew out the measuring line up to the northwest of Jerusalem, and described where the new city would be built. I built a church in the heart of it. Thirty years before there were not half a dozen houses outside of the walls of Jerusalem, and the gates were locked at sunset, and no one dared to stay outside of the city for fear of the Bedouins and other robbers; there were lots of them within an hour's ride of Jerusalem among the native villages. But Jerusalem has spread abroad as towns

Mr. Thompson

without walls, with a multitude of men and cattle in them. In spite of all the German banks could do to boom the land down on the old plains of Rephidim,—they burst their banks in an attempt to sell that property,—all the while the property was selling like hot-cakes up at the place where Jeremiah said the city would be built.

As a boy, I preached a sermon to children, and this was my text, "And the streets of the city shall be full of boys and girls playing in the streets thereof." Haven't you preachers preached on that text to children too, and told them of the glories of heaven, and what a wonderful place they are going to if they will just be what they ought to be? But I went to Jerusalem, and meanwhile God had opened my eyes to interpret prophecy a little differently. I went through the city and I did not see children playing in the streets. I remember a day when I came back from downtown, and cried out with a sheer cry of agony, "Would God I never had to look down on the streets again;" for the wailing cry of Jerusalem had pierced to my very soul. I think it may have been that very day, that my own wee bit of a lad whom we had carried in our arms to Jerusalem, started to cry. I listened, and he was crying like those other children. He wasn't "bawling" as your boy bawls; he was wailing the plaintive wail of the children of Jerusalem. I cried, "Stop that, John!" and he wailed more. Again I ordered him sternly to quit it, and the little fellow wailed worse than ever. He knows all about Arabic, and his keen ear, trained from babyhood, can mimic them to a nicety. It is too plaintive, too minor, for an American who is not a practiced musician, to attempt. I said, "Well John, cry if you want to, but cry as they do in America." He had bawled as a baby up in Canada, and here in this God-blessed land, but he had learned that most awful wail of the East.

One day I was riding the little Arabian mare that my brother gave me, coming in from the surrounding hills one Saturday evening. The sun was almost setting, the Sabbath was over, and the strict legalism of Judaism, which is known in Jerusalem, had been released. I rode into the suburbs, and lo, the street of the city was full of Jewish boys and girls playing in the streets thereof. The sadness and bitterness went out of my soul, and I put my finger down on the prophet Zechariah, and said, "Thank God." That had a fulfilment in Zechariah's time, and it will have a yet more glorious fulfilment, and I have begun to see it. That is only the beginning,—the one by one regathering.

There is another regathering, when the nations shall bring Israel home. As sure as you live, the same pen that signs the treaty of peace, will sign the restoration of the Jew. There was one thing I was sure of when I left Jerusalem, and that was that when I returned, not the star, the characteristic symbol of night, would be floating over the Tower of David, but the dear old Union Jack, the flag that has been waving for a thousand years as the emblem of the free, which means liberty and freedom and protection to the poor and the oppressed wherever it flies, would be on that old Tower. Thank God it is there to-night. But there is another thing, of which I was sure, and just as sure, that whatever this war accomplished, or failed to accomplish, it would result in the restoration of the Jews. I said this because for years I had been watching what God was doing in the world, and reading what God had written in the Book, and I was sure we had come up to that time. But now Balfour has said it. That is the second stage of the regathering. But thank God, it is not the last.

There may be some of you here who agree with the teachers who think that this return is going to result in the wholesale conversion of the Jews. I do not see it written in the Book. They will be regathered in unbelief, and they will live in unbelief. It is not because of their love to Christ that they will break with the antichrist; it is because the Jew has learned to say "Jehovah, the Lord, is One." They learned that in captivity, and have never forgotten it; and whatever the Jew may do or not do, he will not bow down and worship an image, much less bow down and worship a man, and he will break with the antichrist when antichrist declares that he is God. When a man seats himself in God's temple declaring that he is God, it will be too much for the Jew. He will not need to be a Christian to break with the antichrist at a point like that, and he will live on and suffer, suffer for his faith in Jehovah, not knowing that Jesus is Jehovah.

But there will be a third stage in that restoration, and Oh, how glorious it is! You remember Zechariah's picture of the Jew restored. You know how rapidly that is moving on. I need not tell you what is being done in this country, nor remind you of the Pittsburgh convention the other day, or the constitution which the Jews drafted there for the Jewish

Mr. Thompson

State, or the tax which they have already imposed on the Jewish people as the first finance for that State. I need not tell you of any or all of these things happening right under our eyes, proving that the restoration is in progress. But I want to take you on to this third stage, and let us see their meeting with their King.

In the first stage, the one by one gathering, I am sure they did not come to their King; they came to the city of the great King, but Oh, how they hated the King. If any of you doubt it, I wish you could have been in Jerusalem and seen some of the scenes that I went through, and seen the Jewish mob around our Jewish mission, when the church was jammed with Jews as angry and bitter almost as they were when they were crying, "Crucify him, Crucify him." They still hated the King; they hate him now.

I think when the Jews are brought back in multitudes to the Land, when they have liberty and freedom, it will be as hard, perhaps a little harder than it is to-day, for us to get them to acknowledge Jesus as their Saviour; but later, in the day of Jacob's trouble, will come that awful Armageddon thunder, with blood running to the horses' bridles in that great two hundred mile battle line that will be thrown around the little land of Palestine, gathering its borders nearer and ever nearer to Jerusalem. The picture that is given us of it is that two-thirds of the Jews will be cut off and die, and the little remnant is ready to perish, when lo, the heavens open, and the King comes, and his feet stand upon the Mount of Olives that is toward Jerusalem from the east; the nation is saved from annihilation, saved by the coming of their King!

They know their king, and they cry, as he said they would, standing upon that other hill, "Hozanna, blessed is he that cometh in the name of Jehovah." Then one comes near, perhaps deferentially, as they still do in the East, to kiss his hand, and he starts, and says, "What are these wounds in thine hand?" And he shall say, "These are they with which I was wounded in the house of my friends."

Read backwards through Zechariah, and you will find the next picture; that man will turn and flee to his room; he will pass his wife in the hallway, sobbing to her as he passes, that the Messiah is Jesus. He will wail, and she will wail, each apart in their chambers, as only Jewish fathers and mothers can wail for their first-born.

The Jews and Their King

"Then," says Zechariah, "there will be a fountain opened to the house of David, and to the inhabitants of Jerusalem, for sin and for uncleanness." Oh, blessed and glorious day, when there shall be a real restoration, a Messianic restoration, when he shall reign with his ancients in Jerusalem, glorious; when kings shall fall down before him, and all nations shall serve him. For out of Jerusalem shall go forth the law, and his name shall not need to be told by any man to his brother, for all shall know him, from the least unto the greatest.

I remember one day in Jerusalem, in what our American Consul called our "little tin church" (he did not often grace it with his presence), a handful of Jewish young men had crept in Saturday after Saturday, to listen while we expounded to them their own Scriptures. That day I was standing there on the little platform, and my attention had become riveted to a young Jew, sitting just over at the side of the humble little tin church. I was telling them this story, of the awful sorrows that their nation was going to pass through, and of the coming of their King, and of the wounded hands. I was just pouring it out in an agony of soul, under the power of the Holy Spirit. I had forgotten that there ever was anybody in the world, for the time being, but myself and Max. He was sitting with his eyes riveted upon me, and I stopped, and said, "Max, what are you going to do about it?" Quick as a flash he said, "I am going to wait and see if he has wounds in his hands."

"But Max, what if you are not the third man?"

"What do you mean?" he asked.

"I have just told you that two out of every three of the Jews are going to be killed before he comes. What if you are not the third man?"

He caught his breath, and his face became ashen, and then he gasped out, "I'll take my chance."

I stopped. I could not say any more.

A few days afterwards I was walking down the street and saw Max coming, and as I came near to him, I was thinking, and he was thinking of that, and as I came by I reached out my hand and said, "Max, what are you going to do about it?"

"I'm going to wait and take my chance."

"Max, what if you are not the third man? What if you are not the third man?"

Mr. Thompson

The next time I saw him we went through the same scene. "Max, what are you going to do about it?"

"I am going to wait and see if he has wounds in his hands."

"But Max, you do not need to wait to see whether he has wounds in his hands. You have 'seen the wounds in his hands; you know they are there, you know that Jesus is your Messiah. Max, what is the matter with you is that you are a coward, you are afraid of your father, and mother, and friends, you are thinking of your bread and butter." (I tell you, it means something to be a Jewish convert in Jerusalem.) "You are thinking that your father will kick you out, that your mother will spit on you, and that they will hold a funeral service and you will be dead, and you will be homeless, and everybody that you know will curse you."

The last time I saw Max, just after the war broke out, it seemed to me that every time I saw him he had gotten older. He seemed to be shrivelling up from a boy into an old man. There he was in the midst of the war, and he was still taking that attitude, that he was going to wait and take his chance.

Are there those of us here, like Max, thinking, "Oh, what it would cost me to crown Jesus King, to make him Lord of my life!" But we know that he has the wounded hands, we know that God has already crowned him with glory and honor, we know that while the nations rage, and the peoples imagine a vain thing, and while the world is saying, "Let us break their bonds asunder, and cast away their cords from us," God is saying, "Yet I have set my king upon my holy hill of Zion." We know that, and what is there that is worth while compared with putting the crown upon our King?

PRAYER THAT PREVAILS

Howard Agnew Johnston, D. D.

"WE would see Jesus, dying, risen, pleading."[1] If Christ be our life, then we must realize what he is doing *now*. We have seen him dying for our sins and accomplishing the atoning work of redeeming love on Calvary; we have had emphasized the resurrection life in him; now let us see him pleading, for this is what he is doing.

Isn't it striking that in Romans 8: 34 we have those three things? There we see him dying, risen, pleading. "Who is he that condemneth? It is Christ Jesus that died, yea rather, that was raised from the dead, who is at the right hand of God, who also maketh intercession for us."

You know how he longed, during his earthly ministry, for a responsive, an intelligent, sympathetic appreciation on the part of his disciples. You know how hungry he was for that, and how little of it he got. And we can see that all along in those years he is thinking of his return to the throne. You remember in the sixth chapter of John, when he was talking to the disciples about rising up at the last day, and talked about eating his flesh and drinking his blood, some stumbled, and did he say to them, "And what if ye shall see the Son of Man rise again from the dead?" That might have been the first logic in the sequence of his thought, but he went one step further, as he often did,—"What and if ye shall see the Son of Man ascend up where he was before?"

Yes, he was thinking of that often times, and so in that marvelous 17th chapter of John, the inscript of his great continuing intercession, looking past Calvary and Gethsemane, he said, "And now come I to Thee." And as he thought of that, he was so anxious that these disciples, who he had been eager to have come into a real sympathy with him in his earthly life, might so understand the life to which he was going, in his great mediation, that they also would be able to enter with him into that ministry of intercession.

So, toward the end of his ministry, he said to them one

Dr. Johnston's message was given on Tuesday evening at Cedar Lake.

Dr. Johnston

day, as we have it in the 14th chapter of John, "Now I am going to the Father in a little while, and I am going to tell you of a great task that you are to begin to perform. You are to begin now to ask God for things." In another place he said, "He that believeth on me, the works that I do shall he do also; and greater works than these shall he do, because I go unto the Father. And whatsoever ye shall ask in my name, that will I do, that the Father may be glorified in the Son."

Now, don't you think that those disciples looked into each others' faces and said, "Why, what a wonderful thing is this!" We must try to realize that those disciples heard so many of the things that are familiar to us, for the first time, and how hard it must have been for them to take them! I think that was one of those times, and they must have looked into each others' faces and said, "Why, what does this mean? Does it mean that this is a marvelous world of power that he is opening up to us, that he wants us to enter into and realize that our God is eager to do divine things through us as he is doing through him, and that this marvelous world of power is to be made available for us now because he goes to the Father?"

Yes, that was what he wanted them to know. And just a little later, in the 15th chapter and the 7th verse, he said, "If ye abide in me, and my words abide in you, ye shall ask what ye will, and it shall be done unto you." I think they looked into each others' faces again and said, "That is just about the same thing he said a minute ago. Can it be this marvelous thing is for us?" And Jesus said, "Yes, that is what I want you to understand. All this abiding life in me, all this new law of love that I am telling you about, is in order that your character may be crystallized into such a victorious life that you shall come to the place of prevailing prayer with God."

Notice again in the 15th chapter and the 16th verse, "Ye have not chosen me, but I have chosen you, and ordained you (appointed you), that ye should go and bring forth fruit, and that your fruit should remain: that whatsover ye shall ask of the Father in my name, he may give it you." "All this abiding life, all this unfolding of this law of love that I am giving you, all this development of your life in me, is that ye may climb up, up, up to the place of prevailing prayer

Prayer That Prevails

with God, in order that ye may have prevailing power with God."

Why did he say it? Go back to the second Psalm, and we have the Father saying to the Son, "Ask of me and I will give thee the nations for thine inheritance. And the uttermost parts of the earth for thy possession." For God only can give the nations to Jesus Christ. But Christ could not ask for them then,—he could not ask for them before his cross, he could not ask for them until he had finished that work here and had gone back to the throne, where he now ever liveth to do that asking.

In the 17th chapter of John I say we have the inscript of his great High Priesthood prayer, and notice he is praying distinctively for his Church, for those who were there, and for all who would believe in him through them—not directly and immediately for the world, but praying that the believing and interceding Church might be faithful, might be true, might be sanctified by the Word, so that through the fidelity of his witnesses, the world might believe.

I am sure that the disciples, as they were with him day by day, were more and more filled with this thought, "What a marvelous power there is in the prayer life of our Lord! What power he has with God in prayer!" Nearly every time there was a mighty manifestation of God's power, we read that it was as he prayed, or that he prayed, and the prayer was the thing that unlocked the manifestation of God's presence, and power, and glory.

So they came to him, as we have it in the 11th chapter of Luke, and said, "Lord, teach us to pray, as John also taught his disciples." They had said their prayers all their lives, just as we have. They had said prayers all their lives, but they knew there was no power in the prayer, and they wanted to know the secret of power in prayer. You know what he does there, how he unfolds the right attitude toward God, and the essence of intercession in that great Model Prayer. Every pronoun there is a plural pronoun. How often we have heard it emphasized; but think what it means in intercession,— all the way through the very plural pronouns themselves mean intercession.

Then he gave them the illustration of the man who had a friend who came at midnight, for whom he did not have bread, and he went to the neighbors to get bread for his friend. It was an illustration of intercessory prayer. The

Dr. Johnston

man was not asking for bread for himself, he was asking for bread for another hungry friend.

Oh, our Father would be so eager to-night if we should come to him, hungry as we are, and say, "Father, give me bread,"—so eager to give us bread for our own souls. But the Lord Jesus says that here is a stronger appeal, bread for another. Then he says, "And I say unto you, Ask, and ye shall receive; seek, and ye shall find; knock, and it shall be opened unto you."

Now just think for a moment of the graphic situation. You know that over there they traveled largely at night. They traveled very little in the middle of the hot day, and it was a very ordinary thing for a friend to come at midnight. Then he went to the neighbor, and the neighbor did not propose to be bothered. His children were in bed. In Oriental countries they lie down on the ground (many of them have no floors) and cover over all the family together. The children do not wake up as easily as the older folks. The man went to this house and began to knock. "Friend So-and-so," he called, "I want some bread for a friend of mine who is come." [The speaker here began to knock on the pulpit and continued knocking through the next sentences.]

"O don't bother me," came the answer, "my children are in bed."

He kept on knocking. He knew what would get his neighbor, that he would say, "Well, the first thing you know the children will be awake. I guess I had better get up and give it to him before the children wake up." He knew what would reach that man, and that is what he was doing,—knocking, knocking, knocking. That is what Christ meant when He said, "Knock, knock." That was the actual graphic thing. Every person that heard those words of our Lord knew exactly what that meant,—"Knock, knock until the answer comes."

It is as if he said, "This is why I am giving you this illustration, that you may realize that this is the importunate sort of prayer that will meet certain laws in the prayer life of my Father, that will release His power to bless."

Now notice another thing. People say, "Well, when you come to the ministry of intercession, you know there is the power to the contrary that is resident in every human will that God has endued with freedom sufficient to resist the Spirit." Ah yes, but do you know what Jesus puts into that

Prayer That Prevails

picture? He puts that very thing into the picture of prevailing intercessory prayer, the picture of the man with the contrary will who does not propose to do it.

In the eighteenth chapter, not long after, he gave them another parable, that men ought always to pray and not to faint, and he gave them another picture, of a man who did not propose to do a certain thing, but had the contrary will; and that woman with her much importunate beseeching, made a condition there that overcame the stubborn will.

That is what Jesus has given us. He knows psychology, and in both of those illustrations of importunate prayer he has pictured that very thing of the contrary will being overcome by importunate and continuing intercession.

. . . .

Here is a great world of power, with conditions laid upon us before we may enter in. Note for a moment those conditions. We go to Matthew 18: 19, 20: "If two of you shall agree on earth as touching anything that they shall ask." Now that Greek verb translated "agree" is the verb "symphonize," and the 20th verse explains the 19th, where Jesus says, "For where two or three are gathered together in my name, there am I in the midst of them." *He is the keynote of the orchestra,* and all the instruments of the orchestra must be symphonized in him in order to meet the condition of prevailing and acceptable prayer. Two lives symphonized in Christ clear down to bed-rock,—that is the condition of prevailing prayer.

With that in mind, we come to those days when they were waiting "with one accord," symphonizing, when Pentecost came. Humanly speaking, we could not have had Pentecost without that "symphonizing." Then for a little while we have a symphonized Church, a wonderful symphonized Church. Discord came in, and some women thought they were not getting their share. What did the apostles do? They came and said, "Brethren, we have been too busy about this thing."

People say, "Isn't work prayer?" No! no! Work that is not saturated and penetrated with prayer cannot be work in which God shall be guiding, and in which we shall be laborers together with him; but work is never a substitute for prayer. What the apostles said was, "We have been working too much at this business of serving tables. You get seven men to do

Dr. Johnston

this thing, and we will give ourselves to continuance in prayer and the ministry of the Word."

Notice,—not first the ministry of the Word, and second prayer, but first prayer, and second the ministry of the Word. Ah, you may be sure that whenever discord gets into any Church or any home, *somebody has not been praying enough.*

Now may I give you one or two illustrations to emphasize this fundamental teaching which I have touched upon? A few years ago, there was a woman in the church to which I then ministered, named Mrs. Munn. She was a woman of prayer. She lived in one-half of a double house, and in the other half lived a Mr. and Mrs. McMurray. He held a very high position in the Rock Island Railroad, and he and his wife were godless people. Mrs. McMurray had never been to Sunday School in her life, and she was in her thirties. Mrs. Munn had a covenant of prayer with one or two of us for Mrs. McMurray. One day she asked her to go and see a friend that she thought she would be interested in seeing.

She took Mrs. McMurray to the home of Mrs. Chapman, a woman who lay upon a sick-bed with a serious spinal trouble that meant great pain. You would not be there very long until you saw her jerking with this pain. There were marks of poverty in the room. The carpet had been given by the King's Daughters, and the invalid's chair to which she was lifted from her bed had been given by the Ladies' Aid Society. Under her bedroom lamp, on a little square table, there was an open Bible, and that sick woman, with a shining face, was talking to everybody who came into that room about how good God was to her.

As Mrs. McMurray sat there and heard this conversation, she was absolutely astounded, and when they came out she turned to Mrs. Munn and said, "Will Christianity do that?"

"Do what?" said Mrs. Munn.

"Well, you know, do that," said Mrs. McMurray. "Why, if I were to drive up there in my carriage and offer that woman a million dollars in exchange for her faith and her joy in all her suffering, for my good health and my faithless life, she would pity me."

"Yes," said Mrs. Munn, "she would pity you."

"Well," said Mrs. McMurray, "if Christianity can do that, I must know about it."

She came to church the next Sunday for the first time, and I met her. I had been praying for her, but had never met

Prayer That Prevails

her. The next week she went to St. Louis for a visit and was gone about two weeks, when she suddenly developed the need of a surgical operation, and came back home scared to death, and sent for me, saying, "Oh, I am going to die, I know I am going to die, and I am not ready to die. I want you to tell me how to get ready right away."

Keen and alert mentally, she had a dozen questions she wanted to know about. I said, "Mrs. McMurray, you are going to the hospital to-morrow, and it would not be wise for us to attempt to try to settle these questions to-night. I could answer you a question that would give rise to a dozen more. Will you please tell me what you do believe?"

"I believe in Mrs. Chapman's God," she said. "I don't know much about him, but I am sure he is a real God."

I said, "Do you think you could catch Mrs. Chapman's spirit to the extent that you would just trust him to take you through this trial, as a little child would trust her father, just to care for you through those days; and, after it is over (they tell me this is not serious), then we will talk about the things that will help you to find Christ. Could you trust him that way?"

"Well," she said, "I could try.

"Will you try?"

"Yes."

We had a prayer together, she went to the hospital the next day, and the next evening they told me it was a very serious operation, and it was some ten days or more before they would let me see her. I went in, and she was still bound down to the bed. As I stepped inside the room she put up a little white hand, and the smile on her face was wonderful, and she said, "Oh, I know all about it now, I am a Christian."

She did not have a Bible, and I knew she did not know anything about the technical message, but as I was about to ask a question, she said, "Now Mr. Johnston, I have a wonderful joy in my heart, but I want you to kneel down here and pray for my husband. I will never have any deep joy until my husband is a Christian."

I said, "I guess the root of the matter is in her," and I prayed for the husband, and thanked the Lord for the wife's new joy, and did not attempt, in her weakness, to discuss things. "Will you bring me a Bible?" she asked. "Yes," I

Dr. Johnston

said, and I did. Every day when I went to the hospital I was asked to pray for her husband, and I promised to pray for him every day.

Weeks went by, strength returned, and she pored over the Gospel. God had touched her heart, and had opened it as a child's heart would be opened. She came into the truth in a very intelligent way, and we received her into the church. There were ten men in that session that night, and after she had told her child-like story and been received into fellowship, she turned to me, and calling me by name, said, "Will you promise to pray for my husband every day until he is a Christian?" Then she named each one of the ten men (no general request for them to pray), and said, "Will you promise?"

On Tuesday after that, I went to see her husband, and told him how glad we were that his wife was with us, and that we were hoping he would be constrained to come. He turned and said, "I don't know what to make of my wife. I have never seen such a change in anyone. When I come home she has the table spread for two, and sits there sobbing. She cannot eat, and says she never can eat, and never can be happy until I am a Christian, although she has a wonderful joy in her own soul. I do not know what to make of it."

I said, "Mr. McMurray, can't you fix that here? Won't you take Christ as your Saviour?"

"No sir," he said, "I am not going to do it."

"Mr. McMurray," I said, "if your wife keeps on praying the way she is praying, I think you will."

He hesitated a moment, and then he said, "Well, I am not going to do it yet."

There is your instance that the Lord gave us in the 11th of Luke. He knew that the power of the Spirit of God, praying with and for that woman, with groanings that could not be uttered, must conquer that stubborn will. He knew it would, and it did. But the next morning she came to me just choking with sobs. "Oh," she said, "you went to see Mr. McMurray yesterday. I was sure that when you went God would give him to Jesus Christ. I have come to ask you to pray more earnestly than you have been praying for my husband. It seems to me I will die if he is not saved soon."

I said, "Mrs. McMurray, if you keep on praying the way

Prayer That Prevails

you have been praying your husband is certain to be saved very soon."

Within two weeks that man yielded his stubborn will to the will of God, and in that home there was established a family altar of real prayer. He knew the reality of the meeting of the conditions that God has laid down for prevailing intercession. Oh yes, that is the real thing.

I have been thinking today of one or two instances out yonder in Asia. When I was in India at Rawal Pindi, some ten girls from Pandita Ramabai's school came over there, and Miss Abrams, one of the teachers, was with them. She said to me at the breakfast table: "I had a wonderful experience last night. I looked over in the tent where the girls sleep, and I saw a light on toward midnight. I thought, 'This is contrary to the rules,' and slipped out and lifted the flap of the tent. The youngest of my ten girls, a girl not yet sixteen, was kneeling in the farthest corner, holding a little tallow candle in her hand, and holding up her list for intercessory prayer. She has five hundred names on that list. You know there are about fifteen hundred girls in our school. Hour after hour she was naming them by name, very quietly."

You know God said, "I will pour out the Spirit of supplication," and that is what He had done upon some of those girls. That is what happened before the Welsh revival. And a Welsh missionary implored his friends at home to pray, pray, pray that the blessing that had been given Wales might be given to India. Evan Roberts told me himself that at the mouth of the pit the coal-miners would come a half hour before daylight, that they might pray for that half hour before they went down, that God would give to a certain section of India, where their Welsh friends were, the blessing that had come to Wales. One day the message came to them, "The blessing has come."

Pandita Ramabai said, "If there is any blessing in India, we may have it. Let us ask God to tell us what we must do in order that we may have that blessing," and you know how God gave her the light. She turned to the first chapter of the Acts of the Apostles, and read those words, "Wait for the promise of the Father, which ye have heard of me ... ye shall receive power, after that the Holy Ghost is come upon you." Wait!

She said, "We have never done this. We have prayed, *but*

Dr. Johnston

we never expected any greater blessing today than we had yesterday." Does that search your heart? Oh, how it put me down in the dust the day I heard it! She said, "We will wait."

That was the middle of January of 1905, and they prayed on through January one hour every day. There was no compulsion, but all who wished to, might come voluntarily for an hour. Through January, no blessing. Through February, and Ramabai said, "We are not ready yet; we need a deeper cleansing, there is some Achan in the camp. We must wait still, and ask God to cleanse these vessels, that He may fill them. Through February, through March, through April, through May, into June. Do you know what James says, "Ye have not, because ye ask not." He did not mean to say that you do not say prayers, but "Ye have not, because ye ask not." Ah friends, this was asking, and this was asking according to the promise, and according to the commandment, and on the 29th day of June, in that meeting, one girl began to pray as no one else had prayed. She prayed for two hours and could not stop. She would say, "And this we ask for Jesus' sake," evidently intending to stop, and then, "O Lord Jesus," and some more. Do you know what she did during those two hours? She not only confessed her own sins, but she confessed everybody's sins that she knew about, and the rest knew about, and no one had been honest enough to confess them. That was the beginning.

Some of those girls had gone over to Puna and carried the atmosphere of this prayer life with them, and they were "waiting," and Puna had a wonderful blessing in the Girls' School there. There was a girl there, the young wife of a Hindu, whose father had threatened to disinherit him if he should become a Christian. He had told some folks that he intended to become a Christian just as soon as his father died, and he was waiting for his father to die. But this little wife of his, whom he had sent up there that she might be educated, wrote to him and said, "I have found Jesus, and I am going to be baptized, and want you to come up here and be baptized with me." He thought he had better go and look into the matter. He got there about ten o'clock in the morning. The girls were in the schoolroom praying, all down on the floor. He sat down and listened, and they all began to pray for him, and they prayed on, and on, and on, one, two, three, four, five, six hours, and at four o'clock

Prayer That Prevails

in the afternoon, that man, who had been resisting the Spirit of God, yielded, and surrendered in a great new joy, and the next day he and she were baptized together.

Let me tell you one more instance which occurred in Shantung Province, where I saw Miss Vaughan. They called Miss Vaughan the Evan Roberts of Shantung. The way God used that woman out there gives her a right to testify to the place intercession should have in the life of the Christian.

Up there in the educational center of the province, our meetings were going on, and the power of prayer was manifestly there, and deepening. It had been announced that on Monday morning at eight o'clock there would be a meeting in the college, at nine o'clock one in the Boys' High School, at ten o'clock in the Girls' School. We went to the eight o'clock meeting. About two hundred college men were there, and after a little talk it was suggested that perhaps they would like to pray. There were a half dozen on their feet at once praying for each other, and then it was suggested that they might wish to pray together, and the same thing took place there. At nine o'clock it was suggested that the meeting could not be stopped, and we sent word we would be at the High School at nine-thirty. We went to the High School at nine-thirty, and left the meeting still going on at the college.

We were there until about eleven o'clock, and the same thing happened in the Boys' High School, and then we went to the Girls' School until twelve. We went to lunch, and our host informed us that the boys had continued in prayer until twelve, gone home to lunch, and were already back at prayer, and the prayer meeting continued until eight o'clock that night. The missionary group met at eight o'clock that night, and someone came to tell us that the men at the college had sent a special request to the missionaries to pray for Dr. Bey. There were seventeen Chinese teachers in this institution; fourteen were Christians, and three were not. Mr. Bey was one of the three and he was the most popular man in the whole faculty, one of the teachers of the Chinese language. Two of the men said they had a conviction that he was hesitating because of the opposition on the part of his wife and family.

There were no addresses that night, just prayer for about two hours, and some prayed on after the meeting. The next morning there was a general meeting in the church near the compound, for everybody. That was at eight o'clock, and

Dr. Johnston

after a little talk, an appeal was made something like this, "Perhaps there are some of you who have really in your hearts believed in the truth as it is in Jesus, believed and hoped in Him as your own Saviour, but you have never confessed Him, for one reason or another, possibly because some of your own family have opposed the step. But you know, if you really believe in Christ, the only thing to do is to confess Him, and ask Him to use you to win the others of your dear ones to Him, so that they also may be saved. If there is one here, just stand where you are."

The President of the college was interpreting, and had not finished talking when Mr. Bey put his hands on the back of the pew in front of him, and as soon as the doctor ceased he stood up with bowed head. Nearly everybody there knew that for twelve hours there had been intercession for that man, and the impression was most profound. God was there, and almost instantly the two younger teachers stood up with him, and in about five minutes thirty of those college students were on their feet; and there in that meeting seventy-five students found Christ.

Dear friends, "He ever liveth to make intercession for us." "To me, to live is Christ." Oh, for me to live, is to enter into the fellowship of his intercession with him, for this is the way he asks now of the Father for the nations,—through us, through us. And do you know, He has gone limping, his body has gone limping through the centuries, because we have not done it.

THE NEXT BELGIAN INVASION

Edith Fox Norton

I HAVE had a vision to-day. I shall never forget that reiterated knock, knock, knock of last night, in the illustration of importunate prayer that Dr. Johnston brought to us. It bore fruit in my life to-day, and in my room, with the world shut out, and no one (it seemed to me) in all the universe but God and my soul, he spread before me the map of Europe, and he showed me Belgium,—Belgium with nine million inhabitants, and only nine thousand Protestants, Belgium never touched by the Reformation, Belgium never evangelized, Belgium sitting in darkness. My husband joined me after a bit, and we prayed as we had never known what it was to pray before; and we asked God to increase that burden upon our hearts. For what?

He showed to us that what he had done in the Punjab, what he had done in China, and in Wales, he could do in Belgium; he would pour forth the riches of his grace, and we could bring it down by prayer. My husband and I have dedicated ourselves to prayer, and we will not give up until that blessing is poured forth upon Belgium, unless he comes first. If any of you are led into that same prayer covenant with us we will rejoice, and it will be your privilege, when the blessing falls on that stricken country, to rejoice that you have had a share in it.

Some time the German invaders are going to be driven out of Belgium, and there is to be another invasion. Two humble servants of God,—"little father," and "little mother," as they have called us the last four years, with our boys about us,—we know at least a dozen of those faithful missionaries upon whom the Lord can count,—are going to invade that country, and by the grace of God we are going to evangelize that country for Christ. We know that he can do, for he is faithful. That little band will go into their country and proclaim to their countrymen the unsearchable riches of Christ.

Mrs. Norton gave this message on Wednesday evening at Cedar Lake, substantially the same as her address at Princeton on Tuesday evening. Mr. Norton followed with his address on Thursday evening, which he gave at Princeton on Monday evening. See note at the close of Mr. Norton's address, page 292.

Mrs. Norton

Those of you who have read The Sunday School Times know about the beginnings of the work in Belgium, and the great opportunity that lies before us, and I am only going to mention that in passing. Many of you have read about Peter, who for four years has been studying the Word, feeding as well as growing; he would compare very favorably with those Chinese Christians of whom Miss Vaughan has told us. Peter has been going through his time of fiery testing, and coming out beautifully true and fine.

As the result of three years of work in the Belgian army, I suppose there are at least five hundred men who are distributing Scriptures and winning souls in the ranks, and I want to tell you the story of several of those workers, those men who are going to rally around the Cross in Belgium after the war.

There is Ami Rene Claerhout—"Ami" meaning "beloved," "Rene" meaning "born again." He has a defective heart, and is not at the front, but at the construction camp in France. He found the Lord in Argentina, and my husband and I had nothing to do with it. His father, a wealthy Belgian, had a large business, and this boy, dissatisfied, stained with sin, found himself at the point of suicide. But one day he saw a man on the street in a curious garb. It was a Salvation Army officer. He asked his mother to invite the man in off the street, out of curiosity, but he found something he had not reckoned on; the man gave him a Gospel and told him a few words of salvation. He decided for Christ, was kicked out of his home, that palatial home, drifted back to Belgium, and allied himself with the Salvation Army, becoming an officer in it. He told in his last letter that he had distributed 400,000 Gospels in four months in Belgium. The seed is being sown and the harvest will be sure.

Simon Pierre is not of quite such high birth as Rene, but what he lacks in birth he makes up in zeal, and it is not always coupled with tact, but Simon Pierre had a wonderful transformation. An outcast, a drunkard, he stumbled into a Salvation Army hall in Brussels. An Englishman was speaking in very bad French, such atrocious French that Simon Pierre was fascinated, and listened. It was the story of the Prodigal Son, and the Holy Spirit sent it home to his heart. Simon Pierre became a Christian, and he too became a missionary and distributor of the Word of God. After the war began, and after he heard of our work, he became a co-laborer with us, distributing the Gospels, and has been put in jail very frequently for it.

At Christmas time Satan tried hard to spoil our plans for the distribution of Christmas boxes. Simon Pierre heard they had taken all the Gospels out of our boxes, and he sat down and wrote the Minister of War and told him he ought to be ashamed to permit such a thing. Of course he was put into jail for ten days. He distributed Gospels in front of the offices, and got into jail for that.

Frank was Peter's fourth convert, "the hardest man in his regiment," so Peter told us. He said, "I hardly thought I could reach him when I gave him a Gospel." But a great transformation came over Frank, and he himself wrote us, "The Gospel has the power to take the hardest man and make him as meek as a lamb."

He was wounded and went to the hospital, and when he was quite weak the priest said, "I hear you have embraced this new religion. You confess to me as of old, and I will give you three months' convalescent leave in England." Frank said, "I will go back to the front and die first." He went, and was captured. He volunteered for a difficult bit of work, and Peter said, "You be careful, Frank." Frank looked at him straight, and said, "Peter, Jesus is with me," putting his hand over his tunic pocket, where reposed his French New Testament.

Frank went out with the others across the little river Iser, where they were to encircle the enemy depots and cut off the retreat. Peter heard Frank's own signal, and wrote back, "Frank is either in heaven or taken captive, I do not know which; but this I know, Jesus was with him, and that is enough." Word came back afterwards that he was safe in a German prison camp.

Frank does not talk much about his own hardships. Just once he told us that he was beaten night and morning. That card filtered through the German censor because it was not well written; but he said something to offset that,—"There is a good German pastor comes and prays with me and reads the Bible every day." That made him happy. Then he said, "Father and mother, you are not forgetting we are counting on you to help us win Belgium after the war." His sufferings are nothing to him, but father and mother must remain true to their tryst with the Belgian soldier.

Then there is Stellfeld. When we went on our visit to the front Stellfeld helped me to run very fast to the air-raid shelter one night when Calais was being bombarded. But Stellfeld does not run for shelter when little mother is not there. He wrote, "Mother, I do my best soul-saving work during the bombardments. The last bombardment was a terrible one, but I had two men on their knees who had never prayed before, and they were won to Christ."

We have two unique members of the League, workers for Jesus Christ in Calais, father and son. The son with both arms amputated at the shoulder, the father unfitted for service at the front because of his health. They are serving as nurses in the Calais hospitals, and have become soul savers, working day and night in the hospitals. Oh yes, they were stopped once or twice, but God graciously intervened, and their work continues. Going down the street one day, the boy walking along, with no arms, the father in front of him, the boy saw a soldier coming toward him with a very sad face. He said to his father, "What a sad faced boy! We must tell him of the joy that we have." They stopped that lonely-hearted soldier with both arms and legs, and told him about the joy they had, and the boy accepted Christ.

Camille Nart will be with us during those days of the new invasion in Belgium. He was the vilest man I have ever read of. His story is almost unprintable, and yet he has been transformed by the grace of God. The Gospel found him in an internment camp in Holland. Some of those men are very near starvation, but their faith is burning, and revival fires are sweeping those camps. It is a marvelous work our Lord is doing these days, and is going to do.

I have told you about the personnel of these workers, and now I want to take you for a visit to the Belgian front, which we made in February, last year. The scene is a very very flat field in Flanders, and that Flanders mud can be sticky and uncomfortable. We landed there the twenty-second of February, Washington's birthday.

Our Christmas boxes had been held up, and all the Gospels had to come out, but the Lord vindicated his doings later;

The Next Belgian Invasion

and so when the order of the day came out for the eighteenth of February, we found that every officer in the army was directed to tell his men that whosoever should receive a Christmas box from Mr. and Mrs. Norton was straightway to answer them. For little cards of greeting, bearing our name and address were left in the boxes, and they were to thank us for the gift. What a wonderful avenue of usefulness and opportunity this opened up before us! Those boxes were distributed to the army, not to the men for whom they were intended, but to thousands of new men whom we could never have reached otherwise.

The government also asked us to have a personal share in that distribution on the twenty-second of February, and there we were on that muddy field in Flanders. I wonder how you would enjoy standing where we stood that day. The guns were pounding away, very very near it seemed to me. I suppose we were just about parallel with the second line trenches, the shrapnel was bursting, and in the sky, aeroplanes, hostile and friendly, went over every few minutes. We saw from our vantage point, along that road, immense wagons rumbling on their way to the lines, and companies of men on the way to the trenches to relieve their fellows, who were coming back mud-stained, dejected and drooping.

We forgot all that when we looked about us and saw fifteen hundred men drawn up in a hollow square, fifteen hundred eager-eyed men. The Christmas box contained some chocolate and other food, which would not mean a great deal to us, but it meant positive luxury to those men assembled. So the little ceremony commenced. The General of the Division was there, General Gillain, now Chief of Staff, the best friend we have in the army. We had had luncheon with him, and he offered me his arm, and we walked around that square, my husband following with a staff officer. In that hollow square every department of the army was represented. We stopped before each commanding officer and were presented,—rather, he was presented to us; and the men saluted as we passed.

Peter was there too. It is wonderful how Peter gets to come with us when we go to the front. I think prayer has a great deal to do with it. We pray earnestly that Peter may come to see us, and then I go to see the General and ask if Peter may come, and Peter comes. And the funny thing is that Arthur and John usually come stringing along too.

Mrs. Norton

They manage to tuck themselves in on that same permission, and I would not vouch for their always having one of their own when they come. But Peter was there at that distribution. Of course he was not walking with us. He is a common soldier, so he stayed at the outskirts watching proceedings, and listening to the remarks of the soldiers.

There was a moving picture operator there, very disconcerting to us, and he was being instructed by Peter the whole time. He said, "Don't pay any attention to the General (that is Peter all over), but get the expression on those men's faces." Peter told me afterwards, "I almost laughed one time, mother, for I heard one soldier say to another, 'I wonder which queen that is?'" when his humble little "mother" was passing by.

The promenade finished, we came back to one side of that hollow square, where great crates of boxes were being unloaded. They were heavy, and the gendarmes passed them from the rear to me and to my husband. The marching column of men passed by, and I handed out one box, and my husband the next one. But they all wanted to take it from me, and sometimes they would not see the outstretched hand of my husband. They would take the box and look up into my face. I knew what they expected to see, a look of bored indifference, from someone out there to get a decoration of some sort for giving away the boxes. But that box was only an incident of the day,—we were out there to show our love to those men, or rather, to reveal the love of Christ. And when they looked up, they saw smiling, loving sympathy. I prayed with every breath, that they would see the love of Jesus there, and I know they did, because he answers prayer. So often the box would fall from their hands to the muddy ground, as the soldiers saw the smile, and one boy, as he looked into my face, and down at the box, said, "Madam, the very first gift I have had from anyone since the beginning of the war."

All the time the guns were pounding, and the earth was reverberating under our feet, but our hearts were light, and the General said, "Madam, you have made fifteen hundred smiles grow to-day." When all was finished they played the "Star Spangled Banner," and Peter choked up and said, "Mother, I almost wept to think how far you were away from home, you and father." Then they played the Belgian national air, the Belgian soldiers broke ranks, those men with heavy

The Next Belgian Invasion

hearts, lonely, without letters from their loved ones, although only a few kilometers interpose between them and their own homes. My husband will tell you how they have held the line for four years, how they have suffered, and how bravely they have endured, and they are making valiant servants for the Lord Jesus.

The ceremony finished, back again to the lines and the little hotel, and then once more back to London. But that was not to be our last visit to the front for this year. We felt satisfied that a good many of our boys not at the front, but at Calais and other places, had not gotten their boxes. The government had sent out a new order prohibiting the putting of literature in food boxes, and we knew we must do something more for those other men at Easter time.

We prayed much about it. We consider our money very precious. My husband has told you some of the sources from which that money comes, from the pockets of dead children, from the pockets of women who work when they ought to be sleeping, to earn a pitiful wage, and so that money is sacred. We prayed much about it, and went back at Easter time to pay another visit at the front. The intervening months were spent in England, where our offices were flooded with letters. Thousands and thousands and thousands of new men were writing us who had never heard of the work. They might have heard of us, but had had no practical demonstration of our sympathy and love. Such touching, beautiful letters as they were, and many were led to the acknowledgment of the Lord Jesus Christ through those Christmas gifts.

Easter time came, and we wanted to go back to the front, but it is not easy to get permission. The General said, "Do not write to the Minister of Supplies, I can get permission more easily for you. Get it from me." We wrote to our friend, the Chief of Staff, and back came permission to stay forty-eight hours at the front, the guest of the Belgian Government, if you please. In the meantime the Belgian Government had sent out an inquiry through the British War Office as to just what our standing was, and they had satisfied themselves as to that before sending us permission.

The German assault was on, and as we rode along, coming from Calais by motor, the last of March, there was a new sense of peril in the air. We had no difficulty in seeing the great yawning shell holes on either side of the road. The

Mrs. Norton

commander sat outside with the military chauffeur, and I have never seen such riding in my life. He said twenty men were killed on that road just an hour before we passed. We passed Adincourt where the lines of communication crossed at the railway station, and we reached LaPanne Easter morning, and had just time enough to slip into the little Protestant chapel and attend a beautiful communion service.

After a bite of lunch at the hotel, we went across the town to see the Queen at her hospital. Some of you are from the Moody Sunday School, and the Queen had a great time the next day when she saw what you had contributed to her children in the hospital. She received us graciously, and made an appointment for the next day.

Back to the hotel we went, and climbed the rickety stairs. Outside the room was a bunch of soldiers waiting for father and mother. Of course Peter was there, and Arthur, and John, and Adolph, and Rene and Oscar. We went into the little room, and had to sit on beds and whatever was handiest, but we were all thoroughly at home. After greetings were exchanged we had to have the news from the front, and then they were all introduced to one another. Peter had to tell his story. But it is a serious faced Peter. He has been going through the fire, but he has never loved the Lord as he does to-day. And he does not love his Lord because of the blessings he has sent him, but just because he is faithful, and he is himself. He had to tell us that he had as yet had no word from home to tell him anything but what he had heard, that father and mother and wife had all been destroyed in an aeroplane bombardment at Antwerp. The news had come to him from home, and he had had confirmation of that news that was authentic. But there was peace in his heart.

Then later came the glad news that all his loved ones were safe.

Adolph told us with shining face, how he had come to London with a big bag of books, studying philosophy, but he found something simple and satisfying, and Adolph is a new man in Christ Jesus.

Oscar told his story, and we prayed for him long; but he is the Lord's.

Then we read the Bible, and, dear me, but those boys have the appetite of boys! And we had to read the Bible and explain, and then read some more, and then pray, and then they did the singing, and we went downstairs for a bite of supper, and back again and read some more, and prayed some more until the lights went out. I said, "Peter, I know there is going to be a bombardment to-night; the lights are out."

"Oh nonsense," he said, "let's read some more."

Easter was a happy day, but the next day was so different. It had nothing to do with talking about the Lord, but it was demonstrating some of his blessed principles. We went to the orphanage where the Queen has gathered five hundred children whose homes have been destroyed, who have lost their parents, maimed through wounds received when their homes were destroyed. We had some gifts to give those children, about $1500 worth, given by our American friends for those needy little folk kept by the Queen, her jewels for the Master. We had this money for the Queen, and the little boxes given by the very little folk of the Moody Sunday School, which we had brought all the way from America, carrying them in our state-room to get them across. There were the little garments given by Susie Lindstroms and Mary, each with the little card written in the childish hand. Each gift bore the name of the donor, and the Queen took up the little garments and read the little cards, and looked up at me, and letting the garment fall which she had had in her hand, she said, "My heart is so touched. This is so personal. This is the sort of thing that gives me joy."

We had been taking a little advantage of her Majesty, for my husband and I had been taking photographs of her, because she said we might, and I know she has a lot to forgive, but she didn't seem to think of it. When the appointment was over, she turned to us and said, "Well, you are just angels, both of you." Never mind, we are much better off than angels. I would not be an angel for anything.

Before the day was finished we did have a battle above us that was very exciting, I must confess, but when a Queen stands before you so tranquil and quiet, you do not show fear. There were two German aeroplanes right overhead, and the children had to be gotten in quickly, for shrapnel was bursting all about us.

Then we had to go on. We had Minister Vandervelde's request that we should give 14,000 gifts to Belgian ammunition workers. We did not do it all by ourselves. They were simple little Easter cards with a beautiful Easter message of

Mrs. Norton

the risen Christ, and in exchange for the end of this card they could get 25 cents' worth of chocolate, two candles and some soap for their Christmas. We could only go to one place to distribute these gifts to a few hundred of the men. The Minister made a beautiful speech, and then I followed. I could not say much, but I said, "You are our children, and we love you, and have you in our hearts, and we have come to show you how much the Lord Jesus Christ loves you." That is about all, but their hearts were stirred, and there were tears in their eyes.

That is all I am going to tell you about the work among the soldiers, but I want to close with two stories. The first is of a Belgian soldier who works for the League, August Bardmar, the other is of a young officer from one of the crack regiments of the British, who came across our path.

Little August is a stubborn little Flemish boy against whose stubborness neither the gibes nor the jokes of his comrades could have any effect. Little August became a worker for the League, and distributed Gospels and Testatments, and preached when occasion required. They made his life pretty miserable, and one man especially, whom they called the jester, was given to taunting him, and made August as uncomfortable as he could. But the Holy Spirit was working in that man's heart, and one day he came to August and said, "If you have any of those Testaments left I believe I will take one." August quietly handed it over. A few days later he was back again, and said, "August, I wonder if you could tell me what this means, and this, and this," and August, taught by the Spirit of God, was able to make clear to him what the teaching was.

The days went by, and the morning came when they went into the trenches, "the bowels of death." Many letters have come to us from "the bowels of death," letters written by men who know the Lord, or from those who want to know him. They say, "We are living in imminent peril, and any moment may bring death to us; but (if they know the Lord) he is our comfort, and we want you to know the comfort we are finding."

At three o'clock in the morning, after a long night of war, when bodies were tired, minds dazed and dulled, and heads aching, August, hardly awake, heard the ping of a bullet singing its way across his head, and saw that the bullet had

The Next Belgian Invasion

lodged in the neck of the *"farcer,"* as he fell at his feet. August saw the blood gurgling through his companion's lips, and knew the end was not far off. He rushed as fast as he could to the dugout and aroused the doctor, and the doctor stumbled out, followed by the chaplain priest. Together they came to the side of the dying boy. Bending over him, the chaplain priest began to perform the last rites. The boy's eyes opened as he heard the voice, and looking up, he saw who it was. With one feeble hand he pushed him away and beckoned to August. August knelt beside him, and he whispered into August's ear, "August, I'm sorry I laughed at you. I did not mean it. Now I believe just as you do, and He is here with me."

Then the stretcher bearers came along and picked up the body, but the spirit had gone to be with God who gave it.

Now the story of the young English officer. Our work is for the Belgian soldiers, but it overflows to the French and to the Italians even, and to some of our enemy prisoners of war. Whenever we can, we do anything possible for the British and Americans, but we focus our efforts upon the Belgians. This young officer I met at the home of his cousin. She said to me, "I do not believe Jack is saved. He is going off to the front Friday this week, I wish you would talk to him." I said I would do it, but when the time came, in the drawing room after dinner, my tongue clave to the roof of my mouth. Of course I told him just as I would have told a soldier, and I have to say that I found less understanding of the way of life from that brainy young fellow from one of the first families of England, than from the common soldiers. He did not seem to know what I was driving at, and he said, "Mrs. Norton, won't you write to me and to Bernard?" and I said I would try.

Then my husband came back from America, where he had been throughout the winter, and this boy came to our little flat and had dinner with us. After dinner he said to my husband, "You know I found Christ, and your wife helped me. Would you like to know how I came across?" We both said eagerly that we would so like to know, and he told us this story.

"It was the night before Christmas. We were going up with the lines and we knew what it meant. We were going over the top the next day. My battalion consisted of a thousand men. We stood up until almost midnight, every man's heart almost as heavy as his boots. We tramped along those frozen French roads, and through a ruined village, nothing left but bare walls. As we marched along, very suddenly a shell was set off, and we saw directly in front of us the wall of a church, and against it the figure of the Christ on the cross. It was not an emblem of our faith, but it was the night before Christmas, and the thoughts of the men flew back across the centuries to one born for them so long ago, and those unsentimental Tommies commenced to sing, all of them together,

"'Oh come all ye faithful, joyful and triumphant,
Oh come ye, Oh come ye to Bethlehem.
Lo, in a manger, lies the King of Angels,
Oh come let us adore Him, Oh come let us adore Him,
Oh come let us adore Him, Christ the Lord.'

"Just there," he said, "I entered in. A thousand strong we went up the line. Seventy-seven of us came back."

So Jack has been living a Christian life through the months. Just before we sailed he came along to see us. My husband brought him in where I was ill, to say goodbye, and as he sat there I said, "Jack, we are going to have a little prayer for you, as we do for our own soldiers." We prayed, and then I said, "Jack, you pray."

He was sad, and before he went away he said, "Mr. and Mrs. Norton, you are the best friends I have on earth. I come just because you talk to me about the Lord. I stay at the barracks as long as I can, and then I come up here to get a change."

High and low, it matters not, they want the Gospel, and shall we be unfaithful in giving it to them? And shall we sin against the Lord in ceasing to pray for them? Oh, grant that we may not.

REACHING BELGIUM'S SOLDIERS

Ralph C. Norton

YOU know the story of the little land of Belgium when the war began, how she rose in her bravery, and laid down her life. The second year of the war as the guests of the Belgian government we were going over those front line trenches, and as we walked over a few kilometers, our conductor said, "You see this grave here, and that one there? They are only indications of what those days of struggle, and wounds and death meant. We were asked by the French to hold back the hordes of oncoming Germans for three days. We held the line for twenty-one days, and over the ground where you are now walking, 60,000 men shed their life's blood, and untold thousands of them were wounded." Then we knew that soil was consecrated in the minds of the Belgian people.

People are constantly asking me, "What are they doing to-day in the war?" The other day, when the left wing of the English army was driven back to Kemmil Hill, and on the right, an American army was menaced, the Germans rushed down twenty to one and moved forward until they were cut off by the Belgians. And the French edition of the Chicago *Daily Tribune*, published in Paris, said, "Belgium saved the day, and saved the left wing of the English army." The General wrote and thanked them for the heroic work they did on that day, when they took 8000 prisoners. I only bring you that side of the war to show you what men these Belgians are, and what they can do if reached for the kingdom of God.

Our work for the Belgians started very simply in England. I gathered a little knowledge of French from the hotel porter and began the distribution of Gospels and Testaments to one man and then another. I shall never forget the first boy, Pierre De Wallens, who had been lying for three months with a bullet through his neck, hovering between life and death. When we took him to our hotel and gave him a Gospel he told us how a Protestant Chaplain had told him

---

This gives the report of Mr. Norton's message at Princeton, Monday evening, and the same address, in substance, was given on Thursday evening at Cedar Lake.

Mr. Norton

the story of the cross, and the freedom from sin, through the death of our Lord and Saviour Jesus Christ. That night we had the privilege of leading him out into a full salvation. The other day we had the joy of seeing our little Pierre married to a beautiful English girl in the Protestant church. I had just one gold sovereign left (we are not allowed to carry gold over there), and I could not resist the temptation of giving it to the first girl we have had come into the "family."

The work began in simplicity, but how it has grown! Last year we put over 254,000 booklets, books and tracts into the Belgian army, and we have had person after person write to say they found Christ through them. We put about 250,000 Gospels and Testaments into the Belgian army in three years, and last year 141,647 Gospels and Testaments. Of these, 26,000 were Testaments in French and Flemish. A few of them went to the French, say a thousand, and those were sent out on requests from the men. Of those who received these Gospels and Testaments, 95 per cent. never saw a Scripture before in all their lives. Again and again we receive letters saying, "I read for the first time the Gospel of the Son of God. Send me a Testament." And then they want a Bible, and hundreds, yes thousands, of those men have thus been led to the knowledge of Jesus Christ.

For the first time they now have several Protestant chaplains in the Belgian army, and the other day Pastor Rondo said to me, "Mr. Norton, you have little conception of what this Gospel distribution has done in the Belgian army. Of the three thousand men on our list as Protestants, fully a thousand, if not more, came in through this work." Although they are only babes in Christ, one boy, Simon Pierre, has been in prison several times for distributing Gospels in the Belgian army. How brave those men are for the truth, when once they get hold of the truth!

Another Protestant chaplain told me that out of the 135 men in his division enrolled as Protestants, 80 of them had come in largely through these Gospel distributions. Another said, "Mr. Norton, we had a disciplinary camp here where men of light offenses, and some of major offenses, were placed for months, and the treatment they receive is exceedingly rigorous; everything is denied them. I went in and began to preach the Gospel and distribute the Gospels and Testaments that you sent me, and so marvelous has been the change in that camp that the men have become docile to the

Reaching Belgium's Soldiers

orders of the leader, and he has asked me to come back and preach the Gospel every Sunday. And he himself is a Roman Catholic." This work has simply revolutionized that camp.

What is our field of work? First, there are the prison camps of Germany. There are 60,000 or more Belgian prisoners in Germany. Their condition is deplorable beyond description, and their sufferings beyond our imagination. They are kept behind barbed wires, poorly fed, brutally treated, beaten night and day in some of the camps, and their sufferings are enough to break a man's spirit and make him wish for death, as some of them do. Andrew Murray received over two hundred and twenty-five missionaries from the Boer prison camps for his work in South Africa. What a field of opportunity—the 60,000 men who are dying of tubercular conditions, and of hunger and starvation in the prison camps of Germany! At Christmas time we sent them 6,500 Christmas boxes, all of clothing. Food cannot go into Germany. We put a reply card in every box. We sent out 6,500 boxes, and we received 5,500 reply cards. We sent them another letter and told them we would send them Gospels and Testaments if they liked. Now 6,000 pocket Testaments have been sent to that army, and men are hungry for the Word of God.

A man wrote the other day, "Couldn't you send me more of those Gospels and tracts? One of my friends comes to my hut and says, 'Let me read them.' Then he says, 'Let me take them back to my hut and read them.' I answer, 'No, Sir, you cannot take them there, I will lose them.'" So we sent him several to give away to his comrades.

Let me tell you about Louis. One day my wife and I were walking back home from our lunch at London. We met a Belgian soldier, and in my beautiful (?) French I asked him to accept a Gospel, and he said, yes. My wife looked around and said, "He looks sad," and walked back and said, "My Belgian soldier, are you sad?"

"Yes, Madame," he replied.

"What is the matter?"

"I came to meet a friend, and missed him, and have nothing to eat."

"Are you hungry?"

We took him to the hotel and provided him with a room and breakfast. My wife turned back the covers as mother used to do in our old fashioned home in Indiana, and bade him

Mr. Norton

good-night. Later I looked in, and the door was open and he was gone. I wondered what was the matter, and asked the clerk, who said, "He came down and said, 'Sir, I do not understand this. I am a poor Belgian soldier, and they took me in and fed me; met me on the street. I cannot understand this.' I told him, 'Well, they love Belgian soldiers.'"

He went back to the trenches and gathered a group of soldiers around him, and oh, what a sweet Christian boy he became. Louis was the champion bicycler of Belgium. What a change the Gospel made in that boy's life! He was taken prisoner, in an attack, and just before we left we heard from a prison camp in Germany, saying, "Send me Gospels to give away." Sent as Daniel to his prison, as Joseph to Egypt, these men like Louis and Frank and others are going to the prison camps in Germany to reap a great harvest for God. We propose to keep in touch with that work for the prisoners and do all we can.

In Holland there are 37,000 interned Belgian soldiers, and oh, the letters we get from the men there! The other day a boy named Boutet wrote and said, "I must write about the work in this prison camp. When I came here there were only a few Protestants, and without exaggeration I can say to-day there are over five hundred men in this one camp who have accepted Christ as their Saviour; and we have learned that we can learn more in suffering than in prosperity. Send me more of the Gospels and Testaments and religious books, that we may reach more of these men."

The other day one of the boys wrote me and said, "Dear father, you will never know what you have done for me by sending me those Gospels and Testaments. We have gone through awful suffering in the winter time; my hands and face were frozen, we have no covering, the food is poor, and we are starving; and I have tuberculosis, contracted through the war, and one day you will hear that one of those hemorrhages has taken me away. But I will be with Him, and the work will go on for Belgium."

There is a great field in the camps in France, and we are working with them and helping them as far as possible. Little Jeanne Baptiste is dying of tuberculosis. He heard about us and asked for clothing. We sent it, and he sent for Gospels and Testaments, and wrote back, "O Madame, can't I call you my little mother?" My wife said, "Certainly." Then he wrote, "I have read the Gospel and have found the

Reaching Belgium's Soldiers

Saviour, and in spite of the hemorrhages I have Him and He is with me. Send me more Gospels and Testaments for the boys."

We have established a work in Paris, a *foyer*, like a hut, a place to congregate and read and write, and one of the Protestant chaplains of France has charge of that. There are often fifteen at a time gathered in this foyer. The other day there were twenty-seven there, and every man took a Gospel and Testament and began to read it with avidity.

We are confining ourselves as much as possible to the Belgian army, but we are receiving letters by scores and hundreds from the French, asking for Gospels and Testaments and books that we have had put into French. We have had some chances to work for our American boys, but of course they are largely reached before they leave, and have the Y. M. C. A. But the Belgians have nothing of the kind, and we are practically the only protestants who are doing any work for them.

Let me quote a few passages from letters culled from tens of thousands:

"It is now nearly three years since I read the New Testament for the first time and arranged my life according to it, and now I, who was proud and disobedient, am much gentler and more obedient to the orders of my superior. The fear of death had seized me, but has gone, and I feel strong. At each charge I say to myself, 'My Lord and my Saviour, protect me.' Courage has returned to me."

"It is now three weeks since I began to read the New Testament, and I am trying to live according to it. I before was rough and disobedient, but am now much gentler and obedient to those under whose orders I am. I am so happy you have taken me into your family of soldiers, and assure you I will always try to be worthy of your confidence."

"I received with great pleasure the Gospels and the two little books about the Holy Scriptures, which came to me very much apropos in these conditions of the life we are living. It makes us happy to think that if we are suffering, He suffered first in order to redeem us from our sins. So often if the thought of Jesus had not come to give me comfort, I do not know that I should not have become mad before now."

Mr. Norton

These are some of the letters from the men at the front in answer to our letters, telling us exactly how they appreciate and value this work. We have in the army 500 men who are on our rolls as distributing Gospels and Testaments. I do not say they are all Christians, but they are seeking the light, and there are 300 whom we think are genuinely saved and are telling the story of the Saviour and his love for men. Some of you know that Peter led over 500 men to Christ, and lost count after that. Another convert has led over 300 men to a definite acceptance of Christ. Another has a decoration on his breast, because when men were dying, he rushed up to his Captain, put him on his shoulders and carried him back; he was given the second highest decoration for bravery, and that boy is just as brave for Jesus Christ, God's Son.

We have made two visits to the front, and had the privilege of interviewing the Queen of the Belgians. She is so grateful to the American people for what they have done. In the first trip to the front I showed her a Testament, and she said, "That is a beautiful book, and it is so good of you to give it to our men. May I keep it?" I said, "Your Majesty, we would be so grateful to you for accepting it." On the second visit I saw a little book in her silk sweater pocket, which I looked at carefully, and feel confident that it was that little Testament. I pray God that it may bring her life and freedom through the Gospel of the Son of God.

Here is a letter from the Minister of War of the Belgian army, who received us and made it possible for us to distribute the boxes, and had a banquet for us: "Our thoughts are with you, and we see hundreds out beyond the trenches who have been gathered in that small village to receive from your hands a splendid parcel, and from your lips a kind word and a smile. They may, in the future, forget the parcel, but will never forget your charming kindness. . . . In the name of our whole division I thank you with all my heart. Good luck to you, and come back as soon as you can." God in his wonderful way has made this man the Chief of the Belgian army, so you can see what a great friend we have there.

Mr. Vandervelde, head of the International Service of the World, and of the Belgian navy, writes: "It is a pleasure to take this opportunity of expressing my gratitude and deepest pleasure to Mr. and Mrs. Norton, who have already rendered us so many services, and who are preparing for another

Reaching Belgium's Soldiers

effort to present our fighting men with presents next Christmas, through the generosity of the American people."

Don't you see the grip Americans have on Belgium? Oh, to-night I see Belgium in her agony, and in her throes of death, crying for political liberty, but the sound that thrills my soul more than that is Belgium crying out for the Word of God; and I believe, before God, the responsibility can rest nowhere else but upon America for giving her the Light of Life, the Bread of Life as well as material assistance, in this trying hour.

I gave Peter a worker's Testament which I always carried, and we put our names in it. The other day I said, "Peter, do you still have that book I gave you?" "Yes father," he said, and pulled it out. I saw something in the back, and thinking it was some secret, closed it, and said, "Peter, would it be wrong for me to ask what that is in the back?"

"No," he said; "I made up my mind no one could read it; but you and mother can."

Peter had left his father and mother and wife, to whom he had only been married six months, to go and fight for king and country, and since then one Gospel had changed his whole life. Maybe someone gave two cents to buy that Gospel, and in heaven God will know who gave it. I read this: "Dear Jeanne: I have found Christ as my personal Saviour. He has been everything to me. Jeanne, if He wants me to live I want to live, for you; yes, but O Jeanne, more I want to live for the redemption of Belgium. But if I fall on the field of battle, Jeanne, my dying wish is this,—live in my place, for Belgium."

Belgium, Belgium, Belgium, oh, that she may know God!!

Fuller accounts of the work of Mr. and Mrs. Norton for the Belgian soldiers are published in the book "Apostles of the Belgian Trenches," and in leaflet form. See page 379.

OUTDOOR EVANGELISM IN NEW YORK

Arthur J. Smith, D. D.

But when he saw the multitudes, he was moved with compassion on them, because they fainted, and were scattered abroad, as sheep having no shepherd. Then saith he unto his disciples, The harvest truly is plenteous, but the laborers are few; Pray ye therefore the Lord of the harvest, that he will send forth laborers into his harvest (Matt. 9: 36-38).

FIFTEEN years ago, a little group of New York's ministers and laymen met for conference and prayer. They were considering ways and means, and methods of work in the summer time, when so many of the ministers are away, and so many of the churches are closed, and yet when more people are in the city of New York than there ordinarily are in the winter time. Our city's population increases in the summer time by the great influx of tourists from various parts of the country.

Those ministers and laymen organized an interdenominational committee known as the Evangelistic Committee. They projected meetings in tents, shops, halls, and on the streets; they literally obeyed the command of Jesus Christ to go into the highways and hedges, into the streets and lanes of the city, to preach the Gospel to the people where they lived, and worked and played.

They put a tent in Little Italy, where 85,000 Italians were living, with only two Roman churches, and one very small Protestant mission. There were more Italians in New York at that time than in Naples. We had more Germans in the city than there were in Berlin, more Irish than in Dublin, more people of various nationalities in New York than in some of the largest cities of the lands from which they came, more Jews in New York City than in Jerusalem and contiguous territory. Out of the million or more Jews in New York City, only 125,000 of them are related to synagogues. They are drifting. Most of the girls living in shame to-day in New York are Jewish girls. A few years ago they prided themselves on the fact that no Jewish girls were in that life, but that cannot be said now. The drift is terrific. The recent

---

Address given on Wednesday evening at Princeton.

Outdoor Evangelism in New York

Rosenthal murder resulted in the execution of three Jews, one Italian and one American. The young men of Jewish families are drifting, drifting away from their religion, and all religion, into infidelity and atheism.

The same is true of the Italians, nominally Roman Catholic. A policeman said to me one night in Little Italy. "These people have no religion. We are glad you are here." The tent was located in the very midst of the Neapolitan rag pickers, and we were obliged to put a twelve-foot woven wire fence around the tent, and have plain clothes men around on the buildings near, to keep the people from throwing firebrands, and bricks, and stones on top of the tent; and there were also uniformed policemen on guard. They black-handed the evangelist twice one summer, and murdered four men in the neighborhood of that tent the same summer. But that evangelist, the late Michael Mardi, with his blind American wife, moved into that district to live, immediately after they black-handed him.

I can remember to-day the prayer of the workers, that a wall of fire might be thrown about him and that his life might be protected. It was, and he continued his work there. After the second summer's work, through the co-operation of the Presbyterian Home Mission Committee, a student evangelist, who had been Michael Mardi's assistant, took charge of the work, and in five years they had a church with eight hundred members, and a property worth $70,000. It began with an open-air meeting held on the steps of a house.

Our committee does a great deal for the people in various parts of the city, but it is now impossible to put a tent in Little Italy because there are no vacant lots. But where we cannot find lots we go into the neighborhoods, with open-air meetings. Some of our open-air meetings are conducted by paid evangelists, and pastors, and students preparing for the ministry; but the larger proportion of our open-air meetings are conducted by volunteers, by representatives of Christian Endeavor societies, Epworth Leagues, Bible Classes, Brotherhoods and other organizations from various churches. Last year there were 1,100 meetings with an aggregate attendance of 263,000 people.

Nearly all of those meetings were held immediately in front of, or adjacent to, the churches with which the young

Dr. Smith

people were connected. The policy of our committee is not to take the young people from their church neighborhoods to some other neighbborhood to do evangelistic work. We believe they should do their evangelistic work in their own neighborhood, where they are known, and where they know the people, for they will have a deeper interest in following up the results.

When we began to develop this work among the young people I was at a loss just how to go about it. I had heard that there was a great deal of work being done by laymen in Great Britain, and I decided late one summer to cross the Atlantic and spend six weeks away from home, giving the time I spent across the sea to studying work done by laymen. A friend of mine decided to go with me, and just a few days before I was to sail my wife decided to go too. I wired him and said, "Mrs. Smith is going; won't Mrs. K. come?" He wired back, "Get another room."

So we went over, and they did the sight-seeing, and I did the studying. Through letters of introduction I got into touch with the leading Christian workers in Great Britain. I was amazed to discover in that year, 1909, that there were less than 10,000 ordained ministers in the non-conformist churches, and over 50,000 unordained men all preaching regularly every week with stated appointments. I found in London 115 missions started and manned by laymen. The laymen not only paid the bills, as the laymen do in this country in missions; they did not employ a missionary or a superintendent, but those men did that part of the work themselves, and the missions were open nearly every night in the week for straight-out rescue work. You could not turn around in London in those days without running into an open-air meeting. Not only were the non-conformist churches conducting open-air meetings, but if you had gone to Portland Square you might have found Dr. Stuart Holden's assistant, or some of the young people from his church, holding an open-air meeting, and a great many other young people of the Church of England doing the same thing.

One church in London had a group of eighteen men who went out two by two after the service Sunday evening, and held nine open-air meetings in the immediate vicinity of their church, evangelizing the neighborhood. The minister might have preached to two or three hundred people in the church; but suppose each of the two of those nine groups

Outdoor Evangelism in New York

that went out, preached to two or three hundred people? Do you see the extent of the ministry? Those men were not educated, trained men, and they were in the habit of repeating the sermon that the minister preached in the church. He preached an evangelistic sermon for the people that came, and for his men that went out.

I found one church of a thousand members, and they boasted that every one of the members of that church had been converted in open-air meetings. *Every member of the church converted on the street.* I came home filled with sadness. Nothing like it in America. But I came home with a prayer in my heart that God might help me to do something toward starting a work that would result in laymen assuming their proper responsibility in the church.

They have established a chair of economics in Columbia University, and they are teaching firemen how to burn coal so as to get greater results out of it, and not waste so much. There ought to be a chair of religious economics somewhere, that would teach us how to utilize the latent forces in the churches, for I am afraid we are just "playing church." The more I think of it, the more I see the multitudes without the Gospel, and the more I see the apparent indifference of the Church it makes me feel that the Church is just playing at the job. The story is told that two colored men met on the street one day, and one said, "Sam, did I see you in Jones' Band last night? I didn't know you could play in a band. Didn't you have a trombone?" "I suah did," said the other. "Can you play a trombone?" "Well, no," he answered, "I can't play a trombone." "Well, what was you doing with the band?" "Well, you see, Jones he gets paid for every man that goes out in the band, and he takes some men that can't play, and gives them instruments, and the men just blow through their noses, and they call them a blank in the band." I am afraid there are a good many blanks in the Church.

On my way back to America I asked God to help me to do something to interest laymen in New York City in definite evangelistic endeavor. Then the trite old saying came to me, "It's a hard thing to teach an old dog new tricks," and having been associated in the Christian Endeavor movement as a state president, and having seen such high types of consecration and willingness on the part of the young people to respond to almost any kind of an appeal from sincere, earnest

Dr. Smith

hearts, I said, "I think I will make my first approach to Christian Endeavor."

I had not been in my office two hours before my colleague came to me and said, "Mr. Smith, I have been waiting for you to come back. I have been approached by the City Union of Christian Endeavor and asked to take the chairmanship of the Committee on Evangelism. I am waiting for you to tell me whether I ought to do it or not." I said, "Do it by all means." I did not think God was working at both ends. But do you know, he always does.

My colleague accepted the chairmanship of the Committee on Evangelism of the City Union, and we went through the City Union of Christian Endeavor and projected an Evangelistic Institute for the study of the Evangelistic Message, and Evangelistic Methods, methods to include personal work, evangelistic work in the Sunday School, in Young People's meetings and on the streets. We had about three hundred in that first Institute, and the Institutes have been conducted since 1909 until the present year.

Two years ago, the year before the Billy Sunday campaign, the average attendance in our Institute was 337. It was held for ten weeks, on Tuesday nights, one night a week, two periods a night, for the study of the message and the study of methods.

The year preceding the Billy Sunday campaign we turned over our organization to the young man who had charge of that department of our work to the Sunday Campaign. He went to their headquarters with all of our records, and took entire charge of their personal workers, and they put on an Evangelistic Institute for the study of personal work, with an average attendance of nearly a thousand. It was our organization just turned over to them.

This year, because of the war, and because of the going of so many of our splendid fellows into the camps, and some of them across the seas, we were not able to put on as strong an Institute in numbers, but I think we had the best Institute of all the series. Mr. Trumbull came over and lectured on "The Evangelistic Message," and the lectures have been published. The book is entitled "What is the Gospel?" and the subjects covered are, Why men are lost, How men are saved, What is salvation?, The blessed hope, and The Victorious Life. We hope to use the book for our Institute next year,

Outdoor Evangelism in New York

and for extension classes in Young People's Societies. What we have done in New York you can do in your society. You can take a book like that and use it as a text-book.[1]

Who does the preaching in these outdoor meetings? Our young men did it in the beginning, but when they began to volunteer, the young women began to fill the gaps. We have a picture in our office of a splendid meeting up Fifth avenue, and a fine Christian young woman giving the message. It is not strange to see a woman speaking on the streets of New York. During the suffrage campaign some of the very finest women in the city were out on the street corners speaking and answering questions. Why should not our consecrated womanhood go out and give the Gospel message to the lost? They are doing it repeatedly.

One young woman only eighteen years of age telephoned me and said, "Mr. Smith, can I come up to the office and see you?" She was away down in the business district, and had just an hour for lunch, but she wanted to confer with me about some open-air meetings in her district, Washington Heights,—a young women with a vision of Jesus Christ, fully surrendered, wanting to do his will and help lost souls out of darkness into light. We conferred, and a program was proposed for that district. She said she would call the officers of the Young People's Societies together and suggest to them to put it on. The plan was to have meetings in a tent, eight churches uniting in the campaign. They were to have short, snappy young people's meetings in their churches, meetings lasting about twenty-five minutes, then to invite the people to the big meeting in the tent. Every night after the meeting in the tent, during the week, they put on an open-air meeting about 9.30 or 10.00 o'clock in the vicinity of the tent, to reach the crowd that did not come to the meeting.

The other day this girl telephoned the office, and I overheard the conversation of the one in the office who answered, who herself is a girl who is taking the place of the young man who had charge of our auxiliary work. "Your leader has failed you?" she said. "What are you going to do?" The young woman who telephoned was chairman of the open-air work in connection with that tent meeting, and here she was with four or five hundred people on her hands, and no

---
[1] See page 379.

Dr. Smith

speaker. She said, "If I cannot get a speaker between now and 9.30 I will speak myself." And she spoke, and did it well. One of our staff was there to help her if she needed it; but she did not need the help.

I remember one beautiful young woman in her first open-air meeting, who did not speak, but sang. She went downtown to this meeting and began to sing a sweet Gospel hymn. A man of the editorial staff of the New York American was in a saloon, had ordered a drink and paid for it and gotten his change. The drink was put on the bar, he had taken the glass in his hands, when that girl began to sing the familiar hymn. He just left the glass on the bar and went to the door, saw that young woman across the street, forgot his drink and his engagement for that evening, went across the street and listened. Something gripped him, and he went into the meeting. He surrendered to Jesus Christ that night. When he dropped into that saloon he was on his way to deliver a lecture on infidelity. He has been in the ministry now for several years. You never can tell what God will do with you, and I do not know of anyone who will have a greater influence on the streets of New York than a pure, consecrated Christian girl.

We have one girl on our staff who was converted in our meetings when she was a child. Her mother, and sister, and brother, and she herself united with a little German Methodist Church. She is only twenty-three. She began to sing in tent meetings as a little girl from the Sunday School. I lost track of her, and upon inquiry found she was working in the lace mills, and her people were very poor. I said, "Minnie, would you like to work for the Evangelistic Committee?" She looked at me and said, "What do you want me to do?" "Sing in the open-air meeting at Madison and Union Squares at noon and at night," I answered.

Minnie has been singing for us, and going to High School. There are other beautiful girls in New York City going downtown as volunteers, and wonderful things are happening. Scores of men and women have been reached through open-air meetings. One "down-and-outer" was approached by a splendid Christian young woman, and through her influence made willing to listen to a Christian man whom she called to deal with him. Although his seemed a hopeless case, he was converted, became a Y. M. C. A. Secretary and has done wonderful work among the soldiers.

Outdoor Evangelism in New York

Those young people in New York City would not be doing the work they are doing on the streets of New York to-night if they had not made a surrender to Jesus Christ. They are not doing it for the sake of doing something. We have been praying that God would help us to bring them into the Victorious Life, and that is why we asked Mr. Trumbull to come over. Out of his busy life he came over to join us in our last Institute, and helped us start a Victorious Life Conference in New York City. There were two messages on the Victorious Life, and one night two of the young people who have been in the experience and living it, came over with him and gave their testimonies. I wish you would pray that God will keep that little fire burning until it spreads throughout that city. We need it more than you may think.

How about your city? How about your town? How about your church? Are the crowds attending your church summer nights, or is the church closed? Does your minister preach to forty or fifty people, ten or fifteen, when you might have a meeting with four hundred outside? What are you going to do about it? Will you go back and start something? Will you go back and agitate until something is done? Do not despise the day of small things. One young fellow said, "I will do it in New York." He represented a conservative uptown church. I did not believe he would be able to persuade the church. He went back and reasoned with them, "We only have fifteen or twenty out at our Sunday evening Young People's meeting all summer. Why not have a little prayer-meeting here and go down to Riverside Drive and 155th St. and have an open-air meeting?" He agitated until he started something. They have been holding an open-air meeting at Riverside Drive for three months every summer since then, and having wonderful results.

That young man was elected Sunday School Superintendent, and out of the group of young men who took that responsibility they have several men on the official boards of the church.

A member of the Christian Endeavor Society of the old First Presbyterian Church said to me after a conference on open-air work, "Will you come down and speak to our Endeavorers if I can get the elders of the church into the meeting?" "Delighted to," I responded. I supposed I would have fifteen or twenty minutes, and they said, "We can only give you five minutes." I spoke for five minutes, but it

Dr. Smith

convinced the elders that they ought to start an open-air meeting, and the First Presbyterian Church started this initial open-air meeting in 1907. One of their leaders had been praying for years that something of that kind might be started in that church. As a direct result of their open-air meetings, the church has built south of the main yard an open-air pulpit of brown stone in harmony with the architecture of the building.

You may start a great movement in your city, but you must do it in prayer. Will you say, "Here am I, Lord; send me?"

THIS MAN RECEIVETH SINNERS

W. B. Anderson, D. D.

> Now all the publicans and sinners were drawing near unto him to hear him. And both the Pharisees and the scribes murmured, saying, This man receiveth sinners, and eateth with them.—Luke 15: 1, 2.

NO MORE wonderful stories have ever been told than the three in this fifteenth chapter of Luke,—God's story of the lost sheep, the woman's story of the lost piece of silver and the man's story of the lost son. But how few from the multitudes whose hearts have been touched by the parables ever stopped in the first two verses to look at the audience and the Speaker. No part of the chapter is more wonderful than these introductory verses.

It is a vivid picture with clear lines, showing the Speaker, the publicans and sinners drinking in his words, and the scribes and Pharisees opposing him and seeking occasion to have him condemned to death. How eager are the sinners crowding about to hear him! How proud and cruel is the little group standing by to destroy him! How strong and fearless is the figure in the center, the most wonderful Man who ever spoke to his fellow men!

It is difficult for one born and reared in a Christian land to get an unobstructed view of this Man. It is an illuminating experience in a non-Christian land to speak with one who has never heard the Name before, and to gather from the reaction of his hearing something of a clearer vision of the Christ. We Christians have so obscured him that we can scarcely see him as he is. We have emasculated him in our art, and wrapped him around with our doctrines, and explained him away by our philosophy until we are startled when we happen upon him in the clear, true light of some gospel incident.

What a flood of light is thrown upon him by the accusation of these scribes and Pharisees. They had been attempting to find some charge against him that would be sufficiently grave to condemn him to death. The one they bring here,

---

The morning sermon on the opening Sunday at Cedar Lake. This message has been printed in leaflet form, including the portions omitted in this report. See page 379.

while not sufficient to condemn him to death, is a serious one before the Jewish law and the traditions of the elders,—"This man receiveth sinners and eateth with them."

Who was the man against whom the religious leaders brought this charge?

He was a Prince. In adapting our notion of Christ to Western social customs and speaking of him in our Western language, we have very much impoverished our conception of him. He is commonly thought of as a poor outcast from society. The words of prophecy and of the Gospels are taken out of their Oriental setting and put into a new environment. Now, Jesus Christ was not a social outcast. He was an aristocrat. He was not only of noble blood, but he was of royal blood. He was hailed by the people of his time as the "Son of David." He was the oldest son in the home and was possibly the coming Messiah. He was known among his people as a prince.

The Eastern idea of aristocracy differs widely from the Western idea. While the West may scorn the aristocracy of the East, Western aristocracy is in turn despised by the Oriental. In the East they say that any one can be an aristocrat in the West if he have only ambition and money, while among them a man must be born an aristocrat. Their aristocracy is inherent in life itself.

Away in a remote district, among bigoted Mohammedans in North India, there lived an evangelist. He was a *sayyad* or descendant of Mohammed, an old man and a wonderfully lovable character. I was itinerating in the district and was going to visit the town where he was the only Christian. He had come out a long way to meet me and we were walking back together. As we drew near the town the headman with several others came out to meet us. They saluted me politely after the manner of their country, and then stooping, touched the knees of Mohammed Ali Shah the evangelist, doing him reverence as they would one of their own holy men. I was a little troubled at their manner of saluting him, and wondered if it were possible that the old man was making any concessions to their religious demands in order to retain his power over them as a *sayyad;* but knowing him and his devotion, I could scarcely believe this. When we had been seated for a little while in my tent the old evangelist excused himself and went into the town on some errand. I then took occasion

This Man Receiveth Sinners

to inquire from the headman why he had shown to the Christian evangelist the reverence due a holy man.

His face darkened with anger as he said, "Yes, Mohammed Ali Shah has become a dog of a Christian, but do you not know that he is a descendant of the Prophet (peace and prayers be upon his name) and that no sin that he may commit could taint the holy blood in his veins?"

Here was the true Eastern aristocracy. It would not be an unusual thing in India for a university graduate to do reverence to some mud-bespattered hod carrier who was a *sayyad* from his own village.

So Jesus Christ, the son of the carpenter, moved among his own people as a Prince,—the son of King David himself.

He was a Rabbi. Not only did he have a high place among his people because of his royal blood but he had also the thing so highly coveted in the East, the distinction of intellectual leadership. He was a Rabbi. In the thought of the East the priest comes first, and then the king, and then the teacher. Christ had not gone through the ordinary process of securing the degree of Rabbi, but the people, recognizing his marvelous grasp of truth and his power to impart it to others had called him "Rabbi."

In the Orient to be a teacher is to hold a place of distinction. To-day a little Hindu school boy playing in the dust by the roadside, on seeing his teacher must rise and stand respectfully facing him as he approaches. Then with palms together and finger tips touching his forehead he must bow low in reverent salutation as he passes, and he may resume his play only when the teacher is well on his way. So when Jews called Christ "Rabbi" it was no empty form of salutation. It carried with it the deep reverence of the people for him and for the truth he set forth. He was a Prince by birth and a Rabbi by virtue of his power to teach.

He was a Popular Leader. In every generation there are a few men, a very few, who tower high above their fellows. They are marked by force of character and by greatness of personality. They are great, strong men of such heroic mould that other men instinctively gather about and follow them. Others naturally love to follow them for they are strong to lead. It is such as these who draw the world up to its higher destinies or down to its ruin.

Dr. Anderson

Jesus Christ was such a man. He stood out high above the multitude. Men gathered about him and asked him what to do. He could have led a revolution that would have swept over all Asia. He had all the qualities of a great leader of men.

He was One whom these very scribes and Pharisees would have enlisted in their own cause if they could have done so. The keenest search in the world has always been the search for a man. These political and religious schemers must have taken the measure of this Man when he first sprang into prominence as a teacher. The political ring in Jerusalem would have been glad to use him for their own ends or would have been glad even to follow him on his agreeing to "play the game." But they have failed to capture his great soul. They have found him opposed to their every selfish end and ambition, and now they see in the success of his teaching the downfall of their own power. So he must be destroyed.

He was the Son of God. Because he was more than a Prince, he did not claim his right to the throne of Israel. Because he was more than a Rabbi, he did not establish a school of theology or of philosophy. Because he was more than a popular leader, he did not put himself at the head of a cruelly oppressed people and lead them out to political and social freedom. Because he was more than one whom the politicians might have used, he did not join any party even for the sake of helping to reform that party. Because he was more than all of these, he laid aside all of their rights and prerogatives. Because he was the Son of God, he became the servant of men. Little did his jealous, blind accusers dream that this One whom they would have squeezed into the mould of a constricted, distorted life was God incarnate dwelling among men as a man. It was because he was the Son of God that he "emptied himself, taking the form of a servant, being made in the likeness of men, and being found in fashion as a man, he humbled himself, becoming obedient even unto death, yea, the death of the cross." Because he was the Son of God, that Son of David, that Teacher of matchless excellence, that idolized Leader of his people stood that day and allowed the religious leaders of the Jews to weave about him the web of death.

The first accusation they made against him, "He receiveth sinners," would not be a serious one in the West to-day. If

This Man Receiveth Sinners

some famous religious leader among us should go out into the street and gather about him men of sin that he might better them socially and morally he would add to his fame as a real teacher and leader. It was not so among the Jews. The religious teacher must be careful to keep himself aloof from those who did not conform religiously, and to maintain his dignity as an intellectual leader. To depart from this ideal would be to break down their whole social order. A man must not associate with "sinners."

His accusers said that this man received sinners. Was their accusation true? Could Jesus Christ be proved guilty of receiving sinners? He was guilty. He did receive sinners.

He received the Canaanitish woman. He received a leper. He received a publican. He received the Samaritan woman. He received the woman of the street. He received the dying thief. His last service in the flesh was to receive a sinner. Not only had the scribes and Pharisees abundant evidence for his conviction on this charge, but here, right at the end of his life was their justification. He did receive sinners.

And I am glad that he did receive sinners, for otherwise he would not have received me, and if he had not received me, I would not to-day be walking in fellowship with God, nor knowing the joy of sin forgiven, nor have had committed to me this wonderful gospel of salvation for sinners. I am glad he did not leave men to discover that he received sinners, but that he himself kept announcing it and inviting sinners to come to him. Not only that, but he declared that this was the only thing for which he came into the world. He came to seek and to save that which was lost. It is worthy of note that immediately after this accusation made by the scribes and Pharisees, he spoke to them boldly the three parables about the lost sheep, the lost coin and the lost boy; and the sheep was carried in, and the coin was found, and the father's arms clasped the boy. If these stories mean anything, they mean that this Man who is God truly receiveth sinners.

The charge that he received sinners was a serious one, yet not nearly so serious as the charge that he ate with them. To the Jew this was a serious charge indeed.

In the West eating is only an ordinary incident of life, but among some of the peoples of the Orient it amounts to a sacrament. For example, to the Hindu it is a vital part of his religion. Food must be taken with scrupulous care, not only as to its substance and kind, but as to its preparation and

Dr. Anderson

as to the manner of eating it. To the Hindu woman, cooking is her worship and the hearth is her altar.

While with the Moslem and the Jew there are not so many restrictions, the whole matter of the partaking of food is surrounded by safeguards. Certain kinds of food are ceremonially clean or unclean. Food must be taken under certain restrictions and certain forms must be observed in the partaking of it. One of the strictest observances is that of the company in which food may be eaten. A Moslem must not eat with an idolater nor with an enemy. He also believes that eating with a person forms an indissoluble bond of friendship or brotherhood.

One afternoon when we had been in India only about two years, we were sitting in the veranda with some friends when a great, strapping Afghan came in. He was a young man of about twenty years of age. In conversation with him I found that he had been a student in the Mission High School for a year or two, that his father was one of the nobles among the followers of the Afghan prince then a state prisoner in Rawal Pindi and that he had just called to become acquainted with the new principal of the college.

While we were talking, tea was served and in passing it to the others present I offered him a cup. I did not expect him to take it and was not surprised when he told me the usual polite lie, excusing himself by saying that he had drunk tea and eaten cake just before coming to call. I knew he was lying and he knew that I knew he was lying, and we had a perfect understanding between us.

Our friendship ripened through several weeks, and one day again he called when we were having tea. In my knowledge that he would not take the tea, I unthinkingly did a very discourteous thing, and did not offer it to him. When I was seated, he turned to me and said, "Sir, may I have a cup of tea?" With due apologies I handed him a cup of tea and passed him some cakes, and was a little surprised when he drank the tea and ate the cakes. After the others had gone from the room I said to him, half jokingly, "Brother, why did you put me to shame to-day by asking for tea, when on your first visit you declined to drink with us?"

Then he told another polite lie, saying, "Well, you know, sir, the first day I came you were not acquainted with me and I did not know whether or not you would wish to have me for a friend." (He meant, "I did not know you very well and did not know whether or not I could trust you as a friend.") He continued, "Now we are acquainted and I thought you might be willing to have me for a friend." (He meant,—"We are now acquainted, and I am willing to trust you as a friend.")

I asked him to explain to me just what this matter of eating meant to him,—why he was so particular about his eating with a stranger. His explanation was as follows: "You see, we take the round loaf of bread and break it in two, and you eat one half and I eat the other half, and we have become the one loaf and never can anything divide us. Now you and I have eaten together, and that means we are blood brothers. It means that if you have a need of me I am willing to give my life for you. Would you give your life for me?"

I thought a minute before I replied, and then I could look him straight in the eye and say, "Yes, I believe I would, brother."

He meant it and so did I.

I have not seen that man for thirteen years, but to-day if I were in India, and if away up there on the frontier there should be war, and if in the midst of it I should be in a place of peril, and recognizing him, call him by name, I would expect him to throw himself between me and death. I believe he would. It is his notion of his obligation to a friend with whom he has eaten salt. He has become a blood brother.

And when Jesus Christ ate with sinners he took them into his family. He made them his friends. They became his blood brothers. He made himself liable to lay down his life for them. The charge was true, he did eat with them, and he took the consequences, and I am glad he did, for there was a day when I needed a friend. There was a day when someone had to throw himself between me and death, and he went to Calvary and received into His own heart the stroke of death. I live because he chose to eat with sinners and to become a blood brother to me in a day of mortal need.

It is possible to conceive of man's friendship with a man. It is possible to conceive of such a blood brotherhood even with a mere human being, but how can one think of having such intimate relations with God himself? It could not have been conceived of if this Man had not come into the world among men and become a man that he might so unite man to God. If Christ had not come to receive sinners, no man would have believed that God could receive a sinner. If

Dr. Anderson

he had not become blood brother to men and by his sacrifice rescued man from the death of sin, man could not have lived to have this fellowship with God.

As it is, this is no common friendship. Man cannot claim it upon an equality, for man with his mortality, with his human limitations, with his life all marred with sin, with his body still waiting for its transformation, is not a creature to aspire to fellowship with the infinite God. Christ comes with his Godhood, his divine nature, his kingship, his authority, his responsibility and all his essential attributes which he cannot lay aside for any reason whatever. The differences in the man who is a sinner and the Man who is God are necessary and not to be ignored, nor does God either ignore them himself or expect man to ignore them. It was because they could not be ignored that the Son of God came in the flesh to make this new fellowship possible.

Still it is wonderful to know that, although there is such disparity between the Saviour and the saved, the friendship can be real and satisfying in every particular. He can remain God and I can remain man, and still there can be the completest fellowship.

Nearly twenty years ago a friend told me an incident which is, as nearly as I can remember, as follows:

A young American missionary went to India and soon after his arrival there met a British youth who had gone out in the civil service. Immediately there sprang up a friendship between the two which lasted through a long life of service in that land. One day when the missionary was an old man and no longer able to stand the heat of the plains in the summer, he was talking to his British friend who had now become the governor of his province and was telling him of his cottage away in the Himalaya Mountains where he went to spend the summer months. The governor was a keen sportsman and inquired about the shooting in the neighborhood of the cottage. On hearing of the excellence of the sport, he told his missionary friend that he hoped that some time he might visit him and spend a day or two in shooting there. The missionary expressed his delight at the prospect and invited him to be his guest.

After some months he received a letter from the secretary of the governor telling him that his honor was touring through the province and that on a certain date he would be in the vicinity of the missionary's cottage and would be glad to accept the invitation to visit him. The missionary said that he knew what this meant. The secretary was expecting him to put his cottage at the disposal of the governor. He immediately sat down and wrote the secretary how honored he would be to give over his cottage to the governor and his suite for the dates mentioned.

The day before the expected arrival, he made sure that all was in the best of order, and then on the morning set for the coming of the governor, he moved out the things he might need for two or three days into a store-house in the corner of the compound, and himself moved into a tiny tent. The old missionary in speaking of it afterwards said, "Do you know the first thing the governor did when he found that I had moved out of my house was to write me a note calling me by my name and asking me that during the time of his visit I should move into my own bedroom and remain there as his guest. I wrote him a line thanking him, and as it was then almost dinner time, I hastily prepared for dinner and went to the house. I had the unique experience of sitting in my own house, at my own table, with the governor at the head of my table and I his guest.

"We had a pleasant meal, but the best time came when the members of his suite went out to their tents in the compound and when he and I went into the little parlor and sat down in the cheer of a little grate fire, remaining there in sweet fellowship away into the hours of the morning. That was an experience to be remembered.

"And do you know that is the way it is with God and me. He came down to me and said, 'Won't you move out and let me move in?' And I moved out and he moved in. And then he called to me and said to me, 'Now, you move in and be my guest.' And I moved in to abide with him. And he is here as my Lord and I am here as his guest, and he sits at the head of the table and we eat together just as he said we would. It is a wonderful fellowship that I have with my Lord."

Yes, it is as true to-day as it was in the days of his flesh. He not only receiveth sinners but he eateth with them. But how many there are who have been received by him, and who know him as a Saviour but who do not know that he is calling to them to be his friends and to eat with him. How many there are concerning whom he is saying to-day, "Behold, I stand at the door and knock; if any man hear my voice and open the door, I will come to him, and will sup with him, and he with me." He longs for the fellowship of every saved man with a passionate longing, but he is still God and Lord, and he must come in as Lord or not at all. He cannot subject himself to any man, but to-day he stands and says to every man, "Won't you move out and let me move in?" And if men only knew the possibilities of this divine friendship, how quickly they would move out and let him move in. With what joy they would hand over the lordship of life to him for the sake of a friendship with God, for no other joy and privilege on earth is to be compared with that of fellowship with this Man who receiveth sinners and eateth with them.

THE PRICE OF A REVIVAL

W. L. McClenahan

THERE is a great hungering and longing in the hearts of many of us for a fuller work of God's Spirit here in our midst. We had a little foretaste of what God could do in a group of twelve or fifteen persons the other day, when God's Spirit came down upon us. If you had all been there you would have recognized it too,—strong men sobbing and weeping over their sins, prayer and conviction running on for two hours. And what God did for us there, when we were not asking for any demonstration of this kind at all, He can do for us all here. And that is our great desire, that God will come in convicting power amongst us, and give us all peace, and joy and gladness in Him.

Four questions have occurred to me in connection with this subject. The first one is, Do we need a revival? or, What is a revival? The second, Does God want it? The third, What may be accomplished through a revival? And the fourth, How is a revival to begin?

What is a revival? I think we may get a description of a true revival, by just having a glance at the early Church. To contrast our Church of the present time with the apostolic Church, we turn to the book of Acts. Towards the close of the fourth chapter we read, "The multitude of them that believed were of one heart and of one soul." The Holy Ghost had shed abroad wondrous unity amongst His people there, and they were of one mind and one soul,—no diversity of opinion, no weighing of majorities with minorities,—one mind and one soul. We were greatly gratified to learn the other day in connection with the Board of Managers of the Victorious Life Conference, that when questions are brought up for decision, a vote is not taken, but there is prayer and discussion, and if all the members of the Board are not of one mind, the thing is left until another time, and then if there is not unity, the matter is dropped. Is there any such thing as the unity of the Spirit, which can be realized in our churches? If the Spirit is there, will there not be unity? Some of us say that there are some that would be recalcitrants,

---

The sermon on the closing Sunday morning at Princeton.

Mr. McClenahan

who could not be brought in, who would not agree; but where there is a Spirit-filled Church, people of that sort will soon find it out and leave, and we will not be troubled with them. That unity is possible.

Then, in the early Church they trusted one another; they had all things in common. Filled with the Spirit, they were ready to give away all that they had, trusting God for the supplying of all their need. There was a spirit of loving confidence in one another, begotten of God's Holy Spirit, and by God's Spirit alone. They gave to those that were in need, so that none among them lacked.

How much the Church is criticized in these days! How little influence and power she has among a certain class of people! For example, the socialists, who look on us and our wealth, and keep apart from us. They see our neglect, they see it as contrary to Christ, and we consequently have no power with them. When God's Spirit comes into a man's or a woman's life, he sees the need, and gives wherever there may be need, to all parts of the world.

We read in the same connection, that the word of the disciples was in great power, and many were added to the Church. They had favor with the people, a thing which seems almost to be lost in these days in our churches. I had known something of the littleness of results in some of the churches in America, but was astonished this morning, in taking up a Year Book of one of the foremost denominations of our land, noted for her zeal and misionary activity, and evangelistic effort, and discovered that while the membership of this Church is something like 158,000, the net gain last year was only 520, which means a gain of one in every 305 of the membership, and this after all that has been done in the way of evangelistic campaigns, and evangelistic movements in this past year, one for every 305 of the membership. Where are the children of the Church? The children of the Church that are brought into it ought to have amounted to more than that! Is it any wonder, when we see such things as this, and know that the natural population of the world is increasing at a far greater rate than is the spiritual birth in the world, that some of us cry out for the coming of the Lord?

Another characteristic of the apostolic Church was the performing of miracles by the hands of the apostles. Many signs and wonders were wrought. Just recently I came across

The Price of a Revival

this statement by Dr. A. J. Gordon, who is quoting Leiter, the great theologian: "He calls the dictum that miracles ceased with the Apostolic Church an extraordinary assumption of Protestant dogmatism, and a postulate which both history and experience entirely contradict." *The Church does not perform miracles these days because she has lost her faith.* God has not changed; he is "the same yesterday, to-day and forever." The apostolic Church was a Church which worked miracles, *and whenever like faith is exerted on the part of His people in this present age, the same miracles will be repeated.*

"Great grace was upon them all." Of how many of our churches and assemblies can it be said by the outsiders, the great world round about us, that great grace is upon us, that we are distinguished by graciousness and loving kindness, that we are really different from the world?

Perhaps we ought to mention too, that the early Church was a pure Church. They did not allow anything defiling to come in or to stay in. Offending members were not allowed there. Those that were acting and believing contrary to the rule of the Church were put out, put out doubtless in love, and yet they were not allowed to associate themselves along with the believers.

The last thing which I think of in this connection is that Jesus Christ was the center, the Holy Ghost was in control. If we take up the case of Ananias and Sapphira, we find that their sin was in trying the Holy Spirit. They were trying, as it were, to see whether the Holy Ghost was really in control, whether he was really there. Of how many of our Churches can it be said that it is the Holy Ghost who is in control? We acknowledge, perhaps, that he ought to be, that he is the leader; but as a matter of fact how rarely do we think of deciding things as "seems good to the Holy Ghost and to us." Sad to say, the Church in these latter days has come to decide these matters largely on other principles, after discussion, after saying this and that, without looking directly to find out what the Holy Ghost would have them do. A great contrast, the Church of the present time, to that of the Apostles.

That, as I understand it, is what a real revival is,—a return to apostolic principles, and practices, and conditions,—getting back to God's ideal of his Church.

In the second place, may we attempt to answer the question

Mr. McClenahan

as to whether God wants this condition to-day? *Does God want a revival?* It will help us greatly in laboring for a revival, to know whether God wants a revival. If we are to judge by the prayers of Christians as they gather together in their churches, and even in conferences like this,—a revived Church, a return to apostolic conditions, is not very much on the heart and mind of God's children. How rarely do we hear prayer for revival, Spirit guided and Spirit impelled prayer for revival! God grant that the dear friend who the other day sent in a request for prayer for a revival, may have his desire speedily granted.

We have almost forgotten the idea of revival. There have been reasons for that. In the case of some of us it has been a hope long deferred, which has made the heart sick. We have prayed, we have prayed, and we have prayed, and have seen no answer, and have stopped and given up. Then we have concluded that it is not God's purpose to give a general revival in these times. Oh, how hardening is what we call "dispensational truth," if it is not held in conjunction with this more abundant, victorious, Spirit-filled life. How we do limit God, and put things down for this age, and certain things down for the age to come. How we get our thoughts centered on the truth (which is a truth) that God is at the present time calling out a people for his name, and forget that God has at the same time great and glorious purposes for the whole of humanity! We give up. I have known of that experience myself.

Does God expect to give a general revival in this age? Now let us get very clear on this subject. God does want it. If he wants it, a revival, for individual souls, and I think we are all convinced of that here this morning, he wants it for his whole body, *his whole body.* Others are just as dear to him as we are. We sometimes forget that.

He speaks of his Church in the fifth chapter of Ephesians as "a glorious Church, without spot or wrinkle." Now the connection there may indicate that God is speaking about practical duties, the practical life of the Church, but as we look at the context, I think we are warranted in believing that God is also thinking of the Church at the present time in its relation to others. He wants it to be a perfect Church "without spot and without wrinkle," which is a Spirit-filled Church, a revived Church, an apostolic Church, a Church which knows what we call here "the victorious life;" and

The Price of a Revival

it is only through that kind of a Church that He can fully work. We can never accomplish the work which God has for the Church, in the world, unless we are Spirit filled, unless we know Jesus Christ in his fulness.

Now God wants this revival,—he wants it. Some of us may have been terribly discouraged over this thing, but "if God be for us, who can be against us?" Let us just keep on praying. Let us remember how Daniel's prayer was offered, and how he had to wait because there were obstacles in the way; but that prayer was recorded, there is remembrance in heaven, and I do not believe God is ever going to disappoint us when once we have prayed a prayer for revival in faith and expectation. Let us pray for it this morning, and take fresh courage. God wants this revival, and he is, in his own good time—perhaps not immediately, but after years —going to answer our request.

Now, what would a revival accomplish? It would be the means, as nothing else would be the means, of making Christ known in the world. This subject of revival is very much on the hearts of those that have been in the neglected parts of the world. They feel that is the one thing, the great thing that is needed in the world to-day,—a revival of the home Church.

Some of us have known what it is to be shocked by conditions, when we return to America after an absence of some years, and see the diminished attendance in prayer-meeting, and other changes which those who remain on from year to year do not notice because they are so gradual. There is nothing that would so gladden the hearts of your missionaries as to see a real revival here at home, spreading throughout the country. It would help to make Christ known, because at the same time, this revival which God would give us, would bring great love for the heathen, and they would be no longer strangers to us, but would be as our brethren.

The reason it is so hard for us to get money, to get what we need in the way of equipment, and to get workers, is because the love of God has not been shed abroad in our hearts, as a Church, by his Holy Ghost. This is the only impelling power for all these things, and when we get a revival in the Church, there will be no trouble about funds. Instead of going to people for money, and asking for their subscriptions, and taking up collections, they will come to us

Mr. McClenahan

and say, "Where can I spend this? Where can I put this?" That is what will take place in a revived Church.

Think how it would please God, who is longing so for the salvation of the world, that they all might know of His love, as we have known him. Let us just think of how this would please our great and gracious God, a revival in our midst!

In the fourth place, *How does a revival begin?* It does not begin with the many. It begins with the few; it begins with the one or two. Perhaps you have seen this prayer, "Lord send a revival, and begin in me." That is where the revival has to begin,—to begin in each of us individually. It is only what we have to overflow from our lives that will go to others; it is only this overflowing blessing that will benefit others at all. If we are not overflowing, we will have no influence or effect on others whatever. It is only when the joy comes up to our faces that people will see that we have something inside that is worth while. It is from an overflowing life, a revived life, that this revival is to begin generally in the Church.

I want to speak briefly about this Victorious Life. There may be a number here this morning who are as yet strangers to it, and are wondering what it is, and how to get it. We have had so much able discussion, so much study of it in these past days, but people can never see this without the enlightenment of the Holy Spirit. May I speak first of the effects.

One of the effects of the Spirit-filled life is abounding love to all of our fellow men. It may be that some here this morning are lacking that very thing,—that this is the one thing they do not have for people who have wronged them, or people who have wronged the cause of God. Oh, how subtle is the sin, to be so zealous for God's truth that there is just something between us and the other person who is not receiving it, and is not going on with God. Well, when this fulness of Christ comes into our life, it casts out all this feeling of distance from fellow Christians. The love of God is so shed abroad in our hearts that we love the whole world. Are we loving the whole world? Are we loving the unlovely? That is one of the tests.

One of the other marks is peace, "the peace of God which passes all understanding." How hard it seems to get this peace. We worry. Business men are beginning to feel this

The Price of a Revival

as they perhaps never did before. They tell us, "We are all in a nervous strain. Life is moving at a more rapid pace than ever before. Time is being taken from our devotions and the reading and study of God's Word, and our peace just ebbs out." Well, thank God it is possible to get perfect peace with God. I wish you could all have heard the testimonies of the business men here, how God is able to keep them in perfect peace. I do not know that lack of peace is the trouble of business men only, because we are all of the same clay, and all have our difficulties and troubles, but it is possible so to be filled with the fulness of Jesus Christ, that there is no anxiety to trouble or harass,—perfect peace, perfect peace. God is able to give this to us.

Joy is another mark—Oh yes, *joy*. The early disciples were filled with the Holy Ghost, and there was great joy. They took their food with singleness of heart, and with gladness. God's Spirit is shed abroad in our hearts in its fulness, and we get this more abundant life, and we cannot keep it in, and everybody is going to see it. There is joy. Oh, how God would like to see the face of everyone of us light up here this morning! How he looks for it, and it is possible for us: "My joy I give unto you." You can have it in wonderful, abundant measure.

And in this abundant life there is relief, relief from the power of Satan, relief from the power of sin, from those things that so harass us, over which we have no power; this particular temptation over which we never could get victory,—it is possible for us to get complete victory over it, complete victory. Many of us can testify to this. And to put it all in a nut-shell, we get completely satisfied with the Lord Jesus Christ.

A large number of us here this morning know that perfect satisfaction. It does not mean that we are not going to learn more about him, that we will live without fault, not to stumble; but at the present moment, because Jesus is in our hearts, we are perfectly satisfied.

> "I have seen the face of Jesus,
> Tell me not of aught beside.
> I have heard the voice of Jesus,
> And my heart is satisfied."

That is the Victorious Life, *to be perfectly satisfied with*

Mr. McClenahan

Jesus, so that you want nothing else. "The Lord is my Shepherd, I shall not *want*"—any good thing. He gives us this victory and satisfaction, just as we abide in Christ. If we step out of his will, if anything creeps into our lives which ought not to be there, we instantly lose the love, the joy, the peace, the satisfaction that there is in the Lord Jesus Christ.

In closing, may I say that for revival in our churches, and for individual revival, we have to pay the price, and for some of us it has been a great, big price. We have had to give up everything, the last thing that we held dear in this life. It may mean for one thing that you will have to separate yourself from former associates. It may mean that you will have to give up the person that you hold dearest in your life. It may be the hardest thing that you ever did in your life, the giving up of that which is most precious; but I tell you, if you want this Victorious Life, if you are convinced in your hearts this morning that you must have it, you must go all the way with God, you must give up everything he would have you to give up. If he is putting his finger on one thing in your life which you know is not according to His will, you must take the knife and cut it right off; and if you do, God will pour out a blessing on you such as you will not be able to hold, an overflowing blessing into your life, a life of rest, a life of love, a life of peace, of power, of fruitfulness; because "The eyes of the Lord run to and fro throughout the whole earth to show himself strong in the behalf of them whose heart is perfect toward him."

Yes, the revival which we want in our churches, in the churches throughout the country, must begin first in us. It may be that God is asking some one of us here this morning to begin a revival in our community, or in our town. It will have to begin with us perhaps. Let us be willing to pay the price, and go the whole way with him.

THE LEADERS' TESTIMONIES

How They Found Victory in Christ

The messages given at the informal outdoor Vesper meetings at the conferences have been largely of the nature of personal testimonies. At Cedar Lake it was suggested that in one of these meetings the Conference leaders should give brief messages on how their own Christian life was changed. Accordingly in a Vesper meeting at Cedar Lake eight of the Conference speakers gave four minutes testimonies, which are here reported. Mr. Trumbull was asked to lead the meeting and introduce the speakers. He sounded a clear note of warning that it should not be supposed that other Christians need have experiences of the same sort, except that complete surrender and complete trusting which is common to all of them. Following Mr. Trumbull's testimony are included others which were given at various other Vesper meetings at Cedar Lake or Princeton. Mr. Borton's testimony, Professor Kimber's, and Philip Howard's, follow under separate headings.

W. H. Griffith Thomas.—I was born and born again, in the same little town in England, on the borders of Wales. I found Christ when I was seventeen, on March 24, 1878, at about nine o'clock in the evening. I could take you almost blind-fold to the very place where that occurred, and it was a clear-cut, definite conversion, as clear-cut as anything could be. I got a birthday book, and thought I would put my name in that book on my "first birthday," and when I wrote in it on my second birthday, what do you think the text was? "I forgave thee all thy debt."

I had a very blessed, and happy, and glorious time with my Bible. I was very much alone, dependent largely upon myself, and the Lord and my Bible, apart from human teachers, for weeks and months. I devoured everything I could find in the way of reading,—sermons by Spurgeon, Talmadge and the rest,—wherever I could lay hold of them. I enjoyed my Bible constantly, and had a good time. But as time went on there was an up and down experience, and

Dr. Griffith Thomas

I had sometimes joy and was on the mountain-top, and sometimes I had not joy, and was in the valley.

I was conscious of a good deal of wandering from God,—not into open sin, but I was not satisfied, I felt there was failure. One day, about eighteen months after my conversion, I went to my Bible, and said, "Lord, I cannot stand this any longer; I want to have this settled, and I want to be right." I prayed, and was led to two texts, and those two texts always will stand out from all else in the Bible, in connection with my own experience, because they represent the two words that helped me. One was in Romans 6: 13, the word "yield,"—"Yield yourselves unto God." I felt that that was what I had to do, to present myself again to God, as though I had never done it. Then I was led to 1 John 2: 28, "And now little children, abide in him." That means "stay where you are." I thought that was the next thing I had to do, and those two words, "yield," and "abide," were blessed of God to my soul, and I entered into a new experience, and realized as I never had before realized, what Christ is in the believer's life.

A few months afterwards I picked up a monthly magazine called "The Life of Faith," and for the first time read about a place called Keswick and the Keswick Convention. I read some of the addresses, and said, "I know all about this, it is perfectly familiar to me," and devoured it from cover to cover, metaphorically. I said to others in England, and elsewhere, "I don't like to call it 'Keswick teaching;' it is 'New Testament teaching.'" From that time I began to read "The Life of Faith," first as a monthly magazine, and then as a weekly paper, and those two words, "yield," and "abide," have been with me ever since, and it is about thirty-eight years ago since I entered into this new experience.

Now comes the question, Has there been failure since then? Yes there has, but there is this difference betwen failure now, and failure before. I did not know then, I do know now, how to get right when I fail. There ought not to have been failure, there need not have been failure, but I do believe there is this vast and fundamental difference, that when you have accepted Christ as your victory, the Lord Jesus Christ as the Master of everything, you do know how to get back after you have failed,—it is again "yield," and again "abide." And the secret of abiding in this walk will be found in the Quiet Hour, and the way we spend that time with the Lord

The Leaders' Testimonies

every day. If we have the Quiet Hour, and use it as we should use it, we shall not only *not* backslide, but go from strength to strength, and from glory to glory. Praise God.

Miss LOUISA VAUGHAN.—I was born in the little village of Hillsboro, Ireland, in 1866, December 29th, and I was born again when I was thirteen, in a little Moravian prayer-meeting, at a Moravian boarding school that I was attending. I promptly went back to my own family, a family of seven. My people were extremely worldly, lived for the world, and loved the world, and I, a child, went back into the world with them, and did not know any better. Because of this the Lord had to deal with me very severely as I grew up into young womanhood, and when I was twenty-six years of age I had gone through some very heavy trials, and very grievous disappointments. When I was twenty-seven my father died. I loved him very much, and he was the last beloved object that the Lord took from me, and then I was willing to turn to Him with my whole heart.

At twenty-seven, I was in Christian work in the Y. W. C. A., learning to be a Secretary, acting as Assistant Secretary to the one then in charge. I happened across Andrew Murray's book "Absolute Surrender," read it, and was greatly blessed. I knelt in the quiet of my room, and absolutely surrendered to the Lord, and on that occasion, I knew that the Lord Jesus Christ was revealed in my heart as the Son of God, and my companion.

The Lord then led me to give my life to him for the foreign mission field, and I was willing, and in a year, or less than a year, he led me out to China. He was very precious to my soul, and I knew him, and he gave me souls all along the way; but it was when I was in my first class of women in China, when I was up against the most tremendous problem of my life, in great agony of soul, that I prayed to him to know what to do with those women. He again revealed himself to me, this time perhaps, not so much in my heart, as that he gave me a revelation of himself, the risen, glorified Son of God, with all power in heaven and in earth. He gave it to me in those verses of Scripture, John 14: 13, 14, "And whatsoever ye ask the Father in my name, that will I do, that the Father may be glorified in the Son. If ye shall ask any thing in my name, I will do it."

Oh, there is no joy like knowing that the Lord is going to work for you. I had gone out to China, thinking I was going to work for him, and I found out instead of that, that he was going to do all the work for me. Ever since that time he has been working for me, and I have been rejoicing in looking up to him in every thing.[1]

W. L. McCLENAHAN.—It was away back in 1893 or 1894, while I was a student in the Theological Seminary at Allegheny, Pa., that I began to hear about the Keswick Convention. I at once became interested in its teaching of the deeper life, but it was not until a good many years after that, some eighteen or twenty, that I had the privilege of being at Keswick in person.

In the meantime, shortly after leaving the seminary, I was appointed a missionary to Egypt, and in Alexandria, in those early years, I became acquainted with a very remarkable band of young men, who were known in Egypt as the Egyptian Mission Band, men mostly from Belfast, Ireland. None of us were married, all of us were young missionaries, having gone out in the same year, and we saw a great deal of each other. One of the first things that impressed itself upon me was that there was a difference between the lives of those young men and my own life. When I was in their house they would be up early in the morning, reading and studying the Word, and studying it the last thing at night. I could not help seeing their life of prayer. It was a home of prayer, and they called it "The House of Praise."

I saw how they were winning souls, and how they had great joy in their lives, something I did not have. I became concerned, and although I was as old a man as I was, an ordained minister from a theological seminary, out there on the mission field, I doubted my own salvation. Finally, through the study of the Scripture, the help that they gave me, and the help of God I came to see that I was saved, a child of God, but that I did not have what God was ready

---

[1] Further details of the results that followed Miss Vaughan's new view of Christ will be found in her little book, "Answered or Unanswered?" See page 379.

The Leaders' Testimonies

to give me. After some little time of study and of conflict, and of prayer, I came out into this which we call here the Victorious Life. That was in 1899.

While I have come out into this life, and life for me has been different since that time, and there has been a most decided change, it has not been without lapses. There have been lamentable failures, unfaithfulness on my part, but I have never lost the sense that I had the power within me, that it was available, that I was the victor, that I was not defeated, that Christ was within call, and that sin was no longer reigning in my life. I praise God that since that time I have known victory, and when there has been defeat, it has been because I have not taken advantage of the morning hour, and have neglected prayer,—neglected the means God put in my hand. The old nature was never blacker, and never darker, and it has come to the surface and appeared from time to time, but praise God, there is Jesus Christ, our perfect righteousness, to whom we can look.

BENJAMIN F. CULP.—I definitely gave my heart to the Lord when I was about twelve years of age, but I cannot remember any time in my life that I did not love him as my Saviour. I have been more or less active in Christian service all my life, but five years ago, when the Lord brought our dear friend, Mr. Trumbull, to our community, he was showing such a radiant testimony of what the Lord was doing for him, that it appealed to me. I felt at once that he had something that I did not have, and we had a great many intimate, personal conversations along the line of this life of victory.

The summer following his coming to our community, we found ourselves together at the conference at Princeton, and on one of the first early evenings of the conference, after the supper hour, we strolled off together for a walk and a talk. Neither of us went to the meeting that night, because we became so absorbed in what I was seeking. I said, "Well, I believe, Charley, that the Lord is fully able to do anything and everything in my life." Then the Lord, through him, so lovingly and tenderly began to plead with me to let Him do it then and there, and he very forcefully called to attention the thought of God's faithfulness.

We came back to his room and knelt together in prayer, asking that the Lord would just come into my life in the way that He wanted to. I did not have any great wave of emotion, or of ecstasy come into my heart at all, I just had to believe that God meant just what he said. And, praise his name, he has been faithful, and since that time life has been so different to me. I have had such a sweet fellowship with him; I have had such a joy in allowing him to work through me; prayer has meant so much more to me; his own Word is richer and more precious to me since that time, and I have been rejoicing in him ever since.

Like the rest, I have had failures, but it was when I failed to remember His faithfulness, but I have learned that it was just an instant restoration when I turned again to him in confession of sin; and the Lord is so gracious, so "faithful and just to forgive us our sins, and to cleanse us from all unrighteousness." Praise his name.

DR. H. VIRGINIA BLAKESLEE.—I had been a Christian for a number of years, but as I read the Word, it was like a sharp two-edged sword, and I would be condemned for things in my life that were sin. I tried to put them away, sick and tired and disgusted with them, and tried to crucify myself the best I knew how. Then I would go out and straightway do those same sins again, and come back so provoked at myself. I would get along two or three days of a week, and then fall again. I always had to do things in cold blood; I never had these "hallelujah feelings" that some people have. I had to believe the Word and stand on it with my two feet, whether I felt anything or not, knowing that because God said a thing it was absolutely true. I saw that self must be crucified, and Andrew Murray's books were a great blessing to me in bringing light. After floundering around for months, I invited Christ to come and dwell in my heart, and fight my battles, and do those things for me. But down I would go, because I did not count on him to do things.

I have lived so long in Africa, where I have had to think in child terms, living among those primitive, child-like people, that this matter is clear to me in the simplest child-like terms. It is as I used to feel when I was a little girl and went to walk with my father. Sometimes there would be a slippery place, and I would tear away from my father to walk across that place, and fall down and hurt my head. Up would go

The Leaders' Testimonies

my feet, and down would go my head, and I would cry, and would have a headache. After that experience I would go back and take hold of my father's hand, and I can feel even now, the pressure of my father's hand. He had a large hand, and was a large man, and I thought all the power in the world was at my father's disposal. I can feel now the satisfaction I had when, a tiny girl, I put my hand in my father's and it would close over mine. Whenever I got into danger, I learned to put my hand into my father's, and instinctively, just as naturally as breathing, I knew that every ounce of strength my father had was at my disposal the moment I put my hand in his, and I walked along over the icy places in perfect confidence, trusting in my father's great big manly strength.

I have bumped my head a great many times trying to do things, but when I let the Lord come in, I learned to say, "Here is this thing I cannot overcome, and this burden I cannot lift, but thou art here, Lord Jesus, and I reckon on you to do it."

———

E. J. PACE.—I derived from some source a highly emotional nature, therefore my conversion was very violent and pronounced, and was so completely revolutionizing, that I was indeed a new creature in Christ Jesus.

I went as a missionary to the Philippines, and departed from the living God, when I departed from his Word, and followed some of our Higher Critics. I thought that the thing to do was to be up-to-date, and so I went after ——— and all the rest of the same kind of higher critics, until I lost my faith, and lost my Christ, and almost lost my soul. I kept getting farther and farther away, and it was a desert experience I passed through. If you think missionaries occupy pedestals, disabuse your minds of that thought, for we are just as much possessed of the Old Adam as anybody.

A man did me a great wrong, and it almost sent my soul to hell. I would be riding my horse in the mountains of the Philippines, and I would jerk the reins of that horse's bridle in a perfect frenzy of rage, and say, "I will strike him just as he struck me." Then I would collapse in the saddle and say, "O God, I am a Christian missionary, and listen to me talk like that. I cannot overcome it, I cannot

Mr. Pace

overcome it. Why can't I overcome it? Forgive my enemies? I cannot do it."

It got where I could stand it no longer. I was coming up on the train from Manila, hungry for God, and praying that at the coming conference, when all our native workers would be gathered in, that we might find God in a new sense. I said, "Lord, put an end to my desert experience." When I got up to San Fernando depot, one of the missionaries said, "You are to preach at the opening session." I began to hunt through the Bible for a text, and hunted, and hunted, and hunted, and hunted, and could not find any text, and thought Achan and his sin would be most appropriate. For I was well acquainted with Achan. I preached on Achan and his sin. And all the time I was conscious that I was Achan.

I went home very sad of heart, and went to sleep. The next morning the missionary came to the door and said, "Oh, Brother Pace, I was on the point of waking you to get up during the night and come and pray with me. I have had no sleep all night. I have been seeking God." The tears streamed down his face, and he said, "Oh, I am so hungry for God, so hungry for God." I said, "I am too. Why didn't you waken me?"

The workers gathered at eight o'clock in the morning, and he said, "Brethren, won't you pray for me? I don't know anything of God; I want to know his fulness." When he said that, it was a cry out of the depths, and I suggested that we all go apart, each one of us, to seek the Lord that day in a whole day of prayer and fasting. I went out on the beach and began to pray, and pray for myself. Then I began to pray for the native workers, and did not seem to get anywhere; my prayers seemed to fall to the ground. Then I prayed for my fellow missionaries, and then I said, "Lord, I don't know what to do." Then I thought of a man up in the mountains, a great granite block of a human being, the governor of one of the head-hunting provinces of the Philippines. Such a burden of prayer came upon me as I never in my life experienced, and I prayed for two hours for that man, and forgot all about E. J. Pace, and it seemed as if I could take out of the very treasury of God's grace, and put it on that man; I could see all of his needs and put the grace of God upon him.

The upshot of it was, that everything I prayed for that man, God gave to me in rich fulness.

The Leaders' Testimonies

Mrs. Alice E. McClure.—My daughter said a few months ago that she never heard people pray for those who were glad, and she wished there was a prayer for those who were glad. I feel that this was true of my own life. As a girl I had the happiest girlhood a girl could have. Never a sorrow until I had to postpone my graduation one year on account of typhoid fever, which was not very much after all. But in the midst of all that gladness, there was a great yearning in my heart. You will pardon me if I speak very frankly, and truly, and honestly, and say that girls have a thought that when they meet the man they are going to marry that yearning will be satisfied. I met the man whom I married, and that yearning was not satisfied.

I had heard Dr. Torrey give a talk on the Holy Ghost, and when this yearning would come deep in my heart, I knew why there was that yearning. Even when I was in India, and had spoken the message that I believed God had given me, it had no power, and no women were interested in my Lord, and I knew that my word was without power, because I had not given Christ complete possession of my heart. My husband used to pray that at any cost, on any condition, God would fill him with His Holy Ghost. I would not pray that prayer, and I said, "No, I have given over my loved ones at home, to come to India, and I think God ought to give me the Holy Ghost," and I would not yield everything.

I only went to India in the first place, because I loved my husband, and I thought I could not live alone in India. God brought me to the place where I prayed that prayer. But when we got up from our knees, I said "No, I will have to take it back; I am afraid."

In two years and four months God took my husband. For one year I lived in terrible doubt and darkness, even while I stayed on in India. I had prayed that God would spare my husband, and he had not done so. I had pleaded his promise, "The prayer of faith shall save the sick," and all I knew of God I knew in this way. This crisis came when I was 12,000 miles away from my father and mother, and I doubted if there was a God.

I went into the study one night, and knew I would come out of that study either an unbeliever, and go home, or I would believe and stay in India. I do not need to go into details of how God showed me that he is, and that Christ is his Son, and that the Bible is the Word of God, but God

Mrs. McClure—Mr. Trumbull

proved it to me. He showed me through the Bible to begin with, and as soon as I recognized and assented intellectually to the fact that Christ was my Saviour, I surrendered my will, and handed my life over to him in utter and absolute surrender, and wrote out a consecration of myself, and my daughter, Lois, and all I had, and ever hoped to have, to be the Lord's forever. I asked him to fill me with his Holy Ghost, and I have never doubted for one instant, this fellowship with Christ.

The way has not been a path of ease, I have been brought through a very rugged, arid, hilly, stony way, but he is the chiefest of ten thousand, the altogether lovely one to my soul.[1]

CHARLES G. TRUMBULL.—I was forced to recognize that I needed something that I did not have, though I had been for twenty-five years a professing Christian. I was forced to it by the realization that as I was growing older, and more active in Christian service, I was defeated by the same old sins that I had had for years past; and I was not having the fellowship with God that I wanted, in any sustained way; and I was not seeing the results of my Christian service. Although I was busy for the Lord in all sorts of ways, in Sunday School work, teaching, writing, speaking, personal work, I was not seeing results in lives transformed. Those three things,—my defeats, my lack of fellowship, and my lack of results in service,—forced me to see that there was something I did not have.

Just about that time, nine years ago, I began to hear addresses and sermons, during the course of about a year, several of which were apparently talking about one and the same thing. They were talking about Jesus Christ, and they were talking about the believer's relation to Christ in a way that was new to me. I had always believed in Christ, I had taken him as my personal Saviour, the only Son of God, crucified for me, many years ago; but these messengers were talking about Christ in a different way, and I could not understand it at all.

I listened attentively, and after about a year I heard an

---

[1] The full story of Mrs. McClure's experience is told by herself in the leaflet, "An American Girl's Struggle and Surrender." See page 379.

The Leaders' Testimonies

address on Philippians 1: 21, "To me to live is Christ." It was the same truth I had been getting in other directions, until I finally came to see that what Christ was trying to tell me was that he was not merely an omnipotent helper, not merely an omnipotent one to stand alongside of me to help me do something, but that he was my life, actually my life, just the way the vine is to the branch, that Christ and I were one, as the branch the vine—one organism, and that he had taken me to himself.

I stopped trying to work for him, and stopped asking him to help me, by saying, "Lord Jesus, you are doing it all," and by rolling the burden on him. I at once had a new fellowship in victory, a new fellowship with God, a new Bible, a new prayer life, and wonderfully new results in service, when I stopped trying to serve him, and asked him to do it all.

So I passed into a victory which has continued whenever in the eight years since then I have trusted him to do it, and when I have not trusted him, there has been defeat.[1]

ROBERT C. McQUILKIN.—When I found the Lord as my Victory, seven years ago, it was as definite and clear-cut as a business proposition, without any special emotion. I made a surrender of everything that was questionable in my life, I surrendered my ambitions and my loved ones. I surrendered my past, because that was worrying me a whole lot. Then the Devil said (that is, the thought came, and I attribute it to Satan), "It is all right here at the conference, where everything is beautiful, but wait until you get back to your office!" I was working for a building construction company at that time, and I thought that was about the hardest business in the world in which to live up to the highest ideals of the Lord. I had to go back to serious problems at home, and in my church, and the thought came, "What about the future?" Then came another thought, which I knew was from the Lord, "You are making a surrender, are you not? Had you not better surrender the future?"

"But you forget that you do not understand this Victorious Life clearly, and there are those questions you have about the

---

[1] A fuller account of Mr. Trumbull's personal experience will be found in the leaflet, "The Life that Wins." See page 379.

Mr. McQuilkin—Mrs. Norton

Bible," said the other voice. "Hadn't you better wait until you get these questions settled?"

Then came my decision: "This is a complete surrender, and I will surrender those questions, I will surrender my intellect."

When I got to the end of that surrender, there was nothing left except Jesus. Everything else was put in the background,—my ambition, my plans, my church work, the girl I loved, everything was moved away and there was nothing left but Jesus. And then I said, "Lord, give me this gift of Victory." The next part of the transaction, since the Lord wanted to give the gift, was just to thank him for it. It seemed as if I were on a precipice, about to jump down into a place where I did not know what would happen,— "But Jesus is there, and he will catch me."

I had been a church member for thirteen years, in Christian work, leading missionary classes, telling people about Christ, had even given up the possibility of making a lot of money in business to prepare to be a missionary; yet that was the first day that I ever really knew the meaning of faith. I saw a picture of myself as standing on a shore with one foot in a boat, and the other foot on the ground; I wasn't quite sure of the boat. But it seemed that day that I got both feet right into the boat. I told the Lord Jesus, that because his Word said so, I believed his grace was sufficient, and this wonderful, miraculous gift of victory and joy and peace was mine.[1]

EDITH FOX NORTON (MRS. RALPH C.).—This same blessed life came to me three years ago, not at any conference, but just by myself. I didn't have very much victory over sins; I took my sins as a necessary evil, and thought I had to sin a little. But I wanted to walk with the Lord, so I just met the conditions, let everything go, and he came in and filled me, and he walked with me, and gave me victory over sin. I found all that I had to do was to reckon myself dead to the sin as it came along, and give him my life, and he wrought my victories for me. When I put my own hand on the helm again, as I did now and then, of course I fell, but I just confessed my sin and trusted him again.[1]

---

[1] A fuller testimony of Mr. McQuilkin's experience will be found in the leaflet, "Taking God at His Word." Mrs. Norton's experience, which was given in an address at Princeton in 1910, is printed in the leaflet "Just Himself." See page 379.

The Leaders' Testimonies

RALPH C. NORTON.—My father was a member of the Episcopal Church, and my mother a Presbyterian. I went one night to a Quaker church, and was converted, and I could show you the exact spot, and can tell you the exact minute. When the Lord Jesus Christ came into my life for victory, I do not know. My wife does not know where she was converted, but knows the spot where the Lord gave her victory. It was the opposite with me.

Ten years ago I read Hannah Whitall Smith's "Christian's Secret of a Happy Life," and had a rich experience then, just by faith. I am not sure that was the time when victory began with me. A life of consecration and surrender began, and I know that particularly in the last three years he has been with me all the way, and it has been victory, and joy and peace. Although many a temptation comes, he is doing the fighting, and he is with me, and I abide and rest in him, Peace is mine, and he is conquering. Praise his name.

ADDISON RAWS.—Seven years ago the Lord saw fit to take my godly father Home, and to call me to take up the work he laid down. I rebelled, thinking I was not equipped for the work; but the Lord did not cease to call me, and I said "Lord, if you will give me the assurance that you will lead me one day at a time and give me the strength, I will." I am glad to testify, that through his great life and strength, and guidance, he has allowed me to remain in that work.

Five years ago, just before the first Princeton Conference, some members of the Board of Managers came to our institution (the Keswick Colony of Mercy in New Jersey) and spent the week end with us. I went to the Conference at Princeton that year, and played the cornet like a good fellow the first two days, and enjoyed the services. Then I realized that there was something wrong, and that something would have to be done or I would have to leave the conference.

That third day, after the last service I went down under one of the shade trees for our prayer-group. We opened our hearts to one another frankly, about the things in our own lives, we went to prayer, and I poured out my heart to God and asked him to come in in all his fulness into my life, and first to wash out those awful sins that I knew were there.

I am thankful that he answered that prayer, and the years since then have been the happiest years of my life, and I

Mr. Norton—Mr. Raws—Miss Stockwell

have had great joy in his service. Since that day I have never doubted the fact that Christ is able to do anything in our lives that must be done, and to meet every circumstance.

I became proud of the victories, and then awful defeat came, but the Lord showed me that I did not have to struggle for victory, that Christ would live in me and be my very life. The problems of our institution were heavy, and I had an awful habit of worrying, but he gave me victory, and when our buildings were threatened by a great forest fire, I marveled at the way I went through that crisis without a bit of worry, just resting in his will. Our property was saved by a miracle. "Thou wilt keep him in perfect peace, whose mind is stayed on thee: because he trusteth in thee."

Miss Bessie Stockwell.—"There remaineth therefore a rest to the people of God. For he that is entered into his rest, he also hath ceased from his own works, as God did from his." Heb. 4:9-10.

Oh, how much those words have meant to me! From the early days of young womanhood my life seemed to be under the sway of the tyrant, Speed. In business college our work was timed to the second-hand of the watch, and the ambition of teachers and pupils was speed, speed, speed. In the business world promotion was gained through speed, and there was the daily struggle to turn out the mail in time for certain collections. My life had been surrendered to the Master, and nights and Sundays and noon hours were so filled with Christion "duties" that there was the constant necessity for haste, until I was tired out, and went away for a six weeks rest at Grandmother's New England homestead. There, seated on a great rocky ledge overlooking Long Island Sound, I would sit in the morning sunshine watching the boats slowly, peacefully moving upon the calm waters, longing for the time to come when I should enter into God's rest at the end of life's journey.

All too soon, a telegram summoned me back to "the land of speed," and some years later the door opened for training in the Moody Bible Institute. There also, the four weekly practical work assignments, the numerous hours of Bible study required, the daily domestic training, and other things, kept one busy night and day. It was there, in the midst of great discouragement and spiritual darkness, that

The Leaders' Testimonies

the Lord spoke to me in the words of Philippians 1.6, "Being confident of this very thing, that he which hath begun a good work in you will perform it until the day of Jesus Christ," and I saw that it was not my work that the Lord wanted, but that he wanted to work in me and through me.

After going into Christian work I met defeat again, for when the trials came up (and they were many), I thought they came upon me through my own lack of wisdom, or because God wanted to chastise me. Finally I was privileged to attend the Conference at Cedar Lake in July, 1916, where Pastor Paul Rader of the Moody Tabernacle preached on Psalm 66:10-13, showing that God allows the Red Seas, the Bitter Waters, the trials, the nets, the afflictions, the burnings to be placed in our pathways, in love, that he might teach us the joy of looking up and trusting him in the hard place, and that he might bring us into "a wealthy place,"—a place of satisfaction,—in himself. I asked God then and there to forgive my lack of faith and surrender to his will in the hardships, and although there have been many failures since then, I have never known the darkness and discouragement of earlier years, and have proved him, in every crisis, to be sufficient for every need of mine.

This blessed truth I found portrayed in a picture on exhibition at the Art Museum in Chicago. Upon first glance it appeared to be a daub of white, blue, and grey paint. I ejaculated, "What in the world is that doing in an art gallery? Is it a study in the mixing of colors?" As I looked again, I discovered that it represented a mist rising from the Sea of Galilee, and when I looked the third time, more intently, in the midst of the mass of vapour I could descry the form of the Lord Jesus Christ, with his hands outstretched in loving tenderness.

Oh, how I praise his name, that he has shown me that always he is in the midst of the cloud, with his love reaching down to help us go through to the place of satisfaction in himself, and that we do not have to wait for our heavenly home to find the rest which God hath prepared, but that here and now, moment by moment, we may know that rest of simple child-like faith in the sufficiency and the presence of the Lord Jesus, who is himself, "the rest which God hath prepared for his people," and we can say with Frances Ridley Havergal:

Miss Stockwell—Mr. Heinze

"Just to leave in His dear hand
   Little things,
All we cannot understand,
   All that stings!
Just to let Him take the care
   Sorely pressing,
Finding all we let Him bear
   Changed to blessing.
This is all! and yet the way
Marked by Him who loves thee best!
   Secret of a happy day,
   Secret of His promised rest."

OLIVER R. HEINZE.—The last six years of my life have been crammed with all the loving kindness of the Lord. Six years ago an event took place in my Christian life which stands out like a great mountain-peak from which I can never look away.

Previous to that time my Christian life had been very unsatisfactory. As a young man I had given my heart to the Lord, and knew I was saved, and for several years I had a blessed time of fellowship with him, and loved prayer and Bible study; but I did not know the Lord in his fulness, and I had an up-and-down experience; I was not making any progress and wondered why I was not growing in grace. Then trouble came into my life, and the Lord used that trouble to bring me to my senses spiritually, showing me that these troubles were due to heart-wanderings, lack of surrender to him. He showed me sin, and portrayed all of my failings in such an indelible way upon my heart that it humbled me and drove me to earnest intercessory prayer for myself. The Spirit caused me to mourn because of my sins, and on top of that came a wonderful blessing from God, for he says "Blessed are they that mourn: for they shall be comforted. . . . Blessed are they that hunger and thirst for righteousness: for they shall be filled." I found as I reached out after God, that this hunger increased more and more, and I was led to make a full surrender to the Lord Jesus Christ, and to ask him to cleanse my heart and make me clean, and just to let me have him in all his fulness.

He did it, and I had a "violent" blessing from God that fixed me up in my Christian life in such a way that I never went

The Leaders' Testimonies

back to the old life. The heart-wanderings ceased, and a great love for prayer came into my life, a great love for service, a great passion for the world, and for other Christians, that I had never had before.

I was sorry that during all those years I had not had the fruit of an active Christian life, and asked him that he would make up to me those empty years, and he is doing it. The last six years have been so full of blessing, and glory, and victory, and sunshine, and service, that it has been my joy to live for the Lord, and live for others. The Bible is a new book, prayer is a new power, and I have never known such sweet communion, and such beautiful victory, and such glory in my soul as since that memorable 25th of March, 1912.

A BUSINESS MAN'S VICTORY

J. Harvey Borton

IT was in 1910 that our friend Mr. Trumbull had been across the water to the convention at Edinburgh, and after he returned, he wrote me, from New Wilmington, Pa., telling me that something had happened to him there that changed his life. When he came home we had luncheon together in a restaurant, and I tried to get him to tell me about it, but he said there wasn't time. I was hungry for something in my own spiritual life, and insisted that I was coming out that night to see him.

For about six weeks I met him every few days and had lunch with my friend, but I did not get very far, and finally determined to take a day off and settle the problem. That night on the ferry I met a prominent man of Philadelphia, and told him I was going to take a day off, and that he thought he was too important to his business to do it; he called me on the phone the next morning and asked me take a horseback ride with him. I came back, after the cross-country ride, went into my room and read the book of Ephesians, and prayed, but nothing happened.

I called up The Sunday School Times and asked Mr. Trumbull if he could see me, went down and first had a talk with my friend Mr. Howard, the publisher, and found out he also had something he hadn't had before. We went upstairs into Mr. Trumbull's little office, and he asked me if there was anything in my life which would prevent my having this experience, if there was anything I had not surrendered. I told him I didn't know of anything, but supposed there must be something or I would have the experience. He said, "Let us pray," and we knelt down, and he asked God that I might have the blessing, and then thanked God that I had it. Mr. Howard prayed, and then I prayed and asked God that I might have it.

I got up and said, "This is delightful fellowship, but nothing has broken inside of me. I have had no new experience that I know anything about. Charley has had a wonderful

---

Mr. Borton's testimony was given at a "business men's vespers" at Princeton and also at Cedar Lake.

A Business Man's Victory

experience, and Phil has had a wonderful experience." Then Mr. Trumbull said to me, "Harvey, what you need is to believe that you have it, and accept what God offers." The Spirit said, "That is what you need to do, get down and thank God."

We got down and thanked God that I had accepted Christ in a new way. There was no emotion about it. It was a cold blooded transaction, just like a business transaction in my office. Going up Walnut Street after our conference, I said to Mr. Trumbull, "I cannot understand why you and Mr. Howard should have such a wonderful experience, and I haven't had anything." "If I wanted to borrow five dollars from you tonight," he said, "would you want a promissory note?" "Of course not," I answered. "Well, God doesn't have to give promissory notes."

We separated and went home, and before I reached home I picked up one of Andrew Murray's books, and read it on the train, turning to this chapter, "He will complete that which he has begun." The next morning I started to read Ephesians again, and I was ten days getting through it. There were such glorious things there that I had never seen before that I simply could not absorb it fast enough.

Now if any of you are waiting for some emotion, or feeling, remember that God does not have to give promissory notes. The next morning Mr. Trumbull called me over the telephone, and I said "Oh, I am so thankful, Charley, that God did not give me any feeling last night, because if I had had it, and it had left me, I would have been concerned about it, but I haven't had it, so I never need to be concerned about my feelings."

All through these eight years God has been giving me such joy and happiness as I had never known before, and when I have made mistakes, and fallen into sin, I have known that instantly I could come back into his presence again and accept all that he offered me. There has been no hopelessness since then.

Our business is a large one, running into millions of dollars a year, with interests extending over a good deal of this part of the country, up and down the Atlantic Coast, and on the Pacific. Last year I had the most difficult situation to cope with in this business, but since I accepted Jesus Christ in his fulness, he has just taken care of these things, has changed men's hearts, and switched things around, and brought

Mr. Borton

things out to his honor and glory. All I had to do was to use the common sense which he gave me, and then stand back and marvel at what he was going to do, and is doing. God has given me great responsibilities, but I would be almost ashamed to tell the stockholders and directors of our company how little I have thought of the place since I came here.

I had to face the proposition of whether I would leave the business to which I had given nearly twenty-eight years of my life, leave my associates, and start over again, but God just made the way easy, and I was perfectly willing to do it, if he wanted me to.

Since this war the pressure upon business men in this country is increasing almost every day. The work piles up, and the work on Christian committees, and conventions. When this pressure becomes greater and greater, the Quiet Hour is the last thing we can afford to give up. Business men say they haven't time, but I notice they have time to do the things they want to do,—to eat three meals, read the papers, talk to their executives in the office. My hours are long; I start at 5.45 in the morning, and keep it up until late at night, but I simply would not give up my Quiet Hour if I am able to hold my head up.

If there are business men here who have not time for the Quiet Hour I want to say you must find time if you are going to know Him. You have to reckon something as loss, yea all things as loss, "for the priceless privilege of knowing Jesus Christ, our Lord." Then he comes to us in our busy lives, and gives us what we need. There is a sign in my office, "It can't be done.—But here it is." You cannot take the Quiet Hour; but here it is. It can be done the same as you can do other impossible things in His strength.

FIGHTING COLLEGE DOUBTS

Professor J. A. Morris Kimber

I HAD, up until my freshman year at college, the ordinary sort of a Christian life that most church members have. I had been brought up in a family of Friends, and it was the regular thing to attend church. At college I met Mr. McQuilkin, and he was kind enough to ask me to have a prayer group meet in my room, and we went to some Student Volunteer conferences together. I had to attend the prayer group because it met in my room.

In that college, a certain course and a certain book started me into a period of doubt, from which I did not emerge for a period of several years. It was supposed to be a Bible course, where I hoped to get the greatest light and benefit. At the end of that year, largely to get me away from college, and the things going on there, I went abroad with our family, and over in Jerusalem, on the anniversary of the night that Christ spent in the Garden of Gethsemane, looking up at the beautiful Passover moon, I did not know whether that story had any truth in it or not; I did not believe there was anything in the atonement, and the only consolation I could get, was the thought, "Well, the event did not happen here, Christ did not rise, but people have worshiped that place for hundreds of years, and consequently we ought to go to see it, not because resurrection life was purchased here, but because people have thought so."

I went through the Billy Sunday meetings, attended a Bible class in our dormitory, did various kinds of Christian work such as leading singing, even at a Holiness Camp Meeting in Massachusetts,—in the middle of all those doubts, living on my past reputation, and my family's reputation. I even accepted a pastorate and spent the summer working in it. I wrote my sermons, and tried to believe them. Most of them were along social service lines, community uplift, and all that sort of thing, without any real power behind them.

I determined one thing, however, that if there was anything in the orthodox position, the deity of Christ, the inspiration

---

A testimony given at one of the outdoor Vesper meetings at Princeton. The same message, in somewhat fuller form, was given in a Vesper meeting at Whittier.

Professor Kimber

of the Bible, the atonement, I at least was going to be square with those questions, because thousands of people had believed them, and results had been produced in lives. I had heard of the Bible Institute of Los Angeles, and had read Dr. Torrey's books, and so I decided that instead of going on with my graduate work, I would go to the Institute a year. I had all kinds of doubts, but the messages of those Institutes are really substantial, and they took up those doubts in a satisfactory way. But still I could not get straightened out. Toward the end I said to myself, "I am not going to bother any longer, but just take the orthodox position."

Then a strange thing happened. The college at Whittier asked me if I would come out and take up several branches that one or two vacancies had left open, and when they learned that the Professor of Bible was not going to return I was asked to take the Bible Chair at Whittier College. I wrote them that I would take it.

After an interview with one of the leaders of the Victorious Life Conference, and reading "The Life that Wins,"[1] I got a real surrender that lasted for quite a while, and went to Whittier and taught the year through. I took the orthodox position all the year, and referred the students to good books, and helped many a student, who hadn't the slightest idea that I ever questioned, and they came into a much clearer position than I was at the very time. Toward the end of the year all my doubts began to swarm on me again.

I came to the conference at Princeton last year and was perfectly miserable, but decided we must have a Victorious Life Conference at Whittier. My students must know the truth. So I talked with the leaders about it. During my interview with Mr. Trumbull, I told him I could not settle the question of the inspiration of the Bible and the deity of Christ. I had no idea that a person could have victory and not understand these things, even though I saw a student come into the Victorious Life who had not been sure there was a God. Mr. Trumbull asked me if I would simply take that promise "My God shall supply all your needs," and believe it. I argued all around it, and brought up this question and that. But I was held to that one decision: "Is God supplying my needs or is he not? Does God tell the truth?" Some one was coming, and I got down on my knees and thanked God

---

[1] See page 379.

that he did meet all my needs. Later temptation to doubt came, but the Lord showed me that the step I took here I just had to take over again, and that he was meeting all my needs. I want to say to college students, settle it on this basis. Do not read philosophy books to get straightened out, but just believe, "My God shall supply every need of yours," and it does not make a particle of difference what the need is.

IN THE ARMY CAMPS

Philip E. Howard, Jr.

LIKE many of you, I was brought up in a Christian home, came to Christ at an early age, struggled along, falling, and getting up again. But finally I saw the truth in 2 Corinthians 12: 9, "My grace is sufficient for thee." I laid the whole thing at Jesus' feet, even my faith and trust, and He gave me faith to believe that His grace was sufficient for me. The day after my new decision, as I was talking to a very dear friend about it, having had no emotion whatever, two things came over me just like waves of the ocean,—the fact of my own foolishness and worthlessness in trying to fight it out in my own strength, even with Christ's help, and the fact that Christ's grace was infinitely more than sufficient. What joy I felt in the fact that Christ was my victory, and strength and life. I loved to read the Bible, and study it, and the glorious truth of the Second Coming came and filled my life, and he gave me the power to speak to other people.

I believe this was all preparation for my first year in college, my testing time. The college was supposed to be orthodox. I knew there was Higher Criticism, and people who did not accept God's Word, but the insidious way in which they stripped God's Word of everything it meant to me—I never saw anything like it. But God gave me grace to get up early in the morning and listen to him speak through his Word, and talk to him in prayer, and Christ was giving me victory all through each day. There was one Senior with whom I had fellowship, and we would slip into a classroom at night for prayer, the best times I ever had. Towards the end of the year we got a prayer group together.

Then came the summer, and the Conference at Princeton, and at the close I went away feeling that God wanted me in some definite Christian work. The way did not open, and I went back to college. Three weeks later the Lord definitely called me to go into work for the soldiers, in which I have been throughout the winter, with Mr. George Davis,

---

A message given at one of the outdoor Vesper meetings at Princeton.

In the Army Camps

who had been working with the soldiers in the training camps in England, under the Pocket Testament League, asking the soldiers to take the Gospel and read a chapter every day, and making an evangelistic appeal, asking them definitely to accept Christ as their Saviour.

We started through the South, working under the auspices of the Y. M. C. A. Every night Mr. Davis would tell of his experiences on the other side, and make those two appeals. We went to the Mexican border, and farther west in New Mexico. We were gone four months and twenty days, and 14,000 men took those little Testaments, and 3,500 said for the first time that they would take Christ as their personal Saviour.

Then we came back to Philadelphia, and to Camp Merritt. We also visited the Missionary Institute at Nyack. There I heard the missionary appeal, but thought I was all right, being in Christian work, and left the volunteer card they had given me at home. But the appeal kept coming and coming to me, and every time I came to a missionary verse in my Bible reading, it hit me like a stone. Finally one morning I heard a fellow singing. It wasn't the hymn that brought me to it, it was Christ himself; the song was, "Beneath the Cross of Jesus." I was thinking there was so much to give up, I loved my home, and luxuries, but I thank God that he finally gave me the power to make the decision. One phrase helped me, "I ask no other sunshine, than the sunshine of his face." When I thought of that, I couldn't stand it any longer, and said, "Lord, here is my decision to go as a foreign missionary."

After that the way marvelously opened for Mr. Davis and me to go to Camp Merritt as Barracks workers, simply doing personal work before the soldiers embark. A wonderful opportunity.

I went up to one fellow and asked, "Would you like a Testament?" His face brightened up as he said, in a Southern voice, "Oh, yes, suh, I'd like one." He said it in such a way that I wondered at the tone. Then I thought of something that might be hindering. "Can you read?" I asked. "No," he replied, with a quiet smile. "I've been trying to learn for a long time, but I can't do much. But I'm awful glad for what I do know."

He seemed so interested that I said, "Suppose you take one and try to get someone to read it to you each day." "I'll

Philip E. Howard, Jr.

certainly do all I can with it," he said. So I signed a card for him, and he took the Testament. Then I spoke to him about Christ. He spoke out then in such a way that I knew the Lord was working. "Come over by this coal box," I said, "away from the crowd." He followed, and then told me something like this:

"I never made a decision for Christ, but I want to. God has been dealing with me a long while. For the last three weeks I've been seeking after the Lord and praying to him every night. I saw a fellow make the decision at the 'Y' the other night. But I can't get away from the old cussin'—I gave up drinkin'. Many a time I've been in jail because of drink, and I know that if a fellow goes across the pond, and gets killed, if he isn't saved he's goin' straight to hell. But if he is saved, it's all right. Many a preacher has been after me for ten years. But always there's something holdin' me back."

As he talked he broke down and pulled out his handkerchief. Then I talked as I very seldom find myself talking. The Lord gave me many verses to use. I told the fellow a little of my own experience. Finally he said, with his voice trembling, "I'll take him," and he gripped my hand hard. Then I said, "Will you write that here in the corner?" I had forgotten he could not write. He said, his voice still trembling, "You write and I'll touch the pencil." So as I wrote "I accept Christ," he laid a firm, warm hand on mine. Then he gripped my hands again, and thanked me for coming down.

Morning after morning, as I got up and looked out my window, I heard a sound like rushing water down on the street,—the click of the iron-clad shoes of those men, thousands of them, going to the boats, and as I saw those brown helmets going down the road, and those rifles bobbing up and down, I said to myself, "How many of those men are saved? How many of those men have I spoken to?" There are so many going out without him, so many workers giving them the Testaments without a word, and they do not know what they mean; but if the question is put to them, "Have you accepted Christ as your Saviour?" the Lord works with them, and you would be surprised to see how the men will open up. The Lord has taught me the wonderful lesson, "Just put the question."

LOOKING UNTO JESUS

Robert C. McQuilkin

On the closing Sunday afternoon at each of the Conferences the delegates gathered for the "Say-So Meeting." Testimonies half a minute in length, or little more, were given, and the meetings went on for three hours or more, with no sense of weariness. Necessarily the testimonies were confined largely to the new blessings received during the week. But in practically all cases the happy delegates in their testimony "exalted no name but the Name of Christ, and no place but the Mercy Seat." The chairman of the meetings was asked to give an opening word to gather up the teaching of the Conference. This message (Looking Unto Jesus), was given at Princeton, and also at Cedar Lake. The testimonies that follow are selected from those given at Princeton and Cedar Lake. The many like blessed testimonies of the Whittier Say-So meeting are not included, as no stenographic report of these were taken.

A "SAY-SO MEETING" is for two purposes,—to give a testimony or to get a testimony. For there may be some who begin the meeting without a testimony. Those who give a testimony give the testimony to the Lord Jesus, and those that need to get a testimony can get the testimony from the Lord Jesus. It is the redeemed *of the Lord* who "say so" (Psalm 107: 2).

We began our conference with the Master, and at its close the same Master is here. In that other place where there was much green grass, and companies of men sat down, in number about five thousand, this Lord of ours said to his disciples, "Give ye them to eat." And the disciples did that very thing, *having first received from him*. Now the Master who worked that miracle is the Master who is here this afternoon to give us a testimony; we want everybody to have a testimony fresh from Him, whether there is opportunity to speak it this afternoon or not.

It was after the feeding of the five thousand, and after the feeding of the four thousand, that a very strange thing oc-

Mr. McQuilkin

curred,—a break-down in faith; the Master had to rebuke his disciples for their little faith (Matt. 14:31; 16:8-11). Shall He need to rebuke any of us, after this week of his presence and his miracles of grace, for our little faith?

Before we bring our testimony, I have been asked to give a little picture of the Victorious Life, which may help some who do not know Christ as their Victory, to understand the simplicity of it, and to get a testimony to the sufficiency of Jesus Christ to meet every need now. So I bring to you that scene on the Sea of Galilee, just after the feeding of the five thousand, when the disciples were tossed on the waves, and practised seamen though they were, they found themselves helpless to get to land. In the fourth watch of the night, Jesus, who has been yonder on the hills praying for them and for us, comes walking on the water. The disciples cry out with fear, and the Lord says, "Be of good cheer; it is I; be not afraid."

"Lord, if it be thou," says Peter, "bid me come unto thee upon the waters."

Do you see the Lord Jesus walking on those waters? He actually did it. Here is our picture of the Victorious Life. "Lord, if it be thou." The proof of the presence of the Lord Jesus Christ is the working of miracles; the proof of the presence of the Lord Jesus Christ in my heart is the accomplishing of something that could not be accomplished unless the supernatural power of the Son of God were doing it. "Lord, if it be thou, bid me come unto thee upon the waters." Peter was asking Jesus to do something for him that was supernatural. That is the first thing; the Victorious Life is a miracle as much as the walking on the water was a miracle for Peter. If we get that settled we will not *try* to live the Victorious Life; if we get that clear, we will not be bothered about helping Jesus to give us the victory, but we will *let him do it all*.

Jesus said to Peter, "Come." Peter was *looking at Jesus* on the water, waiting for His word. Peter was a good swimmer, and he doubtless knew how to "tread water," but Peter had never walked on the water. And Peter had never seen any other man walking on the water. But there was a Man actually doing it before his eyes, and he said to Peter, "You come and do the same thing."

That is the situation this afternoon. There are those who

Looking Unto Jesus

say, "I never saw anyone living the Victorious Life. I have heard people talk about it, but as I have watched their lives, I do not consider that theirs is the Victorious Life." Peter might have said that; he might have said, "I never walked on the water, and I never saw anyone else walking on the water." *But there was one Man doing it.* Oh, may we turn our eyes away from every speaker we have heard, and turn our eyes away from the friends who are taking Christ as their victory, and get our eyes fixed on the Man who is living the Victorious Life, the Lord Jesus Christ, and he is asking each of us Christians to do the same thing. He is saying to each of us, as to Peter, "Come, do this impossible thing."

He is saying to us, "In nothing be anxious." Can we do it? He is saying to us, "Love your enemies." Are we doing it? I wonder if we are loving our friends? He is saying to us, "Love one another as I have loved you." He is saying to you and to me, "Love the Lord Thy God with all thy heart, and with all thy soul, and with all thy strength, and with all thy mind." He is telling you and me to have complete victory over sin, and put everything evil out of our hearts. Do you catch the point? It is just as impossible for you and me to do this, as for Peter to walk on the water. Just before Peter walked on the water he had seen five thousand people fed with five loaves and two fishes. Jesus had said to his disciples, "Give ye them to eat." Think of it! Five thousand men, and —"Give ye them to eat." The disciples might well have said, "Lord, if we are to give these people to eat, we must first get it from you." And so was the miracle wrought. Peter and John one day passed a man lame from his mother's womb lying at a door of the temple. He asked for an alms, and Peter said to him, "Silver and gold have I none; but what I have, that give I thee. In the name of Jesus Christ of Nazareth, walk." "Rise up and walk?" the man might have said; "that is exactly what I cannot do. If you had asked me to do anything else I might do it. But I was born this way. I have never walked." He did not say that; by faith he started to do the impossible thing, and immediately his feet and his ankle-bones received strength.

Oh, do you see it? The Lord is saying to you, "Here is this wonderful life of victory, and you have never lived it,—it is the one thing you cannot do; but I say unto you 'Rise up and walk.' 'Come, walk on the water.'"

Mr. McQuilkin

What shall be our response? Here is the critical test. Some of you are probably saying, "Suppose the thing does not work? Suppose I go back and have a failure? Suppose I say I am trusting Jesus for victory, and my friends see that I have failed? I had better try this thing out before I take Christ as my victory." Peter might have said, "I have never walked on the water; I have never tried this thing. I had better see whether the water will hold me up." I picture him then turning around and saying, "Andrew and John, hold on to this leg of mine," while he sticks one foot out on the water to see whether it will hold him up. We smile at such a thought, but that is what many a Christian does about the matter of victory. No, Peter did not do that. What did he do? A friend of mine says that usually we think of Peter beginning to sink because he got his eyes off Jesus, but there was something before that: "Peter went down from the boat and *walked upon the waters.*"

Shall we not do that now, step out in answer to Christ's call; having cast off every weight by a full surrender, dare to trust the miracle to Him.

The next part of our picture gives the secret of *continuing in victory.* Some have stepped out and taken Christ as Victory, and they have fallen into sin, and become confused, and discouraged. "Why, I thought I started in the Victorious Life, and here I am going into sin." I thought I was dead to sin and a dead man can't sin, can he?" They thought it was done once for all. No; it is more precious than that. There are three ways Peter might have walked on the water. First, the Lord might have frozen the water and turned it into ice so that it would bear Peter's weight. Second, the Lord might have taken the weight out of Peter's body, so that the small surface of his feet would have been sufficient to bear him up on the water. But the water remained just the same; and the weight of Peter's body remained just the same. How was the miracle accomplished? Peter walked by faith, sustained by the invisible supernatural power of Christ. Peter's part was just *looking.* The Lord Jesus did the whole thing, and the miracle was effective just as long as Peter kept his eyes on Jesus, not doubting that the Master was doing it.

How many of you would like Jesus to do something for you that would make it impossible for you to sin again in this world? Would that be a message of glad tidings, if we

Looking Unto Jesus

could tell you truthfully that that is what the Bible says? That would not be good news to me. God could make such a provision but do you not see what we would lose? The message is, that only as long as we keep in that close, loving, intimate touch with Jesus, the miracle continues in our lives. It is the walk of faith,—looking unto Jesus.

Then suppose failure comes? We have heard the leaders testify, "I have had many failures since I entered into victory," and some say, "Of course I expect to have failures." Suppose Peter had said, before he started on the water, "Of course I do not expect to go all the way to Jesus. I may be able to take a few steps"? Peter was not saying that when he walked on the water, because he had faith. But when Peter looked around on the waves and the winds,—the attendant circumstances,—and got his eyes off Jesus, then he began to sink. He cried, "Lord save me," and *immediately* Jesus stretched forth His hand and saved him. And then the Master looked with loving rebuke into the face of Peter, and what did he say? Just what Jesus says to you and me every time we fail in the Victorious Life after we have started, "O thou of little faith, wherefore didst thou doubt?" It was when Peter's faith failed that he sank. So, while there is always the possibility of our failing, to say that we expect to fail would mean that we were not trusting the Lord's power to continue his miracle that he had begun.

If a failure should come, remember the instant restoration that is ours. It was *immediately* that Christ heard and answered Peter's call to save him.

I am gloriously glad to-day that we cannot stand here and say that if you surrender and believe, you will be dead, so that you will never sin again. That would make it mechanical and take away the preciousness of the contact with the living, loving Lord every moment as we walk. As we look unto him we keep reckoning self dead unto sin and alive unto God. Be of good cheer, then. It is Christ. Be not afraid. The Victorious Life (on our side) is just as simple as this: look unto Jesus—and KEEP ON LOOKING.

AT THE "SAY-SO" MEETINGS

The Word of Their Testimony

What He Will Preach.—I am a young preacher, and I am going back to my parish, and to my people, by the grace of God to live a victorious life, and what I believe is better still, to preach a victorious Christ to my people. Praise his name.

Afraid of Personal Work.—One of our day verses was, "That I may know Him." I said to myself, "Do I know him? I know a lot about Him, but do I know *Him?*" I praise the Lord that now I do know Him. I came here afraid to do personal work, but I handed that over to the Lord while here.

A Happy Family.—A medical missionary was coming to visit our home, and I was explaining to my little boy what medical missionaries do in foreign lands. I told him very carefully that they were living for Jesus over there, as we were living for Jesus here. To my astonishment and dismay, he said, "Are we living for Jesus, mother? Well, I never knew that before." I realized as never before that we had been living only a kind of a Christian life. We surrendered ourselves, and the little boy and his sister gave themselves up to foreign missionary service. Another son has surrendered too, and the little daughter of eight years is trying to understand, and thinks that she does. I came here expecting a great deal, but I am receiving a great deal more.

Two Words.—I thank God that He has answered my prayer in giving me a clear understanding of the fact that Christ's grace is sufficient for me *now*. He has shown me two things this week very clearly, the two words "Christ," and "is."

Jesus=Victory.—I praise God for the flash of light He gave me in one of these meetings, that everything was done for us on the cross in Jesus' finished work, and the victory

---

See note at the opening of article on page 346, also note on page 320.

The Word of Their Testimony

is His; that Jesus is victory, and Jesus and His victory are inseparable.

When Sailing was Delayed.—My husband and I are booked for Africa, and expected to sail in June. In God's providence He has permitted us to stay for this Conference, and we are so thankful, because we have seen Him face to face.

It Lasted.—Last year I came here and accepted victory, and had a joy that I never had before, and a joy which has lasted. My face is turned toward Africa, and I hope some day my body will join my heart over there.

Recommissioned.—I came here weary in body, and worn out from the continuous service in a Gospel mission work, where our work is largely with soldiers and sailors, and where we see conversions every night in the year. I thought my work was practically ended, but since I have been here my spirit and soul have been so renewed that I feel recommissioned for service. This past year I started fighting to keep my head above water, trying to be a Christian. I could not do it; and I thank the Lord for bringing me here.

Absolutely Weak.—I want to thank God that He has shown me how absolutely weak I am, and that He has shown me that His grace is sufficient for me, and has taught me how to trust Him for everything.

Lieutenant Barnhouse's Word.—Last Sunday night when I had to go back to camp, I was disappointed that I could not stay through the Conference. I was thinking of the 78th Psalm, and of God furnishing a table in the wilderness. God can give you a conference in your own heart any time, and that is the secret that can keep you from being let down after you go home. I praise God that the battle is already fought and won, and no matter where you are, in camp, or in your own church or home, or surrounded by things that seek to pull down, it can be victory, and will be victory, because He is the Victory. Pray for the Christian men in

At the "Say-So" Meetings

the camps. The time is short to reach the thousands of men whose names might soon be in the casualty list. For the first time in their lives most of them are away from home, and they are facing temptations which they never dreamed of. But God can furnish a table in the wilderness. I would rather have one private living the Christian life than half a dozen secretaries and chaplains, because it counts more, and you can see it every day.

Not Far Away.—He has become real and vital to my life. He seemed far away, and I never realized what He was until I came here.

Came for Temporary Relief.—I came here praying that I might have a small blessing, a little temporary relief from something that had troubled me since childhood. On Thursday night I surrendered to the Lord, and He has given me peace that passeth all understanding.

Dr. Griffith Thomas' "Portion."—I should like to pass on the little message that came to me in my portion this morning, Acts 27: 25: "I believe God, that it shall be even as it was told me." Whatever the Lord has told us this week, *it shall be.* Secondly, "I believe God," and with that I would couple, if I may, two passages, not strictly literally, but I think they are sufficiently near to make it worth our while to put them together: Corinthians 10: 13, "God is faithful,—that ye may be able," and 2 Corinthians 9: 8, "God is able,—that ye may be faithful."

Seeing After Believing.—I praise God for showing me that believing is seeing, and not seeing is believing, because after we believe He opens the way and we can see.

Our Cornetist's Tree.—Four years ago under a tree on the campus I asked the Lord to take away my sins. The other day I walked over to that place, and there is a big pile of coal there. But if the Lord had left my sins there there would have been a bigger pile. I thank the Lord that He did not leave them there, but buried them in the sea of His forgetfulness. The years since then have been the happiest years of my life. He has been my constant guide, and I have trusted Him and never once doubted that He was able.

Consciousness or Himself?—I have always had an earnest desire for a consciousness of the Lord, and never had it. Now I am glad I have found out that I do not have to have it, but I have Him just the same.

Better than Consciousness.—I feel very much like the newsboy who, when he first heard of Jesus Christ, and found Him as his own, did not know how to praise God, but he just threw up his hat and hollered, "Hurray for Jesus Christ!" I came here to find the blessedness of the consciousness of His presence, but found I had to yield that desire that I had had for eight long years. I gave it up and just accepted Him in cold faith. I did not have any feeling when I got up, nor for some time afterwards, and the Devil said, "This is just mockery. You have just said yes, and there is no change." But the Lord gave me a verse showing that Christ was my victory, and I said, I "know He is true." Then I was flooded with the joy of the consciousness of His presence, and have been hardly able to keep still ever since. He is going to keep on blessing me, I am sure."

A Word from the Leader.—These friends are finding that there is something better than the consciousness of Christ's presence, and that is the fact of His presence. But I do not believe consciousness should be confused with feeling; we may have a continued "consciousness" of Christ's presence, in the sense of *knowing* he is with us. Let the feelings go up and down as they will, but carry with you the conscious knowledge of the fact that Christ is here, because He said so. Let us not be fooled by feeling, though we praise God for the happy feelings when they come.

Found the Saviour and Victor.—Since I have come here this week for the first time I have taken Christ as my per-

At the "Say-So" Meetings

sonal Saviour and my victory. I do not understand, but I have given Him all my doubts, and I trust Him, and am happier than I have ever been in all my life.

Her First Testimony.—This is my first testimony for Jesus. I could never get up before, until that young man said, "I am not ashamed of the Gospel of Jesus Christ, for it is the power of God unto salvation." I said, "I am going to get up and thank Jesus for all the spiritual food I have gotten this week." I thank him for my material food, and have gotten so much spiritual food that I want to thank Him for that.

A Good Time and - - - -. I came here last year to have a good time, and the folks around knew it. This year I came with the idea of getting a real blessing, and asked God that He would give it to me, and that He would let me see Him. I hadn't gotten a real look at Him in all His beauty before. I thank Him that at this Conference I have seen Jesus—just Himself. The speakers have gotten out of the way, and I have seen Him in all His fulness. I thank Him for it.

A Week-ender Takes.—I had a real hunger and desire for Christ and for victory. I just came in on the week-end of the Conference, and I had my question answered in one of the afternoon meetings, and took Christ by faith.

An Assistant.—God has given me a little corner of service, and He has shown me here that I do not have to be responsible for it, neither for workers, nor for the money, nor for the souls that are won; but it is His work, and I only have to be the Assistant, and have to keep looking unto Him and do what He tells me.

Two Pictures.—I want to thank the Lord for two wonderful new pictures He has shown me this week,—one is a new picture of His great love, and the other is a picture of the great world need. This last picture may cost me a great deal, but I will go where He wants me to go.

The Word of Their Testimony

A Pastor Comes 3000 Miles.—God brought me three thousand miles to attend this Conference, and I am going back with such a knowledge of supernatural service as I have never known before.

> "Ready to go, ready to stay,
> Ready my place to fill;
> Ready for service, little or great,
> Ready to do His will."

Mothers!—If there are any mothers who have daughters who are going to the mission field, if you could know the joy He gives when you give them up you would give them gladly.

A Business Man is "Shown."—God has shown me here this week things that I never have seen before,—my sins of unlove to God, and to my fellowmen, pride, selfishness, self-will, censoriousness; and I praise Him that these things have been washed away in the blood of Jesus Christ. He has shown me His wonders of intercession; He has made plain to me things in regard to prayer that I have never known before, and He has also shown me how, when we step to one side and get out of His way, He works.

Richer as Days Go By.—I thought I had had rich fellowship with Him at other conferences, but there have been richer things here than I have ever known before, and I know He has still richer things in store for me, as I trust Him.

Reinstated.—I came to this Conference because I felt a great need in my own spiritual life. Some years ago I surrendered to the Lord Jesus Christ, and for a number of years lived as near to Him as I knew how; but I allowed Satan to turn me aside, and grew careless in my prayer life and Bible Study, and knew what it was to be defeated. I came here to be revived, the Lord has met me, and I have yielded to Him, and He now fills my heart and life.

At the "Say-So" Meetings

That Bodily Hindrance.—Two years and a half ago I asked the Lord to come in and dwell, and He gave me wonderful victory over worry and selfishness; but when my body was in a certain condition, it seemed as if God were really dead. At one of the meetings, it came to me, "Why not let Him take that conditon, take the whole situation?" I did, and it was just as though I had been holding on to something and had let go of it. The confusion all disappeared.

One Foot on Land.—I have been a worker for a great many years in city mission work, and have not had this victory. I have had glimpses of it, but have tried to live it in my own strength, and it seemed as if I had one foot in the boat and the other on land, and was going to be sure I had a part in it. Now I am going to let Him live it.

Satan on Hand.—I do not have to wait until I get home to be tempted, because right here on the grounds Satan has waited for me at the door of the tabernacle. When I have come out of the finest meetings, I have found Satan outside. But I have found that Jesus is able to overcome.

His Volunteer Declaration.—For four years a question has been bothering me, and now it is answered. I am going to be a missionary, and expect to go into training next month.

At the Cedar Lake Toboggan.—As I went down the bathing toboggan slide victory was made plain to me. A lady ahead of me said, "I cannot go down." Two children came along, and without hesitation, went rushing down the slide, and I thought, if I am going down I must go down as they did, so I let go with both hands, and was as safe as could be. I thought, "That is the way the Lord wants me to live in victory. He is going to do it all for me, and I do not have to be afraid."

Christ Marveled.—I wasn't here twenty-four hours before the Lord gave me a picture of my life, and the reason for it. At the early Sunday morning prayer meeting the leader

The Word of Their Testimony

told the story of Christ visitng Nazareth, His own home, and that He did not many mighty works there, save putting His hand on a few sick folks and healing them; and *He marveled because of their unbelief.* There was a picture of my life,—He marveled at my unbelief; and now I have found the way out.

Lazy and Stingy.—I was living a defeated life. I was lazy, and did not want to get up in the morning. I was stingy, and did not want to give God all the time or all the money He wanted. Since I have given the Lord my all, it has not been hard to make a donation to the Lord, nor to get up in the morning. I have not made any special effort, but the Lord has awakened me between five and six o'clock and sent me to the prayer tent, and I have had a real blessing in intercession, because of this victory that is Christ.

Wanted Some Great Experience.—I have been trying for years to live the Victorious Life, and have been defeated, and here I found the reason why, that it was simply unbelief. I wanted some great experience, and have always wished I had been born a heathen so I could have a great experience. I had to surrender to the Lord that desire for a great experience that had been holding me back from accepting what He would give me. Then I thought I had to hold on through my faith, but learned through one of the speakers that if I would give myself up wholly to Christ, the faith was in Him. I have given up, and am trusting Him even for my faith.

Not in "Meetings."—I have been in Christian work for years, and have been wanting this Victorious Life. I have sought it in holiness meetings, in consecration meetings, wherever I thought I should find it. But I thank God I have found it in Christ Jesus, and in Him alone.

The Heathen in Her.—I thank God for showing me some of my sins. I thought I was pretty good, and I found that I was just as bad as the lowest heathen. I had pride, and unlove, and indifference, and had failed in giving God His

At the "Say-So" Meetings

share of time in Bible study, and prayer. I thank Him that I can commit to Him all these things, and that He is able to keep them.

Moved Out.—I came here a happy Christian, but now I am a *joyful* Christan, because I have moved out and Christ has moved in.

His "Shortcomings."—I thank God that what I used to call "my shortcomings," I am now calling "my sins."

Not Optional.—I have learned that the Victorious Life is not optional; that it belongs to every Christian, and that an *unvictorious* life is a hindrance to the Church and a dishonor to Christ.

Ralph Norton's Thirteenth.—This has been a time of great refreshing and joy. This is our thirteenth Bible Conference, but it has been the climax of them all. Dr. Chapman used to say, "I used to look at some men and I thought they had a monopoly on God; but after I learned to know those men, I learned that God had a monopoly on them." When we let God have a monopoly on our lives, what wonderful things He works!

Costly Prayer.—This week I have feasted, and drunk deep, and the Lord has given me a new longing to share His burden for a lost world. He has shown me the power of intercessory prayer, and that it is worth while to pay the price that true prayer costs. He has given me true confidence for the immediate future and the far-off future. I do not know what it holds, but He does, and I am trusting Him to show me where and when He wants me on the foreign mission field.

Mrs. Woolley's Verse.—"I will pour water upon him that is thirsty, and floods upon the dry ground: I will pour my spirit upon thy seed, and my blessing upon thine offspring" (Isa. 44: 3). We are taking the first part of that verse for ourselves, and the last half for our children. I am trusting

The Word of Their Testimony

Jesus to make them victorious in the life that is theirs ahead, and we are taking victory ourselves, now.

Mr. E. Y. Woolley's Thanksgiving.—I have much to thank God for this week, it has been so full of rich blessing. There have been so many answered prayers, that have ranged from weather to finances, and from people to salvation, from little things in our sight to big things in our sight, though I do not know how they stand in God's sight. I praise Him for the fellowship, so full and free, and for such great blessing poured out upon us all. The outstanding fact to me personally was an increased revelation of God's grace, His undeserved love to me—the least of the saints, that He should be willing to take me as I am, willing to lead me, willing to cleanse me under the blood, willing to let me run His errands, hew the wood, and carry the water.

A Friend in Sorrow.—Lately a great sorrow came into my life, and I came down here very much crushed; but God has spoken to me, and I have laid my burden at His feet, and I have lost my anxiety, and He has given me a quietness, and a peace and a joy, and I can say this afternoon "He walks with me, and He talks with me." I am glad we have eternity to try to tell all that He has done for us.

He Upbraideth Not.—I knew all the teaching about the Victorious Life, but drifted into defeat, becoming so busy in my teaching in a Bible School that I gave up my alone time with Him. God never asks us to give Him up for His work, and the old nature deceived me into thinking that if I came back to Him He would upbraid me, and I dreaded my alone time with Him when I did try to take it. I went to my Bible, deciding that after all, that was the only place I would get relief, and there in James I found "He unbraideth not." I am giving Him His time now, and thank Him for victory.

A Business Mistake.—I am one of the busy business men who did not have time to come to the Conference. I was so crowded in business that I worked before daylight and

At the "Say-So" Meetings

after dark, until I crowded out prayer and Bible reading; but bless God, I am going to give more time to Bible reading and prayer, and less to business. I have only come today, but God has wonderfully blessed me, and the next time I want to be here the full week.

Found a Testimony.—I came here without a testimony, just for the afternoon, hoping I would have some startling experience that would make me over. I came here hungry, and I saw Jesus Christ on the grounds as soon as I came. I thought perhaps this victory was not for me, and sat here quite miserable, when it came to me, "You foolish creature, it is only Jesus after all, and He is for you as well as for the rest, who are testifying." He is my victory after all, and I am going to praise Him with the rest of you.

In Chicago's Loop.—I am glad that I have proved that in the heart of the loop in the big city of Chicago, among many wicked men, those who do not know Jesus Christ, He is able to give victory every day in the year, and keep us with a heart made pure, and garments white, and Christ enthroned within.

"It Shall Be."—I thank God that He has shown me some unbelief in my heart, and He has given me this word, "It shall be as it was told you." I am going back expecting God to do impossible things.

Medicine.—I was badly in need of a rest, and prayed that God would direct me to the right place. On Thursday I was asked to come up here, and it has been more than food or medicine or anything else, what I have gotten at these meetings. I am going back to take up my work with a renewed spirit. I have something new to give the girls in our rescue home.

Dr. Thomas' Two Minute Sermon on 2 Timothy 1: 12.—It is the rule in the British army to ask each man what his denomination is. A soldier was asked that by a sergeant, and gave some answer that did not quite satisfy the man. At last the sergeant asked, rather impatiently, "Well, what is your persuasion?" The man answered, "I am persuaded that He is able to keep that which I have committed unto Him" (2 Tim. 1: 12; also Rom. 8: 37: "I am persuaded.") The apostle said in Romans 8, "I am persuaded that nothing shall be able to separate us from the love of Christ." That of course means His love to us,—not our love to Him. An old clergyman was lying on his deathbed, and someone quoted, "I know in whom I have believed." He said, "Don't let a preposition come between me and my Saviour, 'I know Him whom I have believed.'" In that text, 2 Timothy, 1: 12, there are three stages of the Christian life, and we have been having them all this week. I think this is the eighth conference I have been at this summer, and it is the best of them all, but I would like to leave these three points with you—believing, knowing, and being persuaded. When we believe we begin to know; when we begin to know Him we soon are persuaded that He is able. Praise God.

Eyes on Folks.—Looking unto Jesus, who is the author and finisher of our faith! I had my eyes on other folks, and had my ears open to what they had to say; but now I have my eyes on Jesus, and will do His will, and listen to Him.

From Seventh to Eighth.—It does not take very long for the eye to travel from the seventh of Romans to the eighth chapter, but I have been twenty years getting from the seventh into the eighth, and I thank God that He made it possible for me to come here this year. I have known of the Victorious Life for years, but it took five days at the conference here to make me realize that it was a fact I needed, not a promise, and as soon as I realized that Christ Jesus could and would do it all, I was safe. "As ye have therefore received the Lord Jesus, so walk in Him."

A Missionary's Conviction.—The revival in India would have been impossible if Mr. Hyde had not prayed. For ten days he scarcely took his clothes off, so great was the burden of prayer upon him. God has shown me at this conference

At the "Say-So" Meetings

that He is limited by us because we will not pray, also that we must be instantly obedient in intercession until the victory is gained, and He will take care of the body, not for long life, but that we may meet the crisis that must be met in these next few years; also that instant obedience, at any cost, will release power.

Zero Snowflakes.—All week long I have been shrinking, until I have become nothing, and He has become greater and greater, until He is all and in all. Mr. Pace reminded us of the fact that the most perfect shape of the snowflake is just at zero, and all the way down from that it gets less perfect. So it is when self is at zero that the Lord can begin to work His grace.

At Any Cost—Pray!—What I have learned in this conference as never before, is the importance and the place of prayer, and I am resolved, by the grace of God, to continue more faithful, and to give more time to it in the future than ever before, at whatever cost, and cost it does.

Are You in this League?—I think there is no mission in this world that I know of, that is doing more in the sight of God, perhaps, than the Great Commission Prayer League of Chicago. I would suggest that all who want to know more about the prayer life, and to be led out into intercession for the world, get into touch with this League, at 808 N. LaSalle street, Chicago.

Settled.—"God said it, Jesus did it, I believe it, and that settles it."

Will Revivals Start?—The lines that go out from Cedar Lake will reach to the ends of the earth, and if we continue in the confidence we have expressed in our testimonies, revivals will be started here in America and on the foreign mission field.

"AM I READY FOR HIS COMING?"

Robert C. McQuilkin

AS we close our Conference shall we not face this simple question: "Are we ready for our Lord's coming?" Let us to-night think of just Himself, not about our particular theories of his coming, nor of all the hard questions connected with his coming, but just about himself, and his coming, and this question: "Am I ready for his coming?" Can I have boldness or will I be ashamed before him at his coming? Those words in First John 3: 3, "He that hath this hope [this hope of his coming] set on him [set on Jesus] purifieth himself even as He [Jesus] is pure" present to us the great *incentive to holiness* or a life of victory, and at the same time they give God's *standard of holiness* and suggest God's *secret of holiness*.

The next great new event in God's program for the world is the coming back to earth again of the Lord Jesus Christ. The last chapter of the Old Testament is concerned with that second coming, and the last message of the New Testament points forward to that coming. The last word of the Old Testament is the word "curse,"—"Lest I come and smite the earth with a curse," and the last message of the New Testament is the word "grace,"—"The grace of the Lord Jesus Christ be with the saints." He is coming again with the curses of judgment for his enemies, and with the blessings of grace for his saints. The last recorded words of our Lord Jesus Christ are those words of promise, "I come quickly;" and the last recorded prayer of the people of God is our hearts' glad answer to that promise, "Amen: come, Lord Jesus."

A good many of the saints have their hearts stretching out in anticipation of that coming, and expect to see the Lord before they die; and a great many reasons are given that seem to point toward the near coming of the Lord. We do not know whether he will come in our generation, or hundreds of years from now, but one of the signs of his near approach

---

A closing message given Sunday evening before the Communion Service at Princeton. The same message, in fuller form, was given at Whittier. See note on page 34.

Mr. McQuilkin

that I like to think most about is the work of the Spirit that seems to be going on all over the world to prepare believers for his coming and give them a great hunger to be ready for their Lord.

A noted Bible teacher was recently speaking of the "signs of the times" that might point to the near coming of the Lord Jesus Christ, and he said something to this effect: "When the Lord comes we are going to be caught up to meet him in the air; but first, all the dead saints are going to be raised from the dead, and we shall be caught up together with them. There will only be a few of us living saints in comparison with all of those who are raised from the dead, and all the rest of them are going to be very much interested in us. They will come around and ask us just how it happened, and just what we were doing when he came, and just how our bodies were transformed." Then the preacher said, "You know some of us won't want to talk about that. We will want to change the subject. We would rather not say where we were; we would rather not say what we were doing when Jesus came."

That is what is meant here, I am very sure, when we are warned against being ashamed before him at his coming. Not that we may fail to be caught up to meet him, for that is part of the gift of Grace for every believer, but that we will not have boldness before the Lord Jesus at his coming.

Are we ready for the coming of the Lord Jesus Christ? Can we have boldness before him at his coming? Now honestly, would we like Jesus to come to-night, or would we like to have a little more time to prepare for his coming,— time to see that friend whom we have not treated quite right, to write that letter to one who we have wronged, to get rid of that money which belongs to the Lord? Would we like to have at least a month to show the Lord Jesus that we really love him? "Every one that hath this hope set on him purifieth himself." Yes, this Hope is the great incentive to holiness that the New Testament holds before us.

Are you ready to-night for the Lord Jesus to come? Well, if you and I are not ready to-night for the coming of Jesus, we are not ready for the presence of Jesus. Because Jesus is here. Did you notice at the close of that third chapter of First John those words, "If our heart condemn us not, *we have boldness* toward God: and whatsoever we ask we receive of him." If the coming of the Lord Jesus Christ is a

"Am I Ready for His Coming?"

great incentive to holiness, the presence of the Lord Jesus is a great incentive to holiness. If we need boldness before him at his coming, that very same boldness we need as we bow before the throne of grace,—boldness to ask and to receive whatsoever we ask.

"But," we say, "we are to come before the presence of his throne of grace with humility, not surely with boldness." Yes, with reverence and humility, yet with boldness.

A number of years ago I heard a big fatherly looking man preach in our church. I forget all of the sermon except one story. He told us that one night he was standing on a corner in Pittsburgh, waiting for a car. Across the street was a drug store, a good place for getting ice cream sodas. He noticed a little lad who was rather poorly dressed, acting as though he wanted to ask him something. He came closer, and the boy said, "Say Mister, gimme a nickel to go and get a soda." The big man started to walk toward him, when suddenly the poor little street urchin turned around and ran away. He lost his courage, and he did not get his soda.

A few weeks later this minister was standing on the same corner, and another little lad came up, a boy of about the same size, and *he* wanted a soda. He walked up to the big man, took him by the hand, led him across the street and into the drug store. They sat down and the boy ordered a soda, and drank it, and the big man paid for the soda. Then the preacher said, "You know the secret? *The second lad was my own boy.*"

Don't you suppose that boy honored his father? He had a true father heart, and I am sure the boy had honor and reverence for that father,—but oh, what boldness! He asked and he received because he was a son. And that is the boldness the father-heart of our God is eager that we should have with him. If we have this boldness to come into his presence, then we shall have the boldness to be ready for his coming.

Now, what is God's *standard of holiness?* *"Even as He is pure."* Jesus Christ himself is the only standard of holiness and of victory set before Christians. Anything that creeps into our heart that is contrary to the Spirit of the Lord Jesus Christ, we must put down as sin, and confess it, and have it cleansed away in his blood.

It would be a comfortable thing if we could look at the

Mr. McQuilkin

fellow-Christians in our church to get our standard. A lot of Christians are doing that. "So-and-so considers herself a good Christian, and I would not think of doing the things that she does. Why, she talks about her neighbors. I wouldn't think of doing that!" "Look at that man, the things he does in business. I would not think of doing business that way and I do not profess to be a very good Christian." Without understanding, we compare ourselves one with another. If that were our standard we might all feel comfortable, because we are always sure to find somebody that does things we would not dream of doing. Let us get our eyes off folks and on to Jesus, remembering that the kind of holiness God wants of us is the kind that his Son has. That is why the Victorious Life is "the life that is Christ."

If that is so, does it mean that we are perfect, just like Jesus? Where does growth in grace come in? We read that when we shall see him we shall be like him, for we shall see him as he is, and that he that hath this hope purifieth himself. And so the Word tells us that we are to be pure now, and that when he appears we will be like him. There seems to be a contradiction here, doesn't there? How can we grow more and more like him, and yet have his purity at this present moment?

In Romans 3: 23 we read, "All have sinned, and fall short of the glory of God." In Romans 5: 2 we read that having been justified through Christ, "we rejoice in hope of the glory of God." Now this glory of God is just the character of Jesus and at his coming we shall be perfectly conformed to his likeness.

Paul goes on to say this remarkable thing, "hope putteth not to shame." What does that mean? If some millionaire came to me and said, "I am going to give you ten million dollars ten years from now, and will put down the date I am going to give it to you," I would have hope of getting that, and would say to some of my friends, "Mr. So-and-so is going to give me ten million dollars." My friends would laugh and say, "We have heard him say things like that before. We will wait and see." My hope would put me to shame. But if that millionaire should say, "I am going to turn my estate over to you ten years hence, and as an earnest of that am depositing to your credit now one million dollars," then I could say to my friends that ten million dollars were coming to me, and I should not be put to shame.

"Am I Ready for His Coming?"

In like manner the world may say to us Christians: "You are expecting Jesus to come and when he comes you expect to be like him. But what about now? Do you have perfect peace? Do you love your enemies? Do you have victory over all sin?"

"Oh no, but when I get my resurrection body, that will be all fixed up."

A young college friend said to me, "I am trusting Jesus for my salvation, but it does not do me any good now. I hope to go to heaven when I die, but meanwhile I don't have much satisfaction." That is a hope that puts to shame. Now why does our hope not put to shame? "Because the love of God hath been shed abroad in our hearts through the Holy Spirit" which he will give to us when Jesus comes? Oh no, it does not say that; it says this: "the Holy Spirit which was given unto us."

The Holy Spirit is our earnest. The earnest of what? The earnest of our inheritance. "The love of God shed abroad in my heart,"—what is that? That is just Jesus Christ in you the hope of glory, and when the love of Jesus is shed abroad in our heart, we are like him. And this present likeness is the earnest, or the proof, that when he comes I will be perfectly conformed to his likeness. If I have the evidence of this present likeness my hope does not put me to shame.

How then do we grow in grace? As we behold Jesus, we are transformed into the same image from one degree of glory to another degree of glory, becoming more and more like him (2 Cor. 3: 18). And so the nine-fold variety of the fruit of the Spirit (Gal. 5: 22) we should have produced in us all at once, perhaps in a tiny little measure, but as we keep on growing, transformed from one degree of glory to another, we have more and more of the wonderful things he gives to us, love, joy, peace, and all the rest.

Our present standard of holiness, then, is Jesus, and if we find anything in our heart or life in our ways or our thoughts, which is not of the Spirit of Jesus, let us get down and confess it as sin, and his blood will cleanse it away.

Now a final word about the *secret of holiness,* the holiness which will make us bold before him at his coming. We need not dwell on that, because this secret is what we have been studying right through the days of the Conference. "Every one that hath this hope set on him purifieth himself," our

Mr. McQuilkin

verse tells us. How can I purify myself? We purify our souls, Peter tells us, by obedience to the truth (1 Pet. 1: 22). But how am I going to be able to obey the truth? The second chapter of First Peter goes on to show that obedience to the truth is nothing more and nothing less than *believing the Word of Good Tidings*, the truth of the Gospel that was preached to us. They that believe the good tidings are obedient to the truth; they that disbelieve are disobedient. And this applies to sinners who need salvation and to saved sinners who keep needing the "much-more salvation" or the Victorious Life (Rom. 5: 10).

Andrew Murray has beautifully and simply pointed out the difference between the Old Covenant and the New Covenant: Under the Old Covenant God said, "Obey me, and I will be your God." There was man's part and God's part. Man failed in his part, the covenant was broken. Then God made a New Covenant, and said this: "I will put my law in your heart, *and ye shall obey me.*" What is the difference between those two covenants? In the Old Covenant there were two parties, in the New Covenant just one party. In the New Covenant Jesus Christ takes the whole responsibility, and man's part is to believe that He does. The trouble with most Christians is that they are living under the Old Covenant, and they say, "If I obey God I will live the Victorious Life." That would not be Glad Tidings. If I said to-night, "You ought to go out and live lives of victory, you ought to live in freedom from all worry, you ought to go and win souls, or do this or that," that would not be good tidings, would it? But if I say, "Jesus Christ is offering to come and put his law in your heart, by coming in himself to dwell there always, so that as a result of his indwelling you shall obey him," I tell you *that is good tidings;* and my part is just to believe the good tidings.

I hear some of you saying, "I know that Christ will always do his part, but I am weak, and I know that I shall often fail to do my part." The whole heart of the New Covenant is that Jesus Christ assumes the whole work. In spite of my weakness,—nay, more, *because* of my weakness, Jesus guarantees to do the whole thing in the matter of victory over sin. If I had not had that weakness the Old Covenant would have sufficed. Had it not been for my weakness there would have been no need for a New Covenant, and if that New Covenant of grace does not operate in spite of my weakness

"Am I Ready for His Coming?"

there was no point in God's making the second covenant. We have victory by grace, and grace means Jesus Christ is doing it all.

The great *incentive to holiness,* then, is Jesus. God's *standard of holiness* is Jesus. And God's *secret of holiness* is Jesus.

The first time the word "victory" is mentioned in the Bible is in First Samuel 15: 29: "The Victory of Israel will not lie nor repent." That first mention gives the key: *Victory is a Person.* In the New Testament the Greek equivalent of that Hebrew word for victory in First Samuel is used in First Corinthians 15: 57: "Thanks be to God who is giving us the victory." The same word in a different form is used in First John 5: 4: "This is the victory that overcometh the world, even our faith." In First Corinthians the word means the Victory itself; in First John the word indicates the means by which we lay hold of Victory. Christ is the Victory. By our faith (which also is His gift), we lay hold of Him.

Have you so laid hold that you are ready for his coming? You may be ready just now, by resting in Christ's full sufficiency, both for his presence with us and for his coming in glory. As we join together now in feeding on his body broken for us, and his blood, shed for us, may his Spirit in a new way make this a living reality to us to-night, that we may eat and drink together with great joy and with a longing in our hearts for the hastening of the day when he shall come and we shall see him as he is, face to face.

RESURRECTION DAYS

Philip E. Howard

The Post-Communion Message at Princeton

THERE is a deep pathos about the life of our Lord in those closing hours of it. No one was quite so lonely as he; no one knew the truth as he did, and he had gathered about him a group of those whom he was going to trust to a degree disproportionate to anything that the human eye can possibly see in the men whom he trusted. That is so today. You and I never can draw near this Feast of Remembrance, this holy sacrament of the Lord's Supper, without a renewed consciousness of our utter unworthiness because of anything that we have. But on the other hand, we can never draw near it in spirit without recognizing the joy of it.

It was he, himself, who said that he had come that the joy of his friends might be made full. So it is not strange that this beautiful feast has been called the Eucharist, the Glad Feast, the Feast of Rejoicing. Indeed I am sure that is precisely what it is for us tonight. If we were to think over the last week of questionings, of debate, of eager searchings, of doubtings, and of glad surrender, it would be a complex picture in our minds, together too difficult for us to put into words; but thanks be unto God, it is not needful that we should do that, for tonight, here, in simplicity, in this testimony to the New Covenant, we may indeed look to the Covenant-making, and the Covenant-keeping Christ as our souls' sufficiency.

This feast looks forward, and I have been thinking tonight of that Resurrection Day which it typifies quite as much as it typifies the death on Calvary. You remember that on the very day of resurrection, two of Jesus' friends were walking out from the city toward the little village of Emmaus, and they were talking over the events of the days just past. You remember that a stranger joined them by the way, and began to question them about their conversation. They exposed their very hearts to him. They told him what had transpired, of their depression, of their disappointment, all that seemed so strange about the story in those days.

Resurrection Days

Then, in his quiet, loving way, he asked them a few simple questions. "Isn't it just what ought to have been?" he asked. "Isn't it just what you might have expected?" And so, as he walked with them, he told them the story of the old, old plan of God, and unfolded to them the things they already knew, but had forgotten.

Shall we ever forget in our heart of hearts, the little gathering around the table in the humble home, when Jesus' pierced hands brake the bread, and in that very breaking of bread the two men recognized him, and he disappeared from their sight? Do you remember what they said as they were talking it over? "Did not our heart burn within us while he talked with us by the way?"

Indeed, dear friends, as we have been gathered here about this table tonight, looking back over the precious days of this Conference, did not our hearts burn within us as we think of what has transpired here on this old campus, in the midst of these buildings, which are themselves a testimony to the Faith?

What shall it mean to us in our life when we go away tomorrow? There will be the same rush of duty, the same tasks, the same homes, the same offices; but I believe I interpret the situation truly for you and for myself, when I say that our friends are not going to see just the same persons in us whom they saw when we came here. Will there not be a difference? Are we not divested of many of the things that have made life hard for some of our friends because of our presence among them? Are we not divested of many of the things that have hurt the heart of our dear Lord? Is not this communion service to remain in the memory of all, for its influence in our lives, because we have taken this Covenant Lord as our Victory?

A dear old friend of mine said to me once, after a long, busy life, "Howard, just one thing has held me fast through these years of many trials. Not the fact that I was holding on to God, but the fact that God was holding on to me." Praise His name that that is true!

Oh, my friends, let us give over our petty questionings about the great truths that have been set before us here. Have you heard the wind moving through the trees? Do you know where the wind comes from? Can you explain it? No more than Nicodemus could. Do you understand the mission of the Spirit excepting by experience and by the

Mr. Howard

testimony of the Word and by the testimony of the Lord Jesus? Oh, may God give us the sweet child-like open-mindedness of those who have passed through deep experience and are willing now, at last, once and for all, to let self die, and to let Christ live within. And it will be more beautiful day by day. The victory is important, but the results of victory are so wonderful, so enormous, so blessed, that we shall not reach their end in all the ages.

One evening at our dinner table, the littlest girl in the family stepped down from her place, came to my chair, climbed up beside me, and whispered something in my ear. I said "Dear, I could not quite hear. Won't you say that again?" She said it again, but I could not hear. I said, "Won't you step down beside me, and look up at me, and say it so I can see you as you say it?" As she stood there beside me, looking up into my face, she said, "Sweeter as the years go by."

"Dear, do you know that hymn?" I asked. "Yes, I know one verse of it," she answered. The family were all listening by that time. I said, "Won't you say the verse?" She said, as she straightened up to her small height, and looked into my face, what to her was the whole verse, "Sweeter as the years go by." And that was all.

I gathered her up into my arms, and said, "Yes, indeed, indeed it is so,—sweeter as the years go by," and I believe that because of this precious week we have had together, and because of this holy hour tonight around this table, we shall have sweeter memories than we have ever had in our lives before, memories of consecration, memories of victory, and memories of that ever-increasing store of untold benefits for us who are undeserving, bestowed by One whose resources are infinitely loving, infinitely patient, and never hidden from us.

PRAYER

Oh our Father, thou knowest what it in our hearts tonight. We thank thee for the quiet of this hour with thee, and that we have been able to look at thee and see no man but Jesus only.

We thank thee that thou dost break down with thy loving but powerful touch, the barriers of pride, of self will, of conceit, of impurity, and that thou dost open wide the doors through which we may pass to service beyond

Resurrection Days

anything we have asked for or dreamed of. Lord, thou art trying to tell us tonight that thou has work for us, some in distant fields, some in very humble ways about which the world will never know; but thou hast led many of us here to step out in faith, victory, joy, blessedness and peace in the life that is Christ.

Now Lord, we do ask thy blessing upon every one of us, and upon that widening circle of loved ones; upon the friends with whom we work; upon the Sunday School classes and the churches we represent; upon the dear ones on the front line of missions; upon those who are gladly meeting the foe across the sea, who are laying down their lives perhaps this very night.

Oh our Father, make our hearts very tender. Teach us to be uncritical. May we be glad to see others preferred before us, and may we learn the profound blessing of taking a little place,—not with any pride because of our humility, but with a sincere joy of heart that others are preferred.

Bless to us the moments that we have spent around the table of the Lord, and may his shed blood, and his broken body, be to us the type and the reality in our spirits of all that it can be for us in the glad new covenant of grace, in which our weakness has made way for his strength, and his life is lived out in us. In his blessed Name, Amen.

A CALL TO PRAYER

For Future Conferences

This prayer call has been distributed in leaflet form and it is reprinted here as it may be used even after the 1919 Conferences are over. It is planned to issue revised Prayer Calls from time to time, and copies for distribution among those who wish to be prayer helpers, may be had from Victorious Life Conference, 600 Perry Building, Philadelphia.

THE Board of Managers desires humbly and gratefully to acknowledge that our Heavenly Father wonderfully answered prayer for the three Victorious Life Conferences held last summer, in Whittier, Cal.; in Cedar Lake, Ind., and Princeton, N. J.

We take this opportunity of thanking all those who by their intercessions helped to make these conferences bear "much fruit."

Plans are now being made for a Mid-Winter Conference in Philadelphia, January 2-5, and for three or more summer conferences.

We are early laying before you some of the needs with the hope that you will become *a daily intercessor for the Victorious Life Conferences of 1919.*

In order that we may enter into this service intelligently, the following objects for Thanksgiving, Confession, and Intercession are suggested:

Thanksgiving

For God's unspeakable Gift, Jesus Christ, and that with him God freely gives us all things and in him supplies all our needs.

For the undeserved and wonderful blessings and results of the 1918 conferences.

For the large use made of the previous prayer calls and the abundant answers given.

For God's care and protection of all who attended the conferences with no serious accident or illness.

A Call to Prayer

For the provision God has made for funds to enable us to meet all our financial obligations promptly.

For the remarkable use God has made of the book "Victory in Christ" and other such literature.

Confession

For our sin of lack of love to God, to one another, and to our fellow-men.

For our sin in failure to do our full part toward taking or sending the Gospel to the non-Christian world.

For our sin of selfishness.

For our sin of pride.

For our sin of unbelief—at which Christ marvels as he did of old. (Mark 6: 6.)

For our failure to give Christ always first place in our lives.

For our failure to avail ourselves of all that God offers us in Jesus Christ, our risen Lord.

For our sin in not availing ourselves of the promises and possibilities of prayer.

> "And whatsoever ye shall ask in my name, that will I do, that the Father may be glorified in the Son.
> If ye shall ask any thing in my name, I will do it."
>
> John 14: 13, 14.

Intercession

For all those who attended the conferences who have since met with defeat, that they may be completely restored.

That all of us may continue to grow in grace and in the knowledge of our Lord and Saviour Jesus Christ, and to this end that we may hold faithfully to the daily Quiet Time for Bible study and prayer—365 days each year.

That God will teach each one of us how best to profit by criticism of our own personal lives as well as of the Victorious Life Conferences.

That God will lay on many persons a continual burden of prayer for the 1919 conferences.

For Future Conferences

That the teaching and preaching of the truths which are particularly emphasized in these conferences may be clear, sane, complete, convincing, and scriptural.

That the Board of Managers may be kept very humble and teachable, and that they may have a clear vision of the possibilities of the conferences and act accordingly.

That God will open the way and provide the places and accommodations for such conferences as he may wish for 1919.

That Christ's own program may be planned and carried out, including the teaching, preaching, praying, testimonies, singing and recreation.

That all who are directly responsible for the success of the conferences may be given grace, wisdom and strength completely to fulfil their obligations in love and humility.

That God will make us all realize the vital need of proclaiming by our lives as well as by our lips the message of Victory in Christ, and that we may begin now trying to get people to attend the 1919 conferences.

That God will continue to provide ample funds so that the Board of Managers may be enabled to continue to meet all the financial obligations in accordance with the very best business practices.

That there may be in the conferences a great manifestation of the Holy Spirit to convict of sin, to save the lost, to reestablish and adjust the saints, and to give us all a more complete and satisfying appropriation than we have ever before known, of the living Christ as Saviour from sin's penalty and power.

That God will give us a vision and sense of the world's needs that we have never had before, and enable us, as individuals, to make our rightful contribution toward meeting these needs, whether in time, service, money or our lives.

That God will open the way and provide the funds for holding in the near future Victorious Life conferences in the foreign mission field, and that he will qualify persons of his own choice to carry the message.

That God will abundantly bless and fill with the Holy Spirit all the missionaries who have been at our conferences in the past and who are now laboring in their respective fields.

A Call to Prayer

That God will show each one of us our obligation and privilege to become faithful intercessors. (See John 14: 13 and 14.)

That God will take the new book called "The Victorious Life," containing the reports of the three 1918 Summer Conferences, and through it speak to tens of thousands of hungry souls and satisfy them by leading them to accept Christ as their life and victory.

That if it be God's will the way may be opened for the publication of a Praise Book containing Psalms and Hymns particularly appropriate to the message of the Victorious Life.

That all Victorious Life Literature may be abundantly blessed to all who read it.

We do not desire by the foregoing in any way to limit the scope or range of prayer for the conferences. Let our prayers be in the Spirit, remembering John 15: 7, and 1 John 5: 14, 15.

Selected Lists of Literature

The books and leaflets included in the following lists cover topics specially considered at the Victorious Life Conferences. In most cases the books or leaflets have been written by Conference speakers, or were strongly recommended by them. The lists, therefore, are in no sense exhaustive, and many excellent titles have been omitted.

Any of the books and leaflets mentioned may be ordered from Christian Life Literature Fund, 600 Perry Building, Philadelphia, or from Bible House of Los Angeles, 643 South Olive street, Los Angeles, Cal., unless otherwise stated.

REFERRED TO IN PRECEDING PAGES

The Holy Spirit of God, Dr. W. H. Griffith Thomas..........$1.75
Life Abiding and Abounding, Dr. W. H. Griffith Thomas...... 60c.
What Justification Is and What It Does,
   Dr. W. H. Griffith Thomas... ....3c. or 30c. a doz.
Sanctification—What It Really Is,
   Dr. W. H. Griffith Thomas....................3c. or 30c. a doz.
What Is the Gospel? Charles Gallaudet Trumbull
                          (cloth) 50c. (paper) 35c.
The Life That Wins, Charles Gallaudet Trumbull.2c. or 20c. a doz.
When the Spirit's Fire Swept Korea,
   Dr. Jonathan Goforth........................5c. or 50c. a doz.
Victorious Life Studies, Robert C. McQuilkin.................. 25c.
God's Way of Victory Over Sin,
   Robert C. McQuilkin..........................3c. or 30c. a doz.
Taking God at His Word, Robert C. McQuilkin...2c. or 20c. "
This Man Receiveth Sinners, Dr. W. B. Anderson.
   (This pamphlet is not sold, but may be had, while the supply lasts, by sending 2c. postage to Mr. George Innes, Land Title Building, Philadelphia.)
Preacher and Prayer, E. M. Bounds (cloth) 50c. (paper)...... 15c.
Pray Without Ceasing, Andrew Murray....................... 10c.
Answered or Unanswered? Louisa Vaughan................... 85c.
Getting Things From God, C. A. Blanchard................. 75c.
Sundar Singh, The Apostle of the Bleeding Feet.. .... 15c.
Apostles of the Belgian Trenches, J. K. McLean.............. 50c.
Under Shell Fire at the Belgian Front,
   Mrs. Ralph C. Norton (free leaflet).
American Girl's Struggle and Surrender,
   Mrs. Alice E. McClure........................3c. or 30c. a doz.
Just Himself, Mrs. Ralph C. Norton..............3c. or 30c. "
Jesus Is Coming, W. E. Blackstone.................... 35c. net
The Lord's Return, J. F. Silver........................$1.15 net
What Do the Prophets Say? C. I. Scofield..................... 75c.
The Return of the Lord Jesus, R. A. Torrey................. 25c.

On the Victorious Life

20 VICTORIOUS LIFE LEAFLETS

The following set of twenty leaflets or booklets on the deeper spiritual life may be secured from the Christian Life Literature Fund, 600 Perry Building, for 25 cents. The prices for individual leaflets are also indicated.

Victory .... 5c.	a doz.	30c. a hundred
Himself, A. B. Simpson......................20c.	"	2c. each
Himself (poem), A. B. Simpson........... 5c.	"	30c. a hundred
Just Himself, Mrs. Ralph Norton........30c.	"	3c. each
What It Is Not, A. B. Simpson............10c.	"	60c. a hundred
Are You Satisfied? A. B. Simpson........10c.	"	60c. "
The Life That Wins, C. G. Trumbull....20c.	"	2c. each
The Indwelling Christ, A. B. Simpson...10c.	"	60c. a hundred
Others May, You Cannot................. 5c.	"	30c. "
Taking God at His Word, R. C. McQuilkin.20c.	"	2c. each

God's Easy Way of Holiness,
  A. B. Simpson.......................10c. "   60c. a hundred

Is Victory Earned or a Gift?
  C. G. Trumbull......................20c. "   2c. each

God's Way of Victory Over Sin,
  R. C. McQuilkin.....................30c. "   3c. "

Real and Counterfeit Victory,
  C. G. Trumbull......................30c. "   3c. "

What is the Victorious Life?
  R. C. McQuilkin.
    This leaflet, which is a reprint of the first chapter of the author's "Victorious Life Studies," is not sold, but may be had from the Free Literature Department of Christian Life Literature Fund.

Secret of the Victorious Life,
  F. W. Barker........................20c. a doz. 2c. each

How I Ascertain the Will of God,
  George Muller .... 5c. "   30c. a hundred

What Can the Holy Spirit Do for Us?
  John McNicol ....20c. "   2c. each

Bible Study on the Life of Victory,
  Mrs. J. Goforth......................15c. "   2c. "

An American Girl's Struggle and Surrender, Mrs. Alice E. McClure..........30c. "   3c. "

ADDITIONAL TRACTS

What Is Your Kind of Christianity? C. G. Trumbull.3c. or 30c. a doz.
Thirty-one Kings, or Victory Over Self,
  A. B. Simpson....................................3c. or 30c. "
Must Christians Sin? W. H. Griffith Thomas....... 6c. "
The Rest of Faith or Soul Rest, A. B. Earle........5c. or 50c. "
More Than Conquerors, Paul Rader.............5c. or 50c. "

BOOKS ON VICTORY AND HOW TO ENTER IN

Victory in Christ at Princeton Conference, 50c. and postage.
Victorious Life Studies, Robert C. McQuilkin, 25c. postpaid.
The Christian's Secret of a Happy Life, H. W. Smith, 50c. and postage.
The Christ Life, A. B. Simpson, (cloth) 60c., (paper) 30c.
The Threefold Secret of the Holy Spirit, James H. McConkey. (This book is not sold, but may be had free from Silver Publishing Co., Bessemer Building, Pittsburgh, Pa.)

SUPPLEMENTAL BOOKS

Full Blessing of Pentecost, Andrew Murray .... 75c.
The Two Covenants, Andrew Murray .... 60c.
Kept for the Master's Use, F. R. Havergal .... 50c.
Life More Abundantly, A. B. Simpson .... 60c.
Walking in the Spirit, A. B. Simpson .... 30c.
Deeper Experiences of Famous Christians, J. G. Lawson $1.00
Grace and Power, W. H. Griffith Thomas 1.00
Life Abiding and Abounding, W. H. Griffith Thomas .... 60c.
Deliverance From the Penalty and Power of Sin, O. R. Palmer .... 15c.

On Prayer and Revival

With Christ in the School of Prayer, Andrew Murray .... 50c.
Preacher and Prayer, E. M. Bounds (cloth) 50c., (paper) ..... 15c.
The Christian Science of Prayer, Mrs. Horace Porter .... 75c.
Method in Prayer, W. Graham Scroggie .... 75c.
Answered or Unanswered? Louisa Vaughan .... 85c.
Getting Things From God, C. A. Blanchard .... 75c.
The Ministry of Intercession, Andrew Murray .... 75c.
Pray Without Ceasing, Helps to Intercession, Andrew Murray 10c. (A pamphlet with monthly prayer cycle, taken from Ministry of Intercession)
Dynamic of All Prayer, Fleming $1.00
Studies for Personal Workers, Howard Agnew Johnston ...... 60c.
Taking Men Alive, C. G. Trumbull .... 60c.

Prayer and God's Infinite Power, Armstrong ..... 5c. or 50c. a doz.
Intercession, Henry W. Frost .... 2c. or 20c. "
Is Prayer Fundamental or Supplemental? .... 2c. or 20c. "
Responsibilities and Conditions of Availing Prayer, Wm. H. Richie .... 3c. or 30c. "
Intercessory Foreign Missionaries, Alfred E. Street.2c. or 20c. "
Focused and Fighting .... 2c. or 20c. "
Cycle of Prayer of the Student Volunteer Movement .... 5c. or 50c. "
A Great Awakening, Charles G. Finney .... 5c. or 50c. "
Suppose. This and other leaflets on soul-winning and revival are supplied free by the Great Commission Prayer League, 808 La Salle street, Chicago.

(See Next Page)

www.ingramcontent.com/pod-product-compliance
Lightning Source LLC
Chambersburg PA
CBHW050329230426
43663CB00010B/1795